The

PATHFINDER

This Is the Perfect Book for You If:

You've walked a city street with other people on their way to work. Most of these people have strange, taut, resigned expressions on their faces. They are definitely not looking forward to their work day. Suddenly you realize that you are not just an observer. You are one of them.

or

You entered the job market with high hopes that you would be starting a terrific career. By now it is painfully apparent that you have made some sort of misjudgment: Somehow you have found yourself in the job from hell—or even worse, you are bored most of the time with the daily grind of tasks that don't even begin to make use of your intelligence and abilities.

or

You used to really enjoy your job. It used to be full of challenge. When friends sang the career blues it never crossed your mind that anything like that could ever happen to you. But now your gum has lost its flavor on the bedpost.

or

You have visited your local career counselor and read numerous books on career and personal growth. You have done everything you can think of to find your true vocation. You know much more about yourself. Dark clouds still obscure your future direction.

or

You are a mindful young person. You and your friends are trying to figure out what to do with your lives. You want to have a career that really sings, that soars, that gives you a real life. Your friends are doing the same things to decide their fates that their parents did—and you know how that turned out.

or

You are good at your job. Nothing has really gone wrong. You just don't seem to have a sense of purpose anymore. You want to do something that means more to you personally. You may close your eyes and imagine pounding through stormy seas at the helm of a Greenpeace rubber boat just inches ahead of a Japanese kamikaze whaling ship. But then the vision fades. When you open your eyes you are back in your day-to-day life. Sure it would be exciting on that boat, but it doesn't seem very realistic. Nevertheless, you definitely want to do something with your life that matters.

or

Like a leaf in the wind, you have been blown into jobs by the winds of circumstance and by decisions that seemed like the thing to do at the time.

The PATHFINDER

HOW TO CHOOSE OR CHANGE YOUR CAREER FOR A LIFETIME OF SATISFACTION AND SUCCESS

NICHOLAS LORE

A FIRESIDE BOOK

PUBLISHED BY SIMON & SCHUSTER

Fireside
Rockefeller Center
1230 Avenue of the Americas
New York, NY 10020

Fireside and colophon are registered trademarks
of Simon & Schuster Inc.

Designed by Barbara M. Bachman
Illustrations by Mac Lore
Digital art by Nicholas Lore

Manufactured in the United States of America
11 13 15 17 19 20 18 16 14 12

Library of Congress Cataloging-in-Publication Data
Lore, Nicholas.
The Pathfinder : how to choose or change your career for a
lifetime of satisfaction and success / Nicholas Lore.
p. cm.
"A Fireside book."
Includes index.
1. Career changes. 2. Job satisfaction. I. Title.
HF5384.L67 1998
650.14—dc21   97-36944   CIP
ISBN 0-684-82399-3 (alk. paper)

For Mitra

....

Whatever you can do, or dream you can, begin it.
Boldness has genius, power, and magic in it.

—JOHANN WOLFGANG VON GOETHE

CONTENTS

The PATHFINDER

Part 1

LIVING A LIFE
YOU LOVE

You have never used a book like this before. It is designed to actually take you through the process of choosing your future career rather than just reading about doing so. As you continue through *The Pathfinder,* it will become your personal career coach and guide. Many people say that this book seems to be speaking directly to them alone. Of course this is not true, but you will find that you have an opportunity to develop a very personal coaching relationship with *The Pathfinder.* This relationship will make it possible for you to deal successfully with everything you need to consider, as well as learn practical new ways to move forward from your present uncertainty and design a career that will fit you elegantly, perfectly, like a custom-made suit. I hope you will choose to be a participant, and not just a reader. If you've made the decision to change your life, then you've found the book that was written just for you.

CHAPTER 1

•

THIS CAN BE YOUR GUIDE

Once, I was in the same situation you are facing today. It was time to decide what to do with my life. I committed myself to doing whatever was necessary to make a truly excellent career choice because I passionately wanted to wake up in the morning looking forward to going to work each day. This is the book I searched for then but did not find.

I remember an extraordinary, imaginary book that first framed my boyhood vision of what I hope *The Pathfinder* will be for you. Each month, Donald Duck's nephews, Huey, Dewey, and Louie would find themselves in the middle of a full-tilt comic book adventure. When things got completely hopeless, when the forces of chaos seemed sure to win, they always pulled off a miracle. Out of their knapsack came their infallible guide and problem solver, *The Junior Woodchuck Handbook*. It had an absolutely perfect, creative solution for every situation they stumbled into, no matter how obscure or difficult. It was the complete guide to life.

Since then I have passionately sought those rare volumes of chuckery that surface in the real world. Every once in a while one appears, the seminal guidebook to some aspect of life. Inspired by these wonderful books, *The Pathfinder* is intended to be one small chapter of *The Junior Woodchuck Handbook*: how to decide what to do with your life. Whether you are in midcareer change or are making career decisions for the first time, it is designed to get you successfully through the process of planning your future.

How can an intelligent person, committed to choosing a new career path, decide exactly which direction to pursue? That is a question I began asking many years ago. At the time I was restless and bored with my job. I ran a conservation and solar energy company on the coast of Maine. I had written and been responsible for the passage of legislation that saved thousands of beautiful historic houses from destruction and had recently been commended for excellence by the White House. My office looked out on a beautiful harbor where lobster boats and foghorns greeted the new day. Yet I had trouble getting through the workday. Even with an extensive background in psychology and Eastern philosophy, I had difficulty understanding why my workday left so much to be desired. How could it be that working on interesting projects in an idyllic setting and making a positive difference in the world and getting recognition could get boring? It was an absolute mystery to me.

I then searched all over New England to find a career coach to help me solve my problem. I called nearly every counselor in the region. I told them I was seeking to choose a new career where I would be able to wake up in the morning and look forward to work. I said I wanted to find a vocation that was challenging, creative, and that I would passionately enjoy, where I could use my talents to their fullest, doing something that mattered to me. None of them seemed to know what it took to have a really phenomenal career. In fact, I could tell from their voices that many of them didn't seem to love what they did either.

Finally, I took my problem to a wise old man who was a fellow member of my boat club. As it turned out, I was lucky enough to pick the ideal supporter, R. Buckminster Fuller. Many people have heard of Bucky because he invented the geodesic dome. The building at EPCOT Center that looks like a huge silvery ball is one of his many revolutionary designs. Bucky was much more than an architect. If you can imagine Obiwan Kanobe and Yoda combined in a real person who was at the same time a master futurist, scientist, engineer, architect, inventor, mathematician, philosopher, and mystic, you get a little hint as to who he was. I struggled with my dilemma for what seemed like eons. Ultimately, with his encouragement, I decided to dedicate my life to tackling the very problem I had so much trouble solving myself. I founded an organization dedicated to developing more effective ways to help people make career and education choices.

Since 1980, that organization, Rockport Institute, has been a pioneer in developing programs that successfully guide clients through the process of career decision making. These programs consist of clear-cut steps that help clients choose a specific career that will be highly satisfying, give them the opportunity to reach their goals, use their talents at the highest possible level, and be practical and achievable. From the beginning we have been committed to developing the best tools to help people make the best decisions. Rockport Institute has helped many thousands of clients from all walks of life: young and old; rich and poor; professionals in career change; artists, students, and people reentering the workforce. We have had the opportunity to serve as personal career consultants to several national and global leaders, CEOs of *Fortune* 500 companies, senior policy makers of three presidential administrations, and people in nearly every field of endeavor. Our clients have one thing in common: a strong desire for a very fulfilling career.

For the last seventeen years, as Director of Rockport Institute, my single-minded passion has been to create methods that help intelligent, complex people like you choose the perfect career and stretch beyond the circumstances and perceived limitations that hold them back from living lives of deep fulfillment. I have written this book to, as closely as possible, duplicate the experience you would have if we were to sit together in the same room and work step by step until you reach your goal, knowing for sure what you will do with your life. In these what mattered the most to each of us: self-expression, adventure, power, enjoyment, being a member of a team that's going for it 100 percent, making beautiful things, personal growth, solving problems, healing, teaching, machismo, raising a family.

The secret of success is making your vocation your vacation.

— MARK TWAIN

If you were to look around, there do seem to be some people involved in careers that include all the elements we valued as children. There is a satisfied minority that actually looks forward to going to work. Sure, they call it "work" in front of other people. They are being polite. Let's take a look to see how many people have careers that fit like a custom-made suit.

Reality 101—What's Really Going On out There?

Most men would feel insulted if it were proposed to employ them in throwing stones over a wall, and then throwing them back again, merely that they might earn their wages. But many are no more worthily employed now.

— HENRY DAVID THOREAU

When I was a boy, my friends and I would watch the men in dark suits walk to the train station for the ride into Philadelphia. We were, in our blessed state, Tarzans of the jungle pretending to see the "civilized" world for the first time from our hidden vantage point at the edge of the bamboo grove. The men seemed to drag enormous, invisible weights along with them, as if they were sucked toward the city by some mysterious, invisible magnet. We imagined they were zombies answering the call of the voodoo master. We did not have to stretch our imaginations very far. They did look a little like zombies. They had lost the joy of living.

Every once in a while, I take a ride on the subway during the morning rush hour. Even though I no longer watch from the edge of the jungle, I still observe people on their way to work. At first glance, they seem fine, concentrating on their newspapers or lost in thought. But look again, with the eyes of a child. What's really happening here? Perhaps resignation is the best word to describe the general mood. Many of these folks are enduring, submitting. My friends and I were being theatrical in imagining zombie magnets pulling people to dark fates, but, hey, let's face it: These people are definitely not looking forward to going to work. Maybe they are still half-asleep? Might they awaken by the end of the day? Take the same

From *How to Go to Hell* ©1990 by Matt Groening. All rights reserved. Reprinted by permission of HarperPerennial, a division of HarperCollins Publishers, New York.

subway when people are on the way home from work. Any improvement? Actually, if anything, it has gotten worse. Now there is fatigue mixed with the resignation. Some of them look like they've just done fifteen rounds in the ring.

The trouble with the rat race is that even if you win you're still a rat.

— LILY TOMLIN

To make these observations a little more scientific, I have also ridden the subway when people were on their way to see their beloved football team play. The train is filled with a spirit of excitement, enthusiasm. People talk and joke with others they have never met before. The mood is playful, with the channels of communication open, the passion for life obvious. It's irresistibly delicious. So now we know, after careful scientific inquiry, it is not the subway ride that darkens the riders' lives. It must be something about their work.

Not everyone on the subway is dreading work. As a matter of fact, many people are more satisfied than they look. They are hiding it. Try stepping on the subway one morning filled with enthusiasm, doing a little soft-shoe routine, whistling, radiant, alive. People will shoot you looks that suggest that you must be on the way to the Mad Hatter's tea party. You are a threat to their resignation. If there were more people like you around, they might have to wake up and get a life. They want to make sure you do not disturb their somnambulism, so they fire little glowers in your direction to stop that infernal dance that's intruding on their dark daze. So the people who love their work play it cool. They camouflage their enthusiasm. They try to look as resigned as everyone else.

If you divided the subway riders into categories, based on overall career satisfaction, you would discover a wide range of levels of fulfillment. Many surveys have looked into this question over the years. Some of them paint an overly rosy picture because people tend to respond to casual "How's it going?" questions with "all's well." In-depth psychological surveys suggest that most people are not satisfied with their work. At Rockport Institute we surveyed 1,500 people in an attempt to get at the unvarnished truth. Here's what we found. (We did round off the numbers a little.)

The chart on the next pages contains some very good news as well as some very bad news. First the bad—40 percent of American workers are at least somewhat unhappy with their jobs. Ten percent are in a condition I call "career hell," a condition very dangerous to their well-being, their health, and to everyone around them. If you include the Neutrals, fully 70 percent of us go to work without much enthusiasm or passion.

Career Satisfaction Scale

0 to 10 scale	Estimated % of population	General Description	Effect on Personal Life	Contribution to Workplace
10	10 %	**WORK OCCURS AS PASSIONATE PLAY** Looks forward to going to work, work seen as vehicle for full self-expression, fun and pleasurable; difficulties interpreted as positive challenges, considerable personal growth and contribution to self-esteem linked to work; little distinction between work and rest of life, sense of purpose and making a difference, uses talents fully; work fits personality, usually exhibits eagerness and alacrity.	Self-actualized lifestyle, generous with self—often participates in "service" to others; loves life; active participant in all aspects of life, goes for the gusto, playful; high level of personal integrity, self-esteem is rarely an issue; very significant increase in longevity and disease resistance.	Work is an expression of a clear personal purpose; self-generating, does not need supervision; very trustworthy—will persist until objective is reached, almost always contributes and is appropriate; takes correction as an opportunity; the presence of a person living at this level raises others with whom he or she works.
8	20 %	**POSITIVE** Enjoys work most of the time; satisfaction dependent on circumstances, basic enjoyment of work tempered by difficulties; feels useful; usually has a sense of purpose or meaning regarding his or her job, career meets perceived needs, contributes to positive self-esteem; good fit between work, talents, and personality; high level of competence; value appreciated by others; would say work is "pretty good. I like my job."	Satisfying career enhances other areas of life, often has success in relationships, family and projects, positive self-esteem, increased longevity, increased resistance to disease, enjoys life much of the time	Usually makes a positive contribution to the organization and other people; effective worker, fairly flexible; needs a minimum of supervision but not fully self-generating; handles responsibility well; decision making usually based on what's needed rather than personal agenda.
6	30 %	**NEUTRAL** Often accepts work situation without struggle; can appear to be a valued worker in a procedure-driven organization. This is the typical employee of a government agency or large, stable corporation. Some may say they like their work, others may grouse. If so, complaining is often simple socializing in an environment where complaining is a preferred mode of communication.	Leads a life that has no real positive effect on the community, but usually has no significant negative effect either. Relationships and other aspects of life outside work may be "normal" but narrow.	May produce quality results in repetitive tasks; contributions are mechanical; little potential for real leadership, initiative, or creativity; resists change; conservatism affects judgment, at best, furthers own ends; would always hire the person with the best résumé rather than the best candidate, destructive when placed in a position beyond grasp.

4	30%	NEGATIVE Goes to work because forced by circumstances to do so; actively dislikes significant parts of job; daily routine marked by struggle, suffering, resignation; clock watching, resentment, resignation; areas of life other than work may be satisfying; work either doesn't use abilities fully or requires talents not possessed; may be clash between personality or values and environment; complains about job; fear of job loss; may actively attempt to improve lot; may accept some personal responsibility for the situation.	Even though other areas of life may be healthy, career stress usually has negative effect on relationships, health, and longevity. May spend considerable portion of spare time recovering from work. Some erosion of self-esteem contributes to resignation or feelings of powerlessness in other areas.	Destructive to the workplace. Even if lack of satisfaction is hidden, it spreads to other employees; contributions, even when well meant, are outweighed by liabilities; is not really effective because usually wants to be somewhere else; motivated by need rather than choice. Needs supervision to produce consistent high-quality results.
2	10%	CAREER HELL Work is a constant struggle, takes an act of will to go to work each day; strong sense of resentment, deep suffering; major clash between talents or personality or values and requirements of the job; symptoms similar to people between 2 and 4 on this scale except that here the dissatisfaction is more intense and the person feels completely trapped; each day at work erodes self-esteem; profound negative effect on other areas of life.	Because work is so enervating, little psychological room to do more than survive; reduced capacity to support others; difficulty in maintaining healthy relationships; marked hostility or resignation toward workplace; life shortened by several years; diminished immune system.	Dangerous and very destructive to environment; liability to self, others, and workplace; resistance (may be passive) to supervision, poor concentration; agenda is always at odds with organization's purpose; feels vindicated by the failure of others; completely untrustworthy; actively enrolls others in own agenda. Needs constant watching.

Death is not the greatest loss in life. The greatest loss is what dies inside us while we live.

— Norman Cousins

The good news is that about 30 percent of us have at least a moderate degree of career satisfaction. To me, the most exciting news is that about 10 percent of people report that they love their work. This significant minority has somehow managed to pull together all the important elements to have their dreams come true. So often we imagine things going well for a distant and mysterious group of people, the ones we see on TV—the movie stars, writers, and Nobel Prize winners. To have fully 10 percent of people operating at the highest levels of career satisfaction gives hope that you can do it too. After all, how difficult can it be to be in the top 10 percent if you dedicate your energy to achieving that end?

The American Way of Career Selection

Before we begin to delve into how you can make a career choice that fits you perfectly, let's take a look at how people usually decide. The American way of career selection goes something like this. During your junior year of high school, the tribal elders, consisting of your parents and your guidance counselor, initiate you into ancient secrets learned empirically over many generations. They whisper the secret in your ear: "Start to think about what you may want to do." You, as green as the jolly giant, don't notice that this meager advice might be insufficient to plan a brilliant future. You begin your quest. That night you pry your attention away from teenage angst and raging hormones long enough to follow their sage advice. You "think about what you may want to do." Perhaps some ideas for potential careers appear out of the mist, like distant, mysterious mountains. Perhaps they don't. You get no really useful guidance from school guidance counselors or your parents, none of whom realize that such an important and personal decision must be based on knowing much more about yourself and the world than you do at this tender age.

Much later you find yourself in a line. It is the close of your sophomore year of college and you are queued up to pick a major. You remember the mantra, "Start to think about what you may want to do." By the time you reach the head of the line you have decided. Years later you will tell friends that your major in Polynesian philosophy "seemed like a good idea at the time." Years pass. Like the majority of college graduates, you will have embarked on a career that has nothing at all to do with your college major. How did you make that final choice? "Well," you say, "it seemed like a good idea at the time."

If you are a student, you may think that I am exaggerating. I wish I was. Ask some of my older, midcareer readers who are hit-and-run victims of this process. Look closely. You will know them by the tire tracks across their souls.

Here are the results of two studies done by Rockport Institute for all of you statistics lovers: Over 70 percent of successful professionals surveyed thought they could have done a much better job of making decisions about their lives. They said that they had not known how to go about making choices in a competent way. In another survey, 64 percent of college seniors questioned said they had serious doubts that they had picked the right major.

Many people put more energy, creativity, and commitment into deciding which house to buy or where to go on vacation than in deciding what to do with their lives. More often than not, they drift into a career direction that doesn't really fit their talents or live up to their dreams. Others get stuck along the way and spend their lives making unnecessary compromises.

Since the do-it-yourself method, without professional assistance, often fails, what about career counselors? Some colleges have extremely competent job-hunting assistance, but I have yet to hear of one that does an excellent job of helping students decide on a career direction. In fact, I have met only a few people who said their college career center was useful as a source of decision-making tools and coaching. The vast majority agree that college career counselors are well meaning but just do not have the necessary tools at their disposal to be really effective. Of what real value is a career center that is good at helping graduates find jobs they don't really want?

Most professional career counseling is not much better. Several years ago I conducted a survey of people who had used professional career counseling services in New England. Most said the counseling was helpful, but 68 percent said they had not been able to decide what to do with their lives. Even though most career counselors are well intentioned, the methods they use were developed thirty to fifty years ago to help an unsophisticated public deal with simpler decisions. You may have been exposed to these outdated methods in school or in subsequent attempts to make career decisions. How effective were these methods in helping you? It becomes more obvious every year that, in these complex times, the traditional methods of choosing life direction and career path are pitifully inadequate.

If you have worked hard trying to pick a satisfying career and it hasn't worked out, please let the following sentence seep into the very core of your being. IT'S NOT YOUR FAULT! Nor is it the fault of a psychological shortcoming or some fatal flaw in your character. It is simply that the tools you have been using aren't adequate to the task. If you have felt frustrated or depressed that you have been unable to choose well, that is completely normal. It's got to get to you after a while if you try to pound in nails with a wad of Silly Putty instead of a hammer.

How Well Does Your Present Career Fit?

1. Go over this list. Check the statements that are true. If you check almost all of them, you are doing pretty well. The ones you left unchecked show where you could use some improvement. If you left several of them unchecked, you are in the wrong career; and you are reading the right book.

___ You feel like a duck in a pond. Your work is a natural expression of your talents and personality.

___ Your job fits you so well that, often, work is play.

___ You are proud of what you do and enjoy telling other people about it.

___ You are highly respected at work because you are so good at what you do.

___ You do not have to pretend to be someone else at work.

___ Your own best and most natural forms of creative expression are what you are paid to do.

___ The environment you work in brings out your best efforts.

___ You enthusiastically look forward to going to work most of the time.

___ Your job rewards your most important values and allows you to fulfill your goals in terms of personal growth, achievement, income, stability, etc.

___ The result of your efforts makes a contribution that personally matters to you. You don't spend your days working for something that you don't really care about.

___ Your job directly fulfills your work-related goals. It does not create barriers to realizing your other goals.

___ You like the people you work with.

___ You are on a winning team that is having a great time getting the job done.

___ A day on the job leaves you feeling energized, not burned out.

2. Which of the unchecked statements do you want to have in your future career? Write them in your notebook.

3. What work have you done in the past that was fulfilling in ways that are missing in your present career? Think back and notice what was it that made it so satisfying?

Every aspect of your life is directly related to how well your career fits you. People who are engaged in satisfying, challenging careers that match their talents, personalities, and goals usually achieve a higher degree of success than people who do not care passionately for what they do. They are healthier, live longer, and tend to be more satisfied with other aspects of their lives. They feel their lives are meaningful and a source of joy. An ill-fitting career contributes significantly to stress and depression, and has a profoundly negative effect on self-esteem.

We are what we repeatedly do.

— A R I S T O T L E

Whether you are midcareer and contemplating a change or at the beginning of your work life and making a first choice, it is extremely important to make the best possible decisions. If you choose well, your life will be enriched in many ways by your work. If you make a mistake now, you place an unnecessary burden on your shoulders that may be difficult to carry and equally hard to put down.

You spend more time working than doing anything else. Since making the best possible career choice has an enormous impact on the overall quality of your life, attempting this adventure without expert guidance can end in disaster. Left to their own devices, people often find themselves in careers that don't match their talents and desires. To someone who has never worn shoes, there would not seem to be much difference between size 10 and size 9. However, if you have size 10 feet and spend your life wearing size 9 shoes, you would be constantly aware that a small miscalculation makes the difference between comfort and pain. Some people wind up bored or burned out. Some are successful yet remain unfulfilled. Midcareer people who take the risk to improve their lives by making a career change often find their new careers are not much of an improvement. Others pick something impractical or unrealistic, without considering how they could go about making the shift to a new field. These people have done their best; but their best wasn't good enough.

If you do not feel yourself growing in your work and your life broadening and deepening, if your task is not a perpetual tonic to you, you have not found your place.

— O R I S O N S W E T T M A R D E N

The Benefits of a Career That Fits

- **You enjoy better health, a longer life, more vitality.** Read the obituary notices on the "Milestones" page in a few issues of *Time* magazine. Notice how many celebrated (and notorious) people live into their eighties and nineties. Other than inheriting good genes and taking care of your body, leading a satisfied, purposeful life is the most effective thing you can do to live a long, long life. Most of the people whose deaths are reported in *Time* dedicated their energy to the wholehearted pursuit of something that mattered to them. That's why they became so successful that their death was worthy of mention in a national magazine. You may also infer that they must have found an elegant fit for their talents to have become so accomplished in their fields. Even the gangsters and dictators must have excelled at their evildoings to generate such worldwide notoriety. People whose work is fulfilling are more resistant to disease and heal more quickly when they do get sick. Why not turn your sick days into vacation days? People die in disproportionate numbers within three years of their retirement because they have nothing exciting to live for.

- **You have enhanced personal and professional relationships and are more fun to be around.** If you want great relationships, live your life fully. Others want to be around people who lift their spirits out of the petty pace of day-to-day routine. Your enthusiasm will spark those around you, who then become better company themselves. Having your working life be a major source of satisfaction and self-esteem has a powerful positive effect on the other areas of life, including your relationships. You're more fun to be around.

- **You're more successful and more productive.** There is a close relationship between career satisfaction and material success. People who enjoy their work put their heart and soul into their careers. How much do you accomplish when you are completely immersed in a task that you are really enjoying? Compare this with your productivity when you are forced to do something you don't want to do.

- **You have heightened self-esteem.** We have managed to turn self-esteem into something mysterious and complex. Simply said, self-esteem is the reputation you have with yourself. How much do you admire people who grumble about their lives, blame their circumstances, and resign themselves to a life of mediocrity? If your career is not satisfying and your self-esteem is low, you're probably not neurotic. You're just being honest with yourself! Create a future you will be proud of. Spend your days doing something you love.

- **You become a better role model for children.** How can you teach your children, or any young person who looks up to you, to live their lives fully if you don't live yours fully? They watch your actions. When your words don't match your actions, they know instantly that you are full of "caca del toro." Your children will model themselves after who you are and what you do. If you want to be proud of them, live so you are proud of yourself.

Nothing has a stronger influence psychologically on . . . children than the unlived lives of their parents.

— C A R L   J U N G

- **You lead a life that counts.** Your career is your best opportunity to make a contribution. Somehow, it's not the same thing spending your life in a job that is meaningless to you and then trying to make a difference in your spare time.
- **You look forward to life.** And, just as laughter is infectious, so is listlessness, dissatisfaction, and boredom. This ennui will follow you home from work and infect the other parts of your life. Having a career that fits perfectly restores the enthusiasm that came so naturally early in your life.

I think that what we are seeking is an experience of being alive, so that our life experiences on the purely physical plane will have resonances within our own innermost being and reality, so that we actually feel the rapture of being alive.

— J O S E P H   C A M P B E L L

- **You have a deeper, richer, more authentic sense of humor.** Humor that wells up from a core of well-being and satisfaction is very different from the cynical jokes of those trapped in a life of resignation. Wouldn't you rather have your wit be generated in happiness than in desperation? You might even find yourself smiling and snapping your fingers when you're stuck on the thruway during rush hour, happy with thoughts of work well done and the joy of living.

I N Q U I R Y   3

W H A T   W O U L D   I T   B E   L I K E   T O   H A V E   A   C A R E E R   T H A T   F I T S   P E R F E C T L Y ?

1. Imagine waking up in the morning with excitement and enthusiasm for the coming workday. Imagine spending your life doing something that you care about deeply, with most of your time engaged in activities that use your talents fully.

2. What would it be like to attain a high degree of mastery and success while engaged in activities you enjoy? Take a minute now and actually imagine what it would be like. Close your eyes and visualize yourself in a career you love. Make it as real as possible. Try to actually see, feel, and hear yourself in the midst of working happily at this new job. What would it be like to have a career that fits you perfectly?

The Costs of Having a Career That Fits

- **You would have to control your impulse** to constantly remind your friends how much you enjoy your career.
- **You might have to get new friends.** When you begin to live from a commitment to have your life work brilliantly, you might discover that you have outgrown some of the bottom feeders who will champion their lack of fulfillment until their dying day.

Keep away from people who try to belittle your ambitions. Small people always do that, but the really great make you feel that you, too, can become great.

— M A R K   T W A I N

- **You would lose some of your best reasons to complain.** Most of us have a certain investment in complaining. If you think this doesn't apply to you, try to completely refrain from complaining for the next month. An unfulfilling career is ideal raw material for this hobby. You would have to find other things to grumble about.
- **People will talk behind your back.** When you are just one of the herd of moderately dissatisfied people, you don't attract much attention. When your career really takes off, there will be plenty of jealous gossiping.
- **You will not be a member of the biggest, most popular club.** You will be in a minority, and perhaps feel slightly out of mainstream, like a monk in a bordello.
- **It takes more heart, more energy, and more commitment** to have a career that really sings. You would have to ask more of yourself, inquire more deeply, put more time and energy into choosing your direction.
- **You would have to exchange comfort for vitality.** This is by far the biggest reason people pay the terrible price that having an ill-fitting career exacts. If you want a full life, you have to give up whatever addiction you might have to comfort, to not rocking your boat, and to avoiding the feelings of fear and uncertainty that are always one's companion on journeys outside the safety of

the daily routine. A passionately lived life is not always comfortable. Going for it involves being open to all of life—the joys, the sorrows, the mundane as well as the magic, the splendid victories, the most abject defeats. You might even stop closing your eyes during the scary parts of the movie.

Are You Up for It?

It takes courage in the face of cynicism to stand up for the possibility of a life lived fully. Making a definite decision to have a career that is highly satisfying may seem like naive optimism to many of the people around you. Unless you have managed to create a circle of rather extraordinary close friends, you will most likely discover that very few of the people around you will provide any substantive support or encouragement. Many will be threatened by your insistence on a life that, for them, is just a faded dream. Think about it. Aren't you a little envious and uncomfortable when someone you know takes off like a rocket while you are left sitting in the same old spot?

So, the question on the table is: Are you up for it? Please don't be glib in answering. The reason people have so much trouble changing or choosing careers, losing weight, or quitting smoking is that they are unwilling to venture into new territory, to be a little uncomfortable and uncertain, but that's what it takes to get out of the same old groove. So, take your pick. Each choice has its advantages.

—— **I'm going to go for it!**
—— **I want to go for it, but I'm not sure I'm quite ready to definitely commit myself yet.**
—— **Not now. Maybe later.**

OK. If you have decided not now, please put this book away for the time being. You can't ride if you won't take up the reins. Put it somewhere on display in your library where you will see it often. If you like, you could even surround it with flashing lights and large neon arrows. Each time you notice it, it will remind you to ask yourself, "Is it time yet?"

If you want to make the commitment but are not quite ready, read the chapters entitled "Why You Don't Get What You Want" and "The Power of Commitment." Then see if your answer is the same. If you're ready to rock and roll, let's get on with it!

CHAPTER 3

•

HOW TO DECIDE

The time has come to pack up our tents and get the show on the road. This chapter is the basic instruction manual for designing your career and using *The Pathfinder* to do just that. It is the road map for your journey. If you are like me and never follow instructions as a matter of principle, please, please follow them just this one time. I promise you will not regret it. As you continue through *The Pathfinder,* you may find it useful to return to this chapter and reread it from time to time. I will do my best to make this book as complete as possible. But a book can be only a part of the process. You can't learn to master the art of making love or choosing a career by reading a book. It takes enthusiasm, dedicated effort, and constant practice. A book can never be more than a guide. No matter how carefully you absorb all the material here, reading will not lead you to a satisfying career. Reading about position number sixty-six is not the same as joyfully experimenting with it. It takes committed, high-energy, full-tilt-boogie participation to have the kind of life you want. If you treat this book like the huddle in a football game and then go out and play to win, you will do just fine.

Creating Your Future, Step by Step

Choosing a vocation that is not a compromise need not be a terribly daunting task, if you go about it in a way that is effective. Basically, it is simply a process of posing questions and then answering them. It is a little like buying your first house. You start the house-buying process by making a commitment to yourself that you are going to own your own home. Then you start to explore. You really don't start from square one because your mind is already filled to the brim with wishes, dreams, feelings, preferences, prejudices, and everything you already know and believe about houses. As you go through the decision-making process, you may alter some of your dreams and hopes. You may discover that some of what you think you know about houses is not necessarily so. The more you dig into the subject, the more you learn. The more energy you give to the project, the more likely it will be that you will have the skill to buy a house that does not turn out to have terrible flaws you didn't notice when you chose it.

At some point, you will probably realize that doing a great job of picking a house is a lot more complex and demanding than you thought. You discover that there are many important questions to consider that you hadn't even thought of previously. After lots of careful consideration, you begin to make some smaller decisions. You may decide that the house absolutely must have four bedrooms, or a large country kitchen, or that it must be located on a quiet side street. As your explorations continue, you make more and more of these smaller decisions. As you make them, other pieces of the puzzle come together naturally and usually fit together perfectly. While all this was going on, you would be out there in the real world, looking at houses, checking out the realities of how much of a mortgage you could get and doing other practical research. Each of the pieces contributes to the others. The research helps you make decisions. Each decision helps you explore the areas you have not yet made decisions about. And continuing to explore helps you make more decisions. The house you eventually decide to buy may be quite different from your original idea because its features are the result of in-depth exploration and an ongoing process of decision making.

One thing that is very important to notice is that your definite decisions have a much more powerful effect on putting together the pieces of the puzzle than do your preferences. For example, if you have decided that the house absolutely must have four bedrooms, then you would not even bother to look at houses with fewer bedrooms. Your preferences do not have the same effect. In fact they often make things more confusing. Let's suppose you have lots of strong preferences but no clear commitments. You might dream of a house with five bedrooms, two fireplaces, a huge backyard with a stream, nice friendly, quiet neighbors, a big party room, and a large Dutch windmill coming out of the roof. That's a wonderful dream. But since you are living in the ephemeral world of dreams, you are highly susceptible to becoming lost in the twilight zone. When the real estate agent shows you a house with a large Dutch windmill coming out of the roof, you jump for it. After all, if you don't grab it today, someone else will. Only later do you discover that the neighbors file their teeth to a point and raise cobras. When you return to reality, you discover that the house has only two bedrooms, the fireplace doesn't work, and the stream is actually sewage outflow from your neighbor's house.

You could easily make the same mistake in choosing your new career. To make sure this does not happen, please take a minute now to get completely clear about how *The Pathfinder* will guide you through this process. It is not complicated if you employ the principles that are illustrated in the Eskimo illustration that follows. If you spend the time now to completely understand these steps, burn them into your memory, and keep them in the forefront of your mind as you go through this journey, you will not lose your way.

Take a look at the Eskimo illustration on the next page. To the right of letter "A" there are eight boxes. Each of them represents an important area that is worthwhile to consider fully as a part of deciding what you will do. They will each be described a little later in this chapter. The many inquiries in this book are

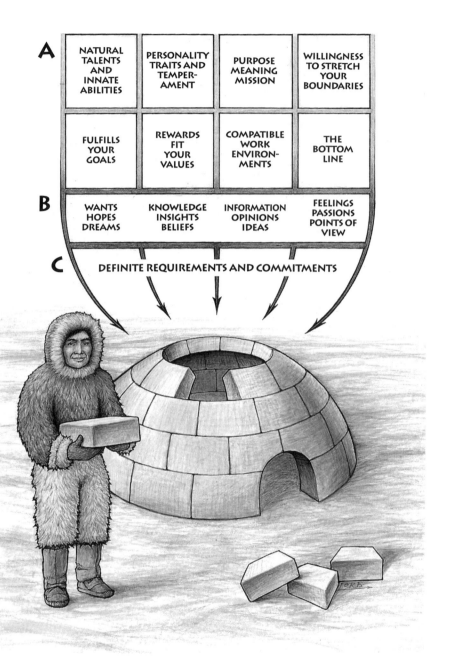

A

NATURAL TALENTS AND INNATE ABILITIES	PERSONALITY TRAITS AND TEMPER-AMENT	PURPOSE MEANING MISSION	WILLINGNESS TO STRETCH YOUR BOUNDARIES
FULFILLS YOUR GOALS	REWARDS FIT YOUR VALUES	COMPATIBLE WORK ENVIRON-MENTS	THE BOTTOM LINE

B

WANTS HOPES DREAMS	KNOWLEDGE INSIGHTS BELIEFS	INFORMATION OPINIONS IDEAS	FEELINGS PASSIONS POINTS OF VIEW

C DEFINITE REQUIREMENTS AND COMMITMENTS

designed to help you explore each of these areas in depth. They are different from the usual career explorations you may have done in the past. Most traditional career exercises just help you sort out what you already know about yourself. You wind up with more information but not any closer to deciding what to do. Why does that happen? Because everything we know, see, think, etc., occurs in a "domain." For example, a chair is only a chair in the domain of furniture. If you put a chair into an environment where a tribe has no furniture and doesn't even have a concept of furniture in their language, it would not be a chair. It would be whatever they said it was. Perhaps to them it would be a hat or a sculpture or whatever. We think they are mistaken. We think they are so out of the loop that they don't even know it's a chair. But it really isn't a chair in their world.

Our thoughts occur in domains, too. Our minds are continually running in a nonstop stream of impressions, memories, information, hopes, dreams, opinions, feelings, passions, and ideas. You could think of it as the domain of the soap opera, the never ending parade of thoughts flowing by. When you dump more information about yourself or about potential careers into this cauldron of random quicksilver thoughts and impressions, the information becomes more flotsam and jetsam, just more stuff swirling around in your head. Have you noticed that thoughts about your future career (and everything else) seem to pop up in your mind as concerns, uncertainties, as thoughts that flow by and then disappear without getting anything important decided? This is shown at "B" on the illustration. This is the perfect domain in which to write love poetry, converse at parties, and live the everyday parts of your life. Without it, life wouldn't be much fun. But, it doesn't work very well as the place to conduct your career choice process.

The Inquiries in this book give you an opportunity to go much farther. To make a leap to a completely different domain, the domain of certainty, of definite requirements and commitments. A domain where the big question is not, "What do I want" but, **"What am I sure will definitely be an important component of my future career?"** This domain is shown at "C" in the illustration. The Inquiries in *The Pathfinder* are designed to provide an opportunity for you to break all the important questions down into small pieces and then actually make smaller decisions, commitments that add up, one at a time, into the final big career decision, like the blocks the Inuit (Eskimo) is building into a nice, solid, igloo.

The Pathfinder will guide you through a series of steps that lead toward the final goal of deciding exactly what you will do with your life, or at least as much of your life as you want to decide about now. Each of these steps builds toward that final goal. Let's take a look at each of them now. I've broken down the career-choice process into several steps for the sake of clarity. In reality, deciding what you will do is not quite as neat and linear as that. You will be engaged in several of these steps: research, making some smaller decisions, investigating, asking new questions, all at the same time. But as time goes on, you will find that you are more and more focused, and that you are coming closer to the final goal as you fit the pieces of the puzzle together. And then, one day soon, you will have put enough of the pieces together that you will see the light at the end of the tunnel.

1. **Make a commitment to decide on your future vocation.** The first step is to decide to decide. Wanting to decide will not get your plane off the ground. What do you suppose the glazed-over, office-bound people you see on the subway on their way to work are thinking about? Probably they are thinking the same sort of things we all think: "I wish my life was _____." "Wouldn't it be great if I could _____." "What I want is _____." It can be very entertaining to think this way. But, no matter how much they wish and hope and dream, they keep getting on the same subway each morning and going off to the same old job. You want to become so certain about your future that you can take potent and resourceful action to make your commitments become your reality. The way to do that is to step out and make definite commitments that you are willing to keep, even when you don't want to. Start by making a promise to yourself that you will choose your career direction and use *The Pathfinder* as the tool to coach you through the process. (You will have a chance to do that down the road a piece.)

   If you are one of those people who has trouble with the C word, don't worry. We will handle it together. It is one part of the career-choice process that gives everyone the heebie-jeebies. You will find everything you need in *The Pathfinder* to master the art of creating and keeping commitments.

2. **Begin by looking in.** The idea is to design a career that fits you rather than trying to squeeze into something the wrong shape or a few sizes too small. To do that you must turn your attention inward. Get to know yourself thoroughly. Inquire into every aspect of your nature and personality. When you have achieved some internal clarity, then turn your attention to matching your vision to the realities of the outside world.

3. **Seek full self-expression.** You would be wise to honor every aspect and each domain of your life. Consider each thoroughly if you want your work to be balanced and harmonious. Full self-expression doesn't necessarily mean swinging from the chandeliers. It means including all the important parts of your nature and your intentions. A career that fits perfectly demands that you be who you are fully and do what you do naturally.

   All other creatures on the planet, from the lowest amoeba to the great blue whale, express all their component elements in a perfect dance with the world around them. Only human beings have unfulfilled lives. Only humans suffer from career discontent. But, then again, we are the only inhabitants of the earth that get to decide what we will do with our lives. Since we have the option to choose to be the authors of our destinies, why not do it well? The reward for taking on the adventure of choosing and creating a career is a life of fulfillment. There is nothing mystical or magical about this. It is simply a function of learning to have all aspects of your nature play together in harmony, like the instruments of an orchestra.

So without any intentional, fancy way of adjusting yourself, to express yourself freely as you are is the most important thing to make yourself happy, and to make others happy.

— SHUNRYU SUZUKI

4. **Break down the big question, "What am I going to do with my life?" into smaller, more manageable chunks.** If you are like most of us, when you attempt to make career decisions, you imagine careers that might be interesting (doctor, lawyer, Indian chief). Your mind hops from one potentially interesting career to another. Your romantic imagination kicks in. You think of all the positive aspects of the job: "Let's see, I really like the idea of becoming an Indian chief. It seems like an exciting job, working outside, nature all around, not a boring desk job, great clothes, etc." Then, after a while, you have an attack of negative considerations, an attack of the "Yeahbut" thoughts: "I'm allergic to feathers, those cold winter nights in the teepee, and what about cavalry attacks?" You are left with a veritable blizzard of mental images and opinions about potential careers yet are no nearer to making a definite decision about which one to pursue. What's worse, using this method, things tend to get foggier rather than clearer.

When you first think of a new potential career, it is an idea as pure as newly fallen snow. Then as you think about it more, your opinions, both positive and negative, tend to get stuck onto the original picture. After a while, whenever the thought of that particular career surfaces in your mind, all you see is all the stuff stuck to it. When you think "Indian chief," up pops a picture of a cavalry attack. The way the human mind tends to approach career decision making is not very effective. It is like eating peas with a knife. Although people find ways around this situation (like coating the knife with honey so the peas stick to it), it works better to have a really effective, road-tested method to make decisions. When you break the "What shall I do with my life?" question down into small chunks, everything gets easier. It's like eating peas with a big, deep spoon.

As you wind your way through *The Pathfinder,* you will have a chance to look into everything you need to consider in order to pick the best possible career, including some things you might not give sufficient attention to, left to your own devices. Later in this book, the big question, "What will I do with my life?" has been divided into smaller components, each a distinct domain. You will have an opportunity to consider and explore each of them. Some have an entire chapter devoted to them. Each is a vitally important component of making the perfect choice. Leave one out at your own peril. These correspond with the eight boxes you saw in the Eskimo illustration. Within each of these domains there is much to explore and many questions to ask. Let's take a brief look.

Natural talents and innate abilities Everyone is born with a unique group of talents that are as individual as a fingerprint or snowflake. These talents give each person a special ability to do certain kinds of tasks easily and happily, yet also make other tasks seem like pure torture. Can you imagine Robin Williams as an accountant? Talents are completely different from acquired knowledge, skills, and interests. Your interests can change. You can gain new skills and knowledge. Your natural, inherited talents remain with you for your entire life. They are the hand you have been dealt by Mother Nature. You can't change them. You can, however, learn to play the hand you have been dealt brilliantly and to your best advantage.

Personality traits and temperament Many people are engaged in careers that make it necessary to suppress themselves at the job. An elegant fit between you and your work includes and supports the full self-expression of your personality. Telltale signs of a career that doesn't fit your personality include: the necessity to assume a different personality at work, restricted self-expression, activities that conflict with your values.

Purpose, meaning, mission People who are enthusiastic about their work are usually engaged in something they care about and are proud of what they do. They feel they are making a contribution. They may need to go to work to pay the bills, but that is not what gets them out of bed in the morning.

Willingness to stretch your boundaries One of my clients was a forty-year-old woman who decided to pursue a career in medicine. Her previous college record was insufficient for entry into medical school. She had no money to finance a medical education. Her willingness to stretch beyond what seemed possible was so strong that she went back to college and completed prerequisite courses. She gained admission to a fine medical school and managed to creatively finance her education. Other clients are unwilling or unable to make more than a modest stretch in a new direction. I encourage you to stretch as far as possible toward a career choice that will not be a compromise. At the same time, be completely realistic. It makes no sense to make plans you are unwilling or unable to achieve.

Fulfills your goals To have something to shoot for is an important part of the joy of working. A custom-designed career supports you to fulfill your life goals and gives you a sense of challenge on the job.

Rewards fit your values Like a biscuit you give a dog, rewards are the motivators that help keep you happily performing your tricks at work. Some rewards mean more to you than others. That is because they are linked with your values. If recognition for doing something well is a value important to you, then it may also be a necessary reward to motivate you to keep performing well. Doing without adequate recognition will slowly erode your well-being on the job.

Compatible work environments Each person flourishes in some work environments and finds others stressful or otherwise inappropriate. Several different aspects of the environment that surrounds you play a vital role in the quality of your work life. You live in a certain geographical environment. The company you work for has a particular organizational environment, style, and corporate personality that affects you every minute you are there. On a smaller scale, your immediate work environment includes the physical work setting, the tone or mood of your office, and your relationships with others including your supervisor, fellow employees, and clients or customers.

The bottom line Are the careers you are considering really suitable, doable, and available? Do they really fit you? The decisions you make about your career direction are no more than pipe dreams unless they are achievable and actually turn out as you hope they will. Research is the key to understanding the reality of potential future careers.

5. **Ask resourceful questions.** The quality of your life depends on the choices you make. Your choices stem from how well you answer fundamental questions about yourself and your future. The quality of your answers directly depends on how focused, how succinct, and how clear you are willing to be when posing important questions.

Questions are the creative acts of intelligence.

— FRANK KINGDOMY

Like most intelligent people, you may have already learned a great deal about yourself. Many people who know themselves well still have difficulty making the best decisions. Getting a Ph.D. in psychology has never made anyone well-adjusted or happy. However, *the way* you understand yourself and *how you use* this knowledge is often more important than *how much* you know about yourself. The art of inquiry is an essential skill in designing your life. The better the job you do of framing the question, the better the answers will serve you. In fact, when you frame a question perfectly, the answer often seems to fall from the question naturally and easily, like rain from a thundercloud.

One secret to successfully asking and answering important questions is to break them down into small chunks. Answering the question, "What shall I do with the rest of my life?" is a mammoth endeavor. The only possible way to tackle it is to break it down into small, manageable pieces. As they say, the way to eat a mammoth is one bite at a time. Instead of trying to leap directly from the swirling uncertainty of an internal storm of impressions, wishes, hopes, dreams, preferences, and information to a definite career choice, take it one step at a time. That way you can consider each important piece of the puzzle thoughtfully and carefully.

6. Delve into all important questions, using inquiry tools and self-tests that help you become absolutely sure what the elements of your future work will be. As you continue on through these pages, you will come upon many guided assignments and exercises called "Inquiries." Some of them are like telescopes or microscopes. They allow you to look farther or deeper. Some are a bit like the transporter room on the starship *Enterprise*. They give you access to new possibilities and new worlds. Others serve the function of a crowbar, prying you off the rock you are clinging to for dear life. Each is designed to delve into one important area in a way that allows you to get clear enough to make some decisions. You must remember that these tools are only little black squiggles on white paper. They will not do it for you or to you. Only your commitment, energy, and work can make anything happen.

As you go through *The Pathfinder* you will focus on the issues that are most important, both the ones you are already thinking about and ones that have never crossed your mind before. You will explore what is unique about you. Some of the eight domains may seem more important to you than others. That may be true. But don't neglect the others. They will almost certainly turn out to be more important than you think.

Several chapters focus on developing a good working relationship with those aspects of human nature that are common to all of us. Some of those aspects get in our way, causing us to throw up barriers that complicate the process of making choices. These chapters will help you become more effective in making the best possible choices by successfully dealing with indecision, confusion, uncertainty, and fear, pushing through procrastination, and turning your dreams into reality. There are specific solutions to the problems you will run into and answers to many of your questions. There are also chapters that are minicourses on some of the things you need to go through this process. They address such subjects as: why you don't get what you want, how to get what you want, decision-making and job hunting.

7. **Design your career one piece at a time. Build with definite commitments.** Often, people attempt to hold back on making decisions until they have done all the research and answered all the important questions. They have mounds of information but nothing definitely nailed down. They try to manage the wild herd of mustang dreams, needs, wants, insights, and goals stampeding through their minds. Every good cowperson knows you can't get the whole herd through the corral gate at once. Like an Eskimo building an igloo, build your future career one block at a time. Build it from solid chunks, made from definite commitments.

There is a big difference between *wanting* something and *making a commitment* to achieving it. Wants and commitments may seem very similar in nature. The wording may be almost identical. The statement, "I want a glass of water" seems very similar to, "I am going to have a glass of water." Yet they are as different from each other as a tree is from a picture of a tree. "I want to have a great day today," often produces a very different–quality day than, "I'm going to have a great day today." Tentative decisions engender fuzzy commitments, which in turn give rise to irresolute actions.

8. **Make decisions that shape and define your career path.** At the same time that you are engaged in delving into and wrestling with all of the important questions, you will begin to build the foundations of your future career, step by step. You do this by making decisions. They are one of the main building materials you use to construct your future vocation.

Over many years of road testing with thousands of clients, we have figured out some ways to make decision making easier. One way, as I have mentioned, is to break everything down into small chunks. It is much easier to make a definite decision about how many bedrooms your new house must have than it is to make the whole enormous "which house to buy" decision all at once.

It does not work to put off making decisions until the end. Some people think they need to consider everything carefully before they make any decisions. They think they will figure everything out, then decide. As attractive as this method seems, there is one small problem with it. It just doesn't work! I see a steady stream of clients who have spent years trying to do it this way. They know themselves as well as the canary knows its cage. But they still haven't decided what to do with their lives. The only way I know that works consistently is to build a piece at a time, to make a series of smaller choices that fit together like the blocks of snow in an Eskimo's igloo. It doesn't matter if you make big decisions or small ones. Each is a worthy piece of the puzzle.

Almost everyone could improve their skill in making decisions. Farther on down the road there is a chapter that is a minicourse in how to make the best possible decisions. Both beginners and old hands alike will find it useful. You will see just how many of the decisions you think you make are actually made by preexisting mental programming. And you will learn new ways to make choices that put you in the driver's seat and increase the odds that the decisions you make will be the best possible.

9. Fit together everything you are sure of like pieces of a puzzle. Like the Eskimo building an igloo, you construct your future block by block, piece by piece. The building blocks are made of the one and only element you have to work with that is as solid as the blocks of snow the Eskimo uses: certainty. You build with whatever you have become sure of as you go through this decision-making process. There are really only two ways to be sure of anything. You can look inside yourself and uncover preexisting requirements, elements about which you are already sure. For example, living in a safe neighborhood might already be a definite requirement for you. The other way to be sure is to *decide* that you are sure, to declare some element you want to be a definite requirement. You make a commitment. Once you make the decision that the house you are going to buy must have a large, private backyard, that choice becomes one building block of the larger decision you will make about which house to buy.

Passions, insights, and dreams live in the realm of inquiry, where they serve as guides. But they become as evanescent as clouds when you take them out to the career construction site. If you build your future on a foundation of solid rock, using career components you have become sure of and definite decisions you have made as the building blocks, you will be more able to stand firm when doubts and difficulties arise.

Taking things one step at a time and building from solid chunks is like putting together the pieces of a jigsaw puzzle. When you start assembling a large, complex puzzle, you have a tabletop covered with a seemingly endless number of unconnected pieces. It's difficult to fit the first few pieces together. Once you have fit some together, it becomes much easier to add new pieces. It is also a bit like doing a crossword puzzle. You fill in whatever you can. When there is a piece of the puzzle you cannot answer, instead of getting frantic, you simply go on and work on answering other parts of the puzzle. Then, later on, you return to the part you could not figure out before. Because you have filled in some other, related pieces, it is now much easier to answer the previously unanswerable question. So, we will concentrate on what you can answer.

10. **Go for vitality, not comfort. Be unreasonable.** At every moment you have one essential choice: to let the programming steer the boat or to take the helm yourself. Your present circumstances, your mood, the thoughts that pass by all have a life of their own, independent of your will. You can, at any moment, take flight on new wings into an unprecedented life by making a choice for vitality, for living fully, for LIFE spelled in capital letters. It is, however, an expensive journey. You pay by giving up the familiar, comfortable, everyday ways of living and thinking that are the wages and rewards of going with the flow of your programming. The willingness to feel fear and keep going forward distinguishes the living from the merely breathing. In fact, it is not just the so-called negative emotions that are uncomfortable. When you choose to live fully, your palate of experiences, thoughts, emotions, and possibilities expands. This leads you onto new ground in other areas of your life as well. And, folks, all that newness swirling around just ain't comfortable.

The question is not whether to take risks, but which ones to take. The peril of being reasonable is that you will miss all the fun. It's not enough to cautiously edge your way toward the cliff. Learn to revel in taking risks for the sake of your soul. Every choice you make gives birth instantly to certain risks as surely as your shadow follows you.

There are really only two ways to approach life—as a victim or as a gallant fighter—and you must decide if you want to act or react, deal your own cards or play with a stacked deck. And if you don't decide which way to play with life, it will always play with you.

— MERLE SHAIN

11. **Go out into the world and do research to discover what matches the pieces of the puzzle you have assembled so far.** Now it is time to look out in the world around you and do some research. You need to find out more about potential careers you are considering. You may need to poke

around and see if there is anything that exactly matches what you are looking for. What is the work really like? What is the work environment like? What is the usual mood and tone of the people working there like? What would it be like to do that all day, every day? How well would it fit with the commitments you have made up to now? What would you have to do to make it happen? Where could it lead in the future? What preparation would be necessary? How would you go about making it happen? These are only a few of the things to research and consider. As you combine this research with your continuing internal inquiries and decision making, the shape of your future career becomes ever more clear.

If you point toward the stars while keeping your feet firmly planted on the ground, you will have the best chance to get to your destination. Research and an honest relationship with yourself are the keys. Unless you check in continually with the real world around you, the perfect career may turn out to be no more than a pipe dream.

Although I have research listed as the eleventh step, don't wait to start this phase until you have gone through the previous steps. You can begin to do research from the very beginning, as soon as you have some questions to answer. What seems to work best is a feedback loop where you continually research in the external world whatever you discover and decide by looking within. Then check out how you feel and what you think about what you have learned in your research.

12. **Keep repeating the steps of this process until you have defined enough pieces of the puzzle to be able to make the final decision. Then, make the leap and make the choice!** Once you have put together many pieces of the puzzle there comes a moment of existential choice. It's time to leap, to decide on your future career. For most people, the final answer will not appear out of the fog on its own. You have to make your own final choice. A few weeks or months ago it may have seemed like an impossibly large leap. Now you are ready. Because you have worked so diligently making some of the smaller decisions, it is easier to decide. In the movies, the hero often has to make impossibly long, death-defying leaps from the roof of one building to another. Making the final decision may feel a little like this. But all the work you have done has paid off. It has brought the buildings sufficiently close together so that making the leap is now within the range of what you know you can do.

You may have assembled enough pieces of the puzzle to reveal your final career. For example, if you decided that you will work with lions in a large cage in front of an audience and carry a whip and chair, it should not be too difficult to make your final decision. You still have to make the leap, however. You have to decide to do that which was revealed by all your hard work. You have to commit. Otherwise, all you have is a nice description of a career that fits you perfectly, which you will probably never get around to doing.

13. **Persist in spite of obstacles and setbacks.** Don't stop until you know what you are going to do with your life. If you quit before you reach your goal, you won't reach it. That last statement seems almost idiotically obvious, doesn't it? Yet, it is the number one reason people do not get what they want.

> *Let me tell you the secret that has led me to my goal. My strength lies solely in my tenacity.*

> —LOUIS PASTEUR

Throughout history, men and women who have made extraordinary contributions have been asked the secret of their genius. The one thing that most of them agree on is the power of persistence. No matter how brilliant your idea or how large your dream, without exceptional tenacity it is likely to remain unrealized. The quirk of human nature that makes it difficult to persist when the going gets rough is that most people are more committed to experiencing their habitual, comfortable range of inner sensations than they are to accomplishing what they have said they will do. If you are willing to experience fear, disappointment, humiliation, and embarrassment, you become an almost unstoppable force of nature. As we shall see in later chapters, the secret to perseverance is a simple one: have a bigger commitment to getting the job done than to attempting to control your inner feelings and sensations.

As you travel through *The Pathfinder*, you will discover that your biggest difficulty in persisting, as well as in making the final decision, is something I call "Yeahbuts." These are thoughts generated inside you by a device that seeks to keep you safe by keeping everything in your life the same. You will meet up with it often on this journey. For the time being, begin to notice that you have attacks of thoughts that try to convince you to give up on making any substantial changes to your life.

> *Never give in, never give in, never, never, never, never . . .*

> —WINSTON CHURCHILL

14. Celebrate! When you have decided what to do with your life, celebrate! You owe it to yourself. Or, even better, why not celebrate that you started this process today? Tomorrow, celebrate that you are moving toward your goal. When you get stuck, celebrate that you are stuck. Celebrate when the sun shines and when the cold winds blow. Make this process one of joyful creation rather than a job you have to do.

More Words to the Wise

Please do not believe anything I say or jump to conclusions too easily. Trust yourself. Don't blindly accept the word of experts. As you read along, look into your own life and your inner self to see whether or not what I say seems valid to you.

Start at the beginning, from wherever you are now. Wherever you are on the journey toward a fulfilling career is the perfect place to begin. There couldn't be a more advantageous place for you to start from, because, for you, there is no other possible starting point. Your life has taken you to wherever you are today. It didn't take you somewhere else. You wound up here! This is it! This is what you have to work with. If you are young and shiny and naive, use your enthusiasm to propel you. But look carefully before you leap. If you are crusty and jaded, use your experience to separate wheat from chaff. You will just have to manage cynicism. If all has not gone well so far in your search for the perfect career, use your experience to guide you away from making the same mistakes. Watch out that you are not seduced by the inner voices that speak from resignation. And, wherever you are, remember these great words of wisdom:

No matter where you go, there you are.

— BUCKAROO BANZAI

Participate fully. Throw yourself wholeheartedly into the process of choosing your future career. Make it the most important thing in your life right now. Sometimes, wholehearted participation alone is the key that unlocks the doors to a future of wondrous new possibilities.

How to get maximum value from Inquiries. An *inquiry* is, as the dictionary says, a close examination of a matter in a search for information or truth. That is a perfect description of the inquiry tools in this book. Each one gives you an opportunity to closely examine one specific area closely. Work through them one at a time, step by step. Throw yourself wholeheartedly into participating in each and every suggested Inquiry. Surrender to being magnificently coachable. Explore all aspects of every Inquiry fully until you have resolved and decided all you can about that area. Then go on to another. If you try to handle too much at once, or mix too many elements together, you will get completely confused. Each of these elements is important. It is definitely worthwhile to devote equal attention to all of them.

Use the Inquiries to design your career rather than to gain knowledge or insight. You can do an exercise to learn from it or you can do it with a commitment to have it play a powerful role in actually deciding on some piece of the puzzle. With a commitment to get results, you probably will!

Work through every one of the Inquiries at 200 percent, even if you think it probably won't help you. By 200 percent, I mean giving twice the energy and commitment you usually give to important things in your life. Some Inquiries will have a profound impact on moving you much closer to your goal, some may not. You will never know which ones will be useful unless you do them all and give your all to each of them. Imagine you are locked in a vault with an atomic bomb that is ticking down toward zero. You have a sheet of instructions that tells you how to disarm it. If you follow the instructions in *The Pathfinder*'s Inquiries as fully and carefully as you would the disarming instructions, the results you get will definitely be worth the short-term sacrifice of not doing everything your own way. Please give the same importance and focus to these Inquiries as you would to disarming the bomb. After all, your life really is at stake!

Don't worry if parts of this process overlap one other. You are not merely a mechanical puzzle that can be divided into a few nice, neat components. The eight domains you will explore are just a way of using language, albeit inadequately, to begin to consider the magnificent complexity that is you. There is a great deal of crossover between talent and personality, meaning and reward and so forth. For instance, as you explore the chapter on meaning, mission, and purpose in your work (chapter 22), you may be addressing some of the same issues that will come up in the chapter that follows on values and rewards (chapter 23). *The Pathfinder* is designed so that you will have a chance to explore everything important. That would not happen if there was not some overlap from chapter to chapter. Some themes keep popping up in various places in *The Pathfinder*. In a book that aims to explain or educate, this repetition would be redundant. In the present situation, you and I are in a coaching relationship where the goal is to get you successfully to the far shore. If you find you are reading something similar to what you read in a previous chapter, please assume that it is a concept that is especially important to master.

To have a great career, have a great life. To have work that really sings takes expanding your commitment to excellence to include other aspects of your life. At any moment each important area of your life is either expanding, contracting, or hovering. If most of the other areas are contracting, or hovering, you will find it very difficult to get very far along the path toward having a very satisfying career. To get moving in this career-choice process, you would be wise to up the ante in the rest of your life. If your relationships, integrity, self-esteem, or follow-through on commitments are suffering, your career-choice process will most likely be compromised, and vice versa. As you wend your way through *The Pathfinder,* you will find that sometimes the conversation focuses directly on career issues. Other times it will expand to include your entire life. When that happens, please expand your Inquiry so it is broad enough to consider your life as a whole.

You may need resources in addition to this book. I have done my best to include everything you could possibly need to go completely through the process of choosing your future career within the pages of *The Pathfinder.* Nevertheless, you may find that you need some personal coaching or assistance. Also, one of the most important areas to get absolutely clear about is your natural talents and abilities. The best way to do that is to go through a special diagnostic testing program. Information about this can be found in the "Getting in Touch" section at the back of the book.

Two mistakes to avoid. Most people make one of two mistakes in going through *The Pathfinder.* The most common is to remain in the role of observer. At a championship tennis match the players are participating totally, giving all they have to the game. Everyone else is just an observer. Their minds are commenting on the game, critiquing, as a journalist would. They are not playing the game. They are just watching as the game unfolds. If you remain in the role of observer, *Pathfinder*'s process will not work. As that great guru Yogi Berra said, "You can't think and hit at the same time." *The Pathfinder* is designed to help you hit a home run in the game of your life. Remember, this is just a book. Nothing more than little black marks on white paper. What will make this process turn out as well as you hope is full participation, unreserved, with as much energy and commitment as if you were being chased by a lion.

The other mistake folks make is to get too anally compulsive. You do not need to examine every leaf on every tree along the path of your journey. Don't make this more complicated than it already is. Concentrate on the central issues, the important stuff. Don't sweat the details.

How long will it take? Most people take two to four months to go through this process. Others blast through it in a couple of weeks. I suggest that you allow it to take exactly as long as it takes. Mark your calendar for six months from now. If you still haven't chosen your career by then, it is time to start wondering what is taking so long. No matter what the difficulty, you should be able to diagnose the problem and figure out what to do about it within the pages of this book. Some people move very slowly. They need a great deal of time to let things bubble up. It takes them ten years to decide to marry their lover and all week to decide what to do Friday night. If this describes you, give yourself one year at the most.

What if I get stuck? If you get completely stuck, go on to another part of the puzzle. Sometimes, no matter hard you try, you will not be able to answer some of the Inquiries you are making. Go through this process as if you were doing a crossword puzzle. If you do not know the answer to whatever you are working on, go on to other parts of the puzzle. By completing some of the other parts, you will find that the answers come more easily in the parts that previously had you completely stumped.

I have difficulty making commitments. Why should I think that suddenly anything will change? It can and will change, if you are willing. Most of the difficulties people experience stem from using commitment problems as a shield to hold off the new, the unknown, and the unwanted. So, in fact, what people often perceive as a problem, is actually a solution they concocted to deal with past problems. When you were a child, did you usually have trouble deciding what to do when other kids asked you to come out and play? If not, you are in good shape. Don't worry. It will all work out. *The Pathfinder* is, in a sense, a course on how to create and follow through on commitments. So, you are in the right place, at the right time.

How will I know that I made the right decisions? You won't know for sure until time passes and you have reached your objective. You can't know for sure how anything in the future will turn out until you get there. If you give the career-choice process your best effort, and you are willing to do whatever it takes to arrive at your destination, you can be fairly sure you will make the best choice. If you diligently work your way through *The Pathfinder,* you will have the best possible chance of choosing a career that will be deeply rewarding in many ways, for the rest of your life.

What if I'm not completely ready to decide now? That's fine. I suggest you stick your toe in and try the water in a place you think you will like. If you have issues you want to work on, go right to the chapters that deal with them. If you like the water, dive in head first.

How to Use *The Pathfinder* as Your Guide to the Future

I wrote *The Pathfinder* to be used as a guide that you could continue to use as you move through the stages of your life, making choices and facing new obstacles.

Right now, you may want to use it to design a career from the ground up. In the future, you may want to use it to help you solve a problem or get clarity on a specific issue, whether it is career related or not. As a result, there are different approaches you could take to use it in a way appropriate to your situation.

One approach is to use it the same way Huey, Dewey, and Louie Duck use *The Junior Woodchuck Handbook* to pull a triumphant victory from the jaws of defeat, just before the razor-sharp teeth snap shut. When you have a problem, look up the solution. *The Pathfinder* was written so that each chapter stands on its own, as much as possible. That's one reason why some things get repeated a little more often than you may think is necessary.

If you are planning to use *The Pathfinder* as your guidebook to choosing your future career, this first approach will probably be insufficient to take you to your goal. Another approach is to start at the beginning and keep moving forward, step by step, until you know exactly what you will do with your life. Read every chapter. Do everything *The Pathfinder* suggests. Choosing a fitting career is one of the most important decisions you will ever make. It is always better to look from a beginner's mind, to assume that you don't even know exactly what you need to know, than it is to assume that you've got it handled. The only way you can be sure that you do not forget to cover anything important is to just surrender control and do the whole book, from cover to cover.

Going through *The Pathfinder* from front to back is challenging and takes much time and energy. Sometimes a single chapter may have as many concepts and ideas in it as some entire career books. This book was written to support you to take a stand on the highest ground—to provide the tools you need to have a completely uncompromised life. If that is what you are after, then I recommend that you use the "do it all" method.

Even though the preceding may be the ideal method, to be realistic, we must face facts: even the best intentioned people rarely do things that way. Most of us, me included, do everything our own way, taking what we think we need and leaving the rest. For most readers, I recommend an approach somewhere in the middle ground between the "do it all" and the "Junior Woodchuck" methods. Start at the beginning, work your way through the book, do everything that is appropriate, everything that might be important, but skip chapters or parts of chapters that do not seem important to you right now. If you are looking for the most direct express route, I suggest that you work your way through part 1 and then turn directly to part 3. Spend a few minutes familiarizing yourself with the chapters in part 2 so you have a rough idea of what they contain and can turn to them when you need them. If a particular section or area of inquiry covers something that you have already handled fully, don't feel you necessarily need to slavishly go through it again. Be creative. This is a dynamic, living process, not one to be done mechanically. Do it as a passionate dance rather than as dishes that must be washed.

Hopefully, this process will be a great deal of fun for you. Some chapters will be smooth sailing. Others may challenge every fiber of your being, especially if you are playing for high stakes—a truly exceptional and highly satisfying future. You may feel you are stuck or wasting your time at least once. Expect that you may want to quit, that you will feel afraid, that you will try to talk yourself into compromises you don't really want to make or that you will decide that this method doesn't work. All of this is just good old crazy human nature hard at work, trying to reduce the risks and make you feel as comfortable as a couch potato watching a good soap opera with a big bag of chips.

To Choose or Not to Choose

Sometimes people put off choosing a career because they feel they have some growing or changing to do. That's fine if you are nineteen and need to get to know yourself and the world a little better. It also makes sense if you are recovering from a catastrophe or from some sort of deep-seated psychological problem. If you were born naturally extroverted but every time you tried to play with other children you received an electric shock and were chased away by a pack of snarling pit bulls, you would quickly learn to behave like an introvert. That would make you an extrovert who acts like an introvert to survive in a hostile environment. Later in life, you might want to take a little time to recover your lost extroversion. Here's a good way to tell if you are engaged in a useful self-improvement project or just putting off deciding what to do with your life. If you have a specific measurable personal growth goal in mind and are engaged full-tilt boogie in reaching it, I would say keep at it. But if you are involved in a long-term, broad-spectrum process of growth or recovery, putting off career decisions is probably a matter of avoiding discomfort. If your favorite hobby is exploring your own inner mysteries, consider choosing a career as a professional explorer of inner mysteries. Don't put off deciding what to do with your life until you explore the back passage of your internal labyrinth. Who knows how long it will take or if you will ever do it to perfection.

An Apology

Throughout this book, I will point out the many ways you could go astray. It may seem that sometimes I am treating you like a wild and intractable barbarian. Often people do not reach the outcome they most want because they do not recognize and master those parts of their nature that are willful, opposed to change, and operate invisibly, completely on autopilot. It is not enough to be hopeful. When you are truly committed to making something difficult happen, you naturally take stock of the forces that oppose you so you can deal with them resourcefully. If human evolution were compressed into twenty-four hours, then just two seconds ago our ancestors were hunter-gatherers, using stone tools and eating each others brains. Most of us, me included, are hard cases, either rebellious ("independent thinkers," as we would characterize it) or too quick to succumb to beliefs we have not really investigated ("good team players"). Most of us need to be reminded occasionally to stay on the narrow road to excellence. I am committed to your being spectacularly successful in designing your future career. I will point out many times how you could get sidetracked by the idiosyncrasies of human nature. Please forgive me if I do that when it is unnecessary. There is no way I can be sensitive to you as an individual when we are not working within a close, personal coaching relationship.

INQUIRY 4

LIFELINE

OK, ready to take a look into the future?

1. Open your notebook to two facing pages. You will be using the two pages together as one big page in this Inquiry. Write "Lifeline" in big letters at the top of the page.

2. Next you will draw your "lifeline." One end will represent your birth, the other, the end of your life. With a heavy pen or marker, draw a long line that spans both pages of your notebook. The line can curve, curl, spiral, zigzag, or do anything else that pleases you. Try to leave room for writing on both sides of the line. At one end write, "The Beginning." At the other write, "The End." Draw short lines to mark each decade of your life, past and present, as shown in the illustration. Write "NOW" in bigger letters at the place that represents your present age.

3. Start at the beginning of your life. Write in significant events, from the time of your birth to the present time. Focus on events where you experienced significant growth, a personal transformation, a major life event, went after or accomplished an important goal, and times when your life was profoundly altered in other ways.

4. If you are using a pen, switch to a pencil with an eraser. Begin to imagine your life continuing along this lifeline into the future. What significant milestones do you want to reach at various times in the future? Begin to write them in, along your lifeline, at the appropriate place. You might find

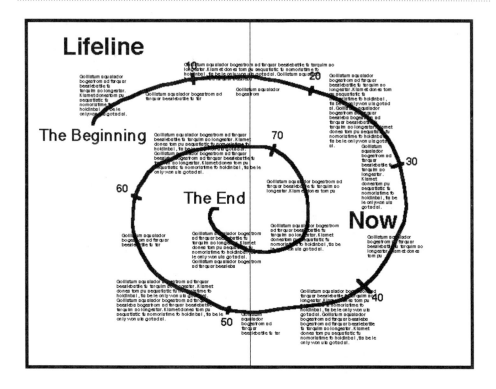

it helpful to frame your Inquiries like this: "What would I most like to accomplish between the years of x and y." "What would I want to have done?" "What would I want to have done that I have not done so far?" "Who would I like to be by then?" "Who would I want to be that I am not being now?" "What would I like to have by then?" Don't let yourself be bound by overly reasonable, practical thinking. This Inquiry is about what you would really like to have. It is not about practicality. At the same time, don't write in entries that you know are just grandiose pipe dreams. You will not find a surgeon who will secretly exchange your brain with Bruce Springsteen's, so that you become The Boss and he winds up stuck forever in your present life. Your favorite movie star will not fall for you and become your love slave. If you are fifty and out of shape, you will not be a world famous ballerina (you might have a chance in opera, though.)

5. Continue to let your imagination fly, where it will, into the future. Keep asking questions that encourage you to visualize what you would like your life to be like. You need not confine yourself to career-related entries. Look in all the other areas of your life as well. Consider things like relationships, personal goals, financial issues, etc.

Your imagination is your preview of life's coming attractions.

— ALBERT EINSTEIN

6. When you are finished, go over your entries. Ask yourself if you are ready and willing to make a definite promise to yourself that you will accomplish any or all of these dreams. Write these commitments down in your notebook. A little farther town the trail you will create a more formal commitment list. When you get there, don't forget to transfer these commitments into that list. Don't worry if you aren't ready to pin yourself down to any specific promises now. That's what the rest of *The Pathfinder* is for. Return to the place in your notebook every week or two to revisit these visions of the future. Each time, ask yourself if you are ready to definitely commit to any more of them.

As you get a bit farther down the road in this career-choice process, you may find it useful to come back and reread this chapter.

CHAPTER 4

•

BEING COACHABLE

Even the Lone Ranger had the support and devotion of Tonto. Everyone needs the coaching, mentoring, and encouragement of trusty companions. You will not be able to do this all by yourself. Why? Because commitments are as ephemeral as breath exhaled onto a cold midwinter window. You must breathe again and again onto the glass or the condensation will quickly evaporate. When you are having difficulties, a single attack of "Yeahbut maybe I should compromise a little for the sake of practicality" can bring an inglorious end to the fulfillment of your dream.

When I was in high school, the coach came straight from central casting, a big rough lout with a whistle and all the subtlety of a bulldog. I'm not sure he had any name other than Coach. My entire relationship with him was one of nonstop passive resistance to his demands that we take a few more laps around the track. Times have changed, and the concept of coaching has expanded into every area of life where people want to be more effective. People striving to be their best have discovered that they can go farther faster with a dedicated and skilled person by their side to guide them, advise them, and keep them on the track of fulfilling their goals. Now there are professional coaches for your financial affairs, voice, relationships, sexual skills, executive development, wardrobe, and spirit as well as your physical development.

If I had been more committed to athletics as a teen, I might have welcomed Coach's input. I might even have learned a great deal from him. But I will never know what could have been. Whatever he told me to do, I either avoided, resisted, refused, or converted to my own interpretation. Professional coaches say that their clients pay them for their expert assistance and then do exactly as I did in high school. Studies indicate that, most of the time, people don't even follow their doctor's advice. How about you? When the prescription bottle says to take one every six hours, do you follow the instructions rigorously or, like most of us, take one when you remember? Authors of self-help books say that they are happily surprised when they meet readers who have actually participated wholeheartedly, from cover to cover. No wonder most readers don't get the results they hoped for.

If you were a master of the art of making career choices, you would not be reading this now. Yet, you are stuck with having to do it yourself. You also, most likely, want to do a really excellent job of designing your future. It all adds up to one inescapable conclusion: If you are going to get the most from this book, you are going to have to play 200 percent! My first suggestion is that you allow me the privilege of being your coach throughout this process. Second, I ask you to suspend whatever degree of uncoachability you suffer from while you go through this process. Surrendering your uncoachability does not mean giving up your independence. During the American Revolution, independence and resistance went hand in hand. In coaching relationships, they make strange bedfellows. True independence means being free from the domination of your own internal automatic behaviors, not doing what you feel like when the urge strikes.

To be truly coachable, you need to master one of the more obnoxious traits of the human mind. We humans believe that the constant opining of the little voice in our heads is the truth. Whatever opinion our mind offers, we accept it as the one and only reality, even in regard to subjects about which we know nothing. Everyone knows that the music they like is really the best music, the people they think are cool are really the cool people, and that the world would run perfectly if all the leaders would just listen to them. Each of our minds is the omniscient god of a teeny, tiny universe. If you were a master of whatever you seek coaching for, you wouldn't need a coach in the first place. A good coach tells you things you don't want to hear and asks you to do things you don't want to do so that you can have the life you most want to have. So, your usual way of evaluating other people may not work since coaches worth their salt will constantly ask you for more than you want to give. The only way you will know if the coach knows anything is to accept and act on their coaching fully rather than to constantly judge and evaluate everything they ask of you. Given the fact that we human beings are usually either resistant or compliant, this is going to take some commitment and practice!

Train yourself to do everything your coach advises, and do it as closely as you possibly can to the way your coach suggests that you do it. To understand this aspect of coaching, watch the film *The Karate Kid*. Whenever you don't understand exactly what your coach is up to, think "Wax on, wax off." If you don't know what this means, see *The Karate Kid* right away. Promise yourself you will follow the coaching fully for some fixed period of time. At the end of that time period, take a look and see if you achieved the objectives you targeted. Give your coach a break. You may have achieved enormous benefits even if you haven't yet reached the final goal. The big question is: "Is this working? Will this get me to my goal if I keep at it?" Then, if it isn't working, fire the coach and get a better one.

The secret to success in choosing your career or in any endeavor is to put out a 200 percent effort and to be 100 percent accountable for the results you get. In doing the exercises in *The Pathfinder*, that means starting by reading the instructions a couple of times, even if you think you got it the first time. After getting perfectly clear what is asked of you, throw yourself into the assignment. Give it everything you've got. Be aware of your very human tendency to resist participating fully. Don't let that tendency run the show. Then, when you are finished doing everything the book asks for, make up your own ways to move the process forward. Never *just* follow instructions. Follow the instructions and then unleash your creativity. After all, no one knows you as well as you do. Trust yourself to make up appropriate inquiries into the most important questions you are facing. Ask yourself over and over again, "What else can I do?" If you are just doing the assignments in this book, without pushing the envelope to break your own sound barrier, you are not participating 200 percent. If you do all of that and it still doesn't work, fire me as your coach. Dump the book in the trash can. Then go find another coach and give it 200 percent again. Don't ever give up on having an extraordinary life.

•

CHAPTER 5

RIGHT LIVELIHOOD

When the sun rises, I go to work.
When the sun goes down, I take my rest,
I dig the well from which I drink,
I farm the soil which yields my food,
I share creation. Kings can do no more.

—ANONYMOUS, FROM CHINA, 2500 B.C.

Right livelihood is an ancient Asian philosophical concept that proposes a perfect working relationship and flow between you and the world around you. Like the farmer who wrote the poem above, when you achieve right livelihood, you are in perfect harmony with creation. You have become ecologically appropriate.

Figure 4 illustrates the flow of energy in any part of the natural world that is ecologically in tune. In and out! In and out! On we go! There is a perfect, harmonious balance between you and the rest of the universe. There is nothing abstract, unrealistic, or mystical about living a life of right livelihood. All living creatures, from gorilla to mosquito do it. Right livelihood does not require green leaves above, soft New Age music playing, or a passion for saving the world. For some of us, working in investment banking in the bowels of Manhattan may be a perfect expression of right livelihood. The thousands of different jobs available do not exist by accident. They are all an integral part of the complex web we humans have spun. On close examination, right livelihood is really a very practical set of guidelines for living. Here's one interpretation of the components:

1. Your work fully expresses all aspects of your nature. It fits your innate talents perfectly. It expresses your temperament and personality fully, even those parts you do not see as positive. It provides the rewards that matter to you. It fulfills your goals. It occurs in an environment that is suitable and appropriate to who you are.

2. The subject of your work is something in which you have a passionate and abiding interest. It is deeply meaningful to you. It continues to appeal to you as the years roll by.

3. Your work continually nourishes you. It provides a natural route for your evolution. Its challenges stretch you to continue to learn and grow.

4. It does no harm to anyone. It is ecologically sound. It does not oppose appropriate stewardship of the earth.

5. It serves humanity in some way. You and I cannot judge what is appropriate service for another person. In the larger scheme of things, an IRS agent is just as important a part of the fabric of humanity as is a teacher, a mother, an entrepreneur.

6. It is freely accepted. You work because you choose to, not because you are compelled to.

7. You are "being" yourself.

Freedom and Surrender

A happy life is one which is in accord with its own nature.

— SENECA

Guarding the gate of the temple of career satisfaction is a grand paradox. On one hand, to be capable of choosing a highly fulfilling career, you must be somewhat of a pioneer, a rugged individualist willing to think for yourself, to be able see through the conditioned thinking and all the conventional wisdom that so often leads people by the nose to decisions that are less than ideal. You must be willing to expand your vision of what is possible as you blaze your trail into the future. On the other hand, you must at the same time do the exact opposite: surrender to the razor-sharp rules of the physical universe in which you live. There are inescapable consequences if you step in front of a speeding bus or choose a career that does not match your talents, personality, and other already existing aspects of your unique makeup.

We live in a time in which one of the most prized cultural ideals is "doing what I want." Many of us wish we were more like the movie stars, the novelists, and other creative types who seem to do exactly what they want. We pity our neighbor who never does. The very thought of being dominated and controlled by the circumstance of our lives conjures up images of dictatorships, slavery, subjugation. There is a big difference between being free to do what you want and having the talent and personality to make it happen. Full self-expression is attainable only when you mix elements of creativity and boundless possibility with the wisdom to pick something that fits who you are and the special gifts you have to offer the world. Let's inquire further by taking a brief look at one of the big questions humankind has puzzled over since the beginning of time: What is the nature of human nature? Why are we the way we are?

Nurture and Nature

For years a debate has raged between the advocates of two different theories of human ability. One group asserts that the personality traits and abilities that distinguish each of us are the result of parenting, environment, and certain events that shape our lives. According to this "nurture" theory, each of us starts life as an empty vessel of potential, a blank slate to be written on by life. The opposing point of view is the "nature" theory. It asserts that we are shaped by our genetic heritage into complicated machines whose behavior is programmed from beginning to end. According to this theory, we are trapped within a life predetermined by our DNA, unable to alter our fixed destiny. Over the years, the battle between these two sides has continued. Each of the two camps continues to insist they are right. Now that the results of many years of scientific study are in, it seems neither side got it quite right. The truth is somewhere in the middle. It turns out that human behavior is a mixture of nature and nurture. As the studies continue to pile up, however, what has surprised much of the scientific community is the enormous weight of evidence proving that we are much more the product of genetics than was previously considered possible. The simple fact is, like it or not, much of who you are today is innate, fixed, hardwired. No one knows exactly how much of your character is hardwired, the result of genetics. No one knows exactly how much was learned or how much of what you learned was shaped over the anvil of your inborn nature.

Whether your most prized qualities are attributable to nature or nurture is not really all that important. It's just water over the dam now anyway. What is important is that you are the way you are: a wonderfully unique collection of talents and traits, points of view, habits, and behaviors. They are now all mixed together to make up the spicy little bit of heaven and hell called you.

If you can let go of the notion that you should be or could be somehow different or better than you are, the whole perspective on education, personal growth, and career choice changes dramatically. Instead of trying to shape yourself or your children into a mold, the task shifts to encouraging growth toward a fully realized expression of one's natural potential. We then transform from small-time tinhorn god to gardener. This is not necessarily bad news. You may find that you enjoy gardening more than godding. Instead of trying to change into something you aren't—a more extroverted person, a more analytical person, or whatever—learn to recognize, appreciate, and express what you have been given. When your work combines your natural strengths and requires only minimum time spent doing things you are not naturally gifted at, it is like swimming downstream in a swift river. To ignore your temperament and natural talents in designing your career will very likely result in a life spent in a never-ending battle swimming upstream against the river of life. Swimming upstream is hard work and slow going. When you turn around and go with the flow, you get farther faster and your journey is a lot more fun. Every once in a while I have a dream where I come upon a man bound from head to foot by thick ropes. When first I see him, I think he looks kind of sad about his situation. Then I look again, and realize that his face is peaceful and quietly radiant. He totally accepts his plight. He is completely free. This is one of the least known secrets of right livelihood.

It's amazing how many people haven't quite figured out how important it is to design their career around the way they are now rather than the way they think they should be or hope they may be in the future. We are all, in some ways, completely free to learn, to change, to improve. In other ways, we are all like the bound man, stuck forever inside our own lives, with the temperament and talents we were born with.

When you begin to design your future career around the way you actually are, you will discover that many of the inborn qualities you considered to be negatives turn out to be some of your biggest strengths. Here's an example. I have always been talkative. At the age when most kids can barely speak a few words, I was holding long conversations with everyone, including the mailman. In the early years of elementary school, I had a great time participating in class fully in my own talkative, enthusiastic style. As the years rolled by, education became a matter of sitting quietly and politely while the teachers transferred their big buckets of facts into our little empty ones. I began to suspect that something was wrong with me. The message being sent was: noisy, playful, and enthusiastic was appropriate only in social settings, not in the serious settings of school and work.

When I made early career decisions, I never thought to design lots of talking into the mix. Naturally, I found myself in work where I had to sit quietly and politely much too often. When I committed myself to choosing a career I would love

and began to design it from the ground up, I began to see all of my various characteristics as the building blocks I had to work with, rather than from a judgmental perspective of good or bad, right or wrong. I got down to the truth: Rocks are hard, water is wet, and I make a lot of noise. So, instead of squishing myself into the same old mold, I designed lots of talking into my career. One of the most powerful things you can do for yourself and your future is to accept and appreciate the whole range of your characteristics, talents, and quirks. They are what you have to offer the world. Then dig in and design yourself a future that is a perfect custom fit with you as you are. Even the things you consider to be your liabilities or psychological shortcomings are worthy of your respect. If you resist authority, maybe you should work for yourself. If you like to blow up buildings, how about becoming a demolition contractor?

The question "Who ought to be boss?" is like asking "Who ought to be the tenor in the quartet?" Obviously, the man who can sing tenor.

— HENRY FORD

I am not advocating becoming complacent about personal growth and self-improvement. Quite the opposite. Remember that joyfully surrendering to life as it is is only one half of the paradox. There may be times when you want to expand your range of possibilities or take on something that stretches you farther than you have ever gone before. That impulse or intention is just as much an element of your makeup, and therefore just as important an element of your expression of right livelihood as your talents. It's terrific when an introverted person joins Toastmasters and learns to be comfortable and capable in front of a room filled with people. They may have great personal breakthroughs as they extend their range of possibilities. They may even discover a previously concealed talent this way. But if they are truly introverted, they are probably not going to enjoy being on stage for several hours every day. In which case it would be foolish indeed for them to choose a public-speaking career.

Rather than try to change yourself, joyfully accept the genetic cards you have been dealt. Then get to work creating new possibilities, if you so desire. Learn new skills. Join Toastmasters if you want to be more comfortable or improve your skills in front of a group. If you are not very good at detail work, get creative and find a way to become competent dealing with the details you have to face. But choose a career with a bare minimum of detail work. If you are afraid of heights, you may want to learn to climb mountains to master your fear. But think twice before you become a riveter building skyscrapers.

CHAPTER 6

•

DIVING INTO THE MIST

May you live all the days of your life.

— J O N A T H A N   S W I F T

When you learn to fly an airplane, you spend some time on the ground covering the basics. The real learning begins once you take off and get your plane up into the wild blue yonder. Up until now, what you have been reading could be mistaken for ground school. After all, what you do in ground school is read books. Just because this looks like a book and quacks like a book, doesn't mean it is a book. In fact, from this point on, *The Pathfinder* is pure, 100 percent high-in-the-sky flight school. If you are not in the air already, it is time to climb into the cockpit, fire up your engines, and take off. Do you feel a little apprehensive? Excellent! That means you are not just reading in the hope that something will happen magically. Whenever you set off on a voyage into the unknown, apprehension comes with the territory. If I was heading out on this journey to decide what to do with my life, I would be more worried if I did not feel some apprehension.

If we were starting off on this journey together, in person, the first thing we would do is get clear exactly what you want to accomplish by going through this process. Please take a few minutes and think about what results you want to get from working your way through *The Pathfinder*. What sort of results would you most want, if you could have it all, without reservations. Then, write them down. Use the spaces below, or, if you are one of those people who, sitting on Santa's lap, would pull out a six-page Toys I Want for Christmas list, fire up your word processor or notebook. Please do not read on until you have completed this.

_____

_____

_____

_____

_____

_____

_____

_____

_____

_____

Very good! You just wrote your first draft. To be skilled at setting goals takes a deeper cut than most of us manage on the first try. Now, let's refine what you wrote until it is so crystal clear that it is like a laser beam of intention, so focused that it will burn a hole through the wall.

Your degree of clarity about your final goal has a huge influence on whether you actually get there and on the degree of difficulty you will face along the way. Let's suppose that you were going to take a vacation. You want to go to one place, get a room, and spend a week exploring without traveling about. You decide you are going to Paris. Since you are quite specific about your destination you can buy a ticket, book a room, and get on with your plans. But let's suppose for a minute that you are fuzzier about your final destination. You still want to spend the week without traveling about. You decide you are going to Europe. Where in Europe? Nowhere specific. Just Europe. You call the airline and try to book a flight. "Where to?" the agent asks. "Europe," you answer. "Where in Europe?" the agent asks. "Just Europe," you say.

As you can see, your difficulties are just beginning. Right now, you may think that this is a ridiculous example. No one would ever plan to go to "just Europe." By the time you get through refining your goal for this process, what you just wrote may seem a little like "just Europe." What's wrong with what you just wrote? Nothing. I'm sure it is a strong and heartfelt expression of what you hope to achieve. Let's just tighten it up a bit. Amelia Earhart's little airplane disappeared forever while on a long journey over the sea, headed to a tiny, distant island. Navigation errors compound over the course of a journey, so, with a small miscalculation, she could have missed the island completely, flown around until she ran out of gas, and plunged into the sea. So, let's spend a few minutes making sure your navigation is on target so you don't miss the island.

You may have written something along the lines of. "Get a better idea of what careers would fit me. Learn more about what would suit my personality. Get clearer about my future work. Become less confused and uncertain. Find the career for me. Gain insight into what careers I might enjoy." All good stuff, but perhaps not quite as clear and sharp as possible. I suggest that you boil it down to one final goal, a clearly defined mission statement. Some of the goals you have written down may be things you want to achieve along the way to the final destination. For example, if what you really want to do is to choose your career, "Learn more about what would suit my personality" is similar to "Have an enjoyable flight to Europe." Both are interim goals rather than the final, main mission statement. They may be important but, if you mix them in with your final goal, they will just muddy the water.

When you are going after anything in life that takes a big stretch, it is useful to be absolutely clear about your intended destination. After many years of working with thousands of people, it still amazes me how easy it is, when confusion and uncertainty mount, to forget about the final goal and settle for an easier, more comfortable interim goal. So, back to the drawing board. Please boil it down a little bit more. What do you intend to accomplish in this process? What is your final goal?

_____

_____

_____

Much better, yes? OK, let's see if we need to take it even one step further. Crafting your goals clearly in words is one of the big secrets of turning them into reality. Language has great power. It's not a matter of using correct form or following some rule, but of saying exactly what you mean. Long before the Beatles had a record on the charts, their goal was to reach "the toppermost of the poppermost." They knew just what this meant, and what they were after. You are not being fussy when you shape the words you use to express exactly what you want to achieve. You are being intelligent. To shape your future, clarify your goals. To clarify your goals, use the power of language as your tool.

In their second draft, many people write that what they want is to "find the perfect career," or something similar. The problem with using words like "finding" is that you are, in effect, placing the source of reaching your goal outside of yourself. When I was a boy, my friends and I spent many a happy summer afternoon turning over rocks in the stream behind my house hunting crayfish. It was there that I learned a great spiritual lesson that goes something like this: "If there are no crayfish under the rocks, you are not going to catch any crayfish." Often, people who have searched for the perfect career for years say it has been like searching for a needle in a haystack. They keep hoping that one day they would run across the golden needle. They have been looking for the answer externally, believing that they will recognize their Holy Grail when they stumble across it. But no matter how hard they search, all they seem to find is hay. They always seem so disappointed when they discover that there is no needle in the haystack. There's nothing there but hay.

The way to design your life is to start with a blank canvas and paint your future on it by making decisions, one brush stroke at a time. So, the way to "find" the perfect career is to give up the notion that you will ever find it, stumble across it, or that it will somehow magically find you, and get to work designing it. If this is your goal, you might want to express it a little more accurately. Perhaps something like this might accurately express what you want to do:

- My goal is to choose my future career.
- My goal is to decide what to do with my life.

Please don't let me put words in your mouth. Take a look and see how you could phrase your intention authentically, so it is as sharp and focused as a laser beam. This puts you in the driver's seat. Instead of wandering around like Galahad and Perceval, looking for the Holy Grail in a haystack, it will be easier to stay focused on what you are up to: deciding what to do with your life. So, let's do it one more time. Work out in your mind exactly what you want to accomplish. Then write it down here.

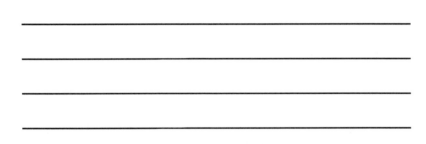

Now for the final step in setting this goal. So far, we have been discussing what you want to get from this process, what result you hope to achieve. Now it is time to take the leap from the realm of wants, hopes, and dreams into the real world of committed action. This leap consists of making a promise to yourself that you will do whatever is necessary to fulfill your goal. Instead of giving over accountability for success or failure to circumstances, the fates, or this book, take it on yourself.

Two common errors trip up folks who hope to have a satisfying career. The first is they set their goals too low. The second is they pass on the opportunity to be 100 percent accountable for bringing their goals to fruition. With this simple existential choice you take hold of the steering wheel of your life. With it alone you can become almost unstoppable, like a force of nature. I am not asking you to extend yourself further than you are ready, willing, or able to. I am asking you to go as far out on the skinny branches as you are willing to go. As every squirrel knows, it is safer near the trunk of the tree, but there aren't a lot of nuts there. All the delicious nuts are out on the ends of the branches. If you want big nuts, you can't cling to the trunk. There is one more reason to commit yourself fully and un-reservedly to deciding what to do with you life now:

> *Until one is committed there is hesitancy, the chance to draw*
> *back, always ineffectiveness. Concerning all acts of initiative*
> *(and creation), there is one elementary truth, the ignorance of*
> *which kills countless ideas and splendid plans: that the moment*
> *one definitely commits oneself, then Providence moves too.*
> *All sorts of things occur to help one that would never otherwise*
> *have occurred. A whole stream of events issues from the decision,*
> *raising in one's favor all manner of unforeseen incidents and*
> *meetings and material assistance, which no man could have*
> *dreamt would have come his way. I have learned a deep respect*
> *for one of Goethe's couplets:*

> *Whatever you can do, or dream you can, begin it.*
> *Boldness has genius, power, and magic in it.*

> — W . H . M U R R A Y

Anyone who regularly commits themselves to making the seemingly unlikely hap-pen, and then goes after fulfilling their promise wholeheartedly, knows exactly what Goethe was talking about. Only when you give up avoiding how foolish you would look if you committed yourself totally and failed; only when you are will-ing to allow yourself to be dominated by a promise you made rather than by the inner voices that always speak for comfort, can you experience the pure magic and unexpected gifts of this most direct relationship with life. Here are some ideas for wording your promise:

- I promise I will choose a lifetime vocation for myself within the next four months, a career that will be highly satisfying, fulfills my values, fits ele-gantly with my natural talents, is something I care about deeply, and al-lows me to reach my most important life goals.
- I promise to choose a form of enjoyable, purposeful self-expression that, to other people, looks like work (and pays like work).
- I promise to decide what I will do with myself in regard to my work within the next month. I will decide whether to quit my present job and seek an-other job in my field or change to a new field. If I decide to stay in my pre-sent field, I will get completely clear what the specifications of the new job will be. I will train myself to not make the mistakes in evaluating potential jobs that I have made in the past. If I decide to change, I will give myself another two months to decide exactly what I will do.

- I promise to try to figure it out.
- I promise to do my best.

Obviously, the last two promises are easier to make than the first two. That's because they are not promises that put your rear end out on the skinny branches. If you fail, you can always say, "I did my best. I tried." They are easy, comfortable promises. But if you are serious about having a life that is not just a series of major compromises, there is extraordinary value in making big promises. If you want nuts, make big promises. At this point, many people say something like, "I never make promises I'm not sure I can keep. I'm a person of my word." The whole point of making big promises to yourself is to make things happen that would not happen otherwise. Promises stretch you out into new territory. Why bother promising something that was going to happen anyway? If you are someone who is always on time, promising that you will be on time is absurd. If, however, you are habitually late, promising yourself you will be on time from now on is a powerful commitment. It will carry you out into the uncharted waters of a future that would not have happened by itself. Little promises are just a way of ripping yourself off. They are a wonderful way to avoid the uncertainty and discomfort of having a life fully lived.

Do or do not. There is no try.

— YODA

Now it's your turn. Are you willing to make any kind of a definite promise to yourself about deciding on a career? If so, write it in the blank lines below.

_____

_____

_____

_____

_____

If you are having difficulty with all this commitment stuff, go check yourself out in the mirror. If you look slightly like a cartoon character who has just been hit over the head with a huge hammer, or if some resistance is surfacing and your countenance is beginning to resemble Yosemite Sam, it is time to read the chapter entitled, "Why You Don't Get What You Want" and the one entitled "The Power

of Commitment." Please do not go on before you have fully handled whatever you need to do to create definite commitments for your Career-Choice Program. This is your life.

Courage

It takes courage to be the author of your life. When you are struggling through one of the difficult parts of turning your dreams into reality, you may wonder why you always get stuck with having to put up with so much fear and uncertainty. Why, you wonder, couldn't I feel more courageous, like those other people do.

You don't feel courageous because courage is not an emotion. There is no such thing as feeling "courageous." It is an imaginary emotion.

Courage consists of doing what you said you would do even when you don't want to.

In the face of danger you have a choice to be the delegate of either your commitments or your feelings. It's as simple and as difficult as that.

Courage is not the absence of fear, but rather the judgment that something else is more important than fear.

— AMBROSE RED MOON

•

CHAPTER 7

YOUR PRIMARY LISTS

INQUIRY 5

YOUR PRIMARY LISTS

---

1. This Inquiry sets up the three primary tools you will use to design your future career. Of course, you will use many other tools, but *you will work with your Primary Lists on a daily basis.* The first is a "Wants List." It is the place to write down all of your wants, hopes, dreams, and passions, The second is your "Commitments and Requirements List." The difference between wants and commitments is that a commitment is an answer to the question *"What am I sure will definitely be an important component of my future career?"* A want, on the other hand, is just a want, a desire, not something you have definitely decided is an indispensable part of your work. The third list is your "Questions List." It is the place to write down all the uncertainties, unknowns, and all the questions you must answer in order to decide what you will do with your life. The Wants List is incorporated into this chapter. The other two lists are explored in the next two chapters. Please make sure you do not skip either of them.

2. Reserve at least thirty pages near the front of your notebook for your Primary Lists. Start with a right-hand page and write PRIMARY LISTS in big letters in the middle of the page, as a title page for the section, Turn the page so you will be looking at two blank facing pages. Write the WANTS across the top of both pages in large letters. Do the same thing across the top of the next few pages, until you have a total of ten Wants List pages. On the first of those pages write this question in even bigger letters:

What do I want, desire, dream of, or wish for?

3. Write COMMITMENTS AND REQUIREMENTS, in big letters across the top of the next six pages. On the first of those pages write this question in even bigger letters:

> ## What am I sure will definitely be an important component of my future career?

4. Write QUESTIONS in big letters across the top of the next fourteen pages. On the first of those pages write this question in even bigger letters:

> ## What questions must I answer in order to choose my future career?
>
> ## My "To Do" List

Now you will start the first of your three Primary Lists.

INQUIRY 6

WANTS

1. Make a list of all of your career-related wants in the Wants section of your notebook. Put down all the wants, wishes, hopes, dreams, and passionate desires that surface in your mind from time to time. Do not just write down your realistic wants. Do not make up new wants. The idea is to get all the stuff you want out of your head and onto a piece of paper so you can look at it all at once instead of having your wants roaring through your head like a speeding locomotive. You may come up with a list several pages long, or you may have just a few things on your list. You may more than fill the pages available, or you may not even fill one page with wants. It is not better or worse to have a long or a short list. If it doesn't arise during this Inquiry, you probably do not want it passionately. Wants are like hair; they are right on the surface. In general, people do not have hidden wants.

2. Highlight the wants that you want the most. Pick just a few from your list, perhaps five or ten or whatever works for you.

3. Go through the few you have highlighted and prioritize them, by level of desire.

4. Go through your Wants List again. Cross off all the wants you know you will not ever make a commitment to achieving. Make another list entitled "Wants and Ideas on Hold." This is the place to store all wants that you know you are not willing to deal with now or at some specific time in the future. Instead of feeling guilty for the rest of your life that you never started that band featuring pipe organ and pedal steel guitars, put this want, this idea, in your Wants and Ideas on Hold file. This is also a good place to store any wants that you know you will never do but are unwilling to give up. For example, if you have always wanted to write a book, know you are unlikely to do so, are haunted by this desire, and are unwilling to throw it away, store it here so it can remain a somewhat real possibility but does not continue disturb you.

5. It may be that what you want is less important than it may seem. The real question is: To what are you willing to make a firm commitment that you will achieve, have, or experience? There are actually some people out there who simply make up a list of what they most want and then commit to achieving everything on the list. Why not save yourself a great deal of effort and simply commit to everything important on your Wants List? If not everything, then what are you willing to commit to? What, of the various entries on your Wants List, are you willing to promise yourself you will definitely make happen, whatever it takes?

6. Do not get upset if you are not willing to commit to anything or much now. If this is so, just ask yourself why not? What stands between you and sticking your neck out and committing to have everything you want?

7. Work with this list regularly. Add newly discovered wants and remove things you no longer want or have already fulfilled.

CHAPTER 8

•

COMMITMENTS AND REQUIREMENTS

Since you seek a satisfying and fully lived life, the following questions may be the most important ones you could ask: What tools give me the most leverage in authoring my life? How can I interact with the present moment so that my dreams are realized and I am controlled as little as possible by programming that occurred in the past?

The most powerful tools we have are two learned skills: the practice of inquiring, questioning, and exploring; and the ability to create new commitments from a ground of being that is sufficient to cause their fulfillment. If life in the present is often directed by preprogrammed mental machinery that seeks to reduce risk and discomfort, then whatever we can do to take the steering wheel serves as an effective tool. To inquire and question gives us a chance to get to know ourselves better, to notice where we are headed, to create new possibilities, to discover answers that move life forward. To create new commitments and give our energies to fulfilling them interrupts conditioned thinking and behaviors. New commitments redirect our attention, replace old patterns and points of view with new ones of our choosing. No wonder they are the primary tools for creating the kind of life you most want.

The Pathfinder is a guidebook to inquiring, questioning, and creating commitments. Nothing more, nothing less. This chapter that you are reading right now is the heart and soul of the book. Other chapters inquire into your commitments and questions at length. This is the place where all the pieces of the puzzle come together, where you design your career, sculpt your life.

The Place Where the Rubber Hits the Road

When you think about a car you like, you may appreciate its color, its design, the powerful engine, or whatever else strikes your fancy. But what is more important than all of these are four little spots we never notice.

These four little rectangles make all the difference in getting your car from one place to another. They are the places where the rubber hits the road. No matter how well designed, how powerful, or how glorious its colors, the car isn't going anywhere unless the tires touch the ground.

In deciding what to do with your life, there is one most vital central question that you will keep asking over and over again as you go through *The Pathfinder*. The question is:

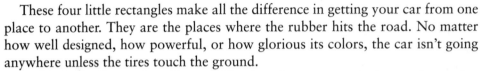

What am I sure will definitely be an important component of my future career?

In other words: What am I committed to? What are my requirements? What promises am I willing to make? **What am I sure will definitely be an important component of my future career?** What am I willing to put at stake? How good can I stand it? This question is the centerpiece and the compass for your journey through the career-choice process. It is the mold from which you create the definite building blocks that combine into your final decision.

Everything you read, explore, consider, meditate on and research is powerfully useful if it leads to being able to define concrete building blocks of your future career. Each of the building blocks of your future career is a commitment to definitely have a certain element be a part of your career. You cannot build your future from wants. They are like smoke and wind; changing their shape from moment to moment.

A *commitment* is, by definition, a promise or requirement to produce a specific result. That's all it means. Its real meaning does not include all the baggage we have added to this word, which spring from failed attempts and broken promises that still haunt us and make us feel cautious and conservative about making big promises in the future. The C word makes people a little uncomfortable simply because feelings of fear and uncertainty guard the gate of paradise. When you get close to the gate, you are supposed to feel these emotions. The key to the gate is committed action. Since you hold the key in your hand as you approach the gate, it is natural to think of uncertainty, fear, and commitment as somehow related.

Some of the commitments that will become pieces of the puzzle already exist inside of you. Think of them as *preexisting requirements*. For example, would you take a job that paid less than $2,000 per year? Take a job that involved harming people or cheating them? Take a job pretending to be a giant sloth in a department store window? How do you gain access to these preexisting commitments that are already lurking about inside of you? By asking skillful questions. Most career-counseling programs work from an assumption that all the answers, all the pieces of the puzzle, are already there, inside of you. They try to help you weave these pieces together into a coherent fabric. The only problem is that this approach doesn't work because you do not have all the pieces of the puzzle hiding somewhere inside of you.

Remember that I said that you build your future career piece by piece, like an Eskimo builds an igloo. If you try to build it just from preexisting commitments, you are going to freeze to death the first cold night. There will be many pieces missing. What you need, in addition to preexisting commitments, are what I call *created commitments*. A created commitment is a promise you make to include some specific element in your career. "In my future career I will ———, because I say so!" You are, in effect, staking yourself to a specific result. A created commitment is a declaration, just like the Declaration of Independence. American independence was not created by revolution but by declaration. The American founding fathers brought a new reality into being through an act of pure invention: They declared it into existence. Then everybody got into action and gave form and substance to their creation.

All created commitments are to some degree an existential leap. You are not merely making a prediction based on past results but proactively authoring the future with your promise. If you had a small company that had just grown enough so that it was time to hire a marketing manager, you would do your best to pick someone who would generate the most growth for your company. If you showed them a chart of your company's growth to date and asked them what they would make happen in the near future, would you hire the person who merely made a prediction, based on the past, or would you hire the person who made a bold commitment to increase the rate of growth of your company?

In the following illustration, A is past company growth. Dotted line B is a prediction. If conditions do not change, your company will continue to grow as it has in the past. C represents a bold commitment to make something happen that wouldn't happen automatically. The whole point of generating created commitments is to make something happen that could not be logically inferred based on the past; to courageously take on a goal and promise that you will do whatever it takes to make it come true.

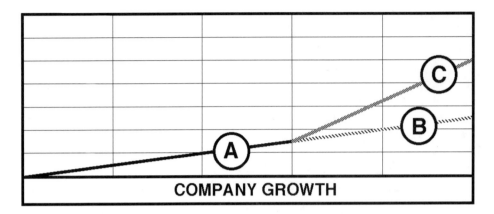

The Difference Between Wants and Commitments

At every moment of your life, you and I think from and speak from a certain "ground of being," a context that shapes the outcome of our thoughts and words. Most of the time, we come from a ground of being that is filled with wishes, wants, hopes and dreams, insights and information, preferences and passions. When we speak from this ground of being, we are, in essence a journalist reporting on what is going on inside of us. "I want a cracker." "I prefer Porsche." I love Meryl Streep." I'd like to go to Hawaii." We are describing an inner feeling or thought. What we do not notice is that what we feel passionately about in this domain of wants often never turns into reality, because this domain requires no action. Shortly after *Dances with Wolves* was released, millions of women were wild about Kevin Costner. They wanted Kevin. They preferred him. They dreamed of him, but most of them did not get in their cars and drive to California to meet him. They were coming from a ground of being of wanting. And wanting requires no action. People often mistakenly think that the more they want something, the more likely it is to happen. Millions of women passionately wanted Kevin. What happened as a result of their wanting? Absolutely nothing.

On the other hand, when you say, "I'm going to go to Hawaii, this year, for sure!" you set into motion a chain of events that concludes with you sitting on the beach in Hawaii. Commitments come from a completely different ground of being than wants. They require you to get into action to make them happen. When you create a commitment, you make a promise to yourself. As you go through *The Pathfinder,* your Commitments and Requirements List is your most important primary tool, because what you commit to actually shapes your future actions, now. The future pours out of your commitments like water from a pitcher. In the domain of commitments, you are not merely a journalist. You are the author of your life, the inventor of your future, the agent of your intentions.

WANTING

COMMITTING

INQUIRY 7

COMMITMENTS AND REQUIREMENTS

This Inquiry is your most important tool for designing your future career. In this chapter you will create several lists that you will use continually as you go through the process of choosing your future career. The most important of these is the following Inquiry, which is a list of your definite commitments and requirements. It is a place to keep track of everything you are sure must be a part of your future career. Each of the components you add to this list becomes one of the solid building blocks of that career.

1. Turn to the Commitments and Requirements section of your notebook, Remember that we talked about how the process of choosing a career is essentially a matter of constructing your future career, one piece at a time, from elements that you have become sure are definite pieces of the puzzle?

Remember the illustration that showed the Eskimo building his igloo from some very solid, definite blocks of snow? This list is the collection of pieces of the puzzle. Each commitment is one of the blocks that, in time, will form the complete igloo. And it is the whole point of working your way through all the many pages of this book.

2. This list will contain two different kinds of commitments, "preexisting requirements" and "created commitments." Here's the difference. Preexisting requirements are commitments you have already made or have absorbed during the course of your life. Some of these come from your parents, from the culture and social environment you were raised within, from your friends, and from your genes. For example, you may already know beyond question that your career will be as some sort of a "professional."

The other kind of commitments are "created commitments." You will spend most of your time in your Career-Choice Program looking into questions that lead to creating new commitments. Throughout the course of *The Pathfinder,* whenever I mention "commitments," I will be speaking of both varieties. Keep in mind, as you continue through this process, that the central focus is on building commitments, answers to the question: **What am I sure will definitely be an important component of my future career?**

First, let's delve into preexisting commitments. Add an additional title, "PREEXISTING REQUIREMENTS," to the first available three pages in the Commitments and Requirements section of your notebook. Begin to write down all the work-related elements that are already definite and beyond doubt. These are your *preexisting requirements,* the things you do not have to wrestle with or research to know they must or must not be a part of your career.

Write down all of them, even those things that might be obvious or that you take for granted. For example, you may be absolutely sure that your future career must be in some, as yet undecided, professional specialty, or in the arts. Maybe you want to use your hands, or manage people, or provide an income large enough to allow you to support a certain lifestyle. You may be sure that you will not get further training, or that you are willing to go back to grad school for x years, if necessary. You could be certain that you will remain in the geographical area you live in now, or you may be sure that you will not wear a tie to work.

Write down everything you are sure of now. Keep working at this and keep exploring to find more of these inside yourself, as you continue through the career-choice process. As you go through your day, keep asking yourself the big question: **What am I sure will definitely be an important component of my future career?** Talk it over with important people in your life. See if they can come up with other elements that you could put on your list. In the "Questions" chapter to follow, there is a long list of potentially useful questions that may bring to light other preexisting requirements. As time goes on, you may discover additional preexisting requirements to add to the list.

3. Now comes the exciting part, creating new commitments. The ability to create promises that call us out into new territory and new possibilities is, I believe one of the most sacred and extraordinary qualities of human beings, even though most of us seldom make use of it. This is the primary tool you have available to invent and shape your future. Nothing really spectacular will happen because you want it to or because you feel passionately about it. It will happen only if you promise that it will be so, and do what is necessary to keep your promise. Write "CREATED COMMITMENTS" at the top of five blank pages in your Commitments and Requirements section. As you go through this book, you may need to label some more pages as either "PREEXISTING REQUIREMENTS" or as "CREATED COMMITMENTS" as the need arises.

What would you like to include as a definite feature or element in your future career? What would you have be a part of your work if you could have anything you want? Would you be willing to definitely commit to any of these? If so, write them into your Commitments and Requirements List. The whole point of creating commitments is to cause something new to appear in your life. You will probably not find enough evidence to support making the kinds of commitments that take you into the most spectacular new territory. In fact, because Yeahbuts are so powerful and prevalent, there will, most likely, be much more evidence that you should not make the leap. But leap you must, if you are to have your life be more than an endless repeat of the past.

4. Poke around the work you have done so far in this career-choice process to see what you might put on your Commitments and Requirements List. Go through your Wants List. Are you willing to select anything on that list as a definite building block of your future career? How about the things you prioritized as most important? If they are important, why not put them on your Commitments List?

5. Keep adding to your Commitments and Requirements List (and the Questions List you will start in the next chapter) as you continue through the process of making choices and defining your future. If you are like me, your tendency will be to get caught up in other parts of the process and forget that this is your primary Inquiry. Find a way to keep your focus on

the big question. When you go to work ask: "What am I sure will definitely be an element of my future career?" When you are in bed with your lover ask: "What am I absolutely sure will be a part of my future career?" When you are in the midst of a beloved hobby ask: "What am I sure will definitely be an element of my future career?" You cannot ask this question too often. Whenever you complete any Inquiry in *The Pathfinder,* return to your Wants, Commitments and Requirements, and Questions lists and see what you can add to them.

6. You may move things back and forth from your various lists as you see fit. There are no rules. Do whatever works for you. But try to avoid putting things in your Commitments and Requirements List if you are not sure they belong. Wait until you are ready to take the plunge.

Commitments should be as specific and as definite as possible. A well-framed commitment usually has a highly specific outcome and a specific completion date built into the words you use to frame it. If I were to say to you, "I will definitely be somewhere at eight P.M. tonight," that would not qualify as a useful commitment. It lacks an important element of specificity. The statement "I will come to your house" lacks another element of specificity, a time frame. A sprinkling of dust from my cremation urn, delivered to your door, would fulfill the promise. "I will definitely arrive at your house by eight P.M. tonight, whatever it takes!" is a much more powerful and specific commitment. Try to avoid fuzzy promises such as, "I will enjoy my work more." Make it specific. For example, you might say something like, "At least three days per week, I will very much enjoy my work. I will be like a kid in a sandbox. On the other two days, there may be some ups and downs, some things I do not necessarily actively enjoy, but essentially and usually these two days will be pleasant and enjoyable." That is a pretty powerful statement of intention. It is measurable. With it, you can consider potential careers to see if they will fit. After you are working in the new job, you can see whether it lives up to your promise. If not, you can get into action to improve it or change it. When your commitments are vague or sloppy, you are left in a cloud bank of uncertainty that makes it difficult to act and correct your direction.

When I work in person with clients, I try to do the same thing a coach does at the Superbowl. I try to get some points on the board as soon as possible. That would be a good strategy for you to adopt as well. Although I am sure that all your commitments are important and valid, some are more useful than others in helping you to decide what you will do. The most useful are those that help you define and shape your career. While it may be important for you to have a window that opens, that statement does not do much to help you decide which career to pursue.

On the other hand, if you decided to work outdoors, teach, never wear shoes to work again, or use a particular talent, you would have added significantly to shaping your new career direction. You would have some very useful points on the board.

There are times when it is useful to mistakenly put things on your Commitments and Requirements List. If you put something on this list that does not belong, it will begin to wriggle and squawk. You will feel that something is not right. At that juncture you will have to discern whether the discomfort comes from something that does not belong on the list or whether you are just having an attack of the Yeahbuts. The way to tell is that if you really want it and you are having thoughts about how difficult it will be to pull it off, you are probably having a fit of Yeahbuts.

Commitments can be conditional. It is perfectly fine to promise to buy a sports car for your chief programmer, if the company makes a profit this year. Or, "I will never wear shoes to work again under any circumstances unless they pay me more than $200,000 per year, in which case I am willing to wear anything, even a chicken costume." Both of these are very clear and specific. But try to avoid too many conditional commitments. You will wind up making everything so complicated that you will never decide what to do with your life. You might be wise to assume that most conditional commitments are actually the Yeahbuts in disguise. You are usually better off deciding specifically what you most want and promising yourself that you will make it happen.

There is no advantage to phrasing your commitments in positive terms. If you feel strongly that "I will never work for a big corporation again!" say so. "I will work for a small company" may not be what you really mean. Put the passion you feel into the words you use to frame your commitment accurately.

7. Remember to work with this daily. As a matter of fact, when you have chosen your career, why not pull out your Commitments and Requirements List every week or two for the rest of your life. You will find no more powerful way to keep your life moving forward.

Captain Neal Parker is owner and skipper of one of the most beautiful sailing ships in the world, the schooner yacht *Wendameen*. She sails from Rockland, Maine, taking a few passengers for an overnight cruise filled with pure magic. Just a few years ago, *Wendameen* was sunk in the mud, a broken, rotting hulk. Major maritime museums with big budgets had pronounced her beyond hope. But Neal fell in love with her and promised himself he would rescue her and bring her back to her former glory. He bought her, got her to just barely float again, and brought her back to Maine, where he was met by laughter and disbelief. The consensus was almost universal that he was engaged in a fool's errand. He worked on her, with little money and scarce resources, all through the icy Maine winters until she was as good as the day she had first been launched in 1912. No matter what obstacles got in the way, Neal found a way through or around them. Now, a few years later, she is the pride of the fleet. And Neal, modest as he is, gets to deservedly bask in the inner pride of those people who have done what everyone said was impossible. Once I asked Neal how he did it. He said, "Once I had definitely decided, there was no turning back. It was just a matter of doing what I said I would do." That is the whole secret of generating spectacular results in any area of your life, and your Commitments and Requirements List is the place to make it happen. If you follow Neal's advice, it will all work out.

•

CHAPTER 9

QUESTIONS

If you could think of every important question that has some bearing on the quality of your future and then answer each one fully, career decision making would be a simple job. In this chapter you are going to have an opportunity to begin doing just that.

Asking Resourceful Questions

As you know, answering life's important questions can be difficult. There is no way to successfully answer these questions without experiencing the confusion and uncertainty that are the unavoidable consequences of wrestling with the unknown. You can, however, make dealing with the questions you face as painless as possible by being resourceful. Most folks never realize that their difficulties in resolving issues are multiplied by their lack of skill in the art of questioning. Some people are masters at answering difficult questions. They are all around you, making significant contributions in every field. They are not necessarily any more brilliant than the rest of us. One of the main sources of their effectiveness is that they know how to skillfully pose the questions they seek to answer.

To resolve an important issue, ask a powerful question. If you are experiencing difficulties in resolving uncertainties, the problem may lie in the questions you are asking. Most of us do not think to hone our inquiries to a sharp point. Most of the questions we chew on just popped into our minds. It never occurs to us to carefully craft our inquiries; that the quality of the question has an enormous impact on the quality of the answers that flow from it. The perfect answer often flows naturally from asking the right question. At the very least, it makes it much easier to get to the answer. Take, for example the question, "Do I need more education?" This may not be something you personally care about, but let's use it as an example because it is an issue many people, young and old, struggle with. You could print this question in huge letters on your bedroom ceiling and think about it every morning and evening, day after day, month after month, and never move an inch toward resolution. Framed as it is, it may be impossible to answer. It may not be the best question to ask to reach resolution. It may not address your real concern. Sometimes you need to look deeply to uncover the real dilemma. Concealed by the apparent question, your real question may be, "Am I willing to go back to school?" or, "Is there any realistic way I could make going back to school work, given my finances and crazy schedule?" Sometimes the real question is just an attack of insecurity like, "Wouldn't I feel completely out of place in a classroom with a roomful of twenty-year-old undergraduates?"

As you work through this chapter, and, for that matter, the rest of this book, see if you can discover what more essential questions are hiding under the apparent ones. You probably don't need therapy to uncover your real life-planning questions. They are in there, just under the surface, bursting at the seams to get out, just waiting for you to lead them out into the light of day. You simply need to poke around a little to uncover them. If that doesn't work, brainstorm. Ask yourself as many different related questions as you can think of. Don't judge. Write down every question, no matter how bizarre. Then put your notebook away until the next day. When you return to the questions, sort through the brainstorms. Checkmark the questions that may possibly be important. Then dig in and see if you can uncover the real question or questions.

Sometimes, there is more than one real question. There may be several distinct questions collapsed into one overly general, fuzzy question. "Do I need more education?" may be covering several other questions such as: "Will it really be worth it? Am I certain enough that x is the ideal career direction that I would risk more years in school? How much suffering am I willing to endure? Is there any way possible to go back to school full time? How long would it take if I went at night? Am I willing to work all day and study every other waking moment? Could I get into the local school that has the courses I need? Would I be willing to move away from Froghollow to get more education?" By brainstorming, you will discover whether or not the apparent question leads to other more pointed questions. If you find more than one question lurking under the surface, see if you can figure out if one of them is the main question, the key to finding the answer or making the decision.

Use your imagination/creativity to broaden your perspective. What else is possible? Is your point of view too narrow? You might ask questions like, "Am I thinking of going back to school because I can't seem to resolve other questions, to delay dealing with real life? Could I get the result I want without going back to school? What have other people done? Am I being too conservative? Am I making assumptions that limit my range of possibilities? Is there any way I could have it all? What qualities, what skills would I have to add to my repertoire in order to have it all?" Improving your skill in framing your questions should lubricate some of your queries and get them moving. Answers will, most likely, come more easily now.

How to Answer Questions

If half of finding the answer is posing a question resourcefully, the other half is answering it skillfully. When we delve into big questions, finding the answer usually seems to be a monumental task. Even figuring out where to look for the answers is forbidding enough to make some of us fold up our tents and go home. Fortunately, there are only three places you can possibly look to find the answers to any question you might ask: inside yourself, in the outside world, or, if the answer does not exist inside or outside, you can always make up the answer. Knowing where to look for the answer to the question you are asking is the first step in finding the answer. You would be amazed how often people get completely stuck in the midst of an Inquiry because they don't know where to look for the answers, or because they keep searching for answers where none exist.

Looking Inside is where to find answers to questions about your preferences, personality, wants, needs, hopes, dreams, ideals, requirements, experiences, etc. Answers to many of your questions, from the profound, through the mundane, to the ridiculous can be found inside yourself: "What matters to me most?" "What would I like to do this weekend?" "How do I feel about squid?" are all questions that could possibly be answered by looking inside yourself. You may discover that you already have some specific, definite requirements for your future career that you can access by simply asking yourself the right questions.

Looking out to the External World is where you will find many other answers. You will not be able to find out if there is a growing job market for acrobats by looking within. Research is the key. (A chapter entitled "The Bottom Line— Research" follows this one.)

Making Up the Answer is what you must do if you need answers and can't find them anywhere else. Many of us search endlessly for answers within ourselves to no avail. I have worked with hundreds of people who have spent years in a futile search to discover their purpose or their calling in life. They wind up tremendously frustrated because they believe that they are here on earth for some preordained purpose. But somehow the answer always eludes them. They are looking in all the wrong places, inside and outside. If they know that, if the answers cannot be found in either of these places, their only choices are to give up asking the question or to make up the answer themselves.

One of the great myths is that you can find all the answers within yourself, if you only know how and where to look. This myth grew out of a reaction by philosophically oriented people to the age of reason and science. Scientists and objective realists say that the answers are found in the external world, and discovered by research. Internally derived wisdom came to be viewed as unreliable and was culturally demoted a few centuries ago. Internally oriented people fought back. This rift continues today, with our culture divided into two camps, the "innies" and the "outies." These days, the outies think of themselves as left brainers and the innies as right brainers. Each side derides the other and looks to its own choir for wisdom. In reality, both points of view are the opposite sides of the same coin. Both depend on the past, on finding answers that already exist.

The real magic comes from the third source of answers, the ability to invent them. This is very good news, indeed. Otherwise, you get permanently stuck in neutral if you cannot find the answer to an important question within you or in the world around you. To invent an answer is to make a choice, to get out in front of the train and lay your own tracks instead of remaining merely a passenger in your life. You make an existential leap.

One way to invent answers is to make up many possible answers and then choose one from the list. Use your imagination and creativity. Brainstorm! Sit down with a pad of paper and come up with many new possibilities. Don't edit. Write down the ridiculous ones as well as the seemingly practical ones. Stretch your boundaries. If your brainstorm is no more than a slow drizzle, or you need a broader perspective, call in a few friends. Not just the ones who think like you. You also want the ones who are least like you. Pick friends with wild imaginations, outrageous or different points of view as well as your most practical, realistic friends. Pose the question to them from different angles. Ask them to come up with lots of possibilities rather than their most sound advice. There is only one ground rule to brainstorming: no evaluating, judging, complaining, commenting on, or criticizing anyone's ideas.

Push your friends to keep coming up with as many ideas as they can. Quantity, not quality. The goal is to loosen up and get the creative juices flowing. Write down everything, no matter how ridiculous. Become an idea vampire. Only when you have drained every drop of creative juice from yourself and your friends is it time to evaluate the ideas you have collected. Don't fall into the trap of believing your own Yeahbuts. More great ideas have been short circuited by people relying on their own prejudices and opinions than for any other reason. Get your friends to play devil's advocate. Whenever you attempt to kill off an idea that may answer one of your questions, have them argue for it. Stretch the limits of what seems possible. Maybe you could do what seems impossible now.

Knowing Where to Look for Answers

How do you know which of the three doors has the answer hidden behind it? First of all, decide if the answer can be found inside or outside. This is usually easy to decide. If the question is, "How do I feel about moving to a colder climate?" the answer is obviously found internally. If the question is, "How much do charter boat captains make in the Virgin Islands?" you will need to ask someone with experience. Where people run into difficulty is in determining if the answer is to be found internally or if they have to get creative and invent the answer themselves. This is unbelievably easy to determine. Here's how you do it. First, look inside. Poke around and see if the answer is in there. If it is, it will appear. You may have to give it some serious thought, meditate on the subject, give it a few days to bubble up, or wait for circumstances to develop.

If you cannot come up with the answer within a few days, most likely you never will. You do not have some cave of answers hidden deep within yourself. (That is just a myth perpetrated on all of us by Freudian analysts fulfilling their deep subconscious need to keep their clients coming back for years so they can continue to make a living.) Most of what is inside you is readily accessible. If you cannot find the answer inside yourself, it is probably hopeless to continue to look there. You will have to make up the answer and decide for yourself.

When you make up answers, you can pick anything you want. You can pick an answer that makes you feel as safe and secure as a bug in a rug. Or you can go for it and make up an answer that would give you everything you want, and more. Making up the answers is quite simple. Here's my favorite method. First figure out what you would most like the answer to be. For example, if the question you have been unable to resolve by looking in or out is, "Am I willing to start my own company?" look to see what answer you would prefer, if you had a choice. Which answer would move your life forward the most? Which answer do you have more passion for? The next step is simply to decide that the answer you lean toward is the one and only answer for you. Then commit to doing whatever it takes to make it happen. That's all there is to it, folks. Inventing an answer can be nothing more than selecting the most desired possibility and then hanging your star it.

Sometimes the answer may involve looking in more than one place. For example, if you are trying to decide what sort of organization you want to be associated with, you may want to look for answers both inside and outside. Unless you are intimately familiar with a wide range of organizations, you are going to need to do some research. Then you will check out how you feel and what you think about what you uncovered in your external research.

Each of us is more comfortable and at home in one of the three places answers can be found. "Innies" introspect. "Outies" extrospect. Hardly anyone is used to making up the answers themselves. You would be wise to leave home base often and put an extra effort into visiting the two areas you are less comfortable with. You will find the answers to your thorniest questions in the places you visit least often.

INQUIRY 8

QUESTIONS

You are now going to begin one of the most important Inquiries in *The Pathfinder* Only your Commitments and Requirements List is equally significant. Remember that the process of career choice, as well as the process of life itself, consists of asking and answering questions. This is your chance to clarify your questions, to get them all out on the table, and to figure out how to get these important questions answered.

In this Inquiry, you will create and keep working on a list of all the questions you need to answer to decide what to do with your life. You will also write down where to find the answers and, finally, what you need to do to get your questions answered. This list of questions is your career-choice "to do" list. What in the world is this man talking about, you ask. Well, if making this big decision is a matter of asking the right questions and answering them, then your list of questions will be, in essence, a list of everything you need to delve into and answer in order to make your final choice. If you do whatever you need to do to answer *all* of your important questions, you will reach your goal (or discover that there may be some questions you haven't thought of yet).

You need to keep track of all the things you need to think about, research, answer, and decide. That makes this list only slightly less important than your Commitments and Requirements List. It is by asking all the necessary questions and doing a really proficient job of answering them that you add to your Commitments and Requirements List. Keep adding to this Questions List and crossing off answered questions for the entire course of deciding what to do with your life.

1. Turn to the Questions section of your notebook.

2. Start by writing down a list of everything you can think of that you might need to resolve in order to choose your future career. Don't try to keep your questions stored in your head. Even if you can leap tall buildings in a single bound, your mind is not the place to keep your list of questions. You need to keep all this information organized enough to work with it effectively. Keep adding to this list until you have every possible question written down. Don't quit after you have written down a few big questions. Keep at it. Write down every question that could possibly have any bearing on your career decision making. You may have some very private questions you do not want anyone else to see. If so, make a top-secret Questions List, put it in code, and store it in a vault. But, WRITE DOWN EVERYTHING, including the trivial and the embarrassing questions! Keep working on this list regularly (every day or two) as you work your way through this process.

   Look through the work you have done so far on considering your future to come up with important questions. Look beneath the surface to see what the real questions might be. After all, if you want something passionately and have not decided to go after it or abandon it as a goal, there must be some very specific questions that you could ask that would break loose your condition of uncertainty.

3. Once you have written down all your questions, turn to the last eight pages of the fourteen pages you reserved for your Questions List. Draw vertical lines on several pages of your notebook to turn them into the form shown here, with a large column on the left, another large one on the right, and a thin column between them. Each of these eight page should have three columns. At the top of the page, write in the main title for the page, "IMPORTANT QUESTIONS." On the line below, title the far left column "THE QUESTION," the small column in the middle "WHERE TO FIND THE ANSWER," and the large column on the right "HOW CAN I ANSWER IT?"

Important Questions		
The Question	Where to find the answer	How can I answer it?

4. Go through your list of questions. Pick out the big, weighty, important ones—the ones you absolutely must resolve in order to make your career decisions. Write them into the Questions column of your Important Questions forms in your notebook. Give yourself lots of room. You may use a lot of space in writing down how you will answer some questions.

5. Then, when you are finished writing down all your questions, take a look at where you would look to answer each of these questions. Write Outside, Inside, or Make up the answer in the middle column, as appropriate. Remember that occasionally you may have to look in more than one place to find the answer. Sometimes, for example, you may have to do some research and then make up the final answer. This step is very important. Knowing where to find the answers makes life run a lot more smoothly.

6 After you have completed the steps above, go back through your Important Questions List with the goal of getting clear what it would take to answer or resolve each of the questions. Fill in the right-hand column, How can I Answer It? Ask yourself: What will it take to answer this question? Be very specific. Remember, the question is "How can I answer it?" not "Am I willing?" For example, you may not be comfortable calling or visiting people you don't know. It may take contacting many people you don't know to answer certain questions. You may have to choose between comfort and getting the answers you need. Don't let your perceived limitations dictate what it will take to answer a question. Write down what would best answer the question rather than what would be easy, reasonable, or comfortable. Look at the question straight on. Don't fool yourself. Some questions may be complicated or take several steps to resolve.

7. Decide if you are willing to do what it takes to answer the question. If you are, put a star on the form by the question to symbolize your commitment to do what it takes to get it answered. If you aren't willing, perhaps you can face up to your unwillingness, find a way around it, or come up with another equally effective way to get to the answer.

8. When you are completely finished going through all the previous steps, with all the questions you can think of by yourself, go on to the next step in this Inquiry, which consists of a long list of questions that you will come across if you keep reading. You may already be wrestling with some of these questions. Others may already have been answered to your satisfaction. Many of them may not matter very much to you. The point of this list is to suggest important questions to you that you may not have thought of. Do not try to answer all of them. Most likely, only a few of them will be important questions you did not think of on your own. Transfer the important ones to your Important Questions List and go through the previous steps.

9. Start working on resolving these questions. If I were you, I would sit down with my Important Questions List every couple of days, or whatever works for you to make your life into a full-time mad scientist's Inquiry lab. It wouldn't hurt to spend a few minutes working on this list every day or two. If you were to do this in regard to your entire life, I guarantee that within a year or two, your life would be functioning at a level you could not even imagine now. Go over everything you have written. Look at it anew. Improve your plan for resolving the questions. Put your plan for answering them in your schedule book for the coming weeks. Remember, this list is your *Pathfinder* To Do List. Keep working on it. Do your other assignments and Inquiries—but DO NOT STOP WORKING ON THIS LIST. Keep working to answer the questions. If you don't concentrate your energy on answering these questions, you will not move ahead.

Please do not read the list of questions that follows until you've written down all the questions you came up with on your own. Why? The plan is for you to do a deep inquiry and get clear what questions are most important to you rather than just browse through a list. This is one of those places where the easy way isn't the best way. For the time being, deal with the questions you think are of primary importance. Answer all of them that you can handle now. Begin to think about and wrestle with the ones you cannot answer now.

The Questions List

Geographical Environment

- Would you prefer to work or live in a specific geographic area, locality, or a certain type of physical environment? If so, based on what?—availability of suitable work, a certain size city or town, demographics, feels like home to you, recreational opportunities, natural beauty, peace, excitement, another family member's needs, the weather suits your clothes?
- How important is this?
- Do you prefer an urban, suburban, or rural environment?

Physical Environment

- Indoors or outdoors—how much of each?
- How much travel required—extended trips, occasional, rarely, or never away from home?
- Your physical location—sit at a desk, visit several locations each day, in front of a group of people, traveling constantly, work on top of a phone pole?
- Do you prefer an office-oriented environment, workshop, medical facility, classroom, etc.?
- Private office or cubicle? A desk in a large office with lots of other people around you?
- How large an office?
- Status of your office space important?
- Are there factors, such as lighting, noise, pollutants that affect you or the quality of your work?

Organizational Environment

- Employee or self-employed?
- Profit, nonprofit, government?
- Service organization or producer of goods?
- Mammoth organization, big, medium, small, tiny, or just you and the dog?
- Organizational purpose, philosophy, style?
- Every organization has a life span. Each stage of its life creates a different organizational environment with different advantages and disadvantages. Is this important to you? If so, what stage fits you?

   1. *Startup Phase*—Being in at the very beginning, maximum opportunity to influence the basic structure of the organization, fewest rules, long hours, pioneering spirit, biggest opportunity to carve out a big chunk of personal

territory and/or significant ownership, most risky, prone to an early death.

2. *Entrepreneurial Phase*—The excitement and rewards of quick growth, risky, unstable, filled with the unexpected, environment tinged with adventure and uncertainty, creative problem solving is highly valued and rewarded, pioneering spirit, opportunity to create the perfect niche for yourself, usually requires long hours, good chance for quick promotion.

3. *Leveling-Off Phase*—Safer, less need for battlefield problem-solving skills but still room for creativity and new thinking, perfect for those seeking to build a well-oiled and stable system and for those who want stability and security as well as growth and creativity, may require long hours.

4. *Stability Phase*—Everything is worked out, organization run by a fixed set of policies and procedures, even keel, everything stays the same, safest nest for the security-minded, lower level of appreciation for creativity and individualism, usually has conservative values, likes the steady step-by-step approach, you feel like a cog in the wheel because that's exactly what you are.

5. *Decline Phase*—Like stability phase in character, except has more pathological tendencies than other phases. Not a healthy place to be for anyone except those who love to save sinking ships. Innovative people are often brought in to try to save the ship, but their ideas are not implemented because the organization is still run by stability-phase management people who would rather sink than change.

• Opportunities for advancement based on performance or political maneuvering or seniority?

Human Environment

• How will you relate with other people at work?
• What combination of extroversion and introversion?
• Describe how often you will be in direct contact with other people.
• What percentage of your workday will consist mainly of face-to-face conversations with a constant stream of people?
• What percentage will be a mix of extroverted/introverted activities? How much introverted time?
• Is your introverted time to be spent alone with the door closed or working by yourself with others around?
• With whom will you relate or be in contact—fellow workers, customers, clients, adults, children?
  • What's the reason for meeting with them?
  • What do you get from being with them? What do they get?
  • What population do you work with or serve: Young, old, professionals;

people with problems or in need; people seeking to purchase something, to learn something, or solve a problem; people from other countries and cultures; people from a particular profession or from a particular background or socioeconomic group?

- If more than one kind of relationship, what percentage of each?
- In what kind of relationship with others?
  - If there is a teamwork approach, what sort of a team? How big? How varied the members' jobs?
  - Degree of collaboration toward a common goal?
  - Degree of independence and interdependence?
  - What sort of people are your fellow employees? What special qualities or characteristics? Professionals, technical, support, blue collar, traditional, liberal, conservative, creative, supportive, cooperative, highly motivated, not dysfunctional, young, etc.?
  - Are you supervised? How much? How often? What style?
  - Type of supervision structure—traditional top down approach or something else?
  - How much structure to your supervision? Clear lines of authority necessary?
  - Will the people you work with be the people you spend your leisure time with?
  - How connected or isolated will your work environment be from the rest of your life?

Work Definition

- Not defined at all
- Big picture objectives are defined.
- Not only are objectives defined but methodology and procedures concerning how to reach objectives are laid out clearly.
- How is it defined for you?

Pace

- Furious, fast, moderate, slow?
- Steady, varied?
- Busy all day, or lots of time to relax?

Decision Making

- How much? All day? Occasionally?
- What kind of problems/issues?
- What kind of decisions?

- What decision-making rhythm? Steady and flowing?
- One decision-making scale has at one end a constant flow of spontaneous decisions. At the other end of the scale is meticulous, deliberative, carefully planned decision making. What point along the scale fits you?

Predictability

- When you show up at work, will you have a pretty good idea of what you will be facing? Possibilities range from arriving at work without the slightest clue about the day's work to total predictability.

Variety

- How much variety is built into the average day?
- How much must work differ from year-to-year, month-to-month, day-to-day, within the day?
- Continual new projects, assignments?
- New problems to face? How often—consistently, daily, occasionally, one new big problem every month or year?
- Degree of routine?
- Emergency fire fighting—how much, how often?

Time Management

- How much of your life will be given to working? When you calculate all the time spent directly at work and then add the other time necessary to fulfill your work obligations, you arrive at a useful estimate of how much of your life will be spent working. Figure in all the time spent—commuting, buying and caring for work clothes or equipment, entertaining, networking, homework, nonwork time spent thinking or worrying about work problems, recuperation time necessary to get back on an even keel.
- What is the ideal expenditure of your total time on work and work-related activities? How close to your ideal are you willing to get?
- How many hours per week are you willing to work?
- How often are you willing to rise to the call of emergencies and special situations that require you to give every waking hour and ounce of energy to your work?
- How important is it to you to have time for family, hobbies, etc. How much is ideal? How much is necessary?

Security

- There are several potentially important aspects to the question of security. The very word means different things, sometimes radically different things, to different people. To some folks, it means a secure nest in a stable organization. To others, carving out their own slice of the pie, on their own terms as an entrepreneur is the only real security.
- There has been a radical shift in the degree of job security available to workers in the last few years. If you want a safe, lifetime nest, there are still places that can offer one. These days, the prevalent philosophy of job security is to be so skilled, so needed, that you will have headhunters lined up outside your door bidding for you. What does security mean to you? What does job security mean to you?
- What kind of security is important to you?
- How important is it?
- What degree of security is necessary?
- Are you looking for a long-term nest, work family, a place to hang your hat for a few years, a step toward some future goal?

Preparation for Retirement

- Do you intend to retire or work until you fall off the face of the earth?
- How long will you work? Some people plan to retire at 55, 45, or even 35, and make it happen.
- How do you intend to be secure in your years of retirement?
- What part will your employer play in saving for your retirement?
- Do you intend to stay with an organization that will provide you with a pension?

Portability

- Some careers, like nursing and physical therapy, are so portable that you can easily find a job on short notice anywhere in the world. Many high-tech careers are also portable. If you decide to move to another city, you will not have great difficulty finding a suitable new job. In fact, in some careers, you move up the ladder by moving from company to company.
- Is it important for your career to be portable?
- If so, how important? How portable?

Degree of Continuing Challenge

- What do you mean by challenge?
- How much challenge do you need?
- What would provide enough challenge?

Other Factors to Consider

- What plans do you (or other people in your life) have that may affect your career?
- Personal plans?
- Are you planning a marriage? A divorce?
- Whose career comes first? Yours or spouse's? Is there some way both of you can win and have exactly what you want? (There usually is, if both of you are willing to abandon "me first" attitudes and are willing to commit to a win-win outcome. You might it helpful to find a book or two on the subject of win-win problem solving.)
- Are there children involved?
- What about your parents?
- Do you hope to move to your dream location?
- Do you want to retire early?

Competition and Cooperation

In a tribe of chimpanzees, every member competes. Apes have differing degrees of competitive spirit for position within the tribe. Each individual chimp also has certain talents that give it certain advantages. The range of talents in the world of apes is much less diverse than in our world. The main factors are size, strength, gender, intelligence, and political ability. Each chimp has a network of political connections. Each ape's position within the tribe is a result of some mix of competitive spirit, talents, and managing the network of connections. Does this sound like another species you are intimately familiar with? An ape could be little, feisty, clever, persistent, and consequently rise to the top of the chimp pile. Another could be huge, slow, and politically naive. There are very dominant, aggressive apes, submissive apes, and ones who avoid the dominance-submission game. But, remember, avoiding competition is just another way of playing the game. Whenever two or more people work together, there is at least some degree of competition. When you have three or more people working together, the politics can get complicated.

There is no way to avoid competition and politics unless you become a hermit. You are going to have to deal with it. There are always people in every workplace who continually stir up competition and political issues. Others folks are put under profound stress when these issues remain unsettled. Some organizations like to keep people on their toes by stirring up competition. It is business as usual in the animal kingdom for individuals to keep testing those just above them on the totem pole. It is vitally important to be clear what supports your success and well-being, what generates sufficient spice in your work life, and what is too stressful.

- How naturally competitive are you?
- Does success involve competing with others?
- Do you thrive in a competitive environment or prefer a cooperative environment?
- How much of each?
- If you seek competition, is the competition between you and fellow employees or between your organization and others?
- If you seek a cooperative environment, what do you mean? How much?
- Is it a problem for you if there is significant competition in moving up to the level you seek?

Future Demand

- Do you need to be in a career field that is expanding rapidly? Steadily? Maintaining the same number of people employed?
- If you go into a field that is not expanding or is shrinking, how can you position yourself so you will be one of the people who gets to keep playing the game?

Difficulty in Getting into the Field in the First Place

- Range: from easy (fast-food restaurant burger flipper) to fierce (movie star or senator).
- How much difficulty are you willing to face?
- How much of a problem is it for you to go after a particular career if there is uncertainty about whether you will be able to get into the field?
- Only a small number of philosophy Ph.D. candidates have faced the fact that just one in ten will find a job in their field. How carefully have you considered this question in regard to fields you are considering?
- If you are considering a very competitive field, what would it take to make sure you are one of the people who succeed?

Rewards

To some degree, your identity as an individual consists of a relationship with yourself and a relationship with the world around you. Any quality you include as an important part of your identity can be fortified or undercut by the realities of your career. Someone who thinks of themselves as a caring person is not going to thrive where they have to constantly get tough with others to get the job done. A job that encourages them to manage in their natural supportive style will offer significant rewards. Primary among these rewards is that they get to be themselves. Useful and positive dimensions of their identity are rewarded and encouraged.

- How important is this to you?
- What are some of the dimensions of your identity that you would be unwilling to have undermined by a workplace that devalues that dimension?
- What careers would you be most proud to be engaged in? Are these on your "Careers to Consider List?"
- How would you like to be perceived by yourself and others in regard to your work? Being perceived by others in a particular way is always an important ingredient of the constant two-way conversation between you and the world around you. One of the important rewards your career bestows is the way in which you are perceived by the other people in your life. How you are reflected in the eyes of the people around you will either nourish or deplete your self-esteem. Everyone has an ego that needs to be fed by the world around them.
- Do you care how you appear in the eyes of others? What careers would be a blow to your self-esteem if your old friends found out? What careers would you be most proud of if others knew?
- How would you like to be perceived by others in regard to your work?
- Making use of your gifts—talents, personality characteristics, etc? (This is an area you need to consider carefully. It is an important reward that has a huge impact on your long-term satisfaction and success, and is often neglected.)
- Solving problems in a particular way, being related with people in the way you relate best, being creative in some specific way?
- Income and income potential—now, in five years, later on?
- Other financial rewards?
- Stock plans?
- Partial ownership of partnership?
- Positioning yourself for the future?
- Acknowledgment, praise, or being noticed for your work by the organization, your supervisor, others, the world, etc.?

Power and Status

- Even if you have not rated power and status as important values, you are still a primate, and to tribal primates it's always part of the game. Your own, individual definition, however, may be nothing at all like the commonly agreed upon definition. You may desire the power and status of having "higher values" than power and status. What does it mean to you ?
- How important are they to you?
- Public recognition or fame?
- Is it important that your work be known beyond your immediate circle?
- Respect, admiration of others?

- Status (at work, in your field, or in the community or society as a whole)?
- Pleasure, avoidance of pain?

What Else Is Important?

- Comfort versus adventure?
- Natural, easy fit with your work?
- Designing your life so you are at equilibrium—your work supports you in being who you are naturally?
- Performing functions that you find satisfying?
- Having fun at work?

Social Impact—Altruism

Some people care that the product or service their employer produces not be harmful or make a negative impact on society. Others really don't care.

- To some folks, it's important that they make a contribution to society or to the well-being of others. What is true for you?
- If it is important for you to make a contribution, what specific areas do you care about most?
- On which specific group do you want to make an impact?
- What kind of an impact?
- How much of an impact?
- Must your specific work make a direct contribution?
- Is it all right if you do not make a direct contribution but work for an organization that does something you care about or believe in?

10. Go back through this long Questions Inquiry. Turn to your Commitments and Requirements List. Ask yourself, **"What am I sure will definitely be an important component of my future career?"** Work with your new Questions List until you have completed every part of this Inquiry to your total satisfaction.

11. Keep working with this list regularly. Every day would not be too often. If I were you, I would keep using this list for the rest of my life, along with my Commitments and Requirements List.

CHAPTER 10

•

THE BOTTOM LINE—RESEARCH

During the first stages of choosing your future direction, you spend most of your time and energy looking into yourself. Once you have put together some of the pieces of the puzzle, it's time to do extensive research out in the real world. Remember, you can answer any question by looking in one of three places: inside, outside, and, if there is no answer in either of these places, you can always make up the answer. This chapter is about the questions you can answer only by looking outside of yourself. You need to:

- Figure out what careers would fit your specifications.
- Learn about fields and career areas you are considering—separate fact from fantasy through reading and getting the opinions of people in the field.
- Find people, especially industry leaders, to add to your network of support.
- Check out your wants and potential commitments to see if they are really what you imagine them to be and within your range of stretch, before you commit to them.
- Find out what you would need to do to get into a new field.
- Identify and learn about potential employers.

INQUIRY 9

CAREERS TO CONSIDER

Make a place in your notebook for a major list, entitled:

Careers to Consider

Below this title, write:

What careers might fulfill my commitments and requirements?

You should leave at least thirty pages for this section. Make the first page of this section a title page entitled "Careers to Consider." This is a place to keep track of all the careers that seem like real possibilities. You will need two pages for each potential career. As you go through the book, you will keep adding and crossing off careers. At the top of the first page in this section of your notebook, write in the name of a career that you consider a real possibility. Continue on, writing the names of other careers that you are considering on other following pages. Do not write in fantasy careers that you know you will not pursue. Every entry should be highly attractive to you, fit all or most of your commitments and requirements, and be within the range of how far you may be willing and able to stretch. Just below the name of the career, make a big plus sign. At the top of the next page, make a big minus sign. As you explore these careers, write in all the plusses and minuses you discover in your investigations.

This is an ongoing Inquiry. If you forget to work on it regularly, your career-choice process may not succeed. You have to keep asking, "What careers might fulfill my commitments and requirements?" over and over again. *Plan to turn to this list at least once a week* as you go through the career-choice process. Keep brainstorming, investigating, asking other people, researching to keep a stream of new possibilities coming in. As your Commitments and Requirements List grows, you will be able to narrow the range of possibilities. This list will naturally become more focused. But don't forget to keep exploring, to see what other careers would fit your specifications. Hopefully, as the process continues, you will be able to pare this list down to two or three possible choices.

Once you have written a career into this list, begin to investigate it at a deeper level. Begin to ask questions about each possible career. Keep adding to your Careers to Consider List. You may also want to write down your list of questions so you can give each career the same thorough scrutiny.

- What makes this career attractive to you? Break it down into separate elements. Which elements are most attractive? Which aren't. Does this suggest any possible commitments?
- How could you learn more about this career?
- What questions arise? What are you uncertain of?
- Does your vision of this career match reality? Just because you are attracted to certain careers or imagine that they would fit you, doesn't mean the reality matches your vision.

- When you compare careers on this list, which ones rise to the top? Which fall? Why? Does this suggest any possible commitments?

When you discover that a career on this list is no longer an option, cross it off. Then ask yourself why it got crossed off. You will almost certainly discover a new commitment or requirement. If you feel strongly enough to kill it off as a possibility, there must be a good reason. Dig in. Get specific. Identify the reasons. Put them on your Commitments and Requirements List.

Information Sources

There are endless research sources. The more you use, the better able you will be to make the best possible decisions. Here are a few:

Your network of friends, relatives, and others should be your primary research vehicle. It is not just a matter of talking to people you know. Get out there and create a wider and deeper pool of people who can inform you and otherwise be of assistance. In a later chapter entitled "Mastering Personal Marketing," you will learn to create this network of supporters. As you read the rest of this list of research resources, note that many of them are really opportunities to get to know people who can help you.

The library is a one-stop resource for a wide range of research tools. Try to find the library in your area with the largest specialty collection of career information. This may be in the career resources office of a local university, a college, or a public library. There you will (hopefully) find a vast array of books on various occupations, the growth outlook for different careers, employer directories, and much more. They may also have job-market studies, local employer listings, and know how to find other information you are seeking. When you read to learn about a field, read a wide range of books that look from different perspectives: books written by people in the field, books about leaders in the field, books about the field by journalists, and textbooks teaching the subject matter you would need to learn. If you aren't interested in the textbooks, you may not be as interested in the field as you thought. But, then again, the book learning and the reality of working in a field may be light-years apart. The business section of your library can provide information about specific organizations, their growth, products, competition, philosophy, and future outlook. Use the library to do periodical searches. You can glean a great deal from doing a periodical search and reading every magazine article written about a career area over the last few years. Many libraries now have extensive computer resources, links to other library databases and the Internet.

The Internet is the biggest library the world has ever known. No matter what you want to locate, from aardvark lovers to zymometers, it's there. Many professions have a "newsgroup," which is a combination of bulletin board and running conversation where people with an interest in a particular area correspond with others who are similarly inclined. Let your fingers do the talking. You will most likely find that people on the Internet are generally very friendly and willing to share what they know. The part of the Net with the most information is the graphically oriented and flashy World Wide Web. You can use special Web sites called "search engines" to search through many millions of pages of information in a few seconds and deliver to you those that meet your criteria. On the Web you can find out about numerous careers, trends, and companies; browse almost endless classified ads for specific jobs being offered worldwide; and identify useful people in the field you are researching. Once you find them, you can E-mail messages to them to enlist their support. Another great thing about the Internet as a research tool is its rugged egalitarian constitution. With E-mail you can reach industry leaders more directly and easily than any other way. If you show up at their offices or call on the phone, you would likely have difficulty getting past the guardians who shield them. But movers and shakers probably answer their own E-mails.

Trade publications are the best way to learn the real inside lowdown about any field of interest. When you read commercial and association trade journals, you find out what is really happening in the field, what insiders think, what concerns and worries they have, what problems you might like to help solve. There is no better way to transport yourself into the pulsing heart and soul of a field. This is the field itself, not something written about it by outsiders or academics. Here you will learn who is who, what topics are hottest, read profiles on organizations and industry leaders, get many, many names to contact. If I were you, I would read at least the last year of the most popular trade magazines in fields you are considering, from cover to cover. Be sure to read the ads, the help-wanted pages, and the news bulletins. They are sometimes more informative than the articles. Use trade journals to find editors of newsletters about the field. Make them a part of your network. Most of them are used to getting several calls per day from subscribers looking for answers to their questions. If you are friendly and respectful, there is no reason why they wouldn't be willing to talk to you as well.

Conferences, conventions, trade shows, seminars and industry-specific clubs are the best place to meet people who work in an industry you are researching. You have an opportunity to meet people at all levels from CEOs on down, speak with experts, visit booths offering a wide range of related products. If you want to learn the most in the least time, this method and the Internet are the two most efficient ways of doing so. Even if you cannot gain admission to an industry event, you can still hang around the hotel where it is taking place, visiting hospitality suites hosted by participating organizations, meeting people in the lobby, and so forth. Participating in professional development seminars that particularly interest you and joining industry-specific clubs are other great methods for meeting people and learning at the same time.

Trade associations are an excellent source of information on the careers within the industry they serve. They often have materials developed specifically for people interested in pursuing these careers. Their more senior employees usually have a stethoscope on the pulse of the industry. You might even be able to talk them into letting you use their libraries, which are often voluminous collections of materials in their area of interest.

Your professional career coach, if you have one, is your partner in research. Most likely, he or she won't actually go out and do the research for you, but will help you design an effective research strategy, suggest resources, point you in the right direction, and help you make sense of what you uncover.

Volunteering and internships take you into the very heart of a field, so you can find out what it is like from the inside. No matter how many people you speak with or how many books you read, there is no substitute for actually working in a field that is of interest. One caution though, volunteers and interns usually are given the lowliest of work to do. If you are thinking of becoming the captain of a Greenpeace ship intercepting whalers on the high seas, licking envelopes in the local office may not give you the authentic experience you seek.

How to Find Out What You Need to Know

Here are three tips to make sure your career research gets to the goal line:

1. **Do twenty times as much research as you feel like doing.** I sometimes have clients come back from doing research as a homework assignment and discover that they have just scratched the surface. It is not enough to talk with one or two people to find out what a prospective career is like. Your two sources may hate a job you might love. It is not enough to read a book or two. After all, you are deciding what to do with your life. The career you choose will be how you spend your days, year after year. If I were you, I would speak with a minimum of ten people in each field of interest, the more the better. I would read extensively. Devour everything you can find on the subject.

2. **Seek to discover new questions as well answers.** The more you learn, the more new and important questions you will uncover. As research progresses, your questions will improve. As the quality of your questions improves, so will the clarity and usefulness of the answers. Keep working with your Primary Lists, especially your Questions List.

3. **Think like a detective, a spy.** You are not writing a college paper here. College trains us to do academic research that often misses the mark when applied to real life. It is very important that you get your finger on the pulse of careers that you want to find out about. Pretend you are a detective and that lives depend on the focus, depth, and accuracy of your research. The quality of at least one life does depend on it. My personal research guru is James Garner's character in *The Rockford Files,* Jim Rockford. Rockford can always come up with a creative way to get access to anyone and anything. I'm not suggesting that you fall in front of the speeding car of the CEO of the company you want to work for, but, then again, it worked for Peter Sellers in *Being There.*

Most research is not very difficult. For example, identifying potential employers is a straightforward task once you have narrowed your search down to a specific job title and geographic area. A systems analyst looking for a job in Portland, Oregon, should have no difficulty uncovering every company in town that might hire him or her. Once they have been identified, a combination of library research, sleuthing, and networking will provide much specific information on each potential employer, the kinds of projects they work on, corporate personality and culture, and so on. It is much more difficult to find out what a potential career is really like. That's why it is so important to think like a detective and do much more research than you feel like doing.

Informational Interviews

In a sense, all the conversations you have with other people about potential careers are informational interviews. The one way you can most dramatically increase the quality of these interviews is to write down and memorize your questions ahead of time. The more clarity you have about what you need to know, the better the answers you will get. Many people have been offered jobs on the spot by an employer impressed with the quality of their questions. Just to get you started, here is a list of generic questions, some of which you may want to ask. Make up your own list. Keep it reasonably short. Keep refining your questions until you are sure you will ask everything you need to know.

- What do you find most satisfying and most frustrating about your job and field?
- What changes are occurring in your field and company?
- Are you expected to take work home at night or fulfill social obligations that eat into time away from the job?
- How often and how much do you work odd hours, overtime, etc.?
- How much of your day do you spend working with . . . (people, speedboats, computers, etc.)?
- What functional skills do you use most?
- What personality attributes, talents, and skills would someone need to enjoy or be satisfied with your job?
- What kind of person does best in this work?
- How often and how do you . . . (use creative problem solving, use a computer, travel overseas, etc.) on the job?
- How much of your time do you spend working with things or information, as distinguished from working with people?
- What kind of interactions do you have with peers, colleagues, supervisors, managers, clients, etc.?
- Who do you go to when you need advice, support? Is there enough available?
- How much and what kind of variety and routine does your work include?
- Do you feel you are able to express yourself at work?
- What kind of challenges does your work provide?
- Do you find your work competitive, cooperative? How so?
- Is it a secure job/field, in terms of income-earning potential, opportunities, future demand, etc.?
- What kind of relationship do you have with your clients, colleagues, supervisor, staff?
- How much do you work one on one with people?
- How much deadline pressure comes with job?
- Is it important to have a detail orientation?
- How much reading, researching is involved?
- How much decision making is involved?
- How much persuading or selling is involved?
- Where do you get praise or appreciation from?
- What sort of compensation could I expect, including salary range and other benefits?
- What is the potential for growth?
- Where do various growth tracks lead?
- Is your job portable?
- What's a typical day like?
- What do you find stressful, annoying, unpleasant about your work?
- Where does the satisfaction come from?

- Why do you feel your work is meaningful, important, valued?
- What administrative aspects are there to your work? How much time do these take?
- How predictable is a given day, week?
- What education and certification and other requirements are required for this type of work?
- What would I need to do to become an attractive candidate for a job in this field? What alternatives are there that require less education?
- How long were you in school, training to learn your profession?
- What is your work environment like?
- What is the best way to gain entrance to your field or company?
- Do you belong to a professional association? How do I contact it?
- What books and trade publications do you recommend I read to learn more?
- If you were in my position, how would you go about getting into this field?
- What employers would be most likely to offer what I am seeking?
- May I contact you if other questions arise?
- Can you refer me to other people in your field who could be of assistance, answer further questions, give a different perspective?

Is It Possible? Realistic? How Far Will I Stretch?

These questions need to be answered if your new career is to turn out to be more than a pipe dream. Make sure. Check out the relationship between potential careers and reality.

Is it possible? seems at first glance to be a question that has some connection with the world outside of yourself, but this is almost always an illusion. The concept of possibility does not live in conventional physical reality. That becomes quite obvious when you take a quick glance back through the history of invention, accomplishment, and human social evolution. All new breakthroughs seem outside the realm of possibility to nearly everyone, until they actually happen. A relatively short time ago, people rode horses or walked. If you had asked them if it were possible that we would, in just a few decades, fly through the air five miles above the surface of the earth to the far corners of the world in huge silvery machines, nearly everyone would have said that it was completely impossible. The history of human life on earth is an ever-swelling stream of breakthroughs into new possibilities that then become a new realities, available to all of us. This exploding pace of invention truly is the evolution of evolution. One-hundred thousand years ago, new possibilities and breakthroughs came at a slow pace. Every once in a while someone would have a flash of insight and invent a slightly more efficient stone tool. Now the ever-expanding pace of breakthroughs pour over us endlessly, one tsunami after another, each wave coming faster than the last. Even if you spent every minute of your life doing nothing but trying to keep up with these breaking waves of new possibility, you would soon find it impossible to do so. Asking "Is it possible?" in this day and age is like asking "Could I get wet?" while standing at the edge of an ocean. A question more to the point is "Am I willing to create this as a possibility?" Nevertheless, you need to ask yourself this question. If it doesn't seem possible to you, then you need to either abandon it or turn it into a real genuine possibility.

Is it realistic? and **How far am I willing to stretch?** are in some ways the same question, and in other ways are completely different from one another. When you ask, "Is it realistic?" there is often a more relevant question lurking just under the surface. Let's suppose you are forty and have been working for all of your adult life for a big company. Now you are thinking of starting your own business. Very likely you will be peppered with a barrage of inner voices asking "Is it realistic?" over and over. The answer depends on what you men by realistic. If you mean, as the White Angel asked, "Is it safe?" the answer is always no. Nothing is safe. Is it safe to stay where you are? What do you mean by safe?

Sometimes when people ask, "Is it realistic?" what they really mean is, "Am I willing to do what it takes to accomplish that goal? Am I willing to pay the price? How far am I willing to stretch?" Only you can answer that question. But remember, there are three places you can find answers to questions: inside, outside, and invent the answer. Most people would look inside themselves for the answer to this question. What is sure to happen when you do that? You guessed it, a huge attack of Yeahbuts. When you ask good old, same old you this kind of a question, you have about the same chance of getting a yes as you did when the teenaged you asked if you could borrow your dad's car the day after you ran over his golf clubs. But, then again, you don't want to make up some hopeful, fanciful, positive answer you are not willing to live up to, either. I suggest that you read the chapter entitled "Making Decisions—A Short Course." Perhaps you would be willing to up the ante and make a truly free choice about how far you are willing to stretch.

"Is it realistic?" can also mean "Does it fit with my commitments?" It may be that you do not have some information you need in order to make a choice. If you are committed to your new career being in a field where there is lots of demand, or where you would be able to reach a certain income level, obviously you need to do some more research. You may not be sure that your picture of this career is accurate. If this is what you mean by "Is it realistic?" you should go back over your commitments to see that they ring true and are adequate in breadth and depth. Then it is just a matter of conducting research, to make sure that there is a good match between your commitments and the career.

•

CHAPTER 11

IF YOU GET STUCK

We will either find a way or make one.

— HANNIBAL

In the midst of trying to decide what to do with your life, you may reach a point where you don't know what to do next. Any of the following might be true:

- You are confused, uncertain, stuck.
- The careers you were considering evaporated when you found out more about them.
- The pieces do not seem to fit together.
- All careers that seem attractive to you seem impossible to achieve.
- Your life has been very busy for the last two months. You just noticed that you haven't really done much to move your career decision making forward.
- You try to work on choosing your future career, but you find yourself just staring at your notebook.
- You can't even imagine what you could do to get moving.

You are stuck, right? Well, maybe not. You are stuck when you fall into a pit of quicksand, sink up to your neck, and there's no one around and no branches available to help you get out. You are stuck when the traffic stops completely and it is thirty miles to the next exit. You are stuck when the forces of evil coat your body with superglue and stick you to the front of a missile that is now hurtling through space. Ninety-nine percent of the time, though, when we say "stuck," we are actually "stopped."

From time to time, we all blame our lack of progress on confusion, not knowing what to do, our impossibly busy lives, a fatal flaw in our psychological makeup, other people, lack of data, writer's block, parents, race, gender, and a world that treats us unfairly, or we blame some other insurmountable circumstance. We attribute the cause of our difficulty to that circumstance.

When you assume accountability for your life, you begin to realize that the whole concept of stuck is mostly a convenient way to justify inaction or lack of commitment. What if there really is no such thing as "stuck" or "stopped." What if they are just two little words and nothing more? At some point in *The Path-finder,* you will, most likely, get very clear that people's interpretations are what creates their reality; that there is not one real interpretation that is the one and only bona fide, indisputable truth. When you say you are stuck, you are unconsciously and unknowingly making another statement: that the circumstances are the cause of your inaction. When you interpret your situation as "stuck," you are helpless, powerless. There is nothing you can do. The circumstances are running the show. When you are willing to shift your perspective a little, you may discover that you are not quite so stuck after all. It is really just a matter of taking on a new and more resourceful interpretation. When you say, "I am stuck'" you instantly become powerless. (Unless, of course, you really are glued to the front of a missile.) When you say, "I am stopped," you automatically put yourself in the driver's seat. The greatest ally you have right now is the power to create a new interpretation. Once you begin to look at your situation from this perspective, you can start to diagnose the problem and figure out how to deal with it.

What to Do When You Are Stopped

What saves a man is to take a step.

— ANTOINE DE SAINT-EXUPÉRY

I used to know a couple who did a very effective weeklong workshop for writers with writer's block. How did they get writers unstuck? Simple, they got them writing. They created all sorts of smoke and mirrors in the form of exercises so that the writers wouldn't notice that the real plot was to get them moving again. Once they started writing again, the writer's block disappeared. So, when you get stopped, when you think you are stuck, when the forces of iniquity have you surrounded, when you have nowhere to go, when your engine dies, your heart stops, when you crash and burn, here is what I suggest: **When stopped, start!**

Yes, gentle reader, this is the only choice you have, other than to stay where you are. Here's how to do it.

- Work on how you interpret your situation. Until you can look from the "I'm stopped, not stuck" point of view, there is nothing you can do. You do not have to resolve your family relationships, grow more willpower or change in any way. You just have to begin to look at it from a new point of view, one where you are the cause of your difficulty, not the helpless victim of the mysterious forces of stuckness.

- Find a way to remind yourself of your new interpretation. Put a big sign on your refrigerator, on the mirror, on the ceiling above your bed, have a flock of trained mynah birds that fly around your house repeating it again and again, get a friend or a coach who reminds you. Write it in big letters: WHEN STOPPED, START!

Here are some of the things you can do once you have created that new more resourceful interpretation:

- Go on to something else. Come back to the part that isn't moving later.
- Do something different. It need not be the perfect thing. Since you don't know what the perfect thing to do is, do anything different. Do something new in other areas of your life to loosen up your brain. If you never go dancing, go out and dance till dawn.

Insanity is doing the same thing over and over and expecting a different result.

—EVA MAY BROWN

- Get professional assistance. Hire a coach. If you just need a coach to support you to keep moving, a trained personal "life coach" will be sufficient. If you also want coaching to assist you through choosing your career, this person must be a highly trained career coach. The training that life coaches and most career counselors have received is totally inadequate for what you need to get through designing your future career with excellence. If you need assistance in finding someone, contact us at Rockport Institute (see the back of the book).
- Reframe your questions. Maybe the way you are asking your questions could be improved.
- Look at your situation from new points of view. Get friends to brainstorm with you. Don't invite those friends who share your perspective. For example, if you are an African American who feels held back because of your race, you might invite friends of other races over to brainstorm.
- Find the most qualified experts in whatever has you stopped and ask them how to get moving.
- Take a course or workshop that opens a new dimension in your life. These three are the cream of all the thousands available:

    Take the Landmark Forum weekend workshop, the finest transformational course on the planet. Ready to have a breakthrough in what is possible for you? Like to skip the twenty-five years meditating in a cave? This is a master course for people who want to dance with life.

    Study NLP (Neurolinguistic Programming). This the best set of techniques to change the programming of your mind that has ever been devised. Brilliant. Way beyond the what most of psychology has to offer.

Get Rolfed! Every year your body becomes older, more solid, frozen, inflexible. This will set your body free. Rolfing (named after founder Ida Rolf) is very popular with professional dancers and others who prize physical freedom.

- Take a vacation in paradise, get some therapy, or find something else that helps you to transform your point of view.
- Study tantric yoga (meditation and sex together, illumination and ecstasy, what could be better?).
- Lighten up! Spend more time playing.
- Ask yourself what benefits you are getting under the table for continuing to stay "stuck." What payoff do you get? Whenever people say they are stuck, there is *always* a secret payoff they are getting that is more important to them than getting moving. Usually it has someting to do with remaining within their good old, same old fixed identity that they drag along with them through their life. Ask yourself, "What is it costing me to stay stuck?" "What would I have to give up if my dreams were to come true?" "What would I get if I got to the goal?" Ask yourself if you would be willing to give up the payoff you get for staying stuck, to have the benefits you would receive if you got moving now.

Diagnosing Your Difficulty and Getting

Moving Again

There are really just a few different kinds of difficulty that can stop you. It's a good thing, too, because these few things do tend to go wrong often. The first step in treatment is to diagnose the disease. Figure out what happened. When you get specific about that and understand the real source of your difficulty, you can, almost always, deal with it.

Look at the figure on the next page, the illustration of a journey to a specific destination, the city in the distance. For you, the journey is to choose your career. The illustration illustrates all the things that could go wrong.

The problems and breakdowns that might occur on the journey to the distant city are the same as those that could get in the way of any journey or project. If you are stopped, it is always one of these:

1. A commitment problem. If you find yourself just sitting in the car reading brochures about the wonders of your destination and not actually putting the pedal to the metal, you have a commitment problem. The way you

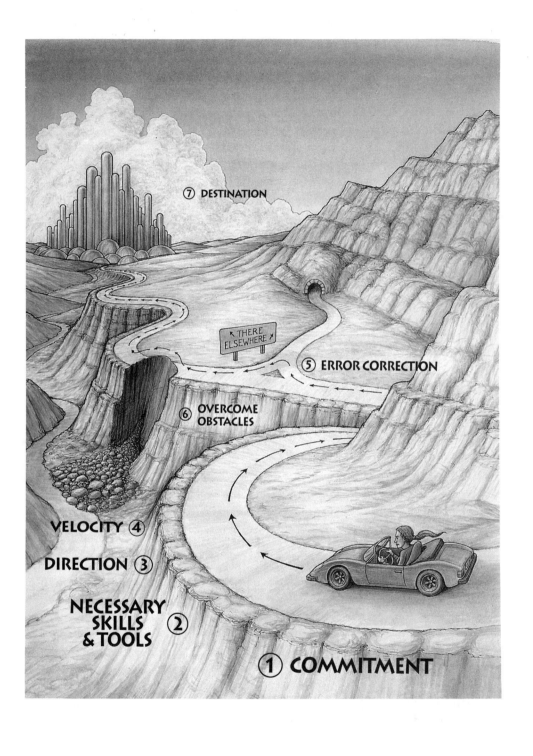

can tell if you are having a commitment problem is whether or not you are actively moving your career-choice process forward. If you are just sitting in the car reading about the destination, talking about the journey, but not in action and moving with alacrity, you are committed to something other than getting there. If someone says he is going to go down to the store to get a bottle of orange juice, and hours later you find him still reading about the relative merits of different kinds of oranges or stirring orange food coloring into a glass of water, it is fairly safe to say he is committed to something other than what he said. When it comes to commitments, actions speak much louder than words. Deal with it by re-creating your commitment. Read the chapter called "Why You Don't Get What You Want," the one called "The Power of Commitment," and whichever other chapters you think may be appropriate to help you focus on declaring what you are committed to and getting into action.

It may be appropriate for you to go back to the chapter called "Diving into the Mist" and reconsider what you wrote there. Did you make a promise to yourself to choose your future career when you went through that chapter? If you didn't then, or you made some other commitment (to try, do your best, or whatever), maybe it is time to up the ante.

2. A lack of necessary skills and tools. Sometimes people get stopped because they simply do not know how to do something that is vital to moving forward. For example, they may not be adept at using a computer hooked up to the internet to do research or they may not know how to type. The bottleneck may be a missing tool, such as a computer, a car, or a good suit. Other times the problem might be more intangible, like a reluctance to cold call people you do not know. Don't let anything stop you or reduce the effectiveness of your career-choice process. Learn what you need to know. Buy or borrow the tools you need.

3. A direction problem. You may be heading in a direction that is not bearing fruit. If you cannot figure out which way to go, go any other way than the way you are going now.

4. A velocity or momentum problem. If you have been driving for a week and you have gone only twenty miles on your thousand-mile journey, you have a velocity problem. At this rate it will take you a year to get to your destination and two lifetimes to choose your career. When you are engaged in an important project such as deciding what to do with your life, a velocity problem is almost always a symptom of resistance to disturbing the equilibrium of your life. The way you deal with it is to speed up. I know this may sound like a simplistic solution, but, can you think of any other way of solving a velocity problem? The way to speed up is to put some urgency into your project. What are the consequences of puttering along at a slow speed? What does it cost you? Are you willing to pay the cost? Making sure you have milestones with dates will pull you forward into the future. Then you need to manage yourself in a way that gets you to your milestones on time.

Sometimes your attention may get absorbed by other events in your life. If you are falling in love, moving, changing to another job in your field, or a close relative has just died, you may want to put *The Pathfinder* away for a month or two, until you have the motivation to get moving again.

5. Error correction. Sometimes it is difficult to know when you are off course. You may be exploring blind alleys or doing what is comfortable instead of what moves your project along most powerfully. What you can do is keep your mind on your goal and keep asking yourself, "Am I doing what is most effective to get to my goal? Is this working? What would work better?" When you discover that you are off course, get back on!

I am not discouraged, because every wrong attempt discarded is another step forward.

— THOMAS EDISON

6. Overcome obstacles. Stopped by a roadblock. Many things can get in your way and bring your project to a screeching halt. Roadblocks and difficulties are just problems to solve. The real culprits in killing off projects are our old friends the Yeahbuts. People abandon their project because "I didn't have the grades to get into the program," "I'm too tired after work to deal with this," "My husband doesn't like the idea," "It just seems impossible," and so forth. It is not the circumstances that stopped any of these people. It is hardly ever the circumstances that stop you, no matter how real they seem and how sure you are that they are the cause of your difficulties. What stops people is nearly always one of two things: your goal was shot down by Yeahbuts, or your commitment snuck off in the dark, absquatulating when your back was turned. What you can do when you face a roadblock is renew your commitment, get out your chain saw and shovel and get the barrier out of the road. No matter what the roadblock is, there is some way through it or around it. It may be that you are unwilling to do what it would take. If so, don't give up. Go back to the drawing board and get to work considering other possible directions and destinations. Sometimes when I point out to a client that there is always a way through or around, they argue for the roadblock. Arguing for the validity of a roadblock is something we all do, which doesn't make us one bit less foolish for doing it. Whose side are you on anyway?

Living in a State of Consonance

There is one other obstacle, besides the Yeahbuts, that is often a major culprit in stopping the voyager dead in his or her tracks: inner conflict. Even though it may seem difficult to resolve these inevitable conflicts, it is actually much easier than it appears to be. Instead of continuing to support a state of inner warfare, create a state of consonance. Consonance means being in agreement or accord, harmonious, compatible, congruous. To achieve consonantal living, all you have to do is create a state, a ground of being where your outside agrees with your inside and the various parts of your personality work together to achieve the same goals. You are not at war with yourself. Your work is in harmony with what matters. Your journey is in accord with your map. You are aligned.

When there is a lack of harmony between your inner and outer life or between important parts of your personality, your integrity is broken. Your personal power erodes. You have less trust in yourself. Other people pick up this dissonance and tend not to trust you either. One of the best example of dissonance, the opposite of consonance, is Nixon smiling and waving as he boards the plane after being driven out of office. Most people are highly sensitive to dissonance. Don't you pick it up instantly when people say they're doing great when obviously they aren't? If you are that sensitive to other people's dissonance, imagine how a lack of harmony in your own life affects you.

The prime tool most people use to deal with dissonance is resignation. If someone passionately wants to do work they care about and doesn't act on their desire, they live every day in a state of jangling discord. This is a most uncomfortable place to be. They find themselves compelled to do something, anything to make that terrible feeling go away. So, they embrace resignation. They submit. They accept their fate as inescapable. They say it can't be done. They find something or someone to place the blame on, so they are let off the hook. From that time on, till the end of their days, no matter what the apparent subject matter, no matter what words they say, they are always talking about one subject: justifying their deep resignation.

All of us experience a lack of congruence sometimes. When you tell your children they must live up to a standard of perfection that you don't follow 100 percent, that is hardly congruent behavior. Sure, you are just doing your best to be a good parent. But your kid picks up the lack of congruence instantly, just like you pick it up in other people. They know that Long Wind speaks with forked tongue. Don't expect that you will ever live happily forever after in a state of perfect harmony. It is not going to happen. What you can do is notice when you aren't in a state of consonance and begin to correct yourself and get back in synch. Just deal with the big stuff, and the small stuff will take care of itself.

There are two different kinds of dissonance. Sometimes the dissonance is a conflict, or lack of communication, between different parts of your personality. For example, one part of you may want to go to the beach while another part thinks you should stay home and finish the work you have to get done by Monday. Or, one part wants you to have an exciting, satisfying career while another part wants you to play it safe. The other kind of dissonance is a conflict between your inner vision and your real day-to-day life, between inside and outside. You may be a cat burglar who hates to steal or the head of a large federal agency with total disdain for beaurocratic environments.

If you get shut down by dissonance, you need an effective tool to resolve your conflicts. The following Inquiry, created at the Esalen Institute in the seventies, is the best method I know for resolving both kinds of dissonance. It coaches you to find creative ways to have your cake and eat it too—to satisfy internal factions that have not found common ground before. It works just as effectively as a tool to resolve dissonance between your dreams and your real life. When you do not follow through in turning your dreams into reality, it is because internal voices have spoken convincingly for another agenda. So all dissonance is internal, a conflict between different parts of your personality. Using this Inquiry, you can negotiate between those parts that look from very different points of view. You can find a way to have all of your internal cast of characters get what they want.

INQUIRY 10

A PARTS PARTY

We have grown up in a culture that promotes the belief that each of us has one personality, one identity. In reality, it is as if each of us is inhabited by a whole cast of characters, each with a singular point of view and agenda. There may be a character who wants to do what feels good now, a hedonist. Another one may be cautious and security minded. Yet another has the soul of an adventurer. Perhaps you are inhabited by some rebellious characters and other more compliant ones. If you think of yourself as a single identity, you are sure to be conflicted. If you realize that you are an ensemble production, it makes it easier to reach a state of consonance. The problem is not that you are inhabited by all these different characters but that they don't communicate. They don't party together. They are like people who live in the same apartment building but never speak to each other, let alone really get to know each other. Your life works best when they all work together to produce aligned outcomes that benefit the entire building and everyone in it. A parts party is the best way to introduce them and get them playing together. You might even start to have regular parts parties, every time internal conflicts arise. Or, you might just like hanging out with your internal menagerie. Here's how to give a parts party.

1. Identify your important internal characters or subpersonalities. Write down their identifying characteristics on a page in your notebook. Then give each of them an apt name such as: Ms. or Mr. Responsible, the Kid, the Rebel, the Saboteur, the Saint, the Whore, the Star, the Beast, Dr. Know-it-all, the Guru, the Mother, the Problem Solver, the Cynic, the Lover, the Creative One, the Philosopher, the Fool, the Hedonist, the Comedian, the Radical, the Conservative, the Good Neighbor, the Basket Case, the Friend, and so forth. They can have different genders, even different species, as appropriate. You may even want to imagine what they look like, or otherwise find ways to distinguish them clearly. You could give them distinctive clothes or physical characteristics.

2. Pick something you feel conflicted about. Perhaps you want a career that is adventurous and provides security, or one that is both meaningful and practical. Create a definite agenda for your party. (As you may have noticed, this party is actually an awful lot like a meeting. Don't tell your more fun-loving characters or they may not show up.) The agenda may be to give everyone a chance to talk about the situation you face, to speak for their point of view, and then to discover a way that all of these characters can get what they want, a plan that generates internal consonance.

3. Schedule a time for the party. You will need an hour or two in a quiet location where nothing will disturb you. Decide which of your subpersonalities should attend the party. Invite the ones most invested in the subject at hand.

4. Select a host/conflict manager to lead the discussions and negotiations. This can be you or one of the characters. If you pick an internal character, pick one who is strong, fair, and diplomatic.

5. At the time for the party, sit in a comfortable, open position and close your eyes. Imagine all the invited internal characters sitting around a big round table wearing clothes that would fit their personalities.

6. Turn the party over to the host. Give all interested characters a chance to speak their minds. What is their point of view, their agenda. What do they

want you to do? Let them argue for their own interests. Let them get clear exactly what the most important conflicts are.

7. Negotiate. The host/conflict manager needs to be especially creative in supporting all parties to come up with win-win solutions. Get each character to come up with brainstorms that would allow them to get what they want, and make sure other character get what they want too.

8. Agree on a unified plan that allows everyone to get their agendas fulfilled.

One parts party may not be enough. You may want to hold one regularly. Who knows, some of your internal characters who don't communicate now may get along so well that they become wanton weasels of love, going wild in your brain.

How to Keep Going Once You Have

Gotten Moving Again

The way to stay in the driver's seat is to get very clear which parts of a project you flow through like a cork in a mountain stream, and at which points you get stopped. You can be sure that you will tend to get stopped in the same place or places, time after time. People who have a commitment problem on one important project will have the same problem arise on other projects. You need to put a great deal of creativity and energy into getting through the rough spots, the places where you are less than naturally proficient. When you are stopped, it's a matter of recognizing that your wheels are spinning and getting out to push yourself out of the mud. The way to train yourself to up the ante and get your project moving is to pay attention to where you fall short. Forget about trying to make sure you are getting positively stroked all the time. Concentrate your energy on filling in what is missing. Nothing gives better strokes than a life lived fully. And nothing contributes more to having a fully lived life than keeping your projects in motion all the way through to completion.

Part 2

How to Get There from Here

Part of the reason so few people have truly satisfying lives is that they simply do not have tools adequate to the task of designing such a life. Even more important is the fact that most of us wouldn't be willing to live such a life for very long, even if we could design it. Our lives are, for the main part, lived on auto pilot. In order to have a truly fulfilling life, you have to design and build your own rocket ship. Then you have to learn to fly it more masterfully every day. After years of experimentation, a few broad, basic truths have emerged that seem to be fundamental principles for choosing the perfect career and living your life in a way that fosters growth and mastery. Each of the chapters in this section is a group of concepts that teaches you to fly the rocket masterfully. If you read the chapters in this section thoroughly and take on the challenges they present fully, you will be well on your way to a life beyond your dreams. I don't expect you to believe me. It all sounds too good to be true. Well, my friend, could it be that there is nothing too good to be true?

I know you are raring to get going on the adventure of designing your life. You may be impatient to start answering some basic, practical questions about your future. Every chapter in this book is an important part of doing a really spectacular job of choosing your career. But if you just can't stand to read anything that sounds the slightest bit abstract and want to start shoveling right away, you could skip this second section and turn to the third section, "Designing Your Future Career." There you can start building the structure of your future career right away. I strongly recommend that you do not do this, but if it is a matter of quitting now or moving into practical action right away, moving to "Designing Your Future Career" is better than quitting. But, please, come back here and read these chapters as soon as you can convince yourself to do so!

•

CHAPTER 12

WHY YOU DON'T GET WHAT YOU WANT

Our doubts are traitors and make us lose the good we oft might win, by fearing to attempt.

— WILLIAM SHAKESPEARE

Nearly everyone has difficulty turning their most passionate dreams into reality. Usually, when this happens, we blame the circumstances or ourselves. Most of us can imagine ourselves doing work that fulfills everything important to us. Yet when we step out of the realm of fantasy and attempt to forge a life that is a major improvement on our current situation, we fall prey to doubts and difficulties. In this chapter you may discover the culprit that keeps some parts of our lives going around and around in the same old groove. The next few pages present a model of how our brains work when we seek to expand our lives into new territory. This is a useful interpretation, not the one and only truth. Looking at your life from this perspective can give you a greatly enhanced ability to have your life turn out the way you want it to. In particular, it will help you whenever you are taking a giant step forward into the future. You do not need to suspend your beliefs about how your mind works. If you think your ego keeps your id from going further than baying at the full moon, fine. Since this is just a useful model, it doesn't matter if it is the truth or not. What does matter is whether or not this model helps you be more resourceful in actually living a life you love. Let's take a look.

An Anatomy of the Human Mind

Take a look at the illustration on the next page. It is a record of someone's satisfaction as they go through life. It could be a chart of satisfaction at work, love life, or any other aspect of life. At the bottom of the scale, below 20 percent, life holds no real satisfaction. You are in the pits. Things seem about as bad as they could be. At the top, above 80 percent, you are completely in love with life. No matter

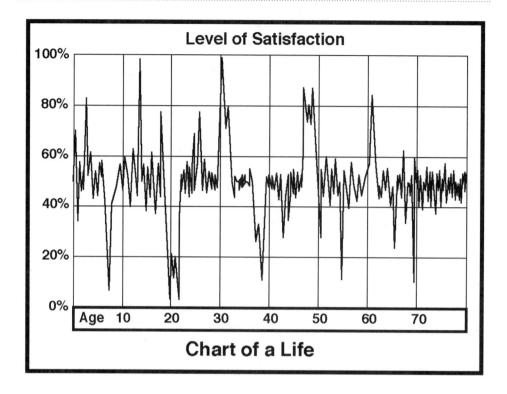

what happens, you see the bright side. When you discover that your wonderful new lover is an ax murderer, you think, "Yes, but, he's so good at it."

Consider your satisfaction with any part of your life in relation to this scale. Let's say your satisfaction in love relationships usually hovers around 50 percent on the scale. Your love life is OK but not great. Then something happens that drives your level of satisfaction down to a 10 percent or a 20 percent. Unlike Humpty Dumpty, it does not take all the king's horses and all the king's men to put you back together again. It just takes time. Sooner or late, you will find yourself back at good old 50 percent again. Rarely do people stay deep in the pits for long. Somehow they find their way back to their usual level of satisfaction. They may change partners to get back to 50 percent or they may work things out in their existing relationship. They will do *anything* to return to their usual, customary level of satisfaction. It is not 100 percent, it's not 90 percent but it is what they are used to. Like a thermostat, we seem to be set for a certain "temperature" of satisfaction.

What happens when a miracle occurs and your love life really takes off? Your relationship flourishes or you fall in love. Suddenly, you find yourself on cloud nine. In this state of bliss, even washing the dishes can feel like dancing through fields of flowers. Life has become perfectly satisfying. You have soared to 90 to

100 percent on our chart. Will it last? Will you live happily forever after? Of course not. Either you will slowly drift back to 50 percent, or you will somehow screw it up so you land with a thud back at 50 percent. You may sincerely want to have a very satisfying love life. It could be something you strive for, work for, care about deeply. But you keep winding up at good old, same old, predictable 50 percent. Why?

Right now, you may be asking, "What does all this have to do with choosing a career?" Nothing at all if your life, your work is as deeply fulfilling as you'd like them to be. Nothing at all if you are willing to leave your life to the ebb and flow of circumstance. If you plan to have a deeply satisfying career, one that goes beyond the ordinary level of satisfaction and success most people accept, then it may be worth noticing that there seems to be a mechanism at work that tends to keep people stuck to the same spot on the flypaper of life. The better you are at unsticking the stuck, the more power you have over how your life will be.

Look at the illustration below. It looks like a seesaw that is balanced in the middle, because no one is sitting on either end. Let's use it to demonstrate how minds work. Don't worry about the little things under the ends of the seesaw. We'll get to them in a minute.

Living things naturally return to a state of balance. When we are disturbed by forces acting on us, our inner machinery kicks in and returns us to a balanced state of equilibrium, just like this seesaw. *Homeostasis* is the word we use to describe the ability of an organism to maintain internal equilibrium by adjusting its physiological processes. Most of the systems in animal and human physiology are controlled by homeostasis. We don't like to be off balance. We tend to keep things at an even keel. This system operates at all levels. Our blood stays the same temperature. Except for extraordinary exceptions, when people find ways to intervene using methods more powerful than our tendency to equilibrium, our habits, behaviors, thoughts, and our quality of life stay pretty much the same too. We say, "I'm in a rut," or "I'm stuck in the same old groove."

Every time something in our lives gets out of balance, our internal machinery

EQUILIBRIUM

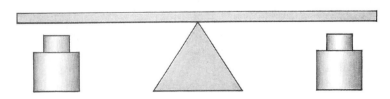

OUT OF EQUILIBRIUM

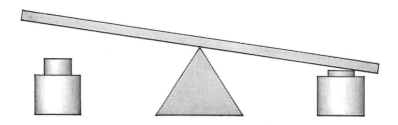

sets off behaviors designed to return us to equilibrium. In the illustration above, the things under the ends of the seesaw are switches. You can see that when balance is disturbed, the seesaw tips a little bit one way or the other and it pushes one of the switches. Pushing one of the switches sets off a behavior designed to return you to equilibrium. Notice that no matter which way the seesaw moves, it sets off one of the switches. So, whether your life has hit the skids or is on cloud nine, powerful forces of homeostasis are at work to return you to equilibrium.

Reptile Brains

To understand how this tendency to return to equilibrium controls our lives let's look back to an earlier time, a time when reptiles and amphibians were number one on the evolutionary hit parade. Imagine a frog sitting by a pond. It's a wonderful, sunny day. Everything is perfect. The air is filled with a veritable feast of delicious flies. All of a sudden the frog notices something large moving nearby. Instantly, it jumps into the pond. What's happening here? Why does it leap? It does not think, "Look at that evil-looking thing heading my way. Maybe I should make myself scarce." It can't tell whether you are a vegetarian or a Frenchman. It doesn't really think at all. Its equilibrium is disturbed, and it just reacts. Look at the illustration on the next page, and please don't get upset because a frog is technically an amphibian and the illustration says "Reptile Brain." They are both the same except that if you were to visit an amphibian neighborhood, you would notice that everyone has a pool in the backyard.

The frog is happily humming along on idle, dreaming of things that only frogs can imagine. All of a sudden its equilibrium is disturbed. The seesaw tips. That sets off a switch and the frog reacts. It leaps into the pond. It leaps for its life. Not

REPTILE BRAIN

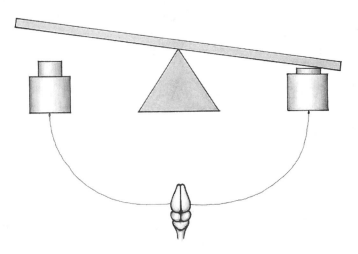

like you, you say. You make carefully thought out conscious choices, you say. Let's imagine you are in town one day. As you cross Main Street, you are dreaming of things only you can imagine. You hear a noise and look to your left. A bus is a few feet away, rushing at you at sixty miles an hour. What do you do? Will you stop to carefully consider the philosophical implications of your plight? No, you're going to do exactly what the frog did. You will leap out of the way. You'll make a mighty leap even if you haven't recently brushed up on your leaping lessons. This reaction to a disturbance is hardwired into your brain. The part of your brain that leaps you out of the way of the bus is not much different from the part in the frog's brain. All of this takes place in a very ancient and primitive part of your brain.

There's not much you can do to alter or train some of these hardwired survival mechanisms. There are very few frog trainers listed in the Yellow Pages (except in California), because you can't train a frog. A frog is basically a sophisticated survival device, programmed, like all of us, with various features designed to increase its odds for survival. Most of the time it exists in a condition of equilibrium. When it perceives a potential threat to its survival, it reacts. Its reaction really has nothing to do with its external circumstances, it is reacting to regain equilibrium.

Mammal Brains

The most basic strategy of the process of evolution is to increase the odds for survival. One of the really giant advances in evolution was the invention of high-tech, advanced mammals. Surrounding the ancient reptile brain, nature built a new brain, a powerful new generation of software with advanced features and extraordinary new survival abilities. See the illustration below.

One of the mammals' most amazing advancements was a greatly increased ability to learn from experience. They could add to their mental software. They could develop specialized survival strategies that made them much more flexible in responding to new environments, conditions, and threats.

A horse ambles contentedly through a field, nibbling at the delicious tips of long oat grasses. Suddenly a lion attacks. The horse wheels and dashes to escape, only inches in front of the flashing claws of doom. It runs for its life. Forever afterward, whenever anything, such as a field of long windblown grasses, reminds it of that threat to survival, it instantly becomes more alert. The memory of the earlier event drives it out of equilibrium and into a survival reaction—superkeen alertness. It doesn't analyze what happened. It simply reacts to regain equilibrium. It has learned to handle a new kind of threat.

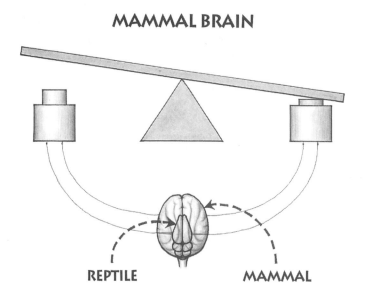

MAMMAL BRAIN

REPTILE   **MAMMAL**

The Problem with the Solution

If you think about it, whenever you are out of equilibrium, off balance, you are in a state of reaction. If you had a few angry bees buzzing around your head, you would likely be in a state of upset, reacting by having all of your thoughts focused on your bee problem. If someone, at that moment, asked you "What's the capitol of Albania?" your brain would be completely unavailable to deal with that question. You would be totally focused on the bees. So, being in a state where you are out of balance may be useful for dealing with the current emergency, but it narrows your ability to deal with other things. Evolution has developed a brilliant solution: the habit.

The Formation of Habits

If you were one of Mother Nature's engineers, charged with improving the design of mammal survival devices, you would try to find some way the animal could come face to face with recurring threats and deal with them successfully without getting so upset that it was incapacitated. That's exactly what nature did. After the mammal has repeated something a few times, it becomes a habit. A habit is an automated reaction designed to keep you at equilibrium while at the same time successfully dealing with a threat. Habits get the job done without all the upset. The horse learns to stay away from the tall grass. When it must travel near tall grass, it becomes more alert without getting completely knocked out of equilibrium. Whatever strategy it used successfully to survive becomes the standard mode of operation rather than a reaction that is triggered only when there is a threat. It is no longer upset. It has learned. Horses take the same path up the hill, time after time. They are creatures of habit, predictable. Much of what you and I do comes from this mammal part of our brains. We, too, are creatures of habit. The first time I drove a car on a narrow two-lane road, the cars whizzing by in the other direction seemed like a huge threat to my survival. Every ounce of my attention was concentrated on them. After a few days' experience, I paid no conscious attention to them. Once anything has become a habit, we don't have to pay attention to it anymore. The rub with this elegant piece of survival machinery is that, generally speaking, we are governed by our habits. When we are not aware that our lives are run by preprogrammed software, it becomes very difficult to captain our own ship.

The Human Brain

The development of our human brain was another major transformation in the evolution of intelligence. One of the new features nature gave us is our ability to project ourselves into situations that haven't happened yet. You and I can stand on a hilltop, look out across the landscape, and think, "You know, it looks to me like that could be a field where lions might hang out." When we imagine walking through the field and being attacked by lions, we feel fear, have a surge of adrenaline, and decide to go another way. This design feature gives us an enormous survival advantage. We can imagine potential threats without having to actually experience them.

Consider this. You come out of a movie theater and discover that it is pouring rain. A dark alley runs back along the side of the theater. You realize that you could save two blocks getting to your car if you cut through the alley. As you consider taking the shortcut through the alley, you imagine muggers hiding in its shadowy recesses. You feel a thrill of fear just thinking about it. You decide to stick to the safer, well-lit main street. What is happening here is that you get yanked out of equilibrium just thinking about walking through the alley. Unlike the horse, you don't have to get mugged to learn.

So, we possess an extraordinary survival advantage. But along with the benefits comes the biggest problem faced by people who wish to create anything new in their lives. The big problem is that the most advanced human parts of our survival systems operate exactly the same way the reptile and mammal parts do. If something throws you out of equilibrium, your homeostasis machinery reacts automatically. The design function of these systems on all levels, from the human part of your brain down to the ancient primordial parts of it, is survival. All the parts of your survival system defend your physical body from harm as they do for the horse and the frog. See the illustration on the next page.

We humans have a lot more than our bodies to defend. And therein lies the source of the difficulties we have in making our most passionate dreams come true. We have an identity. We see ourselves as separate from the rest of the world. Way back in prehistoric times, when you were hairier and your forehead was a half an inch high, your ability to create concepts, to distinguish yourself from your environment, led to having an identity independent from your body. This is what we commonly refer to as the "ego." Your ego, or identity, is flexible. It changes from moment to moment, from situation to situation. It is not as simple as "Me Tarzan. You Jane." To Tarzan, there is more than one Tarzan to identify with. There is Tarzan the King of the Jungle, Tarzan the wonder-filled naive English Lord. There is Tarzan the lonely, horny guy, Tarzan the clever hairless ape, and so forth.

The human part of our survival system is designed to defend our identity as

HUMAN BRAIN

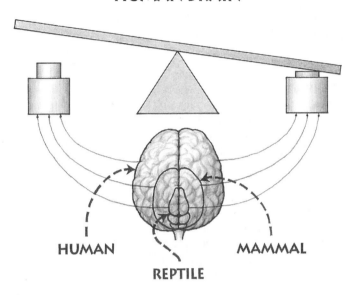

HUMAN

MAMMAL

REPTILE

well as our body. Any time there is even a hint of a threat to the survival of our identity, we are instantly thrown out of equilibrium into an automatic survival reaction. Since we have multiple identities, the system defends whomever or whatever we consider ourselves to be at that moment. Sometimes this works in our best interests. Sometimes it doesn't.

Let me offer a couple of examples. Where I live, a high-speed beltway goes around the entire city. When they built this superhighway, there was an area filled with people so rich and powerful that they had to build the road around their neighborhoods. So the usually straight road gets as curvy and dangerous as a ski run full of moguls. Of course, everyone drives at about seventy-five miles per hour. Here I was one day, zipping along with everyone else, listening to tunes, when I hit the curves. Next to me, in the lane to my right, was a propane truck. On my left was a huge shiny enamel-black Peterbilt eighteen-wheel tractor trailer with "The Nitro Express," lettered in flames on the door. And as we all roared around the corners together, my sunglasses, resting on the dashboard, skittered across to my right. What did I do? Without thinking, I reached to the other side of the car to save the sunglasses, and in doing so risked my own life. When I thought about it afterwards, I realized that, for that moment, I had become my sunglasses. All that existed in my entire universe was the sunglasses. My survival system was willing to sacrifice my life to save "me," the sunglasses.

In medieval Japan, a samurai warrior's identity was his honor. In the code of

Bushido, maintaining one's honor was more important than anything, including life itself. So if something happened that besmirched the samurai's honor, what did he do? He committed ritual suicide. And if he died well, which in that system of beliefs meant he was supposed to look pretty cool on the way out and not allow the pain and horror to show, he regained his honor. Good system, huh? Unfortunately, nobody noticed that there was one small fly in the ointment. The samurai wasn't around to enjoy the fact that he had survived. But losing his life was a small price to pay to regain his honor. His identity survived. Our highly sophisticated survival system isn't intelligent. It doesn't care if the samurai lives or dies so long as his identity survives. Your survival system not does not care about your happiness. It does not care whether you have wonderful, satisfying relationships. It certainly doesn't care if you have a fulfilling career. Sometimes it doesn't even care if your body survives. It's just a bunch of mechanisms running on automatic; and mechanisms don't care. Mechanisms don't think, they react.

Most of the time we don't think that we are our sunglasses or our honor. We usually think we are who we have been. If you woke up in the morning, looked in the mirror, and there was someone else's face staring back at you, it would be an enormous shock. We usually consider ourselves to be that familiar character we have known all of our lives. Good old, same old you. You who likes certain things, thinks and behaves in certain unique ways. You who won second prize in the a cappella yodeling contest. Good old, same old you who has these strange things happen in your love life. If your survival system protects your identity at all costs, it will react if something seems to threaten your identity. *It will do almost anything to keep everything the same.*

If the quality of your love life hovers at around the middle of the satisfaction scale, your survival system will do all it can to return you there if you stray. If everything falls apart, your survival systems will kick in until you are back at equilibrium, the good old, same old middle of the scale. If you find yourself heading toward the top of the scale, in a state of romantic bliss, it will be interpreted as a threat to the survival of your identity. It knows you do not belong in paradise. Sooner or later, you will find yourself back in the middle. Just as fast as the survival system can propel you there.

Your survival system will defend who you have been in the past, in regard to your career. If your work experience has been a fully successful, profoundly satisfying experience so far, the survival system will go balls to the wall making sure it stays that way. If you have been doing work that isn't highly satisfying, guess what? It will work just as hard to defend the status quo, no matter how much you wish it wasn't so. If you are a young person without much work experience, you are not exempt from the system. It also defends how you look at life: your personal philosophy, opinions, point of view, and beliefs. That's why women who believe that all men are pigs always seem to find themselves with piggy guys. If somehow you made up or absorbed and accepted certain rules about work or anything else, your system will make sure your life continually validates your rules.

The Yeahbuts

The frog and the horse react physically to threats. The human part of our brain has another less direct but equally effective way to run from danger, the "Yeahbut." When you think about taking the shortcut through the dark alley, your mind thinks, "Yeahbut, I might get mugged." Whenever you consider stepping into unknown territory in any area of your life, you will develop a case of the Yeahbuts. The simple act of seriously entertaining the thought of expanding your life drives the system out of equilibrium, which triggers a survival reaction, a massive attack of the Yeahbuts.

Don't turn the Yeahbuts into a new enemy. Ninety percent of the time they, like the other parts of your survival systems, are your ally. If you are dancing at the edge of the Grand Canyon, the Yeahbuts warn you of the danger. Remember, without the Yeahbuts, you would have taken the shortcut through the alley. We are designed to be at equilibrium most of the time. People who are usually out of equilibrium are stressed and prone to disease.

Yeahbuts become your opponent only when you seek to add new dimensions

to your life, to take a giant step. When you intend to create something new in your life, the survival system interprets movement toward that goal, or even serious speculation about going after such a goal, as a threat to the survival of your good old, same old identity and launches a Yeahbut campaign to get you back to good old, same old equilibrium. As soon as you consider committing yourself to an improvement in the quality of your life, your system is thrown off balance and the Yeahbuts begin. Think of it as a mental auto immune disease. The salient point is that most of us have very limited skills in successfully intervening in the automatic, mechanical functioning of these systems.

Different people have various degrees of hair trigger. Some people can dream endlessly about possible futures and stay in a state of equilibrium. It is only when they start making commitments or plans that they get attacked. Other people have only to begin to vaguely entertain wisps of thought of something new to trigger an attack of Yeahbuts as massive as the attack on Pearl Harbor.

The Yeahbuts are so effective in getting you back to equilibrium because they are very persistent. They are not intelligent. They just don't give up until you are back at even keel again. Like a persistent fisherman, the system tries out different lures until it finds one that snags you. Anyone that has ever quit smoking or given up any long-standing habit knows exactly what I mean. At the most vulnerable moment, the little voice says, "Hey, have a puff to remember what it tastes like. It won't hurt. I'm in control. I can stop when I want. After all, I'm out with my buddies. I'm having a beer. I always used to have a cigarette when I had a beer. They go together perfectly. It would taste so good right now. I'll only smoke one." It's a very, very powerful force because the system keeps trying new lures until one of them hooks you.

There are endless Yeahbuts that get in the way of choosing and creating the perfect career. Here are a few of my own personal favorites:

- I'm too young, too old, too stupid, too smart.
- I'm the wrong gender; the wrong color.
- I didn't/ don't/ won't have the right opportunities.
- I have lots of energy and sticktoitiveness. It's just so difficult to decide what to do. If only I could decide.
- I'm constrained by my circumstances, my mortgage, my bad back, no time. The circumstances are like a vice around me, holding me here. I can't do anything about it.
- I don't have enough willpower. I'm not a risk taker.
- I'm not committed enough. I have this habit of quitting.
- I couldn't do anything I would really want to do.
- I'm really trying. It's not my fault. Really!
- I don't have enough money. I don't have enough talent.
- I can't do what I want because the fun careers pay less.

- I'm sensitive, an artist. I couldn't possibly have a regular job because I see through the banalities of crass materialism.
- I want to help people, but this is a cruel, heartless world where only the lawyers win.
- It takes putting my nose to the grindstone, year after year, and that's not my style.
- It's hopeless. I have this fatal flaw. It's my karma.
- I'm an immigrant. My English isn't good enough.
- I should have been born in an earlier time.
- I don't have the courage to go out and push and make cold calls and do the things that I need to do to get that kind of job I want.
- I'm over-/under-educated, over-/under-qualified, have too much/too little experience, and all the experience I have is really a detriment because it's in the wrong field.
- I just got out of college. They didn't teach me what Shinola is anyway.
- I went to the wrong college, didn't have enough college, didn't go to college, got a degree in an area that is completely useless in today's marketplace.
- My skills are antiquated, they're outdated, underrated.
- What makes me think I can decide now, when I have failed to for all these years?

Like all of us, you probably have some others besides these little gems. They are the lyrics to the song the townspeople's chorus sings in the old opera, "It's Not Fair." What kind of an opera is it? Hint: It's something you use in the shower.

INQUIRY 11

YEAHBUTS

1. Make a list of the Yeahbuts that have power over you. Get some hints from the list of common Yeahbuts you just read, but do not depend entirely on it. Look back through your memory to times when you had a big decision to make or were considering doing something that was a stretch. What were the objections your mind came up with? What did you worry about? Which Yeahbuts hooked you and succeeded in shutting down your dreams and plans?

2. Prioritize this list based on which of these Yeahbuts usually work best to kill off your dreams and plans. Number one on the list should be the one that gets you nearly every time.

3. Now that you have a list of your top Yeahbuts, your assignment is, for the rest of your life, whenever one or more of them arises, separate it out from the herd of thoughts, like a dogie, and brand it as what it really is, a Yeahbut. Whenever you are considering taking a giant step, you can be safe in assuming that every thought that opposes taking this step is an Yeahbut thrown at you by your internal survival. Because it is a Yeahbut doesn't mean it isn't valid. But, when you recognize a Yeahbut as a Yeahbut, you can consider it to be a problem to solve rather than getting hooked. Whenever you have an attack of Yeahbuts, now you can choose to see it for what it is, instead of getting swept away again and again. Go over this list regularly, once a week or so. Which Yeahbuts no longer have so much power over you? Which ones still hook you, every time? How can you transform yourself so that the ones that still hook you lose their power?

After reading these pages, you might be feeling a little uncomfortable, helpless, hopeless, or uncertain right now. Don't worry, it is perfectly normal. I would be more worried if you were not uncomfortable. The last few pages are not good news. Or, perhaps, they are exceptionally good news. Good news is not necessarily comfortable news. There can be light at the end of the tunnel. It's completely up to you. Now that you fully understand what we human beings are up against, you know why you do not get what you want. It is important to recognize that most of the worthwhile accomplishments of our species have occurred in spite of the powerful grip of this survival system. If this system were as omnipotent as it seems, we would all be back in the cave, wishing there was some way to warm up the place. How can you successfully intercede, so that you can make your dreams come true? You have all the tools you need at your disposal right now. Turn the page. Read the next chapter, "The Power of Commitment."

CHAPTER 13

•

THE POWER OF COMMITMENT

If you really thought about the human dilemma, your human dilemma, as you read the last chapter, it should not be a mystery why so many good intentions go awry, and why, so often, New Year's resolutions vanish like dew in the desert. To slip back to the same old behaviors is not a personal problem. It is a universal phenomenon. It is an especially noticeable feature of human nature because it is the great obstacle to using one of our most extraordinary talents, our wondrous ability to evolve as individuals and as a culture. Even a lowly fruit fly can evolve biologically. Only humans (so far a we know now) can transform their lives and circumstances and evolve into someone far beyond the plan of their genetics. There is not one single human being walking the earth who does not suffer from a serious case of the Yeahbuts when he or she seeks to expand their personal horizons into unknown territory. Most of us carry around the mental baggage of those times when the Yeahbuts frustrated our desire to invent a new future for ourselves and turn it into reality. Some of us have even gone so far as to demonize this aspect of our humanity. Ancient spiritual guidebooks are filled with tales of being tempted by the Yeahbut from Hell. In the Bible story where Jesus was tempted in the desert for forty days and forty nights, it seems to me that his real struggle was with his own internal doubts, not Beelzebub. Otherwise, he would have just said thanks but no thanks the first day, and gone on his merry way. It's not a devil whispering in your ear when you hear words like, "Maybe I will just have one more piece of chocolate." It's just the ancient voice of your flesh and bones speaking to you, trying to fill you up with sugar so you will be a little more comfortable and return to equilibrium.

You could do almost anything within the range of your imagination if you could just decide on a goal and pursue it unfettered by the Yeahbuts. Imagine what it would be like if you could simply choose to pursue a substantial personal goal that seemed nearly impossible to achieve, and were able to go after it without having to do battle with soaring doubts and fears. I'd be willing to bet that the people you most admire throughout the course of human history attained something extraordinary in their lives because they were successful in finding a way to keep on the course of their ambitions. They were so dedicated to their intentions that they became essentially an unstoppable force of nature. These folks had the same Yeahbuts you do. If their projects required much bigger steps than you are considering, they likely had much bigger attacks of Yeahbuts. Even if what you admire about someone is their special talent, believe me, there are hundreds of other people out there with the same talent who never become known for their gift because a bad case of the Yeahbuts got the best of them. Yes, it is wonderful to be able to dream big. But the world is filled with disappointed dreamers.

The real problem with Yeahbuts is that their true identity is disguised. We don't recognize them as the voice of an automatic, internal survival device. They are spoken in your voice, inside your head, so you think they are thoughts "you" are actively thinking. If the Yeahbuts arose speaking in the voice of Bugs Bunny, you would not have a problem knowing them for what they are, rather than taking them for the one and only supreme universal truth. You would recognize that it was not you speaking, but simply a mechanical device playing a prerecorded tape in your head. The difficulty people have with them is not that they occur but that we identify with them. We think we are actively thinking those thoughts of our own conscious volition. But is that really true? Would you say, "I'm doing a really excellent job of keeping my heart beating today." Would it stop beating if you forgot about it for a couple of minutes? Yeahbuts are just as automatic as your heartbeat. They arise on their own, completely beyond your control. They are the output from a stimulus-response mechanism.

So if these automatic internal voices run the show when you otherwise might reach for the stars, what can you do to expose their true nature sufficiently to be able to have some say in where and how far your life goes? Somehow or other you must learn to distinguish your voice from the voice of the Yeahbuts. To do that, you have to get your own voice speaking loudly, clearly, and in words distinctly your own. One way to do that is put some words out onto the playing field of your mind that are definitely not Yeahbuts. Then, practice distinguishing them from Yeahbuts. The only words I know of that are clear and solid and definitely not Yeahbuts are specific commitments that you are totally dedicated to rigorously fulfilling. Since Yeahbuts speak through your voice, they are hard to identify as something other than the authentic voice of your own sweet self engaged in some good old back porch worrying, bitching, and doubting. But one thing you can say with absolute certainty is that they won't be speaking persuasively for making big commitments, taking giant steps, or creating new behaviors. Once you begin to separate your thoughts from the Yeahbuts, you instantly create the possibility of becoming the unstoppable agent of your intentions. Then, you can begin a continually expanding practice of steering your own vessel.

There are various methods you can use to outfox the power of your patterns from the past. Let's imagine that you are a smoker who is thinking you would like to give up the noxious weed. You throw your pack away. The next day you are sitting around the Long Branch having a few shots of redeye and a game of seven card stud. Everyone else around the table is smoking. A voice in your head says, "Why not have a smoke? It won't matter. I'll just have one." And down comes the curtain on your attempt to quit.

Now let's take a look at how creating a clear commitment separates your voice from that of Jiminy Lizard. This time you do it a little differently. When you decide that you would like to quit, you also realize that tobacco is one of the world's most addicting substances. You know the Yeahbuts will have a field day adding the powerful sensations of withdrawal symptoms to their usual repertoire of seductive words. It's going to take more than good intentions to succeed. So, this time you make a promise to yourself, "I am now and forever a nonsmoker." This time you are serious. You mean to keep this commitment no matter what. Next you face up to the reality that, when you are most vulnerable, the Yeahbuts are going to rise up and do their best to seduce you back to equilibrium. You recognize that, in the heat of an attack of Yeahbuts, you may not even remember that you made a commitment to quit. Sometimes the volume can get so loud that it takes over your mind completely. So, because you really mean to fulfill your commitment to quit, you come up with a fiendishly clever plan to succeed. You think of the political figure you despise most. (When I quit I used Jesse Helms.) You make out a check to their reelection committee, in an amount that would really hurt (if you are of average means, perhaps two or three hundred bucks, if you're rich, make it a few thousand). Seal the envelope, address it, and stick a stamp on it. Then you find a friend who is so smart, sharp-eyed, and streetwise that you will not be able to bullshit them. Give them the envelope. Tell them about your commitment and ask for their support. Request that they check in with you every day or two for the first month, then once a week, in person, and ask if you have smoked. If they catch the slightest flicker of concealment in your eyes, or if they sense that you are covering guilty tracks, into the mail goes the envelope.

Later on that week you find yourself in the saloon, at the poker table, a few sloshes of redeye into the wind. When you least expect it, a deluge of Yeahbuts overtakes you. Your every nerve fiber aches for a cigarette. The reasons you should smoke just one cigarette now pound away like surf breaking in a hurricane. "Yeahbut I'll just have one." "Yeahbut a cigarette would taste sooo good right now." "Yeahbut, I have control now. I'm not addicted anymore." "Yeahbut, I'm feeling a little tense and a cigarette would calm me down." "Yeahbut beer and cigarettes go together." Close to drowning, you stick one in your mouth. As you reach for a match, you have a vision of your envelope with little wings on it, flying away toward your worst political nightmare. In a flash you awake from the spell and recall your commitment. You remember that Yeahbuts are Yeahbuts and not your own true voice. You are going to do what you promised. The storm subsides. With nothing but a commitment and a little smart planning, you have reduced it to a tempest in a teapot. A sweet sonata with harpsichords and pedal steel guitars fills the air. You did it!

Another way to outfox the Yeahbuts is to make use of a network of support, people who will help you stay in touch with what you are committed to and keep you from starting down the slippery slope of listening too attentively to your

Yeahbuts. In the stop-smoking story you just read, notice that in addition to making a definite commitment, another person, a trustworthy supporter, was enlisted to help. One of the reasons AA works is that recovering alcoholics are surrounded by a community of support. When you put your shoulder to the wheel and begin to design a new custom-fit career, you would be wise to, at the very least, surround yourself with people who will encourage you to go for it. The last thing you need is everyone else's Yeahbuts joining yours in a galactic strike force totally dedicated to having your life stay exactly the same forever.

The C Word

Along with sex and money, commitment is one of the big three domains of life that is guaranteed to bring out the insanity in everyone. It is a word we all use, yet for the most part don't really know what it really means. Over the course of our lives we have added so much baggage to our personal concept of commitment that it has become a rat's nest of unexamined impressions and illusions. If you are anything like me, your own definition of the word includes the notion that making a commitment involves saying you are going to do something you don't really want to do. Even after speaking with thousands of people about commitment, sometimes I have still have this image arise of teenage me, numb and angry, week after week fulfilling my "commitment" to mow the endless lawn on blazing hot, humid, summer days.

What the word actually means is less complicated. Simply said, a commitment you create is *a pledge to produce a specific result.* It's a promise to do something. In effect, when you make a commitment you bring something new into existence. You speak it into existence. Previously you may have wanted to go to medical school or triple the net of your company or be a rock star, but those thoughts existed only as wishful thinking. With a definite commitment, you find yourself in action on a journey along the path to fulfilling your pledge. If you are willing to master the art of creating and living from commitments, they will be the most powerful tools in your toolbox. Like other tools, they have a very specific purpose. They are the tools you use to make things happen in your life that would not happen otherwise. They are magic wands that can create seemingly miraculous breakthroughs.

Let's look at another example of the power of commitment. Let's say you want to dig a large lily pond in your backyard. You have planned its shape, depth, and location. It is hot and humid outside, but it must be dug today because this is your only free day for the next six months. You also know yourself all too well. You know that if the soil is rocky or filled with roots, you are likely to get discouraged. Perhaps you have the same unpleasant memories of forced child labor in the heat that I do. You know that the way your brain works goes something like this: As you get tired and sweaty, your mind tends to come up with an increasingly compelling barrage of reasons (Yeahbuts) why the pond should be smaller, shallower, maybe even abandoned altogether. But you don't want to look out in the backyard as the years roll by and see a pond the size of a pothole. You want a big, glorious pond. To make it happen, you pull out the right tool for the job, the C word. Remember, a commitment is a pledge to produce a specific result. So, knowing that the pond is likely to shrink the hotter the day gets, you make a promise. The more specific the promise, the better. You might promise yourself something like this: "I will dig the pond and finish it today no matter what difficulties arise. It will be x long by y wide and z deep." With a promise like that, you are more likely, when you start having thoughts of quitting, to be able to contextualize those thoughts as an attack of Yeahbuts rather than the voice of God speaking universal truths to you.

Also, with a clear commitment and a dedication to fulfilling it, something amazing happens. Your commitment becomes an alchemical agent that transforms your Yeahbuts. They change from Jiminy Lizard whispering in your ear into a to-do list. Let's say you and I decide to go on a trek. For the sake of adventure, we decide to walk in a perfectly straight line from one side of the country to the other. We will meet plenty of obstacles that take ingenuity to surmount, but nothing sufficiently confronting to stir up serious Yeahbuts. After many weeks, we find ourselves in the Rocky Mountains. We are looking up at Grand Teton, all 13,766 awesome feet of it. To keep our promise, we are going to have to climb over it. Immediately we each have a massive air raid of Yeahbuts. "I don't know how to do this. I'm not in condition. We don't know what route to follow. We don't have any equipment. We don't have a guide." Without a definite commitment, we would rapidly be swayed by the Yeahbuts and be sucked back to good old, safe old equilibrium. We would think of something we had to do that was much more important than climbing a mountain. Two weeks later we would hardly be able to recall that we were thinking of making such a heroic climb.

On the other hand, let's say we are absolutely, definitely committed to our promise to walk the straight line across the country. We are aware that Yeahbuts will arise, and we are prepared for them. As the Yeahbuts arose, we would hear them differently. We would hear them rattling off a list of everything we would need to do to successfully get over the mountain: "We need to take climbing lessons, work on getting into condition, get a route map, buy some equipment, and find a guide."

When the subject of commitment comes up, most of us have an attack of a Yeahbut that goes something like: "If only I were more committed." Or, "Commitment has always been a problem for me." Or, "If only I had the self-discipline to follow through on my commitments." Let's take a closer look and see if this is really true.

What if every moment of our lives is an expression of our commitments? When your car breaks down by the side of the road, you don't just get out, abandon it, and walk away. You are committed to keeping your car. The fact that you wear a wristwatch is another sure sign that you are a creature of commitment. You could teach your dog to read the hands of a clock, but it wouldn't mean anything to him, because dogs are not creatures of commitment. When the car breaks down on the way to the veterinarian, your dog does not worry that he will be late, as you do. As far as he is concerned, all that has happened is the parade of wonderful smells has slowed down.

The problem is not that we suffer from a shortage of commitment, but that what we are committed to does not live up to our dreams. How can you tell what you are committed to? Just look at your life as it is now. That's exactly what you are committed to. If you are committed to something different than the way it is now, you will be in action making those dreams come true, or you will be engaged in a fierce struggle to change it for the better. You do not get any points for thinking about it. I know this may seem like very bad news, but actually it is the best news you could have. If you want to get somewhere else, you first have to know where you are now.

It takes courage to tell the truth about what you are and have been committed to. Very few people have a commitment to have a truly marvelous career or marriage or anything else. Most of us, for the most part, are committed to comfort, low risk, and equilibrium. Remember, wanting and commitment are two completely different domains. Since you are on the path to having a truly excellent career, let's take a closer look at how you can best influence your life, so that you wind up getting what you want.

Holding to the New Course

Once you have set a new course by creating a commitment, you have a brand-new problem. It is that, even though you have created a new setting for your internal machinery to fulfill your new commitment, your homeostasis system has a memory, and what it remembers is the old setting. So, it will keep trying to return you to the old setting. If you can keep on the new course for two or three months, without slipping back to your old ways, the new setting will get locked into the system. It will become the automatic, preprogrammed setting. This is what we call "habit formation." You will still have attacks of Yeahbuts from time to time, but they will be of reduced intensity. For example, when someone stops smoking, after two or three months they will have established a whole new set of habits. They may still have cravings, but the intensity of the battle with their Yeahbuts will have subsided.

It is the same with creating any new behavior. Dealing delicately and sensitively over a long period of time with things you want to change is nonsense. It doesn't work because you are giving much of your energy to dancing around with and empowering the old pattern. If you want to create something new in your life, commit yourself to the new behavior you most want, not some halfway measure, find a way to gather your forces and allies so you will be able to face the onslaught of the Yeahbuts, and go for it. You must be willing to go through whatever arises for the first few months, until the new habit gets established. The Yeahbuts will fire all of their big guns. You will be battered by storms of emotions. Powerful desires to return to your old setting will arise. You will be offered extremely persuasive sales pitches, spoken convincingly in your own voice. The world around you will continue to argue for the old setting. Eventually, the universe will turn in your favor and completely support your intentions. Since you are not yet trained to dance a fast jig with the physical universe, it might be slow to respond. Sometimes it turns slowly, like a supertanker, but, if you keep holding the wheel firmly, it will eventually come around.

The secret of creating anything new in your life consists of creating new commitments and then holding the tiller to your new course until it becomes established as a behavior. This works equally well whether you want to create a new career that truly fits and expresses you; up the ante in some other way; be more effective, available, awake; create new positive habits; deal with an addiction or other unwanted behavior.

How to Win the Battle of the Yeahbuts

The Yeahbuts are just a nice, normal part of your survival system. They are merely doing their job keeping you on the path to continued survival. They are just in the right place at the wrong time when you attempt to create something new in your life. People who do battle with the forces of Yeahbuts usually get royally screwed to the wall for their brave attempt. The Yeahbuts have a long and successful track record of running people's lives. They have been at it for thousands of years. If you are going to make your own choices and have more say over how and where your life goes, you are going to have to find some other way.

If you are willing to say that the voices that tell you to make unnecessary compromises are just Yeahbuts, then you own them rather than them owning you. Once you start to listen to the Yeahbuts rattle on and on without being compelled to act on them, you have taken some long steps on the path to freedom. You are awake. When you can clearly distinguish them from other thoughts, they lose much of their power over you.

The next problem is staying awake. Even when you have learned to reinterpret some of your thoughts as Yeahbuts, you will still forget when the going gets rough. These Yeahbuts are so compelling, so convincing, that you will get lost in them again and again. You will forget that you decided that the hairs your lover leaves on the sink means that he is generous with the few hairs he has left. You will become lost in paranoid fantasies about the terrible cosmic significance of those hairs. You need to have something that whacks you upside the head and reminds you again and again to wake up and have a little say in your life. Once again, that tool is the C word. By making your commitments clear, writing them down, and having a network of people you can trust to remind you, you can learn to go your own way.

The fastest way to completely alter your ability to deal with the Yeahbuts successfully is to live your life to the fullest by making up commitments that pull you so far out of your comfort zone that the Yeahbuts go into action at all battle stations, attempting to shoot down your commitment to your commitments in full-scale war. Then, if you can see them for what they are, they will just be words playing, like a radio in your mind, and you will have no attachment to them.

Friends

When you transform your life from "I am my psychology, my feelings and interpretations" to "I am my commitments," you may discover that some of your closest friends speak with the voice of your Yeahbuts. Relationships, established groups, and organizations have systems of comparators that are just as complex as those of individuals. They are tuned to keep the status quo shuffling along. When your life really takes off, that event is very likely to be perceived as a threat by some of your friends. They will cajole you to keep within conventional bounds, to be reasonable, to do the right thing.

To me, real friends are those people who will stand for you expressing yourself fully, who will go out of their way to support you to keep your word, to go the extra mile, to get out of the box, to make your dreams come true. The only people who will do that are those who are doing it themselves. Everyone else will be completely caught in the grip of dancing to the tune of their Yeahbuts. Keep them as buddies, but do not ask them to do for you what they will not do for themselves. Nothing is more powerful than a great network of support. In fact, you will not be able to break out of the grip of automatic living without the help of other people. Find new friends who are also willing to stand out in the wild winds. Create a group of friends dedicated to supporting one another to make the entire group's dreams come true. Train yourselves to speak for your friends commitments, rather than from the infinite wisdom of your opinions.

INQUIRY 12

DEALING WITH YEAHBUTS

The two main techniques for dealing with Yeahbuts are ones we have already spoken about: creating commitments and developing a network of people who support you to follow through. Here are some other methods.

You can add strength to your commitments by visualizing yourself in the midst of whatever outcome the commitment is intended to produce. If your goal is to begin a circumnavigation of the globe in your sailboat in two years, actually picture yourself doing it. Make it as real and as satisfying as you can. Hear the sounds, feel the rocking of the waves. Taste the salt spray. See what you would see: the sails, your hands stretched out in front of you on the wheel, bright light leaking in around the outside of your sunglasses. Feel how you would feel. Have a conversation with your first mate. See if you can make it almost as real as actually doing it. Revisit this visualization often, particularly if you are having kamikaze Yeahbut raids. If your goal is merely an abstraction or some words on a page, it becomes easy prey for the Yeahbuts. The more real you make your goal, the more insubstantial the Yeahbuts will seem.

The following methods focus on disarming the power the Yeahbuts have over you. They lose power when you know them for what they are: tapes being played by an automatic system. Everything you can do to reveal them as something other than your own proactively generated thoughts helps to break their spell. Whatever you do to deal with them, make it enjoyable. Have fun. Lighten up.

When you can laugh at ghosts, they disappear. Pick methods that fit your personality. Here are some things you can do:

- Make a list of them. Don't bother with the little ones. Concentrate on the big guns, the ones that could shoot your dreams out of the sky. Carry the list around with you, like you would carry the bird identification field book with you on a birding excursion. Give them numbers or short names. When you have an attack, identify them by number. "Here comes old number 9." "Just as I expected, a Willie and a Pete arriving together."
- Allow them to come into your mind unopposed. Do not fight or resist them. Listen to them. Give them space to exist. Be with them, all the while recognizing that they are nothing more than automatic tapes playing in your head.
- Study them from a distance. Become a Yeahbut scholar. Treat them like bugs stuck on a pin.
- Pretend they are a voice coming over the radio, rather than from inside your head.
- Have them speak in the voice of a favorite cartoon character instead of your own voice.
- Give them a soundtrack whenever they play in your head. Some circus music would be nice.
- Convert them to allies. Turn them into a to do list. When you have having an attack of Yeahbuts, write them down on a page of your notebook entitled, "Yeahbuts Converted to To Dos." Then, imagine how you might resolve them to reach your goal. Thank them for their good advice.
- If none of the above works, you need to really get serious. Find a coach who is a master at dealing with Yeahbuts or, at least, enlist someone you can completely trust to stand with you, to keep you awake to your commitments.

Questions About Commitments

How do I get rid of the Yeahbuts? Perhaps a lobotomy might work.

What if I have trouble keeping the commitment I make? You are in the same boat as everyone else. Half of the problem is thinking that you have a special, unique problem that is not shared by the rest of us. Once you realize that you are dealing with a universal phenomenon, you can quit feeling like there is something wrong with you and get to work learning how to master the art of making big promises and fulfilling them. It is not easy. If you want easy, just let your Yeahbuts keep running the show. It is somewhat like mirrors within mirrors. To learn to keep your commitments, you have to be willing to create a commitment, and live by it, that you will create commitments and live by them. You can do it. You just have to get going and know that you will fail sometimes. Your mind will fall asleep to what you are committed to again and again. The secret is to not give up. Keep picking yourself up, putting yourself back on the path, and starting your two little legs walking down the trail in the direction of fulfilling your promises.

How do I deal with the discomfort, uncertainty, and fear I experience when I am out of my comfort zone? When you create and live from big, outrageous commitments, these experiences are as natural and inevitable as night following day. They are part of the wake-up call, the warning siren your survival system plays to let you know that you are out of equilibrium. They play whether you are really facing a threat to your survival or are creating an exciting new dimension in your life. The system doesn't know the difference. So all you can do is recognize that they are inevitable and stop trying to make them go away. Feel the fear and go forward. If you could make them stop, would you really want to? It would be like disconnecting the buzzer in your car that tells you when you need to put your seat belt on. It is a nuisance, but it's there for a reason.

Isn't it just as mechanical to always keep your word as it is to always do what the Yeahbuts tell me to do? A strange and difficult territory exists in the gap between the master skill of keeping your commitments, no matter what, and being flexible, like bamboo, in the winds of change. On one hand, there is no better way to keep moving your life forward and to live life at a high level of integrity than to make outrageous commitments and to keep them, no matter what the circumstances throw in your face. On the other hand, this practice, when turned into a religion, can rob you of flexibility and the freedom to change your mind. Ninety-five percent of the time, people abandon their commitments, not because it is truly appropriate but because they come down with a case of the Yeahbuts. But the other 5 percent of the time, when you are getting ready to charge up the hill with a tiny force armed with pea shooters to face a vast enemy hoard armed with giant water cannons, it may be an appropriate time to reconsider your promise to "always go forward, never turn back." What you could do is this: Look to see what is the highest level outcome you are going for. What is the real meta-goal behind this commitment? It is probably not to charge up every hill you see. It may be to win the war, to free the slaves, to oust the tyrant, have a career you love. Once you get in touch with, and reaffirm your commitment to the big meta-goal, then you can change your promises with integrity. This way you can find the most effective way to reach the most important goal and in the process become a subtle and flexible force of nature, like the wind itself.

CHAPTER 14

•

MAKING DECISIONS—
A SHORT COURSE

We are educated in a system where we are taught the importance of memorizing the date of the battle of Hastings but nothing about many things that really matter, like: how to think for yourself, how to make decisions, how to change a tire. In the course of this book, you examine all the domains of your life. You consider many things. You may gain powerful new skills and discover potent untapped resources. More than anything else, you make choices; choices, that alter the course of your life. In fact, you will probably make some of the most important choices of your lifetime. One decision can give you a life that sings. Another may turn out to be a mistake that could haunt you to the end of your days. Since the quality of your life depends on the choices you make, it follows that one of the most potent skills a person can possess is masterful decision making. Like anything else, mastery comes most readily to those who look with the eyes of a beginner, and it comes with great difficulty to those who assume they already know.

Because an inquiry into how to make decisions is not offered as a part of our education and because nature abhors a vacuum, each person comes up with his or her own homegrown style of reaching resolution. We absorb various methods through an unconscious process of osmosis. Then we permanently entrust our lives to these methods and never think about it again. It never occurs to most people to question the effectiveness of their way of reaching decisions. And rarely do people consciously decide how they will go about making decisions. If you are going to look with the eyes of a beginner, you might ask yourself: How well do my techniques work? Are you sure that the ways that you arrive at conclusions are the most resourceful? Are they the most likely ways to create the life you want? Let's take a look at how people decide and how you decide. Let's see if your traditional methods are the best tools for the job and, if not, switch to something that works better.

Everyone makes hundreds or even thousands of decisions each day: get out of bed, make the bed, shower, wear the blue shirt or the white shirt, finish the work you brought home or not, give the cat liver or chicken. Mostly decisions are made by your internal decision-making software, without any conscious process. The first decision of the day, to get out of bed or not, is probably made by habitual compliance with the circumstances of your life. If you just roll over and go back to the land of Nod, there will be consequences. If you do it too often, you won't have a bed to roll over in. So it seems you have no choice. Then, to make the bed or not is the next challenge life throws at you. This decision may come from a deep wellspring of personal philosophy like: I'll just mess it up again tonight so, why bother. Or: All good people make their beds. Or, you may make it to avoid that feeling you get when you walk into the bedroom at the end of the day and cast your eyes on this obvious link to your ancestors who lived in caves and painted themselves blue. Whatever the reason, once again the decision is made automatically by your tried and true method. It seems that you have little choice in the matter. Your standard modus operandi for dealing with bed-making situations takes over and does the deciding for you. You never have to stand naked in the face of the existential choice. To make or not to make is rarely a matter of free choice.

Some people always favor one method. Others go through a process that combines methods. For example, some folks may rigorously plot out and analyze every aspect of the available options and then give over the final decision to their feelings. Other people use different methods for different situations. Here are some of the most common methods we trust to do the work of decision making for us:

Logic, analysis, common sense. The thinking man's approach. People who use this method describe this approach as rational, sensible, prudent, moderate, and balanced. You list the pros and cons of the careers you are considering, assign weighted values to them, add up the scores, and, presto!, the career with the best pro/con ratio wins. The only problem with this method is that you didn't make the decision. You gave over the authority to decide to a set of rules. Nothing wrong with that except that I thought you were reading this book because *you* want to decide what to do with your life. It wouldn't be too difficult to write a computer program that could do this for you. Then you wouldn't even have to add up all the numbers. Just type in the answers to a few questions and then go do what the computer tells you to do. The really great thing about letting logic decide is that, if your life doesn't work out as you hoped, you can always blame the computer for your troubles.

Feelings, inclinations, passions. Some folks have their antennae tuned to pick up subtleties of intuition, emotion, sentiment, impressions, attitudes, and hunches. These feelings are the spice of the dance of life, the soul of the arts, and one of the most delightful things about living in this corner of the universe. I wouldn't mind having Spock live next door, but I wouldn't want to exchange brains with him. Once again, the main problem with using this as your decision-making method is that it is not you making the decisions. Feelings are like weather. They come and go. You may not always cry at the funeral or laugh at the punch line. I cried for a year after John Lennon died. I never understood why. You may control revealing your feelings to others, but the feelings themselves have a life of their own. You don't control them any more than you control the weather. Let them be the spice, not the recipe you follow.

Romantic yearnings. People fall in love with imagining themselves in careers just like they imagine themselves in a relationship with that magic someone. They float on a cloud of sweet dreams, envisioning themselves in the midst of a glorious future. They think people who try to talk some sense into them are trying to burst their bubble. (They are.) One of the reasons the divorce rate is so high is that people marry a fantasy rather than a real person. The person or career they imagine exists only in their head. Romantic yearnings are right up there with feelings on the spice-of-life shelf, but they are guaranteed to get you into deep trouble if they are running the show.

Resonance. "I know it's right if it resonates with me" used to be called "going with your gut feeling," instinct, or intuition in pre–New Age times. I have asked many people exactly what they mean by resonance. The first person I asked was a physicist. He said resonance is the increase in amplitude of oscillation of a system exposed to a periodic force whose frequency is very close to the natural frequency of the system. That's when I swore off going to physicists for advice. Everyone has an individual interpretation. Sometimes people say resonance is a warm glow that spreads out from their left gazorch, sometimes a feeling like a soft wind blowing through their head, sometimes a voice that says, "This is right." Nearly everyone reports that when they experience resonance, they are mindful and aware, peaceful and relaxed. Back in the sixties people called that feeling "stoned." If you are on the verge of choosing a career that calls you out into new and unknown territory, that asks you for all you have to give, you are more likely to feel like you are standing by the door of the plane about to make your first parachute jump. You may feel more crazy than stoned. Picking a career that will resonate throughout your lifetime may have a resonance similar to the intestinal flu when you are at the point of choice. On the other hand, there are few clues more useful in the process of sorting out what is most important to you.

External sources. The media, experts, parents, spouses, friends, *Time* magazine, career counselors, common sense, and horoscopes. It's amazing how many people follow the recommendations of others to make the most important decisions of their lives. Whatever you do, don't become a doctor because it would make your mom happy. She will not have to get up every morning and go to work with you. No one can possibly know you as well as you can. No one will ever care as much as you do how well your life works.

External sources are fabulous research tools but, please don't abandon the helm of your ship to them. Magazines often publish articles with titles like, "The Fifteen Super-Growth Careers of the Coming Decade." That's great information, especially if being in a super-growth area is an important commitment of yours. For most people, super growth is not a top priority. Nevertheless, the fact that a certain career is favorably mentioned in the media gives it a special glossy appeal. So does the word of an expert. As zen master Suzuki Roshi said, "In the beginner's mind, there are many possibilities, but in the expert's mind, there are few." Or, as they used to say back in Maine, "An expert? Why that's just a damn fool far from home." So, figure out what is most important to you first. Then use the media, your mother, and the experts to research which careers match your commitments.

Reaction, rebellion, compliance. Do the opposite of whatever you don't like about what you are doing now, the opposite of what you are told or expected to do, or go along with what they want you to do. All three of these turn you into a puppet. One version of the reaction method is common among career changers. Instead of designing a new career from the ground up, they are repelled by the negative features of their present job. Doing something that is the opposite of what is wrong with the current job becomes the most important criteria of the hunt for something else. This is a prime example of an absence of free choice. Yet another form of reaction is rebellion. The third is compliance. If you turn the coin of rebellion over, the reverse side is unthinking compliance. Con men are very good at appraising whether their victims are compliers or rebels. Once they figure it out, they've got you by the short hairs.

Random. Just let it unfold, go with the flow, take the promotion you are offered, roll the dice, choose the major with the shortest registration line, look in the want ads and select a career because you think they might offer you the job. The most insidious form of random decision making is to allow the circumstances to dominate you. Who says you can't go for a walk in the rain? The rain doesn't care. Sometimes we are so ruled by circumstances that we may not even notice that it is possible to go for a walk even though it is raining. You always have a choice, if you choose to choose. You might even love walking in the rain. What can I say? Random is random. You are a leaf in the wind. You go where it sends you. A great way to spend the weekend, but not recommended for a lifetime.

Shoulds and Yeahbuts. People are often propelled into doing all sorts of things they don't really want to do because of the little voice in their head that tells them what they should do and shouldn't do. One of the noisiest of the chorus of voices that natters and chatters away inside each person's head is the one that constantly compares you (and everyone else) to a fixed set of standards and ideals. This voice rates the people we come in contact with by attractiveness, intelligence, class, erotic potential, ability, degree of fit into our social order, and a long list of other criteria. That voice that, if it were played aloud over the intercom at work, would probably get you fired. When you are thinking about possible careers, it babbles and gabbles away, letting you know, in no uncertain terms, exactly what's wrong with whatever you are considering, making sure that you do not miss a single second of its career advice. The problem with doing what it advises is that, because it is just a mechanical comparison device, it has no creative imagination or enthusiasm for possibilities outside the range of your experience. Another flaw in its design is that it is relatively quiet when something fits your standards or ideals. Like the mind of a German shepherd, it is in its glory playing "what's wrong with this picture?" So, it tends to sniff suspiciously at the most wonderful twists of fate that life offers you.

Yeahbuts operate in a very similar way to cloud the decision-making process. Sometimes they make so much noise and are so persuasive that it is difficult to do anything other than what they tell you to do.

There is absolutely nothing wrong with using all or any of the above methods to make decisions. We have used them successfully for many thousands of years. Our civilization is the result. There are, however, two small flies in the soup. The first fly has already been pointed out. When you allow any of the these methods to run the show, you abdicate the captain's chair to the rule of your trusted technique. The counselor becomes king. If you allow your method to do the choosing, you become merely the recipient of the decision. In effect, you become the slave of the method. A slave to your feelings. A slave to other people's opinions. A slave to practicality.

The second problem with relying on these methods is that you may have trouble reaching a final decision. Many people never quite get to the finish line. They reach the point where they know what their trusted method says they should do, but they are not 100 percent sold on the idea. Sometimes they simply get permanently stuck there. Life continues to creep on at its petty pace; but somehow they never quite get to the point of committing themselves and moving forward. Other times, someone caught in this dilemma may move forward on the decision the method made for them, usually saying something like, "Well, I guess this must be the best thing to do." But they go ahead with reluctance. They feel they haven't really quite decided. (They feel that way because they haven't.) Their ambiguity leads to an uncertain commitment, which then results in restrained or unfocused action. There is an old story of a samurai leader who was taking one hundred warriors into battle. He lined them up. He asked that all the men ready to die for him instantly take a step forward. Sixty of them stepped forward. He then had them behead the forty that hesitated. He knew he was better off going into battle with sixty totally committed samurai than with a larger but flakier force. Personally, I think he may have overreacted slightly. I would have gotten the forty flakies jobs in the federal government. But, other than the beheading part, this story contains some very good advice for all of us. To have your dreams come true, make sure you are 100 percent behind the decisions you make. The best way to get 100 percent behind your decisions is to make them yourself by exercising free choice.

Free Choice

Recently we visited a couple, former neighbors who had taken the leap and moved to the beautiful but more remote Eastern Shore of the Chesapeake Bay. Every window of their new home commanded smashing views of the bay. The place was absolutely magical. They had given up many conveniences to make this move. Now the trip to work was a very long commute. Their kids could no longer attend one of the few truly excellent high schools in the country. Looking through a scrapbook of their move, I came across a long pros-and-cons list. I laughed to myself because this was so much like them. These people are logical and analytical with a capital L and A. Looking more closely, I noticed that the pros list for making the move was short and the cons list almost endless. At dinner, I asked how they had decided to make their adventurous move. They said that after making their pros-and-cons list, they both had felt disappointed with the outcome. They realized that logic pointed one way, feelings another. But for this very important decision, they wanted to do the pointing themselves, rather than leave it to either automatic process. They began to inquire into one of the more profound questions a person can ask: Is it possible to make a free choice, and, if so, how?

They wondered if free choice could be as simple as just pointing to one of the options and saying "I'll have that one." After some discussion, they recognized that doing it that way would be more like pin-the-tail-on-the-donkey than free choice. As they looked deeper into the puzzle, they discovered a secret as simple as walking and as rare as diamonds. I'm going to reveal that secret to you in the following inquiry. At first, you may not like it very much. It is too simple. We humans like things to be as complicated and difficult as possible. We like our wisdom to come after years of practice or study or guarded by some significant dragon at the gate. Free choice is a simple sort of wisdom. You can start to practice it immediately without delving into esoteric mysteries or volumes of how-to tips.

Let's start by taking a look at what we mean by free choice. One possible definition of free choice is "to select freely without being ruled by conditioned thinking." Another is "to select freely, after thoughtful deliberation."

The first definition, *to select freely without being ruled by conditioned thinking* expresses the intended result. The trick is to find a pathway through all the opinions, rules, apparent limitations, and considerations that usually blind people to seeing beyond their own noses. If you want to make your own selections from the menu of life, without being ruled by the preexisting programming, you must learn some new skills

PRACTICING FREE CHOICE

1. Pay attention to how you make decisions now. The first step in learning to exercise free choice is to become acutely aware of exactly how you make decisions now. You need to witness yourself in action, sitting right on the handlebars of reality as it hits the curves at a hundred miles an hour. A little bit of direct observation of how you make decisions now is a prerequisite to free choice, because, otherwise, the way you usually make decisions will continue to operate automatically, like a monkey on your back. With a little observation, you can get the monkey around to the front where you can keep your eye on the little rascal. It has then lost some of its power to control you. You will notice when it grabs the steering wheel.

Begin to pay attention to what actually happens when you make a decision. Write down three important decisions you have made over the last few years.

Now write down three less important decisions you have made in the last few months. All of these should be times where you went through some sort of process to get to the final decision.

Start with the first of the six decisions you have written down. Close your eyes and go through the process of making the decision like you are watching a movie, from beginning to end. What did you do first? Then what came next? What occurred after that? What part did the following common decision-making methods play: logic, analysis, common sense; feelings; romantic yearnings; resonance; external sources; reaction, rebellion, compliance; random; shoulds and Yeahbuts? Did you start out with one or more method and then switch to another one later? Did you trust one method above all others? Did you use some combination of methods? Actually follow the process through to the end.

Write down how the process worked for that first decision, like this: "I started by having romantic yearnings, then did research, analysis, and talked with other people, and then made the final decision by going with my strong desire for one of the options."

Go through the same process for each of the other five decisions. When you finish, you should have a very clear idea of how you make decisions.

The next question is: How well does this method or methods work for you? Do you get you what you want? How well do the decisions hold up over time? Do you feel that you made the right decision every time? If not, where did your methods fail you? Do you experience having made the decision yourself, or does it seem as if the methods made it for you? If you switched to another method, could the outcomes be improved?

2. Learn all you can about the matter in question. The secret of free choice is revealed in the second definition: to select freely, *after thoughtful deliberation.* Let's take this one step at a time. First let's deal with the "thoughtful deliberation" part. Later, we'll get to how to select freely.

It would be sheer insanity to attempt to make important decisions without knowing everything you can about the matter in question. The more you know, the better off you will be. Thoughtful deliberation involves rigorous research, discussion, study, reflection, meditation, speculation, calculation, and education. It includes looking into every nook and cranny that could have any bearing on what choice you make. This may seem obvious, but given the reality that some people put more time into researching what car to buy than they do on what to do with their lives, it's worth repeating.

What do you look into and thoughtfully deliberate about? Everything that might be important! Fortunately you already have a full set of powerful research tools at your disposal. The conventional decision-making methods we discussed a few paragraphs ago make the ideal set of research tools. Using them as telescopes and microscopes is completely different from relying on them to make the decision for you. As research tools, they provide you with everything you need to know: access to all the diverse aspects of your personality as well as practical information about the external world. You don't need to be told to use your habitual methods and techniques. That will happen all by itself. Give special attention to the areas to which you give short shrift. If you just look into the areas you are accustomed to considering, you will have a lopsided view of the situation. If you usually go with your feelings, take an in-depth look at the practical and analytical side. If you tend toward a logical approach, delve more deeply into your feelings than usual. If you usually trust the outside world for answers, make sure to give special attention to internal voices, feelings, and insights as well. Explore all of it thoroughly. Look at your potential choices from as many perspectives and directions as you can. Here's how you can use some of the methods that usually dominate the decision-making process as allies to insure that you make the best choices.

- **Logic, analysis, common sense.** Read everything appropriate. Find out all you can. Become an expert on the subject. Read a year or two of recent issues of the trade magazines in whatever fields you are considering. Read books. Make a list of all the important questions you need to answer in order to know enough to decide. Make pros-and-cons lists. Ask your computer. Do some in-depth career testing to evaluate your talents and personality.

- **Feelings, inclinations, preferences, resonance.** Your internal resources provide some of the most important clues. If these are methods you know well, you will have your own methods and rituals to process them. Use the Inquiries and projects in *The Pathfinder* to delve into these areas.

- **Romantic yearnings.** Be aware that your passionate interest in something may color your view of it. If you are the sort of person who keeps falling in love with exciting new possibilities, you may not feel the way you do today next month. The object of your affection will appear different in the light of a new day. If this is so, you can learn to see beyond the sparkling blinders of your enthusiasms, just as you can learn to look from new models. If you are the sort of person who tends toward consistent, long-term passions, you may want to give these yearnings special significance. To have a strong natural liking for something is a powerful clue. But remember, just because you have been passionately interested in snakes for many years doesn't mean you have to become a charmer. It just means that you need to make a choice about pursuing this passion, or in whatever career you choose you will always dream wistfully of cobras dancing in baskets. Also, it might be very different to do something all day, every day than it is to dream about it or have it as a hobby. In Maine, there are very few lobstermen who enjoy eating lobster.

- **Resonance.** Look within to check out whether or not you and your potential choices are on the same or a complementary wave length. What "vibes" do you pick up? Are you called toward a future that is compelling? Sometimes resonance is misleading. If you are thinking of something that is a huge stretch for you, you may simply feel terrified. This is often a good sign that you are on the right track. Check beneath emotions for resonance. Feelings and resonance are two separate domains.

- **External sources.** Ask everybody you can who knows anything about whatever you are considering. Find some experts. You need to speak with many of them in order to form your own opinion. Ask your friends and family.

- **Reaction, rebellion, compliance.** Strong negative feelings and reactions are powerful resources. It's a lot easier to find out how people really feel about things by asking what they don't like than it is to ask them what they do like. People are always crystal clear about what they don't like. Career counselors constantly hear new clients say, "I know what I don't want. But I don't know what I do want." If you have a rebellious streak, turn it into an ally. Many of the great leaps in human evolution, art, and business were created by rebels with a cause.

  If you have a compliant streak, make sure to notice whether it pulls you in a particular direction. Is it fine with you if it makes your choices for you?

- **Random.** There can be a certain magic to randomness. Don't consider it to be worthless as a resource. Sometimes what appears to be random may not be quite as it seems. Over the last few years, the serious scientific study of chaos has begun to reveal the profound depths of this subject, which has been previously thought, by scientists, to be without merit.

The oldest book in the world is the ancient Chinese oracle, the *I Ching*. Over the history of civilization, it has been trusted as a source of wisdom and decision making by rulers of Asian countries as much or more than any other method. To use this book, you go through a ritual that randomly selects portions of the text for you to read and consider. You read the text to glean what wisdom and advice you can about your situation. For thousands of years, people have been amazed how powerfully appropriate and useful the randomly selected passages can be, especially in coming to new ways of looking at a situation. This book is so respected that the flags of several Asian nations contain symbols taken from *I Ching*.

How can you use randomness in your quest? I don't know exactly. You will have to figure this one out on your own. Just remember to consider the events and happenings that seem random as important parts of the puzzle. In a study of stock-picking methods that is a regular feature in *The Wall Street Journal*, throwing a dart at a dart board did a better job of making investment decisions than professional investment advisors. But please don't go too far over the edge with this advice. Remember that it would take a million chimps a billion years to write *A Midsummer Night's Dream* by randomly pounding away at a keyboard.

- **Shoulds and Yeahbuts.** The voices in your head that constantly throw up opposition to new possibilities and compare everything in your corner of the universe with your standards and ideals are great sources of raw data. If you are clear that you do not have to do what the shoulds and Yeahbuts say you should, then you can enlist these noisy voices as allies. They will, at the very least, come up with everything that might possibly be wrong with whatever you are considering. Sometimes they offer practical, down-to-earth viewpoints that are invaluable. To make choices free from the domination of shoulds and Yeahbuts, you need to be very clear about them.

3. Make a choice. After you have looked from every possible viewpoint at whatever you are trying to decide, you arrive at a cliff, the moment of choice. You can leap courageously into the unknown or turn around, go back home, put your feet up, and take a nap. OK, Here's the part you have been waiting for, the part where you find out the secret of how to choose freely. A dramatic drum roll, please maestro! Here's how you do it. You lay all the possible choices out before you. If you are deciding whether to buy the tie with the big pink palm tree or the one with hundreds of mating rabbits on 3D velvet with jimmies, you can do this physically. For choices with less physical substance, such as what career to pick, it helps to write down the different possible choices on a piece of paper. OK, now we are really to the part you have been waiting for all these years. Next, you simply point to one of them and say, " I pick that one." That's all there is to it. At this moment in Pathfinder Career Seminars, there is usually a long stunned silence. Then the muttering begins. The seminar leader has memory flashes of lynch-mob scenes from old cowboy movies. Remember, back there a few pages ago, I told you that you might not like this part at first?

But, you say, what is this choice based on? Nothing, absolutely nothing, zilch, nada. That's why it is free choice. If it were based on something, it wouldn't be free choice. If it is based on something, then you are not making the choice. Whatever it is based on is making the decision for you. That's idiotic! you say. It has to be based on something, or else it is just pure random chance, like drawing straws. In fact, making a free choice is the most advanced way you can go about it. It is not random at all. You have done extensive research. You have become intimately familiar with everything that could, in any way, influence the decision. You have explored your internal universe. You have talked with other people. You have become fully aware of your talents, tendencies, and leanings. You know what is important to you. Now that you have accomplished all that, you are in a perfect position to actually make the choice yourself. So, instead of your decision being based on something, it is a free choice illuminated or informed by your thoughtful deliberation into everything important.

Please don't jump to conclusions about this. Think about it for a while. Give it a chance to sink in. This whole concept seems so radical that many people find it to be completely unimaginable. And please remember that people are generally much more suspicious of things that seem too simple than they are of things that seem too complicated.

Remember the definition of free choice: *to select freely, after thoughtful deliberation.* How else are you going to select freely other than to simply pick after complete and thoughtful deliberation? If you figure out some better way, please let me know.

I didn't say exercising free choice should necessarily be the way to decide everything from now on. You may, like me, prefer to decide which movie to go to based on sheer, primitive, drum-pounding emotion, unclouded by rational thought. For really important decisions, though, like what to do with your life, or whom to marry, free choice is a methodology that puts you in the driver's seat. I never said you would like being in the driver's seat or that it's a comfortable seat. But if you want to play with the big kids, in that place where life is not just the same old thing day after day, it's one of the best ways to get there.

4. Practice by making some small choices to get the hang of it. Start off with something really small and somewhat absurd, like choosing a brand of orange juice to be your regular one. If this seems ridiculous, that is because it is. This is about practicing, not about orange juice. Actually use all the usual decision-making methods to learn all you can about the various orange juices available. Use logic, read and compare the labels, read *Consumer Reports,* ask friends, bring different brands home and try them, check with your feelings, and so forth. Notice if your habitual methods try to push you into a decision. When you have completely investigated the various juices from all points of view, line them up in front of you and pick one. Just point and shoot. You did it! You made a free choice, a decision that is probably much more one of your own authorship than usual.

Next, up the ante a little bit. Use free choice to decide what you will do next Friday night. First of all, notice how you usually decide what to do on Friday nights. Do you have something you habitually do? Do you have a range of only three or four habitual options and then use some method to pick between them? Do you wait for a friend to call and suggest something? Do you decide based on horniness or guilt or practicality? Notice if you somehow get railroaded into the decision by habits, desires, other people. Do the same sort of an inquiry you would do for a big decision such as what to do with the rest of your life—just do it on a smaller scale. Take an hour or two instead of months. Once you have really dug into it and have used the conventional decision-making methods as tools to look into every corner of the issue at hand, you are ready to choose. Write down the possible choices on a piece of paper. Then pick one of them. Yes, just pick one. Then go and do it. It may feel strange at first, like appearing on the stage at Carnegie Hall dressed as the tooth fairy. But you will get over it. Before long you will get to relish having the ability and the skill to make your own decisions. Mastering the art of free choice turns you into a dangerous character. You will find that you are not wimping out in situations you might have previously. You may surprise your friends. In medieval Japan, the samurai who were Zen adepts were the most dangerous foes. They were completely unpredictable because they chose freely, in the moment, rather than relying on habitual pattern of behavior that their enemies could exploit.

Keep practicing. Keep upping the ante. In Walt Kelly's *Pogo* comic strip, the first step to becoming a pianist is to learn to carry the piano. You start with a little toy piano and each day carry a slightly bigger one. Eventually you reach the point where you can carry a full-sized piano. Then you are ready to start to play. That's exactly how you can learn the art of free choice.

5. If there is anything you want to add to your Primary Lists (Wants, Commitments and Requirements, and Questions), turn to them now.

What if I Have Trouble Deciding?

When people have trouble reaching an important decision, they often interpret their difficulty as a fatal flaw in their character. When this happens to you, remember that you are in the same boat with a lot of very gifted people. If you read the biographies of American presidents, you would be reminded again and again how difficult it is to make big decisions. Granted, the decisions they have to make are bigger than yours, but they have also practiced enough that they can carry a gigantic piano. Great artists, famous explorers, and Nobel laureates all agonize over the decisions they face. The things you have trouble deciding are equally intimidating. How formidable they appear is not a function of the size of the decision but of the difficulty you have in making the choice.

Having difficulty making decisions is neither mysterious nor suggestive of a character disorder. There is always a very specific cause. When you can get to the root cause of the difficulty, you can then do something about it. Usually it is much less difficult to successfully get through whatever is stopping your progress than folks expect. To get to the bottom of it, troubleshoot. Dig deep to find the source of the difficulty.

The first thing to consider is to check out how fully you engaged in the "thoughtful deliberation" stage. There may still be important unanswered questions. Make sure you have covered everything to your complete satisfaction. It may be that you have not done enough research. It is possible to come up with answers you still don't feel too sure of. Asking three people what a potential career is like may not be enough. You may need to speak with ten or twenty more experts until you have formed an independent opinion that you would be willing to bet on. The way to find out if there is important deliberation or research still to be done is to turn to the Questions section of your notebook. Write the following question at the top of a new page: "What do I need to answer, find out, or consider in order to decide?" Then do some brainstorming. Write down every possible answer without editing. When you have finished, go over what you have written and cross off the entries that are not matters of life or death, or potential deal-breaker issues. Focus on the important issues. The next step is to go forth and deal with all the important stuff on that list. Then see if you can choose. Come back here if you are still having trouble.

You're back? OK, let's continue the troubleshooting process. Sometimes there are valid reasons to hold off on making the final choice. There are times when you may need to know more then it would be possible to know now. If the person you have been dating for the last month has proposed, it might make sense to wait a few more months until you really get to know them. There are also times when events have not matured enough to provide a framework to weave a choice within. If you are considering an eventual move into an area of developing technology or marketplace, it may make sense to wait and see how things shake out as time passes. In both these examples, it is appropriate to make a decision to wait. There is no hesitation or uncertainty expressed in making such a choice. As the *I Ching* says, "Strength in the face of danger does not plunge ahead but bides its time, whereas weakness in the face of danger grows agitated and has not the patience to wait." The person who holds back when it is more opportune to wait is not avoiding the edge of the cliff. They are awaiting further developments or gathering their forces.

Usually though, if you put off making the choice after doing a reasonably good job of "thoughtful deliberation," you are most likely doing it for one of four reasons:

1. **You don't have much practice in the art of free choice.** It could be that you are somewhat of a babe in the woods in regard to the art of choosing. If you have avoided making decisions because of a lack of skill or practice, reading this book and starting to work out your free choice muscles on some smaller matters will, most likely, be a pathway to nearly miraculous new possibilities. Practice on small stuff and work up to the big choices. In time you will become both the arrow and the archer of your life, able to fire yourself straight toward the perfect apple at full speed.

2. **You are deciding to not decide.** When people say, "I want to think about it for a while" or, "I need to process this further," they are usually fooling themselves or trying to be polite. In reality they are making a covert decision to not decide. For some weird reason, we have a cultural stigma about not deciding. When was the last time you heard someone cheerfully exclaim, "Oh that? Well, I've decided to not decide!" There is nothing wrong with backing away from the cliff. It is not weak or irresponsible. Only a mad person leaps off of every cliff they encounter. The problem is with the covert nature of the decision. To be able to simply acknowledge that you are not jumping off some particular cliff can be an expression of clarity. To obscure the matter with bogus reasons just adds unnecessary confusion and self-flagellation to the situation.

3. **You are waiting for your usual decision-making method to take the load off your shoulders.** Sometimes people reach the cliff of choice and can't decide because their habitual mode of decision making didn't show up for work that day. They don't know how to go about it without help. So they put off the decision in the hope that, sooner or later, their trusty sidekick will show up and do the dirty work for them.

4. **Your temperament is such that you prefer to keep your options open.** People who have closure-oriented personalities do have an easier time of

it. If you prefer to wait and see, let the situation flow spontaneously, hate to close off possibilities, or like to adapt as the situation changes, it is not going to come as naturally is it does for people with a big strong decision-making bone. If your nature is to let it all flow, it might make sense to choose a career where that characteristic fits the work. But to do that, you are going to need to make some decisions, and to pin it down to one career. To have a career that fits you perfectly, you may have to push yourself to get skilled in areas that are the opposite of what comes naturally to you, like picking one thing and sticking with it. You are just being a little naive if you expect that everything you do should come easily. The solution is to make a commitment to making a choice, even if it is difficult to do. Then practice choosing every day until you can carry a full-sized piano.

If you feel that you are cutting off other wonderfully attractive options when you make a decision, you are right. That's true. The reality is that you do it all day long. Right now you are reading this book when you could be making love or racing motorcycles or writing your own book. You could be doing a million other things. You are an expert at picking one thing to the exclusion of countless others. You do it all day long. Not one waking moment goes by that you could not spend doing something else. You constantly make decisions about what you are going to do that exclude everything else. You picked your spouse or lover. By choosing that one person, you decided to forgo the pleasure of the company of billions of other possible people.

The fact of the matter is that you cannot do it all. You are a human being with limited time, limited energy, and a limited life span. Doing something you love, doing it brilliantly and getting paid well for it is a hell of a lot better than pissing your life away trying to do several different things at once. Most people never even get really good at doing one thing. It takes such a big chunk of a person's life and energy to master one thing and make a success of it that you may not have the juice available to get several balls into the air at once. Most of those people you admire do one thing well. They sing or create businesses or make discoveries or whatever. Only a very few people get to play in multiple arenas. Most of them got to up the ante because they completely mastered and succeeded at one game. If you want to have an expansive career that marches in several different parades at once, you need to come face to face with a paradox: In order to have a career that is free from the need to focus your life and attention on one narrow field or subject, you need to focus so completely on one thing that you master it completely and become a resounding success at it. Then you get to expand. It's not fair, but that does not make it any less true. Notice which actors get to be film directors. Isn't it usually the actors who have totally succeeded in their craft that get to expand into directing? Your friend who is struggling to make it in summer stock never gets the chance. Please remember that to choose one career does not in any way limit you or mean that you must compromise. You can, most likely, find a way to combine everything important to you in one career and one life.

Please remember that this advice is not *the* truth. It's just one perspective. There are some people who make multiple careers work. They may have two fulfilling part-time careers. They may have serial careers. But, remember, it is much easier to keep one ball in the air than it is to juggle five of them at once. Usually, when people have trouble settling on one thing, they are just experiencing difficulty pinning down one career. If this is the situation you are facing, all it usually takes to get off the dime is to realize what the consequences will be if you do not pick one thing and put your energy into that one thing 100 percent.

How Can I Tell Whether I Am

Putting Off Making the Decision

or Being Responsible in

Waiting to Choose?

If you are absolutely sure that it is appropriate to wait for some very definite reason, or if you are doing battle with your own historical patterns of leaping too quickly or compulsive decision making, then you may be exhibiting a case of responsible thinking. Otherwise, you are probably dodging the issue. If you are feeling uncertain, confused, or a little ashamed of yourself, you are most likely backing away from the cliff. Just ask yourself. You will know the answer. This is not the time to play dumb with yourself. What are you really up to? Moving your life ahead in the most direct way toward your most important long-range goals? Or are you struggling in the webs of the Yeahbuts?

How Can I Be Sure It Is the Right Decision?

You can't really be sure of anything until it happens. You will not know with absolute certainty how well you chose until you have worked in the career you picked for a year or two. Anything else is guesswork. All the questions you delve into, all the people you speak with, everything else you do to make the best possible choice can do nothing more than make you a master of making educated guesses. Now that it's settled, it becomes quite evident that you would be wise to throw yourself completely into the process of making a wonderful career choice. The best way to increase the odds that you will make the best choices is to increase the quality and quantity of your participation.

What if I Make the Wrong Decision?

If you make the wrong decision, you make the wrong decision. That's all there is to it. There are few guarantees in life. One of them is that you will make lots of mistakes. It happens to all of us. The worst thing you can do is to wimp out and spend your life in suspended animation, wringing your hands and refusing to make a choice because it may not be the perfect one. Go boldly into the future, doing all you can to make good choices. If you make a mistake, acknowledge your mistake, forgive yourself, and plunge into the process of deciding what to do with you life one more time. Make new choices. Then step boldly into that future.

•

WHY YOU DO WHAT YOU DO

The Machinery of Human Behavior

This chapter is for you, if you want to dig even deeper into how your internal machinery controls your life or if you want to run your show with your hands on the steering wheel. If you are tired of hearing about this stuff, go on to the next chapter. If you are still hungry for more, go for it.

When you do not get what you go after wholeheartedly, it is usually because you have not learned the skills to turn your internal machinery in your favor. To know how to make the machinery work for you, we have to have a working knowledge of human behavior. I'm going to present a model that is useful because it works. It is not the one and only truth. The beauty of this model is that it is easy to understand, remember, and to use as a template for figuring our how to deal successfully with whatever is going on at any moment of your life. So, here we go.

Take a look at the illustration on the next page, which I call "The Machinery of Human Behavior." Let's use an imaginary example to show how human behavior works. Please keep referring to the illustration as we go through this step by step.

1. Number 1 in the illustration represents input from the environment around you. Every moment of your life involves an interaction with the external world. Imagine that your office door flies open, in comes your boss, yelling, blaming you for something you haven't done.

2. All input from the outside is filtered through many interpretive, cognitive filters. For the sake of simplicity, at number 2 the illustration shows just a few basic ones: your memory, imagination, and self-concept. The boss yelling is filtered through memories of other people yelling at you, scenes of people yelling from the movies, and so forth. Your imagination makes up explanations of what the yelling means. Your self-concept also influences how you interpret this incident.

3. Once the input has gone through these cognitive filters, it becomes what you could call a "filtered perception," shown at number 3 in the illustra-

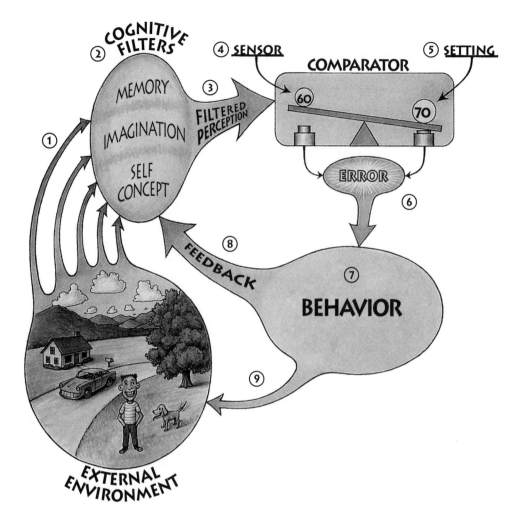

tion. It has been shaped by the cognitive filters so that it is no longer the original input. It is your own personal interpretation of that input. This filtered perception is what you and I call "reality." In fact, it may not bear the slightest resemblance to whatever input came from the outside world. Your interpretation could be: "Wow, he is really upset. I must have made a big mistake. I'm in trouble." Or: "What an asshole." There is no end to the ways you could interpret his yelling. But you can be sure that you do not simply listen to it as information. You attribute meaning and give a certain spin to whatever information he is transmitting.

4. This little nugget of what you call reality then arrives at a device that engineers call a *comparator*. A comparator is an instrument for comparing a measurement with a standard. It is like the thermostat you have in your house to tell the furnace and the air conditioner when to turn on and off. Each cell in your body has some of these little devices built into it. In fact, these comparators are what run every part of our lives, at all levels, from the cellular to the philosophical. Every comparator has a little device for sensing whatever it is supposed to measure, shown at number 4. In a thermostat, a little thermometer reads the temperature in the room. On a biological level, the ones in your body sense thousands of different chemical, electrical, and physical measures, all to keep your body running smoothly. On a psychological level, there are further thousands of comparators tuned in to all the nonphysical things that keep you functioning. More about this in a minute.

5. A thermostat has a little dial on it that allows you to set the temperature in the room. All the comparators in your body and brain also have a specific setting. This is shown at number 5 in the illustration. Some are easily adjustable by you, some are adjustable only by a licensed service representative (your doctor prescribes a medication), and some are not adjustable at all.

6. When the sensor and the setting do not agree, the comparator registers an error, shown at number 6. If your thermostat could talk, it might say, "Setting is 70 degrees, sensor reads 65 degrees, ERROR ERROR."

7. When the comparator recognizes an error, it turns on a switch that starts something happening to deal with the error, to make it go away. In your thermostat, if the sensor reading is too low, it turns on the furnace. If the reading is too high, it turns on the air conditioner. Almost all the behaviors in our lives work the same way. When you go jogging and your blood starts to heat up, little comparators start sending error messages when the sensor registers a temperature higher than 98.6 degrees and respond to this error message by turning on the perspiration and other systems that help to cool you down. In the purely biological parts of us, the comparators turn on biological equipment. In our more psychological domains, various comparators are set for other, nonphysical things. But the system still works exactly the same way. Whenever one of these devices registers an error, it turns on a behavior designed to return you to equilibrium. This is shown at number 7.

Throughout this book, we have encountered this mechanical survival system, that seeks to return us to equilibrium whenever we stray from it, as the force that keeps you and me from getting what we want. On this most basic level, you and I are machines that are designed to survive. Our survival machinery is not intelligent. It just reacts to whatever is pro-grammed into it. Each little comparator in our psychological self has al-ready been set by experiences we have had, decisions we have made, and whatever we have learned in the course of our lives. Once one of these lit-tle guys is set, it usually stays put on the same setting forever. Whenever it reads "error," it reacts and sends a message that turns on a behavior, such as "Danger! Danger! Start genuflection! Kowtow now!" Sometimes the behavior works and helps produce the intended outcome, sometimes it doesn't. If you have a comparator set for "Attention equals love, I must be the center of attention in one-one-one situations," you will react to make that happen when the comparator registers that you aren't getting enough. Let's suppose this comparator got hooked up to a behavior called "throw a tantrum" when you were two years old. Now you are twenty-five and out on a date. Your date seems to be ignoring you and keeps mak-ing eye contact with someone across the room. Your little love and attention comparator reads "error" and instantly pushes the "play" but-ton on your tantrum behavior tape. You may not actually cry, jump up and down, and shake your fists, but, inside of you, there is a major upset happening. Even though you try to conceal it, your date can feel it and be-comes even more distant. Clearly, the behavior that the system turned on did not work to produce the outcome you wanted. Let's go back to our example, the boss yelling at you. If you have a little comparator that is set for "keep this job at all costs," the boss yelling might turn on a completely different behavior than one set for "yelling equals attack equals fight back." Your reaction depends on what you are set for.

8. All of the foregoing affects us by reinforcing our cognitive filters and the world around us. The rest of the universe runs on the same kind of mech-anisms, so however you react tends to reinforce its filters as well. If you yell back at the boss, it will affect how he behaves with you next time. Even more important is that your reaction reinforces your own filters, shown at number 8. We continually reinforce behaviors that work and ones that don't. Our lives essentially consist of habits, both good and bad. We react to situations from our data bank of preprogrammed tapes rather than respond anew to new situations. The whole process of life consists of millions of these cybernetic feedback loops. This is the great wheel of ex-istence. Around and around we go. Where it stops, nobody knows.

How to Get What You Want

If you want to improve or change something in your life, you can work on any part of this cycle of behavior. Every therapeutic methodology that has been designed to help people be more effective or deal successfully with personal problems is pointed at one or more of these areas. Some methods take an environmental approach. If you don't like the weather, move to San Diego. You may be happier there. Others focus on working with cognitive filters. The idea is that if you change the way you filter experience, if you work to improve your self-concept, change the structure of your memories, and so forth, there will be less distortion and you will have more flexibility to respond to life. Some methods concentrate on reinterpreting filtered perceptions. Still others replace behaviors that do not produce the wanted result with more productive ones. Chew gum rather than smoke cigarettes. All of these have their place and are appropriate for certain situations. In the present situation, what we are looking for is the method that will be the most effective to help you make your dreams come true. And that method is to change the setting of the system. Concentrate your efforts at number 5 in the illustration. Back to our example. Let's say, after you and the boss have had several run-ins, you notice that the situation is deteriorating. When you take a look at what you are set for, it turns out to be "yelling equals attack equals fight back." So you change the setting to "I do not take what the boss says personally. No matter what tone of voice he uses, I listen to find out what he is requesting." Now, with that setting, the situation is likely to improve rather than continue to deteriorate. You have completely transformed the situation by making one small adjustment.

The one big problem we all face in making dreams come true is Yeahbuts. If you could just write down a list of everything you most wanted, plan how to make it all happen, and then get into full-tilt effective action, without interference, just think what you could create in your life. But what actually happens is that when we begin to get close to stepping out of our customary boundaries, it triggers an error switch on comparators, which produces a behavior (Yeahbuts) that are designed to return you to equilibrium. A few lucky people have most of their comparators tuned to settings and actions that produce favorable outcomes. This is what parents could strive for in providing their children with a "good upbringing." Most of the rest of us have a smorgasbord of settings that range from resourceful to downright destructive to our ability to fulfill on our intentions.

When you attempt to move forward in designing a career that will turn out to be truly excellent, it quickly becomes apparent that our comparators are set for such things as "comfort," "that which is unknown is risky," "avoid risks at all cost," and so forth. The best way to deal with them is to make up new settings, for example to consciously set yourself for "a life of full self-expression," "a high level of career satisfaction," "choose a career I will love," "do work that makes a contribution," or "win this upcoming election." Don't these sound an awful lot like commitments? That is exactly what they are. Creating commitments is the most powerful way to set yourself to get the results you want. It is how you can most effectively reset yourself to make your dreams come true, rather than get swept away by your ancient biology.

When you understand how the system I just described works and recognize that by creating new commitments you are setting yourself to achieve the result you commit to, you can get much more creative in making up effective settings, commitments, new rules, or whatever you want to call them. In our dating example, if you notice that you go crazy when you are not getting enough attention, and that you are set for, "Attention equals love, I must be the center of attention in one-one-one situations," you can make up a new setting. For example, instead of taking it personally, you could make up a new rule that when a date seems to be getting distracted, it means that you are not communicating effectively. You could take a course in effective communication and in the future, use this situation as an opportunity to master communicating, rather than ruin the evening.

CHAPTER 16

GOALS AND PROJECTS

In the long run you only hit what you aim at. Therefore, though you should fail immediately, you had better aim at something high.

—HENRY DAVID THOREAU

To design your future career or find the perfect job, begin by creating goals and then turn your goals into a project. Let's suppose that you have decided to design and build your own home. At the beginning of the process, you already have some goals in mind that building the house will fulfill. Perhaps your big overall goal is to fulfill your dream of building your own house. Or perhaps it is to have a house that suits you perfectly, with no compromises. When it comes time to sit down and begin designing the house, you would need to get very specific about your goals for the house. You would also need to turn your attention to goal setting in other domains of your life. Your home is an integral part of the web of your life. Decisions about the house will be intimately connected with goals regarding your family, children, career, recreation, finances, geography, self-expression, lifestyle, community, and much more. So it is with your career goals. We often make the mistake of separating life into modules instead of thinking of it as a whole, a complex network of domains that all interrelate and depend on each other. Our culture has taught us to compartmentalize everything. This works beautifully when you are organizing your kitchen shelves, but not so well when you are designing your life.

This chapter is a complete course in the art of goal setting and project management. Acquiring mastery of setting and fulfilling goals takes a deeper appreciation and understanding of goals than most people have. In the next few pages, you will have an opportunity to develop an intimate and effective relationship with goals that will make it easier for you to create goals and smooth the way to turning them into reality. To do a really excellent job of designing your future, you should consider becoming expert at goal setting and project management as a prerequisite. I suggest that you make this Inquiry the most important central project of your life until you have completed it and are totally satisfied with the result. This might take a week, a month, or more. Let's deal with a couple of questions before we get started:

What is the difference between my Commitments and Requirements List, a Goals List, and a project? All of these lists and concepts are no more than ways to look at important parts of your life. Often your various lists and Inquiries will contain the same information. To design your life well, it is very worthwhile to look from several different reference points. The more ways you look over what is most important to you, the clearer you will get.

- Your **Commitments and Requirements List** is the place to declare promises about your future. It is a way of saying that whatever you are committing to will definitely be a part of your life.
- Your **Goals List** can be used in several ways: as a worksheet to explore possible goals, to get clear on your biggest abstract goals like "prosperity" and figure out how to reach them; as an aid to deciding what to commit to; as a way of planning and prioritizing; as a way of deciding what to turn into a project to do now and what to do later.
- A **project** is a goal you have decided to accomplish now or in the near future. Project management is the art and science of taking a project all the way to completion.

A Future of Limitless Possibilities

When you ask the question "What are my options?" you automatically limit yourself to potential choices that are within the range of your vision now. Everyone has options, even inner-city kids. They can join a gang or hide indoors. They have a choice of several strategies to improve their chance of surviving in a hostile environment. They are, however, usually completely devoid of possibilities, with absolutely no training in how to get out of the windowless room. As soon as you ask "What is possible?" you open up a new world that, for you, never existed before, a doorway that takes you out beyond the range of options previously available to you.

There is almost no limit to what you can accomplish when you are willing to step beyond the options before you now, when you get clear what you most want, and commit yourself to making those dreams come true. Many years ago, a fifteen-year-old boy named John Goddard sat down at his kitchen table and wrote out a list of 127 life goals he called "My Life List." Here is his list, with check marks, showing which of those goals he has accomplished so far. (John is now in his seventies.)

This list is amazing, but it actually does not even begin to tell the story of his remarkable life. The point is not to become a goal setter but to live an extraordinary life. Clear goals are the path to that kind of life. Each goal checked off on

John's list was a powerful learning experience for him and many of them were an extraordinary adventure. For example, goal number 1 was to explore the Nile. When John says explore the Nile, he doesn't mean a couple of miles along the bank. He organized the first expedition to explore every inch of the Nile from source to mouth, all by kayak. I consider my friend John to be the world's premier goal setter. When I asked him recently to reveal the secret of his ability to create and fulfill so many amazing goals, he first said to tell you that he is in no way an extraordinary person. He says he is just like you and me. What he does is very simple. He writes down what he most wants to do. Then, he commits to doing it. It becomes a goal, then a project to plan. Then it becomes an adventure to live.

Making big, unreasonable promises to yourself like John Goddard does stretches you out into new territory, and becomes a force that produces extraordinary results.

I once saw a TV news feature story about two professional golfers. They were the same age, looked alike, had gone to PGA school together, each had 2.2 children, cute blond wives, were best friends, and had the same stroke average. Two people could not be more alike unless they were twins. One of them had won several major tournaments that year and was raking in huge sums of money. The other was working as a golf pro at a country club and had never won anything, even though he had participated in tournaments. The point of the feature story was supposed to be something about the fickle finger of fate. But as they were interviewed, it became evident that there was one big difference between the two golfers. The winning golfer, when asked about his future goals said his goal was to be the best, and most successful golfer in the world. The other fellow said his goal was to keep making a living playing golf. One had created an extraordinary vision for the future and was going for it 200 percent. The other was happy to putt around in the comfort zone.

It does not make you a better person to have bigger goals. It simply makes life a more exciting game that stretches your very being. You may be happy in the comfort zone. You may just want to have a decent career, 2.2 kids, retire to Florida, and watch TV until, one day, you don't wake up. If so, I suggest that you really swing out and set some goals about how good a parent you will be, when you will move to Florida, etc. Whatever you want, being clear about your goals makes it much more likely that you will get there.

EXPLORE:

✔1. Nile River
✔2. Amazon River
✔3. Congo River
✔4. Colorado River
5. Yangtze River
6. Niger River
7. Orinco River, Venezuela
✔8. Rio Coco, Nicaragua

STUDY PRIMITIVE CULTURE IN:

✔9. The Congo
✔10. New Guinea
✔11. Brazil
✔12. Borneo
✔13. The Sudan
✔14. Australia
✔15. Kenya
✔16. The Philippines
✔17. Tanganyika
✔18. Ethiopia
✔19. Nigeria
✔20. Alaska

CLIMB:

21. Mount Everest
22. Mount Aconcagua
23. Mount McKinley
✔24. Mount Huascaran
✔25. Mount Kilimanjaro
✔26. Mount Ararat
✔27. Mount Kenya
28. Mount Cook
✔29. Mount Popocatepetl
✔30. The Matterhorn
✔31. Mount Rainier
✔32. Mount Fuji
✔33. Mount Vesuvius
✔34. Mount Bromo
✔35. Grand Tetons
✔36. Mount Baldy

✔37. Carry out careers in medicine and exploration
38. Visit every country in the world (30 to go)
✔39. Study Navajo and Hopi Indians
✔40. Learn to fly a plane
✔41. Ride horse in Rose Parade

PHOTOGRAPH:

42. Iguacu Falls, Brazil
✔43. Victoria Falls, Rhodesia
✔44. Sutherland Falls, New Zealand
✔45. Yosemite Falls
✔46. Niagara Falls
✔47. Retrace travels of Marco Polo and Alexander the Great

EXPLORE UNDERWATER:

✔48. Coral reefs of Florida
✔49. Great Barrier Reef, Australia
✔50. Red Sea
✔51. Fiji Islands
✔52. The Bahamas
✔53. Explore Okefenokee Swamp and the Everglades

VISIT:

54. North and South Poles
✔55. Great Wall of China
✔56. Panama and Suez Canals
✔57. Easter Island
✔58. The Galapagos Islands
✔59. Vatican City
✔60. The Taj Mahal
✔61. The Eiffel Tower
✔62. The Blue Grotto
✔63. The Tower of London
✔64. The Leaning Tower of Pisa
✔65. The Sacred Well of Chichen-Itza, Mexico
✔66. Climb Ayers Rock in Australia
67. Follow river Jordan from Sea of Galilee to Dead Sea

SWIM IN:

✔68. Lake Victoria

✔69. Lake Superior

✔70. Lake Tanganyika

✔71. Lake Titicaca, South America

✔72. Lake Nicaragua

ACCOMPLISH:

✔73. Become an Eagle Scout

✔74. Dive in a submarine

✔75. Land on and take off from and aircraft carrier

✔76. Fly in a blimp, hot air balloon, and a glider

✔77. Ride an elephant, camel, ostrich, and bronco

✔78. Skin dive to 40 feet and hold breath for two and a half minutes

✔79. Catch a 10-pound lobster and 10-inch abalone

✔80. Play flute and violins

✔81. Type 50 words a minute

✔82. Take a parachute jump

✔83. Learn water and snow skiing

✔84. Go on a church mission

✔85. Follow the John Muir Trail

✔86. Study native medicines and bring back useful ones

✔87. Bag camera trophies of elephant, lion, rhino, cheetah, cape buffalo, and whale

✔88. Learn to fence

✔89. Learn jujitsu

✔90. Teach a college course

✔91. Watch a cremation ceremony in Bali

✔92. Explore depths of the sea

93. Appear in a Tarzan movie

94. Own a horse, chimpanzee, cheetah, ocelot and coyote (has owned a horse, ocelot, and coyote so far)

95. Become a ham radio operator

✔96. Build own telescope

✔97. Write a book

✔98. Publish an article in *National Geographic Magazine*

✔99. High jump 5 feet

✔100. Broad jump 15 feet

✔101. Run a mile in 5 minutes

✔102. Weigh 175 pounds stripped

✔103. Perform 200 sit-ups and 20 pull-ups

✔104. Learn French, Spanish, and Arabic

105. Study dragon lizards on Komodo Island

✔106. Visit birthplace of Grandfather Sorenson in Denmark

✔107. Visit birthplace of Grandfather Goddard in England

✔108. Ship aboard a freighter as a seaman

109. Read the entire *Encyclopedia Britannica*

✔110. Read the Bible from cover to cover

✔111. Read the works of Shakespeare, Plato, Aristotle, Dickens, Thoreau, Poe, Rousseau, Bacon, Hemingway, Twain, Burroughs, Conrad, Talmage, Tolstoi, Longfellow, Keats, Whittier, and Emerson

✔112. Become familiar with the compositions of Bach, Beethoven, Debussy, Ibert, Mendelssohn, Lalo, Rimski-Korsakov, Respighi, Liszt, Rachmaninoff, Stravinsky, Toch, Tschaikovsky, Verdi

✔113. Become proficient in the use of a plane, motorcycle, tractor, surfboard, rifle, pistol, canoe, microscope, football, basketball, bow and arrow, lariat, and boomerang

✔114. Compose music

✔115. Play *Clair de Lune* on the piano

✔116. Watch fire-walking ceremony
✔117. Milk a poisonous snake
✔118. Light a match with a .22 rifle
✔119. Visit a movie studio
✔120. Climb Cheops' pyramid
✔121. Become a member of the Explorers' Club and the Adventurers' Club

✔122. Learn to play polo
✔123. Travel through the Grand Canyon on foot and by boat
✔124. Circumnavigate the globe (has done it four times)
  125. Visit the moon
✔126. Marry and have children
  127. Live to see the 21st century

Principles of Goal Setting

1. **Understand that there are three different levels of goals.** At the highest level are big, comprehensive *meta-goals*. The word *meta* means "transcending or more comprehensive." These goals usually express large, abstract ideas, like health, contribution, love, ecstasy, pleasure, security, self-expression, prosperity, satisfaction. From these meta-level (higher level) goals flow *specific goals*. Falling under the broad comprehensive goal of prosperity, you might set specific goals concerning income, saving, investment, retirement, controlling impulse buying, etc. Finally, at the lowest level are the items on your to-do list. Some of these are *action steps*. They are the nitty-gritty, step-by-step plans to make your dreams come true. Other lower-level goals could be thought of as *mileposts*. They are markers along the path to completing a project that fulfills a goal. They tell how far down the trail you have gone.

At the heart of our fondest dreams are our meta-goals. Most people who want to have a million dollars, Scrooge McDuck excepted, don't want all that money because their dream is to have a big pile of dirty pieces of green paper. They have a larger, more comprehensive, abstract goal in mind, perhaps prosperity or security or to win the game of monkey on the mountain. These meta-level goals are the real goals behind the goals we set and work on consciously. To get to the meta-goal behind the conscious goal, ask "Why?" If you are thinking of going to the beach this weekend, and you wanted to get to the real goal behind the conscious goal, you might ask, "Why? What will I get by going to the beach? What do I really want?" It might be that you want the good feeling you get when you recharge your batteries listening to the pounding surf. You might be seeking excitement or to work on looking good by deepening your tan a couple of shades.

Most of the goals you set have a meta-goal behind them. When you buy a puppy, get married, or wash the dishes, you are fulfilling one of them, usually without realizing it. The first step in goal setting is to get clear about these meta-goals. Your relationship with your goals will be much more powerful. Often people don't get what they really want because they don't know what they really want. When they try to decide whether to go to the beach or stay home, they focus on the issue at hand rather than to look behind to see what is motivating their desire. If you know that the real motivating desire is to feel good by recharging your batteries, you can come up with other possible ways to do it. Then you can pick from a number of options. When your inner formula is feel good = reduce feelings of stress = recharge batteries = go to beach, you do not really have any choices except "go" or "not go." That puts you and a lightbulb on a similar level of choice. It has no choice. You have only one, either off or on. By looking to the deeper meta-level goal behind the goal, you get in direct contact with what you really want to satisfy. Looking from that point of view cuts the automatic cause-and-effect relationship between motivation and fulfillment. If you know that the real goal is "feel good," not "beach," then you are free to invent" new ways to feel good.

If your goal setting is simply focused on your to-do list or on specific goals, you will have much more difficulty sticking with the plan than if you understand all three levels of goals. It is not easy to get out of bed and go running on a cold, gray winter morning. Being conscious that this item on your to-do list is a part of your specific goal of "physical fitness," which is part of your big meta-goal of "feeling good and looking good," makes it much easier to pull those sneakers on. What you really want is the meta-goal, not the icy wind blowing in your face. Begin goal setting at the highest level. Go from the general to the specific. It won't work the other way around. You can't figure out your life goals by looking at your to-do list.

Most people's meta-goals are not something they created. In fact, most of us have had no say in choosing our meta-level goals. Remember that advertising psychologists say that what motivates us is: looking good, feeling good, being right, feeling safe, and avoiding pain. With the exception of "being right," these are powerful motivators for our nonhuman neighbors as well. They are already programmed into our internal wiring. If "feeling safe" is a meta-goal, you may have some choice about how to realize this goal, choices about what "safety" means to you, etc. But, you don't have any more choice about the goal itself than you do about your shadow. Like your shadow, meta-goals follow you around everywhere. You can live in the dark and deny they exist, but they will spring forth every time the light shines on you. Many of these higher-level goals will be the same as some of your most important and deepest held values, which will be explored in a later chapter. Once you are consciously aware of the extraordinarily powerful role these meta-goals play in your life, a new possibility arises: perhaps you could start to invent some new ones, alter, transform and even abandon old ones.

The most conscious, evolved people create their own meta-goals rather than just run the software program built into them. For example, Gandhi's nature was deeply sensual, which he abandoned because he thought this meta-goal detracted from his life's purpose. Imagine what people would have thought if he spoke and spun from the grounds of the Himalayan Hedonism Hideaway. When you create a purpose for your life, what you are actually doing is creating the highest form of meta-goal possible. Living from a purpose is essentially surrendering to a meta-goal that you invented, which you elevate to a higher position than the ones already programmed in, and which serves some purpose larger than your self-fulfillment.

2. **Make your goals correspond with what you really want.** If your goals represent what you think you should want, what would please your parents or spouse, your cultural identity, or fulfill your company's goals but are not authentically your own, you will have great difficulty achieving them. Align your goals with your deepest principles and values, and with your most genuine dreams and desires. Let your mother make up her own goals. If you can't authentically take on your company's goals as your own, go get another job in a company where you can. Wanting something passionately does not necessarily mean you must have it. You may be perfectly happy to lust for your favorite movie star from afar. But if you do not have the passion, the desire for something, don't turn it into a goal. Life is short. You don't have time to waste going after stuff you don't really want.

3. **Create goals for every important area of your life.** Remember that each part of your life is interwoven with everything else. Don't stop with career goals. Create goals for your marriage, your hobby, your community involvement. Make up some health and fitness goals, satisfaction and well-being goals, and so forth. Make up parenting goals, but don't make up goals for your children. They are perfectly capable of making up their own goals without your help. Encourage them to become masterful at setting their own goals. If you concentrate on your goal of continually pushing the envelope to be a truly great parent, they might even learn something from your example.

4. **Understand that well-founded goals contain some specific ingredients that boost their effectiveness.** Fuzziness is the enemy of productively moving your goals along to completion. When you are slogging through

waist-deep mud along the path to fulfilling a goal, it is amazingly easy to forget why you were in the mud in the first place. All of your goals should be *highly specific*. Remember back to the "Diving into the Mist" chapter, where you honed your goals for the process you are in the middle of now. That is a good example of how to sharpen up goals so you say exactly what you mean, with no uncertainty remaining and no fluff added. Wherever possible, make your goals *measurable*. If they are not measurable, how will you be able to tell if you are achieving them? Those changing careers may want to enjoy their work more than they do now. But framing the goal using the words "enjoy my new job more than my present one" is both vague and not measurable. With a little thought, it might be sharpened up into something like this: "In my new career, I will actively enjoy my work at least three days each week. During those three days, my job will be enjoyable, pleasurable, fun. I will be like a kid in a sandbox. On the other two days, I don't mind if I'm not completely turned on by what I'm doing, so long as it is rarely boring or highly stressful." Notice that this new goal is much more specific. It is also measurable. Don't worry about attempting to make your meta-goals measurable. They are usually too abstract to hone into measurability. Goals should have a *definite completion date*, if possible.

Sometimes a goal may not need to contain all of these specifications. Use your own judgment. People often wind up with vague, nonspecific goals because they say something like, "I don't know when it will be finished so how can I write down a date?" The whole reason to set goals is to have something specific to shoot for. Goals are an active intention, not a prediction. They focus your energy and direct your attention toward things you desire to accomplish.

5. Frame your goals so they communicate what you really want. Don't worry about being positive (usually). Be true to yourself instead. If what you want passionately is to quit your horrible job within the next month, don't try to sweeten it up by saying something other than what you really mean. Say it as it is, "My goal is to quit my horrible job within a month." On the other hand, there are some times when it is useful to look from the positive side when framing goals, simply because the human mind hates to give up anything. Instead of saying, "I will completely stop eating anything unhealthy." You might say something like, "I will eat food that is both healthy and pleasurable most of the time." Don't turn the part of your mind that loves pizza into your enemy. Sometimes, to set goals you have to think a little like a parent. The idea is to trick your mind into going along with what you want rather than start a war between the pizza-loving part and your willpower. If you do touch off a war, the pizza part will usually win the battle. I realize that I just advised you to do two things that are the polar opposites. Well, all I can say is, sometimes one strategy is appropriate and other times the opposite strategy will work better. You will have to figure out which is best on a situation by situation basis. Some people's minds naturally move toward positive experiences. "I'm going to jump into the pool." Others are more in synch with moving away from negative experiences. "I'm going to get out of the blazing hot sun." Frame your goals to fit your personality and communicate your real intentions.

6. **Write them down.** Your brain is a bad place to keep your goals. Goals are more valuable than anything you have, except your health. If you are anything like me, your brain is it too much like a pocket with many holes in it, too susceptible to hypnotism, somnambulism, and storms of uncertainty and doubt to be the best place to store your goals. If you manage a Goals List you will be able to simply cross off a goal you are abandoning. If you keep your goals in your head, you will have to deal with your psychology and your memory in addition to your goals.

7. **Create both short-term and long-term goals.** Effective goal setting involves creating a comprehensive life plan as well as deciding what to accomplish next week and tomorrow.

8. **Manage your Goals List. Revisit your goals often.** I suggest that, at the beginning of each year, you go over your long-term goals, create new ones, revise the existing ones, toss out the ones you decide not to aim for. Go over the goals you set for the year just ending. Complete each goal by marking it done, transferring it to a time in the future, or declaring it complete as it is, even if you failed to get the result you wanted. Go through the same process at the end of every month and every week, focusing on the goals you set for the month or week that is finishing. The most effective people I know do this every day. At the end of the day, they complete their Goals List for the day that is ending, create new goals for the next day, get complete on everything, and then spend a few minutes looking to see where they could improve their efforts tomorrow.

9. **Meta-goals cannot always be reached by fulfilling lower-level goals.** OK, I know that sounds a little abstract, but stick with me for a minute and it will be clear. Let's say your big, meta-goal is "prosperity." People generally reach for this goal by making great pots of money. But many of them do not experience prosperity because they do not come from a

ground of being that is prosperous. No matter how big a yacht they get, they envy others with bigger boats. They think, "When I move up to the fifty footer, then I'll experience prosperity." When they get it, they then want a sixty footer. They are never satisfied, never reach their meta-goal. If you think you may be caught in the grip of this phenomenon, go down to your video store and rent Orson Welles's *Citizen Kane*. The film's point is the subject we are talking about now. Kane's lifetime of empire building is nothing more than an attempt to reach a meta-goal expressed by a simple childhood memory. No matter how much he achieves, it is always just out of his grasp. At the end of the film, we discover that he had it all the time. He just didn't know where to look. On the other hand, there are people who have little in the way of material possessions, people who experience and come from a ground of being that is prosperous. They do not need more to be satisfied.

You can reach any specific goal, such as "wealth" through concerted action but the larger goal of "prosperity" occurs at an abstract level and sometimes cannot be reached by conventional means. Prosperity issues from within. You have to come from prosperity, to experience it as other than a fleeting feeling. But there's paradox in the ointment: You will never experience prosperity or any other meta-goal unless your actions are consistent with that meta-goal. You can't just wave a wand, declare yourself prosperous, and then pull out the checkbook and write checks for more money than you have in the bank. You have to get to work fulfilling your specific goals through a well-founded action plan in order to experience fulfilling the bigger, meta-goals.

10. **Set goals that take you as far as you are willing to stretch to make your wildest dreams come true, but not farther.** Most folks set goals that do not require much of a stretch. If they wanted to buy a house, they would go after reasonable goals: features that fit their price range, etc. Their main criterion is that their goals be sensible, reasonable. If you want a reasonable degree of success and satisfaction, by all means, create reasonable goals. If you want more than that, being reasonable will constantly block your path.

Nothing is ever accomplished by a reasonable man.

— GEORGE BERNARD SHAW

A good way to figure out how far you are willing to stretch to have your dreams come true is to draw a line horizontally across a piece of paper. At the left end of the line, write down what would be a reasonable goal to go after. On the right end of the line, write down what you really want and would go after, if you did not have to be reasonable, if you were not constrained. This may even be a goal that seems completely over the top and into the realm of impossibility. Then fill in the space between the two extremes with intermediate goals that represent a progression from your more reasonable, safer goal to your outrageous goal.

The only way to discover the limits of the possible is to go beyond them into the impossible.

— ARTHUR C. CLARKE

Then consider how far you are willing to stretch, how outrageous you are willing to be in stretching toward the goal on the right side of the page. You may be willing to go halfway. Or, you might consider going after what seems impossible at first glance. Don't make assumptions. There may a way you could make the impossible happen, with creativity and dedication. Brainstorm. Talk with people who take on and fulfill outrageous goals. Use their experience to come up with possible solutions that shift your perception of your goal from impossible to possible but challenging. Then, again, you may not be willing to stretch far from the reasonable goal on the left side of the page. You have to be completely honest with yourself. Don't set goals based on wishes and hopes, but on what you are ready and willing to make happen, even if difficulties and problems arise. Keep your feet on the ground and your head in the sky.

INQUIRY 14

GOALS

In this Inquiry, you will have an opportunity to look into every area of your life, decide what you most want, and set goals to turn your dreams into reality. This goal-setting process takes you through considering possible goals, deciding which ones you will actually pursue and prioritizing them. Some far distant future goals will be complete at that point. Other goals, the ones you need to begin working on, will become projects, so you that you can develop an action plan to see them through to accomplishment.

Goal mapping may strike you as a time-consuming, involved, and detailed process. If you are as disorganized and spontaneous as I am, you will definitely feel like this is overkill. But, it works. It is better than nothing to just write out your goals on paper in an informal sort of way. But it works much better to give them the dignity of your time and attention and to plan them out fully. That's what you will do in this Inquiry. Your first effort will take some time. Once you have gone through this process the first time, each subsequent goal-setting session will be relatively effortless. You will already be familiar with the process, and you will have most of your long-term goals already in place. Since you are in the process of making career decisions, you will not be able to completely map out your career goals until you have decided on your future career. You can, however, begin the process now.

You may go through this whole process now in regard to your career, or you may wish to do the first parts of this Inquiry now, leave it a little loose, and firm it up when you are farther along the trail. Even if some of your career goals are foggy now, you may want to tackle setting goals in other areas of your life. You may want to set them for every important area of your life. Since your career interacts with all the other areas of your life, the clearer you get on everything else now, the easier it will be to reach final decisions about your career. If you decide to work on only your career goals now, remember to consider other areas that have an influence on your work, such as where you will live or how much time you need for your life outside of work.

You could also tackle working on all your important life goals now. If you think you can work on your goals for other areas of your life in a reasonably short period of time, no more than a few hours over the next few days, go for it. If you tend to get bogged down easily, concentrate only on work goals now. Sometime later you can go through this same Inquiry to work on areas that do not link with your work life.

1. Start a "Goals and Projects" section in your notebook. Then, on one page, write down your big meta-goals. If, like most people, they do not just pop up on their own, you will have to delve deeply to uncover them. A good way to do that is to go through the "Values and Rewards" chapter now. Many of your meta-goals are the same as what you value most, the true values that you will uncover in "Values and Rewards," the things you are committed to live by, things like love, security, adventure, contribution.

2. Write down major-goal categories as headings at the top of blank pages in your notebook, one category to a page. That way, you'll have separate page for each important area of your life. Here is a list of some possible categories. Remember, if you might get bogged down, only work on career-related goals.

Activities	Church	Dreams
Adventures	Clubs	Education
Awards	Communication	Emotional
Career	Community	Entertaining
Career Choice	Contribution	Exploring
Children	Discoveries	Fame
Family	Knowledge	Relationships
Fantasy	Learning	Relaxation
Finances	Love life	Research
Friends	Marriage	Retirement
Fun	Money	Service
Garden/grounds	Music	Sex
Going wild	Net Worth	Skill Development
Health	Parents	Spiritual
Help others	Parties	Sports
Hobbies	Personal Growth	Study
Home	Philanthropy	Travel
Income	Play	Vacation
Independence	Pleasure	Wardrobe
Inventions	Politics	
Investing	Reading	

3. On the line below the category, write in the big, comprehensive meta-goals that are supported by fulfilling goals in that category. You might even want to write them in a different, bright, and cheerful color of ink. The idea is to remember what you most want. For example, you could have a page for hobby goals. When you think about it, you realize that the reason you picked your hobby was for adventure, fun, and relaxation. These are the meta-goals served by your hobby. Why bother with all of this? Normally, folks don't think about the big picture. We tend to get so involved in day-to-day activities that we forget why we are doing them. We forget to make sure we are getting what we really want. It is amazing how many of us are involved in things that no longer—or never did—provide whatever it was we originally picked them for or imagined they would provide. If your goals pages have a direct reminder of the meta-goals that you most want to achieve, then, when you create specific goals, you are less likely to come up with goals that are off the track. Take a look at the top part of this illustration. Notice how the meta-goals serve as a very clear reminder of what work is about for this person.

4. Set up your goals-and-projects pages like the sample on the next page. Draw vertical lines that give you a skinny little column on the left for

completed goal check marks, a slightly wider column next to it for prioritizing goals, and a column on the right for your target date. I'll explain the other parts of this sample—like "action steps"—as we work through this Inquiry.

5. Before writing finalized goals in your goal sheets, do some preliminary exploration. Make two or three copies of your goal-category sheets. Use them to explore possible goals. Start with one of your most important goal categories, career. Write down: "Things I want to accomplish in my career in the next six months." Then, farther down the page: "Things I want to accomplish in my career in the next year" (two years, five years,

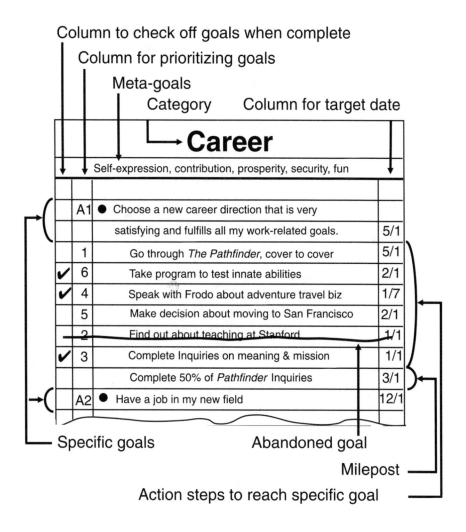

ten years, twenty years, and so forth). Use whatever time frames work for you. It is important to create both short-term and long-term goals.

6. The average American woman lives for 28,000 days, the average man 26,000. At the end of your life you may have a chance to look back and evaluate just how well you have spent those days. Certain things will stand out as the most important successes and failures. Right now you may feel your life has lost all meaning because your new lover just left for Paris in another's tender embrace. Or, you may be devastated that you are snowbound and the town doesn't give your street the correct plowing priority. Your car may not be running perfectly, you could stand to lose ten pounds, you (or your child) didn't get the grades you had hoped for.

When you look back from the end of your life will you even remember today's *Sturm* and *Drang*? Unlikely! What you will probably do is assess whether or not you met some very personal "conditions of satisfaction" for your life. If you have met or reached for these, you will most likely feel that your life has been well lived. Some specific arenas are most important to you. They might include your success or failure in having a loving marriage, making a difference in the world in some special way, generosity, wisdom, spiritual growth, power, money, toys, fun, or whatever else means the most to you. When you try to look forward from your present vantage point, the insistent beat of the current soap opera overpowers your ability to assess the importance of these ultimately more significant conditions of satisfaction. Why? Because you are sitting a foot in front of the screen and the volume is turned all the way up. You need to find a way to get some perspective. Here's what I suggest:

Find a time when you can spend a few minutes without being disturbed. Lie in bed and pull up the covers. Pretend you are very, very old. Actually imagine that you are frail and wizened and that you are near the end of your life. Your loved ones are with you, laughing, talking, appreciating you. You have a chance to reflect on the life you have lived. Look back over all your years on earth, remembering the things you did, your accomplishments, your successes, failures, the contribution you made to others. Ask yourself these questions: "What has been most important to me? What gave me the most joy? Who have I been, what have I done and had that has meant the most to me? What are my real conditions of satisfaction?" What would cause you to feel that your life had or had not been fully lived? What kind of compromises would cause you to be disappointed with yourself?

When you are finished, sit up, and get out your notebook. Title a new page, "Conditions of Satisfaction," and write down what you have discovered. Then, prioritize your conditions of satisfaction in order of their ultimate influence on the quality of your life and other people's lives. OK, you are done. You have just created the perfect list of long-range goals for yourself. If you choose to accept, your assignment is to take on these conditions of satisfaction as your biggest long-range goals.

7. Write down as many specific goals as you can that relate in any way to career. Forget about meta-goals for now. Concentrate on specifics. These are possible goals, not necessarily definite commitments, so write in anything you may want to take on as well as ones you know you are definitely going after. Include everything, both big and small. If you have difficulty coming up with goals you feel strongly about, make up some goals you might like to accomplish, if you could. Make sure you include the important components discussed previously. Goals should usually be:

- as specific as possible
- measurable
- phrased in language that calls to you and says what you really mean
- yours, not someone else's. They should be things you personally desire to accomplish

   Not all of your goals need to be projects that require action or specific results. You could create goals to look at something a little differently, be more present to what your kids are saying, remember to relax, or any number of things that do not fit into the structure of this Inquiry. The suggestions in this Inquiry are not rules. They are just guidelines to make you more effective in getting what you want. Improvise! Be creative. If something you want does not lend itself to specificity, fine. Go for it! Keep at it until you have exhausted your mental reservoir of possible career goals.

8. Go through your list again and do some weeding. Cross off the pipe dreams, the things you know you really aren't going to do, and the frivolous things that do not have much of an impact on the quality of your life. Trim the list down to career goals that are important, ones that really sing to you. Cross off goals you are not personally interested in, but feel obliged to do. Sharpen up goals that are too vague or do not contain enough components of specificity to be clear.

9. Go through the list one more time. Ask yourself, "Am I willing to make a promise to myself that I will definitely do what it takes to make this happen?" Cross off anything that does not meet the test. At this juncture, your list should contain only goals you are definitely committed to.

10. Prioritize your goals using a combination of two criteria: desire and long-term impact on the quality of your life.

   A-level goals have the highest level of desire and impact. These A-level goals are ones that have a powerful, long-term impact on the quality of your life. They are the big, important goals, the ones with profound consequences riding on them, the ones that involve taking risks that will give you the kind of life you want. Most goal-setting methods make the mistake of labeling things you have to do now as A goals. In their way of looking at it, doing your laundry is an A-level goal when you are about to run out of underwear. Think about it. Do you really want to have washing your underwear as one of your top-level goals? The question to ask is: "Which of my goals will give me the biggest return?"

   B-level goals are intermediate in their impact on your life. They may be important for some reason or hold a high level of desire, but they don't transform your life. They don't take you into the stratosphere.

   C-level goals are the everyday, mundane things that have no long-term impact. This is where washing your underwear and deciding what to do this weekend belong.

   A good reason to prioritize goals using this system rather than by need is that it tends to focus your energy on doing things that really matter. That does not mean that you will be walking around in dirty undies. You still have to take care of life's little duties. If you prioritize by desire and long-term impact, you will be able to notice how your time and energy is spent. You might notice that your life is so filled with C priorities that you don't have time to do the A list. In which case, it may make sense to rearrange a few things in your life.

11. Now for the final step in prioritizing your goals. Add a priority number after the priority letter, so each goal has both a letter and number, A1, A2, A3, and so forth. The number serves as a guide to the relative importance or timeliness of the goal. You may want to assign high-priority numbers to goals you want to work on in the near future and lower-numbers to ones that will wait for a while. You may want to give high-priority numbers to goals that are most important, within their category. So A1 could be your most important long-term goal, or it could be an important goal you want to give full attention to now. Be flexible. Use

these numbers to help you focus on how to best use your time and energy now.

12. Now it is time to turn some of your goals into projects. The definition of *project* is "a planned undertaking, requiring concerted effort to reach a specific goal." Any goal that involves planning and a series of steps can be considered to be a project. After this Inquiry, we will get into the subject of project management. Why don't you read that and then come back here and complete this step.

   Go through your important long-term A-level career goals and write down the action steps you need to follow to accomplish them. This is essentially a "to-do" list. Don't worry about getting them in perfect chronological order. Just write them down as clearly as possible. When you are finished, go through the action steps and number them in the order you will begin them. The first step should be labeled "1," even though it may not get finished first. The big advantage of doing it this way is that you always know what to do next. Before I labeled my "to-do" list this way, I tended to look at my list and pick something I felt like doing most. The things that got saved for last (or never) were the things that involved discomfort or risk. That is not the way to get the results you most want.

   So, specific goals get both a letter and a number. Action steps just get a number. They do not get a priority letter because they are all important steps to reach your goal. If this seems confusing, look back to the illustration on page 177.

13. Go through this same process with all the other areas of your life. When you are finished, transfer your goals onto nice, new, clean final goal sheets. Now all you have to do is wake up each morning, look at your lists, and get to work on A1.

14. **Turn to your Primary Lists (Wants, Commitments and Requirements, and Questions), as well as to your Careers to Consider List. What can you add to those lists now? WHAT AM I SURE WILL DEFINITELY BE AN IMPORTANT COMPONENT OF MY FUTURE CAREER?**

Mastering the Art of Accomplishment

Goal setting is the first step in mastering the art of accomplishment. Turning your goals into projects and managing them through all the steps to completion is the other part of the equation. In the next few pages we will look into this second phase. Let's start with the big picture and then get down to the nitty-gritty.

Accomplishment Cycles

Goals are not merely things you want that you have written down on a list somewhere. They are part of something larger, much more grand and exciting. They are the first part of a cycle of accomplishment, the engine that drives achievement. Setting written goals is an extremely powerful way to forward your life, even if you don't understand how they fit into the big picture. You will become a dangerous enemy of mediocrity when you understand the whole cycle. Remember, grasping the principles behind anything is many times more powerful than trying to memorize a bunch of rules or tips. Average fishermen get by on tips. Great fishermen come from the principle: Think like a fish. Fortunately the principles behind accomplishment cycles are much simpler than thinking like a fish.

Almost everything in the natural world is cyclical. All cycles—the tides, night and day, and the great wheel of birth and death—can be broken down into phases. The new moon and the full moon are phases of the moon cycle. Adolescence and old age are phases of the cycle of life. There are three phases in any project: creation, action, completion. If you want to make your dreams come true, it helps to get skilled in going through all three of them.

Creation. This is the first phase, the generation phase of anything you want to accomplish. You get an idea of something you want to do or have. You actually create something that did not exist before, an idea. Then you make a commitment to the idea you had and you are ready to go on to the next step. This combination of idea and commitment is a goal. An idea without a commitment is not a goal. It is just a dream. This is why New Year's resolutions usually don't get off the ground. As an example of the accomplishment cycle, let's suppose that you come up with this wild idea of taking a spur-of-the-moment trip to Bali. You play with the idea for a while and then decide you are going to go for it. You begin to plan. At this point, it is no longer just an idea. It has acquired an existence of its own. It is now a project; a new cycle is underway.

Nearly everyone is better at some parts of the cycle than at others. Some folks are terrific at the first part of the creation phase. They have great ideas but stop when it comes time to commit. Other people may be quite skilled at their habitual day-to-day activities but have trouble envisioning new projects. Having an idea does not automatically start a new accomplishment cycle. There are several things you can do with a new idea: make a commitment to make it happen, delegate it, abandon it, forget about it, sell it, give it away, share it, put it in a file called "Inactive Ideas File." Committing to accomplishing your idea is what gets a new accomplishment cycle rolling. Once you are committed, you move automatically into the action phase of the project.

Action. Usually 90 percent of the time and energy you put into any project occurs in this phase. The action phase begins with planning, designing, and researching; includes everything you do to bring your goal to fruition; and ends when you have just about reached your destination. For your Bali trip, this phase consists of everything from convincing your boss and packing your bags to snoozing on the plane as you wing your way across the sea. As you feel the airplane begin to descend for its landing in Bali, you have just about finished the action phase of your get to Bali project.

Many people get stuck in the action cycle of their projects. They come up with a great idea, commit to accomplishing it, get off to a good start, and then wind up running around in circles. You can tell if you tend to get stuck here if you spend a lot of energy on projects without ever seeming to move them forward with much velocity.

Completion As you sit on the beach, looking out over the sparkling water, it is time to declare your project complete. Yes! You did it. This final phase is not so much a matter of doing anything as it is in acknowledging what you have done and declaring your project complete.

Having great ideas, making outrageous commitments, throwing oneself into action wholeheartedly is only part of the secret of mastering accomplishment cycles. The rest of the secret is to get skilled in the completion phase. Completion generates energy, power, and creativity. Incompletion sucks your energy away. This is not an abstract philosophical principle. This is just as real and as demonstrable as the fact that your car goes faster when you stomp on the accelerator. In fact, the best way to know if you are complete is to check your mental dipstick. When you are complete, you experience increased energy, personal power, satisfaction, and pleasure. Everything that remains incomplete sucks away your precious energy.

Managing Your Projects

The skill you bring to bear on managing your projects makes all the difference in the results you get. Even people with a massive commitment to a specific result often do not reach their goals because they have not managed their commitments as projects. Charging into the breach with bugles blowing will lead to mangled projects if you do not manage them skillfully. Now that you understand the cyclical nature of projects, we can get down to the nitty-gritty. There are a few basic steps to the process:

Managing the Creation Phase

Declare your goal as a project. This begins a new cycle of accomplishment. You enter the first phase of a cycle, creation. As soon as you declare it as a project, the wheel begins to turn. Commit yourself to thinking about it and managing it as a project. Then it is no longer just a goal but enters a new domain. When you consider it to be a project, it occurs differently in your mind. "To create a beautiful flower garden" is a worthy goal. When you turn it into a project, you naturally begin to think of action steps and a time line to accomplish it.

Give it a name. The name should clearly communicate the project's intended result and your intentions in language that calls you to participate. When you read it, you want to get turned on. Instead of "Get a new job," you might say, "Choose a great new job from several excellent offers." You don't have to put a positive spin on it. If you absolutely loathe your present job, use your loathing as a lever. You might name your project "Get out of Zomboid Industries and into an exciting new career by the end of the summer."

Decide on a completion date. Base this on a combination of desire and doability, not just on an analysis of what seems reasonable. That way, you and not the circumstances, are running the show. The average person is driven by circumstance. An intentional person creates his or her own circumstances. Plus, you will be more creative in figuring out how to get the job done. Of course, you can always adjust this date if, after planning, you realize that it is just too much of a stretch to get it done by then. Some of your projects may not need a completion date. If a project is related to a hobby, for example, you may want to just do it when you feel inspired.

Plan it. There is really no difference between a goal and a project, except that a goal lives in the future and a project in the present. By declaring a goal as a project, you are committing to make it happen, starting now. Use the same form as you did in setting goals. The only difference is that in planning a project, there will usually be more details to fill in. First write down the major steps to get from here to there in chronological order, based on start date. Then, if the project is large or complex, fill in the smaller chunks you need to handle to accomplish each of the major steps. Think of the major steps as milestones. A milestone is a marker along the road that tells you how far you have traveled. They are one of the main tools you will use to manage projects. Each milestone should include a specific result and a completion date. For example, look back to the sample illustration on page 177 in the goal-setting section of this chapter. On this goals worksheet the steps are not in chronological order because you were in the midst of the process of deciding on goals. Once your goal has become a project, you want to list all the steps in order, so you can just go down the list and knock them off, one after the other. Some of the entries could be milestones, "Complete 50 percent of *Pathfinder* Inquiries" is an obvious example. It has a specific, measurable result and a completion date. The whole point of having milestones is to reveal to you whether or not your project is on track and on time.

Be unreasonable! Acknowledge that you are likely to plan your action phase around what seems within your comfort range, rather than on what may be most effective. If you want to be really unreasonable, imagine someone other than you doing your project. If there is some extraordinary historical person you feel a special affection for and connection with, close your eyes for a few minutes and imagine you are having a conversation with him or her. Explain what you want to accomplish and what obstacles you face. Then ask what they would do, if they were in the same situation. Then switch roles and pretend you are the person you admire. Answer for them. Let them tell you what to do. Another similar way to come up with creative ideas: Imagine a feature film where the hero is engaged in a life-or-death struggle to complete your project with fantastic results, as fast as possible. An evil alien has kidnapped his children and will devour them if your hero fails. What would he do? How would a hero go about accomplishing your project if he had a commitment that was much bigger than being reasonable and comfortable? Once you have done that, you just have to decide how much of a hero you are willing to be. Then all you have to do is what the hero did.

Create displays. A display is a visual way of tracking or reminding you about your project. In small-town America, a common display is a giant vertical thermometer set up in front of the fire station when the volunteers are raising money for a new fire engine. The goal is printed at the top, with incremental amounts printed up the sides. As the money comes in, the mercury gets painted ever higher, until the goal is reached. Devise your own cheerful, visual way of tracking your project. A good display shows you instantly how you are doing. This just might be your chance to award yourself those gold stars you've always deserved. Make it big, if possible. Bigger than a bread box, smaller than the firehouse thermometer. Another way of using a display is to remind you of your goal. If you want a career that will allow you lots of free time to work on your garden, you might create a collage of magnificent gardens with some sort of a project-tracking chart in the middle. The reason to have displays is to keep your project fresh and sweet in your mind.

Commit to the plan. In this book the word *commit* occurs only slightly less often than *the* and *and* because it works to make definite commitments. Once the planning is done, promise yourself that you will do whatever it takes, no matter how hard the sledding, to get to your goal.

Managing the Action Phase

Begin it. Start with the first thing on your list. Then go on to the second.

Follow the plan, not your feelings. If you keep checking off steps you have accomplished, step by step, you will probably reach your goal. If you do what you feel like doing, you may concentrate on the more comfortable tasks instead of the ones that really move the project forward. Improve the plan as the project progresses. Be flexible, but only when changing the plan betters it.

Track your results on your goal worksheet and your displays. Pay attention to which parts you traverse with difficulty.

Keep going until you reach your intended result. You need to keep plowing forward until your project is complete. When you get stopped, slowed, or off course, make corrections.

The first part of the action phase often involves an input of 100 units of your energy for every one unit of result. You give it your all, but nothing seems to happen. The boulder blocking your path on the mountain track doesn't move an inch. You begin to have massive attacks of the Yeahbuts. If you keep moving forward, eventually you will reach the stage where the boulder rolls down the mountain on its own. In this later stage of the action phase, projects move forward on their own requiring very little energy from you. You can relax while the pilot flies you to Bali.

Make corrections. If you get stopped, slowed, or off course in the action phase, your problem is to figure out what happened. When you get specific about that, you can deal with it. Actually, there aren't all that many things that can go wrong. It's a good thing, too, because these few things do tend to go wrong often. Let's say that you are starting from wherever you are now. Your goal is to reach some distant destination over the horizon. You think it over and commit to the project. You do some planning, get time off from work, put the car in tip-top shape, pack your bags, kiss the dog, and go roaring off into the sunset. Somewhere along the journey, you get stuck. The project is not moving along the way you planned it. What do you do? Turn to the "If You Get Stuck" chapter. It is a guide to diagnosing and dealing with the difficulties that arise in the course of any project.

Managing the Completion Phase

Get "complete" even if you do not get the result you wanted. Declaring your project complete is a choice you make rather than something that happens automatically when you put the last dab of paint on your masterpiece. Your project is not complete because you have finished it, but because you say so. It is a matter of declaration. That does not necessarily mean that the result looks at all like you thought it would look in the beginning. It does not mean that you succeeded in getting the result you planned for. To be willing to declare a *failed* project complete is one of the most powerful skills a person can learn. If you think about it, how often does anything turn out exactly like the original idea you had? If you can't dance with chaos, you can't dance at all. Nearly all of us could use a bit of improvement in our skill at dealing with this third phase of the cycle.

One of the most common ways people get stuck is to finish projects that are not quite to their satisfaction. You replace the light switch cover in the bathroom with one that matches the wallpaper, but you put it on a little crooked. You notice it every time you turn on the light, but never take the time to straighten it out. You are in a hurry when you record an outgoing message on your answering machine. You know the message doesn't really represent you well, but you never seem to get around to changing it. You spend your evenings designing and making a beautiful work table for your office. After six months of work, you are getting tired of working on it. You are planning to put a beautiful multicoat French polish finish on the whole thing, top and bottom. But since you are in a hurry, you decide to skip finishing the underside. After all, no one is ever going to look under the table. No one will ever know but you. Forever after, whenever you think about your beautiful table, what comes to mind is not the intricate inlay work or the spectacular design, but the undone underside.

Another way people stick themselves with incomplete cycles is to abandon projects midstream. They move out of the action phase directly into accomplishment purgatory. The half-knit sweater, the abandoned tuba in the attic, the Ph.D. program you put on hold to have a child and never returned to, that time you broke up with your lover and moved away, leaving much unsaid and incomplete. Each of these is an incomplete cycle.

To Get an Important Project Moving,

Speed Up All Your Accomplishment Cycles

The best way to get any important project moving, including that big project called your life, is to crank up the velocity of your accomplishment cycles in as many domains of your life as you can think of. Especially the ones that are not moving at all. Clean up your desk, forgive your boss for being a jerk, throw away all the junk you have saved for a rainy day but haven't used for years, call up your mom and apologize for being so weird when you went home last Thanksgiving. If you have to do something to get complete about something, do it! Then declare it complete. If you don't have to actually do anything, then just declare it complete. Put the past in the past, where it belongs. You do not have to finish anything to be complete with it. Since completion is a matter of declaration, you can be complete with anything, as it is now. You can wave a wand over the half-finished sweater and declare it complete as it is as long as you really mean what you declare. In fact, it is possible to be complete with everything. The Asian concept of enlightenment is essentially about completion. It is not a blissful, peaceful feeling or an elevated state or something you get after sitting in a cave meditating for twenty years. A Zen master lives face to face in the presence of life itself by being totally complete with everything. You may not have enlightenment as high on your goal list as having a great career, but beginning to practice being complete with your past and present projects leads directly to both.

Power comes in many varieties: charisma, physical strength, intellect, etc. Real personal power is the ability to go through accomplishment cycles with velocity. Nearly all of the people who accomplish a great deal during their lives have learned this secret, and live by it. Yes, you can write off their extraordinary accomplishments as a special gift, good luck, or whatever. They may have talent and luck, but they have definitely mastered the art of accomplishment cycles. They have a great idea. They commit to it. They do whatever it takes to make it happen, with velocity. Then they complete it and go on to another exciting project.

Most people think of their personal energy as a limited commodity. They feel as if they are given so much each day. When they use it up, it is gone forever. They feel they need to lie around recovering, "gathering energy." But it is easy to create unlimited energy. Just get your accomplishment cycles moving. Does that sound overly cosmic to you? Well, if so, I dare you to experiment. Dedicate the next few hours to cleaning up some things in your life that you have been resisting dealing with. Get complete. Then check and see if you have more or less energy for what's next.

It is not as difficult as it might seem to get mired-down accomplishment cycles moving again toward completion. Cycles tend to move naturally toward completion if you give them half a chance. That is not an abstract principle. It is really just a matter observing the natural world around you. Does the moon ever get stuck in the sky or do the seasons of the year ever get stuck (except, of course, in Southern California, where natural laws do not prevail). The only cycles that I can think of that ever get stuck are human accomplishment cycles. It takes a great deal of energy to resist one of the laws of nature, and we do so at a great psychological price. No wonder you experience diminished energy and personal power when you leave things incomplete.

So, as you can see, it turns out that goal setting doesn't work so well as an isolated activity. If you sit down and write out your goals, you will wind up with a nice list. If you want your life to rock and roll, begin to manage the entire cycle of accomplishment. All accomplishment cycles can be thought of as projects. Choosing your future career is a project. So is writing a song, starting a new division or product line for your company, or getting a date for Saturday night. Even making a sandwich is a project, an accomplishment cycle.

Good Ideas

When you come up with a good idea for a possible goal, treat it with great respect. Whether it is an idea that solves one of the world's great problems or is just an idea for something wild to do with your girlfriend this weekend, it doesn't matter. Your ideas deserve your respect because they are the output of your internal creative department. Without them, life would just creep on and on and on. Make a conscious decision about what to do with each idea. Are you going to commit to making it happen, abandon it, delegate it, forget about it, or what? You want your accomplishment cycles to get off to a good start, to be intentional, not accidental.

CHAPTER 17
•
SEVEN KEYS

At the heart of any process you can discover basic principles that are the foundation of that process. These seven keys unlock the door to transforming your ability to generate a new future that goes far beyond what has been previously possible. Even though they may seem like philosophical abstractions to some readers, they are as real, practical, and necessary as the floor beneath you. To begin to practice them, begin to practice them. Sorry, there is no way to learn how, no set of step-by-step instructions. You just have to jump in and begin.

1. Create your future from the present, not the past. Designing the perfect career is like creating a painting that expresses you fully and completely. Rather than add dabs of paint to something you painted years ago, start at the beginning with a blank canvas. Take your time. Consider everything very carefully before including it in the final picture. This is your opportunity to have your life be exactly the way you want it to be.

We are so transfixed by the endless webs of words our minds spin that even great experts often miss simple, obvious truths. For example, most scientists firmly believe that animals don't experience the more complex emotions. But every child with a dog or cat knows better. They may have seen their pet experience joy, embarrassment, pride, or a sense of humor. Their direct insight is on target, unclouded by prejudgment or analysis. Most of the time, we are so busy thinking, categorizing, and comparing that we don't pay attention to what is actually happening in and around us. We don't even notice the most basic truth about our lives, that our lives are operated by internal software that we allow to run the show while we pretend we are making the decisions and authoring the direction of our lives.

A computer doesn't make choices. It just runs a program. Whatever "decisions" it seems to make are no more than the automated processing of data through a set of rules built into the program. If it is important to you to have a great career, you might take a little peek at just how much free choice is actually expressed in the decisions you make. If you think that you actively make most of your decisions, perhaps you are living in a dream world. It's not easy to own up to being an automaton. But, if you want to truly think for yourself, you have to face up to the fact that sometimes (or, perhaps, even more often) we don't. Just because we are the most intelligent of living creatures doesn't mean that most of our decisions stem from exercising this marvelous gift. Just because we can think doesn't mean we usually do it.

Few people think more than two or three times a year.
I have made an international reputation for myself
by thinking once or twice a week.

— George Bernard Shaw

Make a promise to yourself that you will determine your future as free as possible from the domination of your past. It takes a commitment to make your own choices as independent as possible from all the voices of your past: your memories, parents, friends, successes, failures, and the media. That commitment is the key to creating new possibilities and extraordinary results that take you beyond the world you already know. The bottom-line question is: Are you going to design your future, or is your past going to keep doing it for you?

2. Throw away your assumptions. I know it's difficult to throw anything away. We all tend to hold on to our pet notions about life the way some people save twenty-year-old *National Geographics* in the attic. Each of us has an unexamined collection of beliefs, opinions, and points of view about how life works that we trust blindly and completely. We live by a rule book we wrote but have never read. We think we know what we cannot do and what it would be like to do things we have never done. Most of the time, automatically following this internal rule book works just fine, but in regard to choosing one's life's work, it pays to rewrite a few of the rules.

Yes, you may have to make some compromises along the way. But don't start off assuming you will have to make them. Just because you have a 2.0 average doesn't mean it is impossible to become a doctor. Just because you are a middle manager with a wife, kids, two cars, and a mortgage doesn't mean you cannot be a wandering Taoist priest. As you go through this process, you will have plenty of chances to decide what compromises you are willing to make, if any. You will be able to choose them consciously, rather than assuming there is no other possibility.

3. Embrace "not knowing." Imagine sitting on a rural hilltop at night. In the sky you notice a blinking light that slowly circles overhead. You are mystified. It makes no sound and offers no clues to its origin. If you are like me, your mind immediately and automatically comes up with explanations about the source of the light. It's a helicopter. It's a saucer. I'm hallucinating. It's something the government isn't telling us about. It's not easy to allow the light to remain a total mystery. Our nature is to explain, to justify. We like quick answers because we are uncomfortable with uncertainty. Think about it. Wouldn't you rather be thought of as someone who knows than someone who doesn't?

In Japan, they tell a story about a learned professor who hears about the wisdom of the local Zen master. He becomes more and more curious until, finally, he goes to visit the master. As they sit face to face, the professor explains at great length all he has learned during his lifelong scholarly study of Buddhism. As he rattles on and on, the master begins to pour him a cup of tea. The professor is startled when the master continues to pour even after the cup is full. Tea spills over the tabletop. Still, the master continues to pour. Finally, the professor sees himself for the first time. He realizes that you can't put any more tea in a cup that is full. If you go through this career-choice process as a beginner and remain a beginner until the end of your days, no matter how well you know yourself, your work, and your world, you will be able to keep pouring tea into your new cup of wisdom. The difference between a master and a know-it-all is that the master, in any field, brings a beginner's mind, fresh and open to unlimited possibilities, to each new workday.

4. Since you may never discover the truth, invent it. Most of us are very fixated on what everything around us signifies. We want to understand the "real meaning" of events, concepts, and our lives. What did it really mean when he didn't call? What did it really mean when Napoleon put his hand in his coat? We habitually jump to conclusions and instantly assign meaning to everything.

The best way to predict the future is to invent it.

— A L A N K A Y

Once we know what something "really means," we will gladly die defending our point of view. It never occurs to us that, to someone else, it could mean something entirely different. Or it might mean absolutely nothing. If something can mean completely different things to different people who may be even smarter or more experienced than you, then meaning might be flexible. That opens up the possibility that you could get creative about what various things mean to you. When your spouse leaves hairs on the bathroom sink, it's practically impossible to let them be nothing more than hairs on the sink, little hairs devoid of meaning. But we turn them into hairs fraught with great significance: "He doesn't really love me, because if he did he would care that the hairs upset me."

In any endeavor that takes you, the explorer, into new territory, it is enormously useful to keep reminding yourself that all your definitions and judgments are only one point of view. Remember that they seem to be the one and only truth because you are a human being. And almost all human beings think that our opin-

ions and beliefs are the "real" truth. Since you will never actually see the inside of the watch, you will never even know if there is any "real" truth. Even your belief that there is any such thing as "real" truth may be nothing more than your opinion, your own personal interpretation. Once you can accept that all there is, is interpretation, you are free to invent other possible points of view and go with the ones that are most useful, the ones that most powerfully support you to be all that you can be, and more.

Since we have so much difficulty in allowing anything to be completely devoid of meaning, the next best strategy is to become creative in transforming what things mean to you. For example, the woman in our example could invent the interpretation that that the hairs on the sink mean that her man is a powerful male marking his territory. Then, every time she sees hairs on the sink, she can feel proud that she has such a manly male. Is this the truth? Who is to say that it is any less the "real" truth than her original interpretation? Instead of trying to figure out the "real" truth, you might ask, "What possible interpretation would give me a great life? Which is more fun?" If you will never know the "real" significance of anything anyway, lighten up, trust that Einstein knows what he is talking about, and light up your life instead of worrying about what it all means!

Physical concepts are the creation of the human mind, and are not, however it may seem, determined by our external world. In our endeavor to understand reality, we are somewhat like a man trying to understand the mechanism of a closed watch.

— ALBERT EINSTEIN

5. Get to know the realm of possibility. There is a big difference between "options" and "possibilities." Everyone has options. Your options consist of a fixed set of predetermined scenarios, points of view, perceived limitations that already reside in your inner data bank. They are the different things you could do and remain in the same box you live in now. When you ask "What are my options?" you are really asking "What is the contents of my box?" You are taking inventory of your internal stockroom. If you depend on your options to formulate your future, that future will be no more than a rearrangement of your past.

Possibilities are completely different. When you ask "What is possible?" you must stretch your imagination out of the confines of the familiar. You have to stretch your wings, get out of the box, and look around.

If I were to wish for anything, I would not wish for wealth and power, but for the passionate sense of what might be, for the eye which, ever young and ardent, sees the possible. Pleasure disappoints, possibility never. And what wine is so sparkling, what so fraught, what so intoxicating as possibility!

— SØREN KIERKEGAARD

Possibility is the great motivator. A prevailing condition of no possibility is, I believe, more directly the cause of the persistence of our inner-city social problems than is lack of opportunity. To have a life beyond the mediocre, ask not "What are my options?" but "What is possible?"

6. Learn to separate Yeahbuts from original thoughts. For anyone who is committed to having their dreams come true, this is, by far, the one most important skill to master. The natural law that operates and controls the lives of all biological organisms is the law of homeostasis. Your body and mind contain thousands of little switches, like thermostats, that control your perceptions and actions. When you exercise, your body heats up above 98.6 degrees. That throws a switch that produces a whole range of actions designed to get you cooled back down to the temperature you are set for, 98.6 degrees. When your temperature returns to equilibrium, all the machinery working to cool you down stops.

What most people do not usually realize is that the same kind of mechanism makes their decisions for them. Your "comfort zone" is the range of thoughts and actions you can get away with without triggering one of these mechanisms. The internal survival machinery compares what you are doing or thinking of doing with its database of what you have done before. It assumes that whatever you have done, day after day is "safe." Anything outside the comfort zone is perceived as a threat to your survival. It can't distinguish real dangers from personal growth.

When you seek to increase the quality of your life in ways that require you to step out of the safety zone farther than you usually do, these systems react with everything they have to return you to good old familiar equilibrium. They use as their tool a special category of thoughts: Yeahbuts, which are thoughts brought to your consciousness by internal survival mechanisms. For example, when you think, "If I become a doctor, I know I'll be happy," it is automatically followed by Yeahbuts such as, "Yeahbut, I'll carry a huge amount of student loan debt." Their design is to return you to equilibrium as fast as possible. Their power comes from the fact that they are so convincing. They speak with your voice. They have many years of practice in finding the weakest links in your resolve and exploiting the places where you are most vulnerable. When you learn to distinguish Yeahbuts from other thoughts, they lose their power over you. You recognize that what your Yeahbuts consider to be dangerous, and react to so strongly, is actually a great opportunity to step into some new shoes.

Security is mostly a superstition. It does not exist in nature, nor do the children of men as a whole experience it. Avoiding danger is no safer in the long run than outright exposure. Life is a daring adventure, or nothing.

— Helen Keller

7. Dance on the edge of the sword. One needs to master two completely different realms in order to live fully. On the one hand, you must learn to live in the realm of possibility and invention, or your life will be nothing more than a clockworks of gears turning predictably and automatically. On the other hand, having your feet firmly planted on terra firma is the bottom line of actualizing your dreams. If you live mainly in the realm of possibility, you will become a dreamer who does not get much accomplished. Dancing on the edge of the sword is the art of living in both realms at once, perfectly balanced between them. When you lean too far to one side, get your balance back as soon as possible. With practice you will find that you can be present to both at the same moment. Which side do you usually live on?

CHAPTER 18

•

LIVING IN THE PRESENT

Some folks think that the primary tools for having a great life are such things as money, class, beauty, brains. But people with one or more of these attributes live lives that are essentially just the same as everyone else's. Their careers are no more satisfying. Their marriages no more vibrant. They may struggle a bit less. It is easier to get dates when you are gorgeous. Having the right connections does help. When you have a big pile of money, at least you do not live under the illusion that money equals happiness. All of this buys the ticket and smoothes the way to paradise. None of it is paradise itself. What makes life work spectacularly is not what you have but who you are, or, to say it more accurately, who you are being. You are either being nothing more than a bio-computer running the same program over and over and over and over or, in addition to being a bio-computer, you are, as much as possible, the author of your life, a creative expression of your intentions. You are being very skillful at generating the results you want.

Life seems to stretch out like a long scroll that begins in the distant past and ends where it disappears into the mists of the far-off future. Sometimes these memories and these visions of the future seem more real than the present moment. But it does no good to wish that you had not said that foolish thing. The past is gone forever. Memories of the past occur only in the present.

The future never comes. Somehow, just when it seems that it will finally arrive, it mysteriously turns into the present. We live as if the entire time frame we imagine, from past to future, is the stage we have to act our lives upon. But this is an illusion. It is fairly obvious that you cannot change the past. Just as true but less obvious is that you cannot change the future, either. Why not? Because the future is a just a dream. When you look out into it, what you see is a fantasy of your own creation. It seems real because, often, it turns out to look somewhat like we imagined it will. When you think about tomorrow, you imagine yourself at work, doing what you imagine you will be doing then. But between now and tomorrow, all sorts of things could happen that would turn your future in a different direction. You could get laid off, win the lottery, or the aliens could land. There is an old science-fiction movie where the space aliens replaced Hubby with an alien they thought was a perfect duplicate. Wife sensed that it was not really Hubby. He walked like Hubby, talked like him, too, but, like the future you imagine, he was just a replicant, not the real thing. When the future becomes the present, it never turns out exactly the same as the vision you had of it. Every once in a while, it gets as close to the dream as the alien did to the real Hubby. But, usually it doesn't. As John Lennon said, "Life is what happens to you while you're busy making other plans." Even though, when you think about it, the future is no more than a dream, we live as if it were real.

Perhaps the past is no more than a dream, either. We don't notice that we alter our memories of the past to support good old comfortable equilibrium. In a study conducted during one of the lower low points of Richard Nixon's public perception, a couple of years after he had been driven out of office, fewer than half of registered Republican voters said that they remembered voting for him. If they didn't, who did? Must have been Hubby's double.

All of the attention we put on attempting to change the past and future could be thought of as a form of mental masturbation. It may be entertaining. It could even be better than the real thing. But, it is not the same as the real thing. To attempt to change the past or the future is like trying to steer your car by turning the volume knob on the radio instead of turning the steering wheel. Oftentimes, we are so busy dealing with the past and future that we don't notice that it is always the present. When we remember the past, the memory occurs now. When we plan for the future, the planning occurs in the present moment, not in the future we are projecting ourselves into. This moment is all we ever have, to do with as we will. We can either just allow the software to run and animate the somnambulism, or wake up, live in the present, and create our own dance to the rock and roll beat of life.

We cannot put off living until we are ready. The most salient characteristic of life is its coerciveness: it is always urgent, "here and now" without any possible postponement. Life is fired at us point blank.

— JOSÉ ORTEGA Y GASSET

People think that to design a career all they have to do is make some plans for their future. Obviously, planning is very important. But thinking about riding doesn't get you on the horse. What makes dreams come true is to have a powerful relationship with the present. The ability to successfully create anything in your life that stretches you out into new territory is more a function of who you are being in the present moment than what plans you draw up for the future. Let's say you want to change careers and become a successful travel writer. It's easy to lay out a plan for the future. "Let's see, first I will take my vacation on St. John, and while I am there write a book about the Virgin Islands. Then when I get back I will submit it to a publisher . . ." If wishes were horses, we would all smell like a horse. The problem with this plan is that it is a pipe dream. It is not backed up by a commitment that will be kept, no matter what. What typically happens is that we have a wondrous dream of the perfect life, and then have a massive attack of Yeahbuts that shoots it out of the sky. The Yeahbuts wind up running our lives because we don't have a powerful relationship with the present. Only in the present can you say, "Wait a minute now, I'm not going to let these Yeahbuts shoot down my dream." Only in the present can you transform your relationship with yourself to one where you fully support the fulfillment of your dreams.

Part 3

DESIGNING YOUR FUTURE CAREER

The time has come to actually create and design your new career. This section guides you through everything that's important to consider in order to make the perfect choice. I suggest that you up the ante from now on. If you can, put even more energy and commitment into working through this section than you have up until now.

CHAPTER 19

AT THIS POINT IN TIME

INQUIRY 15

AT THIS POINT IN TIME

This first Inquiry in the process of designing your future is a brief look into your present situation. Later on, we will take a deeper look into most of this area. Use this exercise to sort out, clarify, and communicate what is going on at this point in time. Answer each of these questions in your notebook. You may want to toss some of these questions around for a few days. Use this Inquiry as a microscope to look deeper into your present situation.

- What do you do in your current occupation? Write a complete description. Your "occupation" is whatever occupies you most days. Answer this question in a way that reveals as much as possible about what you actually do. Instead of saying, "I am copilot of a 747," it might be more revealing to say, "I spend most of my time sitting around chatting while eating potato chips and Tums while the computer flies the plane."
- Make a pie chart that illustrates how your time is spent over the course of an average month. If your job changes from month to month, you may want to make more than one pie chart. For example, if you write proposals all day for three months, then spend the rest of the year managing projects, you essentially have two quite different jobs. In which case, it makes sense to draw a pie chart for each of them.
- What do you like about your occupation?
- What do you like least about your occupation?
- In what ways does your present occupation fall short? What is missing?
- Why are you considering choosing a new direction at this time?
- What are your strongest talents?
- What would people who know you well say are your most positive or special qualities, attributes, and personal characteristics?
- What do you not do well? What are the areas where you have no talent?
- What would people you know say are the attributes or qualities that can or do cause you the most trouble or mischief in your life?

- Are there issues other than career that contribute to your present situation or the way you perceive it?
- What personal or health problems do you have that affect or could affect your career?
- How is your financial situation? Are you prospering, just making ends meet, falling behind, or going under? How much of your desire for change is related to your financial condition?
- What already-existing personal or professional commitments do you have that you plan to continue to honor that affect your choice of occupations?
- What is your attitude about making a change? Do you feel completely committed, ready, willing and able?
- What are the key elements and criteria for a career/occupation that would be ideal?
- If there were no limits placed on you by your education, skills, finances, etc., what would you be, do or have?
- If you discovered that you had only five years to live, how would you spend those years?
- What are your fondest interests and the most important passions in your life?
- What do you love to do that you did not mention in answering the previous question? This may include work activities and leisure activities as well as activities that you loved doing in the past but are not presently a part of your life.

Turn to your Primary Lists (Wants, Commitments and Requirements, and Questions), as well as to your Careers to Consider List. What can you add to those lists now? **What am I sure will definitely be an important component of my future career?**

CHAPTER 20

•

TEMPERAMENT, PERSONALITY, AND PASSIONS

Making sure there is a match between your personality and your work is one of the most important things you can do to guarantee that your career will be highly satisfying, and stay that way for years to come. Imagine what it would be like if you took a slow and steady plowhorse and switched it with high-strung thoroughbred racehorse. Both of them would fail miserably at their new jobs. The racehorse would feel restrained and come to hate the farmer and the plow. The plowhorse would come in last every time. It doesn't take this extreme degree of misfit between personality and work to drag down your effectiveness and satisfaction. Even a seemingly small mismatch can make going to work much less pleasant. It's like ingesting lead or radioactive substances. There is no safe level. Every little bit adds up. Conversely, the more perfect the match between your work and your personality, the more happy and successful you will be.

Many people believe that personality is flexible, flowing, ever changing. They think that their temperament is like soft clay that can be molded to a new shape by growth experiences or therapy. They may have observed friends who have changed radically, become more caring, more effective, or less constrained by inner demons. Their friends may behave differently, but they have not really changed into new people. What they've done is learned new, more effective ways of living, or have mastered habitual patterns, mislearnings that used to hold them back from full self-expression. They have learned to step out into a fuller life in which they can more authentically express themselves. But they are still the same person, with the same basic temperament.

No one knows what percentage of our personalities is given to us by our genes and how much is learned. Even though the majority of our mental software is learned as we develop through the years of childhood, the basic structure of our personalities, our temperament, is inherent. Scientists can now accurately predict whether a newborn baby will grow up to be extroverted or introverted by observing a few telltale clues in the hospital shortly after birth. If your degree of extroversion and introversion is the gift of your genes, why would someone who is born introverted want to be extroverted? For the same reason people start to smoke cigarettes, to be cool. But there is nothing cool about rejecting one's authentic self. Changing from one thing to another is, at best, extremely difficult. Try changing a table into a chair. It is one thing for an introverted person to learn to become more effective or more comfortable in social situations. It is yet another to try to change into someone else. Although the plowhorse may dream of racing, and may enjoy a hobby of racing with the other plowhorses on weekends, it would not have much fun if it actually had to compete with the thoroughbreds.

Does it sound like I am saying that you should not reach for the stars, that some people are predestined to drag a plow behind them like a ball and chain? Not at all. I used the horse example to demonstrate how deeply our thinking is imbedded in cultural ideals, and how much this subverts our ability to choose a career that fits our own personalities. Even those of us whose natures are slow and steady are going to be more attracted to being a racehorse than a plowhorse. We have ideals and standards about personality, just as we do about everything else. Often, people pick the wrong career because they are paying attention to their standards rather than getting in touch with who they are.

There seems to be something defeatist and elitist in saying a plowhorse should plow and a racehorse should race. We were raised in a revolutionary culture, taught to resist going with the flow and to fight to the top of the mountain. It seems counterintuitive to suggest that wholehearted acceptance of one's own individual nature is a more profound form of personal growth than change. (If you can't be the one you love, love the one you are.) But most of the people we most admire reached their level of achievement not by changing into someone else but by embracing their natures fully and using their personalities as instruments of self-expression. They not only chose work that fit their temperaments but also learned to use their personalities proactively to further their intentions. You do not get very far if you spend your energy resisting or doing battle with your nature. If you have patterns you need to change, points of view or behaviors that do not serve, then master them. But, please, choose a career that perfectly fits your personality as it is now.

In this chapter, you will have an opportunity to take a look at the basic structure of your personality and what career may fit. First, you will have a chance to assess your basic temperament. Then you will take a look at some other important aspects of your personality.

INQUIRY 16

TEMPERAMENT

The ancient Greeks recognized that each individual is born with a distinct personality. They categorized people's temperaments into four types. In modern times, psychologist Carl Jung expanded the concept. More recently, a test called the Myers-Briggs Type Indicator expanded the concept of personality type even further. Back in the sixties, when you walked into a bar, you would find the inevitable lounge lizard leaning over his prey, saying something like, "Hey, baby, what's your sign?" In recent years, the lizards have shifted from the astrological to the psychological. This test has become so well known that you are more likely to overhear them ask, "Hey, baby, what's your Myers-Briggs type?" these days. The test divides human temperament into sixteen basic personality types by asking you which of four pair of opposites is most like you. Each of these sixteen types is described by four letters. Here are the pairs of opposites and the letters that represent them:

E	Extroversion	Introversion	**I**
N	Intuition	Sensing	**S**
F	Feeling	Thinking	**T**
P	Perceiving	Judging	**J**

For example, if your answers to questions about extroversion and introversion leaned toward extroversion, the first letter of your four-letter type would be E, for extroversion.

To decide which of the sixteen types represents your personality, work your way through the four lists of opposite traits that follow. This simple personality-type sorter is no substitute for the most recent, in-depth version of the Myers-Briggs Type Indicator, which I highly recommend. If, after going through this Inquiry, you do not recognize yourself when you read the description of the type this sorter points to, you will find a phone number for the publishers of the Myers-Briggs Type Indicator in the "Getting in Touch" section at the back of the book. The temperament sorter that follows should, however, give you an accurate reading of your personality type. Read one pair of opposites, left column then right column, and decide which statement is more like you. Put a mark next to the statement that best describes you. Don't burn out your wiring trying to decide which is the real you. Use your intuition. Take the first answer that pops into your head. If neither alternative fits, or both describe you equally, don't mark either side. As you finish each of the four sets, add up how many marks you made in each column. Write the numbers in the spaces at the end of each column.

E

Extrovert
Outgoing, gregarious, expansive
Many social relationships
Expressive, congenial
Public
Mixer, mingler at parties

I

Introvert
Attention on rich inner life
A few deep, personal relationships
Reflective, quiet observer
Private
One-on-one conversations

When studying at the library, finds a place near other people	When studying at the library, finds a private place where others will not intrude
Lonely when often alone	Savors and seeks time alone
Easily begins new relationships	Gets to know people more slowly
Discusses everything with everyone	Shares personal life with intimates
Speaks first	Thinks first
Loves to be in midst of things	Loves to close his or her office door
Action	Reflection, quiet times
Works ideas out with others' input	Works ideas out internally
Talks	Listens
Enjoys being the center of attention	Resists being the center of attention
The outer world	The world of ideas
Acts	Ponders
Objective	Subjective
Reality = immediate environment	Reality = ideas and understanding
Easy to read	More difficult to read
___ Number of E responses	___ Number of I responses

N	**S**
Intuitives	*Sensors*
Energy focused on what could be	Energy focused on what is
Possibility, potential	Actuality, reality
Lives in the future	Lives in the present
Conceptual	Realistic, straightforward
General	Specific
Insights, ideas, inferences, hunches	Facts, examples, evidence
Figurative	Literal
Analogies, metaphors	Detailed information
A love for new ideas	Likes new ideas with practical applications
Anticipation of future events	Interacts with events when they happen
Seeks inspiration	Seeks enjoyment
In the clouds	Down-to-earth
Especially aware of sense impressions that relate to inspirations and ideas	Very aware of all sorts of sense impressions
Inventors, initiators	Pleasure lovers, consumers
Often restless	Often contented
Original	Imitative
Seeks future expansion	Seeks to possess

Willing to sacrifice present pleasure to bring future possibilities into existence

Turns achieving goals and building for the future into an art

Strong appreciation of initiative, inspired leadership, entrepreneurship

Learns new skills

___ Number of I responses

Dislikes sacrificing present pleasure for future goals

Turns living in the moment into an art

Strong appreciation of comfort, luxury, beauty, recreation, pleasure

Refines existing skills

___ Number of S responses

T

Thinking

Objective
Principles
Analytical
Logical, cool
Dissect
Clarify
Compare, emphasize
Explaining
Divide
Explore
Laws, rules, policy
Impersonal
Thoughtful
Mainly interested in things other than human relationships
Truthful
Brief and businesslike

Justice
Achievement
Cultivate
Contrast, separate

___ Number of T responses

F

Feeling

Subjective
Personal values
Caring, compassionate, tender
Passionate, warm
Care
Forgive
Appreciate
Understanding
Include
Caress
Extenuating circumstances
Personal
Sentimental
Very strong interest in human relationships
Tactful
Friendly. Has difficulty remaining businesslike

Harmony, mercy
Appreciation
Cherish, adore, nourish, sympathize
Include, relate

___ Number of F responses

J	P
Judging	*Perceiving*
Comfortable after decisions made	*Comfortable leaving options open*
Sets fixed goals and concentrate on achieving them on schedule	*Goals are more open-ended, subject to change*
Decided	*Flexible, curious*
Enjoys having projects framed by definite deadlines	*Feels that deadlines should be adjustable*
Work now. Enjoy if there is time	*Enjoy now*
Planned	*Spontaneous*
Structured	*Vague, indeterminate, amorphous*
Loves to reach completion, finish projects	*Loves to begin new projects*
Product-oriented, wants to get the job done	*Process-oriented. More interested in how the task will be accomplished*
Prefers knowing what he or she is getting into ahead of time	*Very adaptable to changing situations*
Steady, sustained effort	*On-and-off effort*
Decisive	*Puts off decisions*
The present situation must be made to conform to the rules, customs, plans, specifications	*The rules, customs, plans, and specifications flex to be appropriate to the changing situation*
Carefully protect themselves from unplanned or undesirable experiences	*Depend on their ability to handle unplanned or undesirable experiences resourcefully*
Exacting	*Tolerant*
Make the right decision, do the right thing	*Have as many experiences as possible, miss nothing*
As students, may carry out an orderly and systematic study plan	*As students, may put off studying until the last minute*
Sometimes accused of being too rigid	*Sometimes accused of being to indecisive*
Should be, must be, definitely, absolutely	*Could be, might be, perhaps, maybe*
Definite, clear-cut, final	*Tentative, experimental, exploratory provisional, contingent.*

___ *Number of J responses*   ___ *Number of P responses*

Now that you are finished, transfer your scores here.

___ *Number of E responses*   ___ *Number of I responses*

___ *Number of N responses*   ___ *Number of S responses*
___ *Number of T responses*   ___ *Number of F responses*
___ *Number of J responses*   ___ *Number of P responses*

If you have a higher score on one side of a pair, that letter becomes part of your four-letter type. For example:

10 *Number of E responses*   **5** *Number of I responses*
6 *Number of N responses*   **2** *Number of S responses*
5 *Number of T responses*   **12** *Number of F responses*
3 *Number of J responses*   **9** *Number of P responses*

Notice that, in this example, the numbers do not add up to the total number of questions. That's because the test taker, as requested, did not answer questions where he or she was not sure that either answer fit. Since the scores were higher for E, N, F and P, the test taker's type would be ENFP. In the pages that follow, there are encapsulated descriptions of all sixteen types. If you get the same score, or nearly the same score on both sides of a pair of opposites, read the descriptions of both types. For example, if EN and F were all definite, but the scores for P and J were almost the same, read both ENFP and ENFJ. You will probably find that you have characteristics of both types. Remember, the point of doing this Inquiry is not to pigeonhole yourself with a four-letter type, but to get clear on important aspects of your makeup, your personal blueprint. Use this Inquiry as a mirror to see yourself more clearly. If you are in the middle in more than one pair of opposites, don't worry. This is perfectly natural. Many other people have scores in the middle. It doesn't mean you are wishy-washy or undecided. It just means that you are balanced in regard to these traits. That's fine. The only downside is that it makes it harder to come up with a definite four-letter type. But so what, unless you need to have a fast answer for the lounge lizards. If you highlight the traits that best describe you in each of the temperament types that seem to partially fit you, you will wind up with a list of your temperament traits, even if you do not exactly match one type or another.

The careers suggested for each type *are only examples,* not a list from which to choose your future career. Use the recommended careers lists to better understand how your various personality traits might be expressed in your work. These careers are suggested as possible matches for your temperament, not your talents, your interests, or what matters to you. Often, an in-depth look at these other areas suggests careers that are very different from the ones listed here. Some people feel the need to have a career that is a direct expression of their temperament. They would usually be most attracted to careers that were similar to ones listed for their type. Others are perfectly satisfied if they can do whatever they do in a style that allows them to freely be themselves at work, without having to manufacture a politically correct business persona. For example, for someone whose temperament includes a built-in tendency toward helping people to be their best, that tendency could be expressed most directly by choosing a career where that quality would be of profound importance, such as teaching, coaching, or counseling. That trait could also be expressed less directly in many other careers. It is even possible that prison guards could use this trait to benefit their charges. But in some careers, this trait might be socially unacceptable. As you read through the key words that describe your type, ask yourself which ones are most important to express in your career. If most of the key words for your type describe you accurately, and you are committed to work you love, wouldn't you think it necessary to choose a career that would fit elegantly with those descriptive words?

If you want to delve deeper into your personality, I recommend that you buy a book entitled *Do What You Are* by Paul Tieger and Barbara Barron-Tieger. It is an absolutely terrific, in-depth guide to the subject of temperament and work.

What have you learned in the course of this Inquiry? How important is it to you that your career be an expression of your temperament? Turn to your Primary Lists (Wants, Commitments and Requirements, and Questions), as well as your Careers to Consider List. What can you add to those lists now? **What am I sure will definitely be an important component of my future career?** *What would be a highly desirable element of your future career that you are not quite ready to commit to yet?*

ENFP

Enthusiastic, expressive, emotional, warm, evocative, imaginative, original, artistic, improviser, perceptive, affirming, supportive, cooperative, positive, open, responsive, sensitive, playful, fun-loving, multifaceted, gregarious, zestful, spontaneous, idealistic, initiators of new projects and possibilities, agents of change. Their focus is on self-expression and possibilities, "what could be" rather than "what is." Life is a celebration and a creative adventure. Enthusiastic initiators of new projects, relationships, and paradigms. Masters of the start-up phase. Lose interest when the project or relationship gets routine or when the primary goal is well on the way to accomplishment. Often eloquent in expressing their vision of a world where ideals are actualized. They might say the glass is full rather than half-full or half-empty. They are quick to see the potential in people and situations. Frequently have a positive attitude in situations others would consider to be negative. May enjoy a rainy day as much as a sunny one. Management style is focused on the people rather than task-oriented. They encourage and serve as mentors rather than command. Work in bursts of enthusiasm mixed with times when little gets done. Need careers that are personally meaningful, creative, and allow for full self-expression and that contribute to other people in some way. Extremely versatile. They may have friends from many walks of life, a wide range of interests and hobbies, and they gain a professional level of mastery without formal training.

activist: social causes
actor
agent for actors, artists, writers
buyer
clergy in low-dogma faiths
coach: personal growth and
    effectiveness
counselor: relationship, spiritual,
    career
consultant: communications,
    education, human resources,
    presentation personal effectiveness
director/producer, films
entrepreneur
fund raiser
healer—alternative disciplines

human resources specialist
journalist
midwife
ombudsman
passenger service representative
physician: family, holistic
psychologist
public relations
recreation leader
religious activities director
social scientist
teacher
therapist in active, participatory,
    growth-oriented discipline
trainer

INFP

Idealistic, warm, caring, creative, imaginative, original, artistic, perceptive, supportive, empathetic, cooperative, facilitative, compassionate, responsive, sensitive, gentle, tenderhearted, devoted, loyal, virtuous, self-critical, perfectionist, self-sacrificing, deep, multifaceted, daydreamer, persistent, determined, hard-working, improviser, initiator of new projects and possibilities, agents of change. Drawn to possibilities, "what could be" rather than "what is." Values-oriented with high level of personal integrity. Their focus is on understanding themselves, personal growth, and contributing to society in a meaningful way. Under surface appearances they are complex and driven to seek perfection and improvement: in themselves, their relationships, and their self-expression. If their career does not express their idealism and drive for improvement, they usually become bored and restless. Dislike conflict, dealing with trivialities, and engaging in meaningless social chatter. Thrive on acknowledgment and recognition so long as they are not the center of attention. Needs a private work space, autonomy, and a minimum of bureaucratic rules.

activist
administrator: education or social
    service nonprofit

healer: alternative disciplines
health-care worker
human resources specialist

architect
artist
attorney devoted to righting wrongs
clergy in low-dogma faiths
coach: personal growth and
    effectiveness
counselor: relationship, spiritual,
    career
consultant: education, human
    resources
developer of training programs
director of social service agency
editor
entrepreneur
librarian
medicine: family
midwife
nurse
physician: psychiatrist, family, holistic
psychologist
researcher
social scientist
social worker
songwriter/musician
speech pathologist
teacher
therapist
writer, poet, or journalist

ENFJ

Enthusiastic, caring, concerned, cooperative, congenial, diplomatic, interactive, facilitator, diligent, emotional, sincere, interpersonally sensitive, warm, supportive, tolerant, creative, imaginative, articulate, extraordinary social skills, smooth, persuasive motivator, teacher/preacher, verbal, natural leader, active, lively, humorous, entertaining, witty. Values-oriented. Uncannily perceptive about other's needs and what motivates them. Often rise to leadership positions. Concerned with the betterment of humanity and works to effect positive change. They have such a gift for persuasively using language that others may consider them to be glib and insincere when actually they are forthright and openhearted. Does not deal well with resistance and conflict. Easily hurt and offended if their well-meaning crusades meet with criticism and rejection. Takes everything personally. Puts people before rules. Strong desire to give and receive affirmation. Manage by encouragement.

actor
advertising account executive
camp director
counselor: career, relationship,
    personal growth
clergy
consultant
dean
director of communications
newscaster
outplacement counselor
politician
producer: films, television
promotions
public relations
public speaker
recruiter
sales

director of social service nonprofit
entrepreneur
fund raiser
health practitioner: holistic
mediator

sales manager
supervisor
teacher
trainer

INFJ

Gentle, introspective, insightful, idealistic, intellectual, inquisitive, sincere, quiet strength, steady, dependable, conscientious, orderly, deliberate, diligent, compassionate, caring, concerned, peace-loving, accepting, intense, sometimes stubborn, dreamer, catalyst, many interests, seek and promote harmony. Many feel at home in academia, studying complex concepts, enjoying theory-oriented courses. They are quietly aware of the dynamics between people. Because they are gentle and quiet, their gifts and rich inner life may go untapped. Their caring, nurturing nature can remain unnoticed since they may not find it comfortable to express these feelings openly. Consequently, they may feel isolated. Need a great deal of solitude and private personal space. Dislike tension and conflict. Give a great deal of focused energy and commitment to their projects, at work and at home. Although usually compliant, they can become extremely stubborn in pursuit of important goals. Seek careers that further their humanistic ideals and engage their values.

accountant
administrator: health care,
  social work
analyst
architect
artist
clergy
composer
consultant: organizational
  development
coordinator
editor
entrepreneur
human resources planner
judge

librarian
management analyst
novelist
photographer: portrait
physician
physical therapist
poet
psychologist
researcher
scientist
social scientist
social worker
technician: health care
writer

ENTP

Enthusiastic, puzzle master, objective, inventive, independent, conceptual thinker, creative problem solver, entrepreneurial risk taker, improviser, competitive, questioning, rebellious, rule breaker, gregarious, witty, involved, strategic, versatile, clever, adaptable, energetic, action-oriented agents of change. Improves systems, processes, and organizations. Relentlessly tests and challenges the status quo with new, well-thought-out ideas, and argues vehemently in favor of possibilities and opportunities others have not noticed. Can wear out their colleagues with their drive and challenging nature. See the big picture and how the details fit together. The most naturally entrepreneurial of all types. Usually not motivated by security. Their lives are often punctuated with extreme ups and downs as they energetically pursue new ideas. They have only one direction: ahead at full speed, leaving a trail of incomplete projects, tools, and plans in their wake. Their idea of fun and best creative self-expression involves devising new conceptual modeling and dreaming up imaginative and exciting ventures. Need lots of room to maneuver. When forced to dwell on details and routine operating procedures, they become bored and restless. Respect competence, not authority. Seek work that allows them to solve complex problems and develop real-world solutions. Often surrounded with the latest technology.

advertising, creative director
agent, literary
CEO, high-tech companies
computer repair
consultant, management
designer
engineer, high-tech
entrepreneur
industrial designer
inventor
investment broker
journalist
lawyer

manager, leading-edge company
marketer
political analyst
politician
public relations
publicity
sales
software designer
special projects developer
systems analyst
strategic planner
technician, high-tech
venture capitalist

INTP

Logical, original, speculative quick thinkers, ingenious, inventive, cerebral, deep, ruminative, critical, skeptical, questioning, reflective problem solver, flaw finder, architect and builder of systems, lifelong learner, precise, reserved, detached, absent-minded professor. Seeker of logical purity. They love to analyze, critique, and develop new ideas rather than get involved in the implementation phase. Continually engage in mental challenges that involve building complex conceptual models leading to logically flawless solutions. Because they are open-ended and possibility-oriented, an endless stream of new data pours in, making it difficult for them to finish developing whatever idea they are working on. Everything is open to revision. Consequently, they are at their best as architects of new ideas where there are endless hypothetical possibilities to be explored, and no need for one final concrete answer. Their holy grail is conceptual perfection. May consider the project complete and lose interest when they have it figured out. To them, reality consists of thought processes, not the physical universe. Often seem lost in the complex tunnels of their own inner process. Seek work that allows them to develop intellectual mastery, provides a continual flow of new challenges, offers privacy, a quiet environment, and independence. Thrive in organizations where their self-reliance is valued and colleagues meet their high standards for competency.

archaeologist   *historian*
architect   *judge*
artist   *lawyer*
biologist   *mathematician*
chemist   *musician*
computer programmer   *physicist*
computer software designer *philosopher*
computer-systems analyst   *researcher*
economist   *social scientist*
electronic technician *sociologist*
engineer   *strategic planner*
financial analyst   *writer*

ENTJ

Born to lead, outgoing, involved, fully engaged, ambitious, take charge, impersonal, hearty, robust, type A+, impatient, bossy, controlling, confrontational, argumentative, critical, sharp-tongued, intimidating, arrogant, direct, demanding, strategic, tough-minded, organized, orderly, efficient, long-range planner, objective problem solver. Self-determined and independent. Skilled verbal communicators. Firmly believe that their way is best. Hold on to their point of view without alteration or compromise until some brave soul is able to convince them, through extensive argument and definitive proof, that another way is better. They consider all aspects of life to be the playing field for their favorite game, monkey on the mountain. Their energy is focused on winning, getting to the top, beating the competition, reaching the goal. See life and evaluate other people as part of this game. Assess others hierarchically, above them or below them on the mountain. Tend to look down on people who will not engage them in competition. Often generate hostility and rebellion from their employees and children. Show affection for others by helping them improve. Seek power. Learn by fully engaged discussion (also known as arguing). At their best planning and organizing challenging projects, providing the leadership, straight-ahead energy and drive to keep the momentum up, and efficiently managing people and forces to reach the objective.

administrator	*military officer*
athlete	*mortgage banker*
consultant, management	*office manager*
corporate executive	*president*, CEO
credit investigator	*program designer*
economic analyst	*sales*
engineer, project manager	*sales or marketing manager*
entrepreneur	*stockbroker*
financial planner	*supervisor*
lawyer	*systems analyst*
manager, senior level	*team leader*

INTJ

Innovative, independent, individualist, self-sufficient, serious, determined, diligent, resourceful, impersonal, reserved, quick-minded, insightful, demanding, critical, argumentative debater, may seem aloof to others, strategic, tough-minded, organized, orderly, efficient, global, long-range visionary, planner, objective problem solver. Self-determined and independent. Uses resources efficiently. Does not waste their time on trivialities. True to their own visions. Can become stubborn when they are supposed to do things in a way that differs from their own opinions of the best methodology. Oriented toward new ideas, possibilities, and improving systems. Their motto is "everything could use improvement." This includes processes, systems, information, technology, organizations, other people, and themselves. Many use education as a path to success and earn advanced degrees. Usually one of the first to buy the latest computer and upgrade to new, improved software and other technology. Show affection for others by helping them improve. Learn by in-depth study of the subject and by discussing and arguing. May not realize that other, more thin-skinned individuals do not interpret arguing in the positive way that INTJs do. Attain personal growth by confronting anything within themselves that could be ameliorated. Constantly stretch themselves in new directions. Highly competent. Read and understand both conceptual and practical materials. See both the forest and the trees. Excellent at planning, execution, and follow-through They see the big picture, thinking and ably organizing the details into a coherent plan. Often rise to the top in organizations. At their best where they can conceptualize a new project and then push it through to completion; then do it all over again with a new project.

administrator	*inventor*
analyst: business or financial	*judge*
architect	*lawyer*
CEO, high-tech	*pharmacologist*
computer programmer	*psychologist*
design engineer	*physician, cardiologist, neurologist*
consultant	*researcher*
curriculum designer	*scientist*
designer	*systems analyst*
engineer	*teacher: college*
entrepreneur	*technician*

ESFP

"Live for today. Face the consequences tomorrow." Warm, positive, friendly, popular, vivacious, helpful, generous, inclusive, tolerant, enthusiastic, gregarious, action-oriented, robust, zestful, spontaneous, flexible, energetic, alert, fun-loving, playful, impulsive, thrill seeker. Realistic, practical. A great deal of common sense. The focus is on people. Accepting, live-and-let-live attitude, go with the flow. Sunny disposition, love life. Laugh easily, even at themselves. Adventurous, fearless, willing to try anything that involves sensation and risk. Tuned in to and relishes the world around them. Smell the roses without stopping. Plunge in head first. Live in the present, spurred into action to meet today's needs. Seek immediate gratification, harmony, positive experiences. Avoid or repress unpleasant or negative experiences. Do not naturally plan ahead. Dislike routines, procedures, limits, conflict, and slow-moving, long-range projects. Learn by interactive, hands-on participation. Do best in careers that allow them to generate immediate, tangible results while having fun harmoniously relating with other people in the center of the action.

bus driver	*physician: emergency room*
child-care provider	*police officer*

carpenter	producer, film
coach	promoter
comedian	public relations
events coordinator	receptionist
fund raiser	sales
lifeguard	sales manager
mechanic	small business, retail store
mediator	supervisor
merchandiser	teacher: preschool
musician: rock & roll	tour operator
nurse: emergency room	travel agent
performer	veterinarian
physical therapist	waiter/waitress

ISFP

Gentle, sensitive, quiet, modest, self-effacing, giving, warm, genuine, service-oriented, helpful, generous, inclusive, tolerant, people pleaser, considerate, respectful, loyal, trusting, devoted, compassionate, caring, supportive, nurturing, encouraging, serene, easygoing, fun-loving, open, flexible, realistic, practical, independent. Extremely observant and in touch, especially with the sensual world, both externally and within themselves. Savor the sweetness of life. A great deal of common sense. Accepting, live-and-let-live attitude, go with the flow. No need to lead, compete, influence, or control. Seek harmony. Do not impose their values on others. Find their own practical and creative way to do things. Often seek self-expression through crafts or hands-on arts. At their best in work that expresses their personal values and helps or provides a service to others. May forgo college for a practical education in the trades, crafts, or service professions.

administrator	luthier
artisan, craftsperson	massage therapist
beautician	mechanic
bookkeeper	medical-office personnel
botanist	medical technician
carpenter	nurse
chef	physical therapist
computer operator	plant nursery: herbs, other
cosmetologist	specialties
dancer	painter
electrician	potter

forester
gardener
household worker
interior designer
jeweler
landscape designer

secretary
shopkeeper
surveyor
teacher: elementary or adult,
    nature, science, art
weaver

ESFJ

Gracious, amiable, affirming, gentle, giving, warm, genuine, cordial, kindly, caring, concerned, dutiful, reliable, punctual, polite, tactful, socially appropriate, thoughtful, self-sacrificing, nurturer, people-pleaser, efficient manager, event planner, goal-oriented, helpful, cooperative, consistent, extremely loyal, traditional, rule-bound, uncomplicated. Perfectly in tune with others needs and sensitive to nuances, they are world's natural hosts and hostesses. Their presence contributes graciousness, harmony, fraternity, and fellowship to whatever they are engaged in. Both female and male ESFJs relate with people in a way that combines warm-hearted "mothering" and caring, considerate "inn-keeping." So eager are they to please that they put others needs before their own, ignoring their personal well-being as they care for the people most important to them. They seek harmony, avoid conflict, follow the rules, keep their commitments, ignore problems by pretending they do not exist. Sensitive to criticism. Need appreciation and praise. Particularly concerned with etiquette, "shoulds" and "should nots." Family and home are often their central passion. Value stability, harmony, relationships, and practical, hands-on experience. The day-to-day events in their lives are carefully planned and meticulously managed. At their best in professions that provide helpful, caring, practical service to others and do not require them to learn theories. They are particularly good at planning events, organizing people, and managing the day-to-day aspects of projects that deal with producing tangible results. When they learn an effective new method, it becomes standard operating procedure. Their extraordinary effectiveness comes from picking the perfect, tried and true procedure from their internal database at exactly the right time.

bartender
caterer
chef
child-care provider
customer-service representative
event planner/coordinator
fitness coach

manager: office, restaurant, hotel
optometrist
personal banker
real estate agent
receptionist
sales, tangibles
secretary

flight attendant
hairdresser
host/hostess
innkeeper
maître d'

small business, retail store
social worker
teacher: elementary school, special
*   education, home economics*

ISFJ

Warm, conscientious, loyal, considerate, helpful, calm, quiet, devoted, gentle, open, nurturing, practical, patient, responsible, dependable, very observant, sensitive, holistic, inclusive, spontaneous, pragmatic, tactile, respectful, noncompetitive, sympathetic, painstaking and thorough, efficient, traditional. The most service-oriented of all the types. Very much in touch with their inner processes as well as the world around them. Seek harmony for themselves and all others. Serene, appreciative, in tune. Do not impose themselves or their opinions on others. Do not need to control. Find their own creative way to get the job done. Learn by doing. Uninterested in abstractions and theories. Use standard operating procedures only when they are the best method for reaching the goal. Often creative and highly skilled but so averse to imposing that they are easily overlooked and their contributions go unnoticed.

administrator: social services
counselor
curator
customer-service representative
dietitian
dentist/dental hygienist
educational administrator
entrepreneur
guidance counselor
hairdresser, cosmetologist
health-service worker
household worker
innkeeper
librarian
manager: restaurant
massage therapist

media specialist
medical technologist
nurse
occupational therapist
personal assistant
personnel administrator
physical therapist
physician: family practice or
*   receptionist*
priest/minister/rabbi/monk/nun
religious educator
sales: retail
secretary
speech pathologist
teacher: preschool, elementary,
*   adult, ESL*

ESTP

Outgoing, realistic, pragmatic problem solver, action-oriented, robust, zestful, spontaneous, energetic, alert, laid-back style, direct, fearless, resourceful, expedient, competitive, spontaneous, flexible, gregarious, objective. Adventurous, willing to try anything that involves sensation and risk. Plunges in head first; then analyzes. "Live for today. Face the consequences tomorrow." No tolerance for theories and abstractions. Short attention span. Usually have a laid-back attitude, value individual rights and personal freedom. Do not naturally plan ahead. Prefer to deal with what life throws at them. Adapt to the present situation. React to emergencies instantly and appropriately. A passion for tackling tough jobs and winning in impossible situations. Football hero mentality. Break the rules more often than any other type. Often find themselves in trouble in strict bureaucracies. Dislike being tied down. Learn by doing; rarely read the manual. Want a big return for their investment of time, energy, money. Lively, entertaining center of attention. The ultimate party-hearty soul. Always willing to put off mundane tasks for the thrill of something new and exciting. Often attracted to motorcycles, fast cars, power boats, sky diving, and similar quick thrills, the new and the unexplored, tactile pleasures, high-risk sports. May enjoy working with their hands.

athlete	*mechanic*
athletic coach	*military*
auctioneer	*negotiator*
carpenter	*news reporter*
contractor	*paramedic*
entrepreneur	*photographer: combat or adventure*
explorer	*pilot*
field technician	*police officer or detective*
fire fighter	*promoter*
fitness instructor	*real estate agent*
heavy-equipment operator	*sales*
lifeguard	*stunt person*
manager: hands-on, day-to-day	*troubleshooter, problem solver*
operations	*truck driver*
marketer	*waiter, waitress*

ISTP

Independent, reserved, cool, curious, expedient, flexible, logical, analytical, realistic, spontaneous, action-oriented. Adventurous, willing to try anything that involves sensation and risk. Usually have a relaxed, laid-back attitude, value individual rights and personal freedom. Enthusiastic about and absorbed in their immediate interests. Constantly scanning and observing the world around them. Do not naturally plan ahead. Prefer to deal with what life throws at them. Adapt to the present situation. Follow the path of least resistance. React to emergencies instantly and appropriately. Live-and-let-live philosophy, laissez-faire approach to life. Dislike rules, being tied down or imposing themselves on others. Often attracted to motorcycles, fast cars, power boats, sky diving, and similar quick thrills, the new and the unexplored, tactile pleasures, high-risk sports. May enjoy working with their hands. Things or objective information are the focus, rather than people

ambulance driver
athletic coach
bus driver
carpenter
chef
construction worker
dental assistant
diver
entrepreneur
engineer
farmer
field technician
laborer
lifeguard
manager: hands-on, day-to-day
  operations

mechanic
military
optometrist
pharmacist
physician: pathology
photographer: news
pilot
recreational attendant
secretary
service worker
stunt person
surveyor
technician
troubleshooter, problem solver
truck driver
video-camera operator

ESTJ

Systematic, serious, thorough, down-to-earth, efficient, decisive, hard-working, dutiful, loyal, sincere, conservative, aggressive, in charge. Focused, controlled, and controlling. A strong sense of responsibility. Gregarious, active, socially gifted, party goer. Make their points of view known. "Macho" or "macha." Often rise to positions of responsibility, such as senior-level management. Want their work to be practical, pragmatic, immediate, objective, have clear and unambiguous objectives, require follow-through and perseverance, involve facts, and produce tangible, measurable results. Natural managers and administrators. Type A personalities. Keep their commitments at any cost. Think from the point of view of "should" and "should not." Have difficulty appreciating and learning from other points of view. Work first, play later. Drawn to work in stable, structured, hierarchical organizations using standard operating procedures. Follow the rules. Seekers of security. They safeguard and maintain traditions and traditional values. A tendency to trample other people (usually unknowingly) as they plow straight ahead to accomplish their goals. A high percentage of military people have this personality type.

athletic coach
bank employee
cashier
computer-systems analyst
contractor
chef
corporate executive (all levels)
dietitian
electrician
engineer
entrepreneur
funeral director
insurance agent, broker, or
  underwriter
judge
manager: retail store, operations,
  projects, restaurant, bank,
  government

mechanic
military
nurse
optometrist
pharmacist
physician
police officer
purchasing agent
school principal
sales
stockbroker
supervisor
teacher of practical material: math,
  gym, shop, technical

ISTJ

Systematic, serious, thorough, down-to-earth, efficient, decisive, hard-working, dutiful, loyal, reserved, sincere, conservative. A strong sense of responsibility. Very private but learn extroverted social behaviors for the sake of practicality. Want their work to be practical, pragmatic, immediate, objective, have clear and unambiguous objectives, require follow-through and perseverance, involve facts, and produce tangible, measurable results. Often have type A personalities. Keep their commitments at any cost. Think from the point of view of "should" and "should not." Work first, play later. Drawn to work in stable, structured, hierarchical organizations using standard operating procedures. Seekers of security. They safeguard and maintain traditions and traditional values. A high percentage of military people have this personality type.

accountant	*government employee*
administrator	*guard*
analyst	*IRS agent*
auditor	*manager: retail store, operations,*
bank employee	*projects*
bus driver	*mechanic*
chef	*military*
chemist	*operator: machinery*
computer-systems analyst, operator,	*pharmacist*
programmer	*police officer*
corporate executive (all levels)	*school principal*
dentist	*speech pathologist*
dietitian	*surgeon*
electrician	*teacher of practical material: math,*
engineer	*gym, shop, technical*
entrepreneur	*technical writer*
farmer	*technician: lab, science, engineering,*
field technician	*health*

Turn to your Primary Lists (Wants, Commitments and Requirements, and Questions), as well as to your Careers to Consider List. What can you add to those lists now? **What am I sure will definitely be an important component of my future career?**

Before you go on to the next Inquiry, remember to work on your primary lists.

INQUIRY 17

OTHER PERSONALITY TRAITS

Here are some other personality traits to consider as part of your self-assessment.

1. Please draw a mark on the line at the appropriate place on each scale.

2. Write a description of yourself that contains your traits that stand out most in the previous temperament and personality self-assessments. For example, you might write:

"I am imaginative, enthusiastic, cheerful, flexible, optimistic, warm, intimate, confident, persevering, independent, bold. I am a leader, unconventional

Cautious			Impulsive
Practical, down to earth			Imaginative
Serious, subdued			Enthusiastic, cheerful
Unbendable			Flexible
Pessimistic			Optimistic
Unsentimental			Sentimental, kindly, sympathetic
Self-indulgent			Disciplined
Low need to influence others			Persuasive
Suspicious			Trusting
Cool			Warm
Tyrannical			Tolerant, permissive
Expedient			Moralistic
Forthright, genuine			Sophisticated, polished, shrewd
Chaotic			Organized
Conservative, traditional			Experimenting, liberal
Tough-minded			Emotionally sensitive
Reserved, private			Intimate, sharing, open
Panic under pressure			Unruffled under pressure

Highly dependable		Inconsistent
Aspirations do not drive actions		Ambitious
Worrying		Self-confident
Uncomplicated		Complicated
Tendency to give up, fickle		Tenacious, persevering
Concern for others		Self-centered
Dependent		Independent
Loner		Sociable
Submissive, obedient, docile		Assertive, aggressive
Relaxed, tranquil		Driven, tense
Clinging		Self-reliant
Joiner		Socially independent
Shy		Bold
Follows urges		Controlled
Follower		Leader
Conventional, conforming		Unconventional, rebellious
Restrained		Adventurous

and adventurous." Or, "I am a restrained, conventional, shrewd, pessimistic loner." Be honest. Seek the truth rather than stroke your ego.

Turn to your Primary Lists (Wants, Commitments and Requirements, and Questions), as well as your Careers to Consider List. What can you add to those lists now? WHAT AM I SURE WILL DEFINITELY BE AN IMPORTANT COMPONENT OF MY FUTURE CAREER?

Are You a Tribal or a Maestro?

The next few pages look into one of the most important things to consider in fitting together your personality and your work.

The Tribal Personality

Most people (about 75 percent) have a personality type that we describe as tribal. Tribals are group workers, usually most successful and satisfied working with and through other people as members of an organization, group, or "tribe." They have a broad, generalist frame of reference for life, usually getting bored with work that is highly specialized and narrow in scope. They are at their best contributing to the goals of an organization. They are on the same wave length as the group. Like a member of a flock of birds or a herd of gazelles, they move with the flow of the group. This does not necessarily mean (though it often does) that they have a special understanding of human nature and motivation. However, because they are tuned to the tribe, they derive many of their values, goals, and points of view from their tribe. Most of the kids who are members of the "in crowd" in high school are extroverted tribals.

Because they are on the same wavelength as others, many tribals are more gifted than maestros at understanding human nature without specialized training. For example, exceptional sales managers and supervisors are tribals who have an inborn understanding of human psychology, demonstrated by an ability to motivate employees effectively. Their success often depends on their interpersonal abilities or their gift for fitting easily into the culture of an organization. Tribals choose careers in business, management, personnel, high school teaching, training, supervision, sales, advertising, public relations, administration, banking, homemaking, etc.

Extroverted tribals are outgoing, people-oriented individuals who are found where the action is. They like to spend their workday in the part of the beehive where there are plenty of others bees to interact with. Examples: salesperson, receptionist, lobbyist, supervisor, office manager, foreperson, waiter, flight attendant, contractor, restaurant manager, "networker" style of CEO Introverted tribals work in a quieter part of the beehive, where they can close their doors and get some privacy. They work internally for the goals of the organization. Examples: manager of projects that involve more planning than direct supervision, administrator, clerical worker, corporate accountant, patent examiner, underwriter, corporate lawyer.

The Maestro Personality

Maestros comprise about 25 percent of the total population. They are individual workers, preferring to be valued for their mastery of a particular discipline or subject. Their success depends directly on special training or a talent for a chosen field. At work, they like to have people seek them out for their mastery, expertise, or knowledge. They most enjoy being appreciated and valued for the unique contribution they make. Maestros usually gravitate to careers that put them on a raised platform of expertise, like a college professor. They tend to understand the world through a unique, personal, and subjective way of thinking. They are on their own wavelength.

As children, they often delve deeply into interests and hobbies. They often recognize at an early age that their perspectives are different from the group's. This tendency continues throughout life. Maestros who have made the mistake of selecting a tribal career often report that their job "seems like something that anyone could do."

Extroverted maestros are performers. They may not necessarily perform in front of a large audience, but even with an audience of one, they communicate their expertise to others. As extroverts, they are usually in direct communication with other people. Examples: college professor who loves the classroom, seminar leader, spokesperson for a technical subject, courtroom lawyer, politician, actor, comedian, performance artist, dancer, consultant, trainer. Introverted maestros process information related to their special area of expertise internally. Many of the career areas usually thought of as "professional" are filled with introverted maestros. Examples: scientist, artist, college professor who most enjoys the research and writing, technician, medical specialist, accountant, poet, analyst, lawyer, economist, novelist, inventor.

Which Are You?

Hopefully you will recognize yourself as either a tribal or a maestro from the above descriptions. Consider this distinction to be an important piece of the puzzle. Having a clear understanding of which you are is just as important in selecting your career as understanding your talents and temperament. It tells you a great deal about the nature of your ideal career, what kinds of a relationships with other people fit you best, and is a powerful diagnostic tool for figuring out exactly why your present career may fall short. Of course, most people are some combination of the two. Knowing exactly where you are on the scale, what percentage tribal and what percentage maestro, is very useful in picking a career that fits perfectly. If you are not absolutely sure your self-assessment is accurate, or you want more depth of understanding, measuring this scale is a part of the career-testing programs offered by several career-coaching organizations.

Tribals and maestros answer the question "What do you do for a living?" differently. A tribal answers by stating what it is he or she does: "I am a manager at Galactic Communications." Even though they may use the same words, maestros answer from a different place. Their answers are more statements of their identity: "I am a scientist." "I am an artist." If they have chosen their career well, a large chunk of their identity is wrapped around what they do for a living. Of course a part of everyone's identity, for better or worse, is derived from what they do for a living. But for maestros, identifying themselves as "I am what I do" takes up a much bigger chunk than for tribals. Ideally, maestros should choose a subject area they are passionate about, and spend their lives becoming more and more masterful. A maestro without a specialty is like a cat without claws, a bird without wings. The good news is that it is never too late to get started. If you are a maestro and are not doing something that you are passionate about, you had better get to it. You will probably never be satisfied until you do. For tribals, things are a little more flexible. Change is easier. Even though the workplace has become so highly specialized, tribals move from job to job within an organization based on factors other than specialized knowledge. They learn as they go. Their abilities to manage, administer, market, or supervise is more important than technical knowledge.

It is less important for tribals to choose a specific career during their first years of college. Although they often go to college with specific educational objectives, when they look back on their college years later in life, they usually say that what was most valuable was something other than the specific subject matter learned in the classroom. Maestros, ideally, go to college to get an early start learning an area of specialty. A young person with a maestro personality should select a career direction early and obtain the specialized training to become a professional or expert. For them the selection of subject matter is critically important. If they are not passionate about the subject matter, they will not be able to proudly say, "I am a . . ." For tribals, it is often more appropriate to give more weight to other pieces of the puzzle.

Before the revolution in medical care, when the majority of physicians were in private practices, the vast majority of medical students we tested turned out to be maestros. This makes perfect sense because the relationship physicians have with their patients is classic maestro behavior, dispensing wisdom from a raised platform of expertise. Even though the majority of medical students are still maestros, the percentage of tribals has risen dramatically during the last few years, because nowadays many physicians are employees of HMOs or other organizations. So, as the practice of medicine becomes more attractive to young tribals, it becomes a little less attractive to young maestros.

Traditionally, psychotherapists, especially psychiatrists, have been very high maestros, Freudian beard strokers with very little "seat of the pants" understanding of other people. Their understanding comes from their technical training. Frankly, I think this explains why so many are incompetent at coaching their patents toward mental health. If I were the god of therapy, I would design therapists who were right in the middle of this scale. They would be 50 percent maestro, to give them the interest in delving deeply into the complexities of their art, and 50 percent tribal, so that they had a natural, innate understanding of other people.

Many careers do not line up neatly on one side of the line, fitting either tribals or maestros. It is more a matter of being clear what you are like in regard to this so you can pick a career that fits you like a glove. The great majority of retail-store owners are tribals, but a maestro with a raging passion for radio-controlled model airplanes, sewing, mountaineering equipment, or some other specialty where the customers would constantly seek their expertise might love owning such a specialty store. College professors who fall in the middle of the scale, partly tribal and partly maestro, say they would like to pull the chairs into a circle and be more of a facilitator than lecture from the front of the room. Most high school teachers are tribals. They do not have the need or desire to be on the raised platform of mastery that most college professors have. As far as the kids are concerned, a high school teacher is just another person, an older member of the group with the job of teaching. As far as most high school teachers are concerned, this is perfectly fine. In fact, these days, to be a high school teacher is sometimes much more like being a supervisor than a professor. Those schoolteachers who are maestros act like professors and teach like professors. Think back to your high school days. Which of your teachers were maestros and which were tribals?

Like many people in jobs that do not fit them in regard to this scale, you can always try bend the job to fit you. Sometimes this works. In most cases, it doesn't. Secretaries with maestro personalities often adapt their jobs to their personalities by mastering some specialized aspect of the job, perhaps becoming the office expert on the word-processing program. By doing so, other employees come to them for problem solving and instruction, a role that suits their personalities better than the usual work secretaries perform. In choosing your future career, you want to make as few compromises as possible. Generally speaking, picking something that does not exactly fit your combination of tribal and maestro increases the risk of winding up in an unsatisfying career.

Extroversion and Introversion

While it may be useful shorthand to think of yourself as an extrovert or introvert, in truth almost everyone is a mixture of both of these traits. People who think of themselves as either an extrovert or an introvert become confused when they find themselves desiring to spend more time on the opposite side of the coin. The trick is to figure out what percentage you are of each and design your career so you have a harmonious balance between both forces. If you are right in the middle, 50 percent extrovert and 50 percent introvert, and in your job you spend most of your time alone, you will, in time, develop a powerful desire for more people contact. Most likely, you will spend a great deal of your time outside of work in the company of others. If your job has you in face-to-face conversation all day, you will, most likely, want to spend your free time at home, curled up on the couch reading or watching the tube, recovering from your overly extroverted job. When either side is not getting enough of what it needs, powerful inner forces influence you to seek the proper balance.

In my never-ending quest to do inexpensive research studies, I once asked a male friend, recently divorced and spending time in singles bars, to approach as many single women as possible and go through a questionnaire on extroversion/introversion with them. He thought this was a heaven-sent opportunity and applied himself to this volunteer job as a psychological researcher with enormous enthusiasm. What we discovered was that more than 70 percent of the women who frequent singles bars on weeknights said their jobs were considerably less extroverted than they would prefer. After work they felt the insistent beat of powerful inner drums to get out of the house and mingle with others. The reverse happens with people whose jobs are too extroverted for them.

One of the common misconceptions about this subject is this myth that extroverts get their energy from being with other people, and that introverts get theirs from being alone. Nobody gets their energy from external sources. It always comes from within. In fact, it could be said that what you are is energy. But you will definitely feel a loss of energy and fulfillment if your life does not give you the proper balance between these two forces. For most people, it does not work very well to spend time outside of work recovering from an imbalance on the job.

Their after-work activities are the result of a compulsion rather than a free choice. So it is especially important to choose a career that provides the balance you need.

Another myth is that extroversion involves dancing on tabletops as the life of the party, and that introversion means sitting in the corner with a lamp shade over your head. A more to the point way of thinking of these two traits is that the extroverted part of a person lives externally, with attention focused on and interacting with the outer world. The introverted side looks within. This does not necessarily mean being alone. Illustrators who work for graphic arts companies usually lean toward introversion. They often work in the same room as several other illustrators. Even though they have lots of company, most find a good match for their dominant introverted side because their work is internally focused.

The way to discover the perfect balance is to look back through you life, assess the percentage of each trait by reliving various jobs, schools, and what you did in your spare time. What combination of activities gives you the perfect balance? Do your best to turn your insights into percentages. For example, "I am 60 percent introverted and 40 percent extroverted." Then consider how you could achieve this balance at work. Afterwards, turn to your Commitments and Requirements List. Are there any new commitments you want to make at this time?

Combining Tribal/Maestro and

Extroversion/Introversion

Combining both of these scales can provide you with a broad, general sense of what careers might fit you. The examples here may not include careers that you have any interest in. The descriptions may not seem to describe you perfectly. But from these simplified guidelines, you should be able fit these concepts together with your sense of yourself.

Extroverted tribals like to spend their workdays in the part of the beehive where there are plenty of other bees to rub wings with. They often work as a member of a tribe (otherwise called a company or other organization) furthering the mission of their tribe primarily through interaction with others. Examples: receptionists, salespeople, flight attendants, lobbyists, high school teachers, supervisors, contact- and marketing-oriented CEOs.

Introverted tribals enjoy working in a quieter part of the hive. They further the organization's goals by working within themselves. Examples: administrators, chief financial officers, clerical workers, contract administrators, planners, members of orchestras. As entrepreneurs, they like to work in the back room, managing the business.

Extroverted maestros are performers. They want to be up on stage communicating as an expert. The stage can range from huge and global to very tiny and one on one. As entrepreneurs, they are often visionary leaders, with special technical competence, who develop a loyal following of people they have enrolled in their vision. Examples: professors who loves the classroom, seminar leaders, corporate trainers, physicians in high-contact specialties, TV personalities, politicians, orchestral conductors, expert consultants.

Introverted maestros make up a large percentage of the people we think of as "professionals." They are experts who work internally in their chosen discipline. Examples: software designers, artist, CPAs, inventors, dentists, computer repair people, scientists, engineers, writers and poets, professors who love the writing and research most.

Passions and Interests

When most people attempt to pick their future careers on their own, this is one area they usually give attention to. As you know, there is much more to career selection than that. Still, passions and interests are important. Please go through the following Inquiry to clarify them.

INQUIRY 18

PASSIONS AND INTERESTS

You may be passionate about some special activity you do in your spare time. Or, your passion could be reserved for something you dream of doing but somehow never get to. You may feel strongly about the subject matter itself or the state of mind you find yourself in when you are engaged in it. In this Inquiry, you will have a chance to sort out what you feel passionate about, what is the source of the passions, and whether it needs to be a part of your work.

1. Open your notebook and start a new section called, you guessed it, "Passions and Interests." In instructions number two, three, and four, you will be asked to separate the big undifferentiated mass of personal interests into separate categories, based on degree of passion. You have to

make the decisions yourself as to which category your wants and passions fit into. There are no rules.

2. Start a subsection called "Major Life Passions." Write down everything that you feel very strongly about, that is a major strain of passion that runs through your life. Don't make a long list. Just write down your biggest, most important passions. Don't limit your entries to areas that you think you could turn into a career. If you are wildly passionate about lovemaking, but don't envision it as a career opportunity, write it down anyway. Your passion may be for some specific subject matter, such as antiques, baseball, or Mississippi Delta blues. It could be for an activity, such as sailing, reading, or actually playing baseball. It is perfectly fine if you do not have anything that you feel this strongly about. If that is so, just go on to the next instruction.

3. Start a second subsection called "Passionate Interests." Here you will list everything you feel passionate about, that you feel does not quite qualify as a major life passion. This may turn out to be a long list, or may just contain a few items. You are not graded on the length of your list (except perhaps by yourself.) Don't make up answers. The point is to uncover all of your areas of passionate interest.

4. Start a third subsection entitled "Interests, Preferences, and Activities I Enjoy." List areas of interest or preference that do not qualify as passions. Include both subject matter and activities. For example, at work you may not be particularly interested in the subject matter but look forward to getting out of the office and visiting clients. Or you may look forward to shutting the office door and messing around with the computer. Write it all down. If you like it, write it down.

If you get stuck trying to figure out what is interesting, you may want to use some sort of a list to suggest things to consider. One such list is the Yellow Pages for any large city. If you live in East Little Wild Horse, go to your library. They will have Yellow Pages from some larger metropolitan areas. Go through them from front to back. Pick out and write down any area that might possibly turn out to be interesting.

Remember that some folks are naturally more passionate than others. If you don't feel the raging exaltation of Zorba the Greek, that doesn't mean something is wrong. If you have difficulty coming up with any interests and preferences, then either you don't have strong preferences, so this Inquiry will not be an important part of designing your future, or your passions have been beaten into submission. If you used to have more passionate interests than you do now, it is likely that the latter is the cause. If that is the case, you will need to find a way to regenerate your sense of passion, through your own method, career coaching, or therapy.

5. Make a hierarchical list of passions and interests, drawn from the preceding three lists. The first entry should be your area of strongest passion or interest. Then write down the next most intense passion. Continue until you run out of energy, or your hand falls asleep.

6. Ask yourself these questions: "How passionate must I feel about my work? Is it enough to be doing interesting activities? Must I also have a personal interest in the subject matter?" Remember that the answer to these questions may not be lurking about inside of you. When you ask, you may get nothing but a great vast silence in return. What does this mean? It means you are going to have to make the choice yourself, rather than count on some inner preexisting requirement. It means you have some questions to write down in your Questions List. I suggest that you read or reread the chapter called "Making Decision—A Short Course" to get clear on how to make the choice.

   If you are ready, willing, and able to draw a line in the sand in regard to how passionate or interested you must feel about your work, look through the hierarchical list you just made. Then draw a horizontal line at the cut-off point. What you want is to have all entries above the line you draw to be sufficiently interesting to be a part of your career. You may not have the talent, the personality, or the opportunity to participate in some of these things. What we are going for here is simply level of interest.

7. Now go through the list of items that are above the line. Cross off the ones you know you are not going to do. Cross off the ones that you might want to do as a hobby or sideline, but not as your main career interest.

8. Of the ones that remain above the line, which one or ones stand out as possible career areas?

9. Now it may be time to do some research on the areas of passion or interest that are still contenders.

Turn to your Primary Lists (Wants, Commitments and Requirements, and Questions), as well as to your Careers to Consider List. What can you add to those lists now? **What am I sure will definitely be an important component of my future career?**

CHAPTER 21

•

NATURAL TALENTS

*The important thing in life is to have a great aim and to possess
the aptitude and the perseverance to attain it.*

— JOHANN WOLFGANG VON GOETHE

Take a duck. Drop it in a pond. Even if it was raised in the desert and has no
swimming experience, it will be instantly at home in its new environment. In a
matter of minutes it will happily be doing what ducks do to make a living, exhibiting perfect natural mastery. It would be hard to find a more suitable candidate for pond life than a duck, even one with no previous experience. That's
because ducks are designed for the environment they inhabit. They have an ideal
set of talents for their job. They have webbed feet, bills shaped for obtaining the
special foods available pondside, and hollow feathers that act as a raft to keep
them floating high in the water. They have a waterproofing system that keeps
them dry and a layer of down to keep them warm in near-freezing water. All the
beasts of the field and the birds of the air are perfectly equipped for the highly specific way they go about making a living. Over millions of years, Mother Nature
has eliminated all the ill-suited candidates for each niche in the natural world.

One major difference between all the other creatures and human beings is that all
the individuals of most other species are pretty much alike. There are small differences between individuals, but, essentially, each giraffe is pretty much like all the
others. On the other hand, every person is a unique individual, different in many
ways from all the others. We are different from the other people around us not only
in personality, temperament, and interests but also in our innate talents. Each of us
is genetically dealt a very specific hand of talent/ability cards that gives us a knack for
playing a narrow range of roles in the working world with natural ease and mastery.

When you see someone wind surfing gracefully, like a dancer in a high wind,
moving quickly and powerfully across the sea, you are viewing the result of extensive training and a commitment to improve a body that was *born with a special gift
for balance and agility.* People who were born with less coordinated bodies are
rarely the ones out there in the stronger winds. It is more difficult for them to master the skills and usually not as much fun as it is for someone with natural talent.

Everyone is born with a unique group of talents that are as individual as a fingerprint or a snowflake. These talents give each person a special ability to do certain kinds of tasks easily and happily, yet also make other tasks seem like pure torture. Talents are completely different from acquired knowledge, skills, and interests. Your interests can change. You can gain new skills and knowledge. Your natural, inherited talents remain with you, unchanging, for your entire life. They are the hand you have been dealt by Mother Nature. You can't change them. You can, however, learn to play the hand you have been dealt brilliantly and to your best advantage. The better you understand your unique genetic gifts, the more likely you will be to have a satisfying and successful career.

Most of what we usually think of as special talents, such as music, writing, math, science, are each actually constellations of deeper, more elemental abilities that, when well combined, play together in harmony like instruments in a band. Let's use an example. Suppose you needed an operation and wanted to pick the best possible surgeon, someone with a real "gift." Obviously, other factors, such as quality of training and length of experience are also extremely important. But since you are looking for someone who is truly excellent, you want a surgeon who combines excellent training and experience with natural talent. What would comprise the elements of that special gift?

First of all, you would want someone with high spatial ability, a talent for thinking in three dimensions. How would you feel about going under the blade of a surgeon who viewed your body as an abstract philosophical concept? You would want your surgeon to be a natural in something called diagnostic reasoning. This is a talent for being able to leap to accurate conclusions based on just a few clues. If something went wrong during your operation, the surgeon would use this talent to figure out what to do quickly. Another talent to look for is something we call "low idea flow." Some people have minds that move quickly, restlessly, seemingly at a hundred miles an hour. These folks are great at improvising, but have difficulty in concentrating on one thing for long periods of time. Their brains are just zooming along too quickly. They have "high idea flow." Hawkeye, on *M*A*S*H,* is one of those people. He is supposed to be a great surgeon, but this is unlikely because his attention is scattered rather than concentrated. Next time you watch a *M*A*S*H* rerun, notice that his mind constantly leaps from one thing to another. You would want a surgeon who naturally and easily kept his or her mind totally concentrated on the task at hand. You would also want someone with "great hands." Manual dexterity is an innate gift. If you had a choice between a surgeon with superb, average, or low hand dexterity, which would you pick? There are several more pieces to the puzzle of what constitutes the natural talents of a great surgeon. But, hopefully, now you have a sense of what I mean when I speak of innate talents.

Getting to the Source of Career Difficulties

The difference between a career that is just OK and one that really soars and sings depends on fitting together many elements, all of which are important and all of which we cover in the course of *The Pathfinder*. When people complain about work, they usually bitch about fairly obvious problems they face in their jobs: the boss, the money, the hours, boredom, stress, etc. They don't realize that what stands between them and a truly satisfying career may be more complex. The obnoxious boss and the long hours are usually just the tip of the iceberg. When you are willing to put up with an OK career, then solving the obvious problems may be all that matters. But when it is important to have a perfect fit between you and your work, you have to deal with the whole iceberg.

Over the years, I have worked with thousands of clients. Many of them come to me in midcareer with the goal of changing to a new occupation. When they describe why their present careers are less than perfect, they report various factors that they believe are the main causes of their dissatisfaction. As a part of their Rockport Institute Career Choice Program, they take a testing program that measures natural talents and aptitudes. Ninety percent of the time there turns out to be a substantial mismatch between their abilities and their work. So, even if they were to solve the problems that they believe are the source of their difficulties, they would still continue to feel less than satisfied with their work.

What happens when there is a mismatch between your talents and your work? For creatures other than us humans, the answer to this question is extinction. Because we are so adaptable, we survive, but at a terrible cost. What gets extinguished is the pure joy of doing something that comes perfectly naturally. The further you get from fully expressing your talents and abilities, the less likely it is that you will enjoy your day on the job.

When important abilities go unused, people become bored with their work. When the job requires talents they do not possess, people find their work frustrating and difficult. Sometimes, having only one thing out of whack can ruin the chance for career satisfaction.

When someone performs less than optimally at work, his or her supervisor often makes inaccurate assumptions. The supervisor thinks the problem is that the employee doesn't have the right personality for the job, isn't "motivated," isn't smart enough, or has some sort of personal flaw. About half the time, supervisors correctly diagnose the problem. The rest of the time, they fail to understand that what's really going on is that the employee's innate talents don't fit well with his or her job. The supervisor's attempts to correct the situation only make things worse. What would happen if your car's fuel pump was broken, but you misdiagnosed the problem and began to adjust the carburetor? You would then have both a broken fuel pump and a carburetor problem.

The workplace has no monopoly on difficulties caused by talent mismatches.

Imagine a bright high school student with a wild, fast-flowing imagination and a talent for powerful, critical diagnostic thinking. Some kids with this combination may join the debate team, a perfect outlet for these talents that can be a great deal of fun and a major contribution to self-esteem. Others, just as worthy, just as gifted, will make a different set of assumptions. They may get rightfully bored in Miss Peabody's drone-it-right-out-of-the-book history class. To preserve their personal dignity, they may decide to opt out of school and mainstream society. This solution often leads to drugs, early pregnancy, and crime.

The Mystery of Human Talents

Until recently, the entire subject of innate talents and aptitudes was a mystery to scientists. The theories of intelligence that have dominated scientific thinking until recently essentially boiled down to slightly different versions of one single premise: Some people are smart and some people aren't. Intelligence was thought of as a single scale, like a thermometer. You either had it or you didn't. At the same time, the psychological community promoted the notion that the differences between individuals are the byproducts of our parenting, environment, and other forces that influenced our upbringing. If you were smart and well brought up, you did well in school. If you had a less than spectacular academic record, you were thought to be either lacking in brains or somehow psychologically impaired.

In the last few years, scientists have made major breakthroughs in understanding the human mind. The old theories of why each of us is a distinct and special individual are being blown down like straw houses by gale-force winds of creative research. This new thinking has not yet trickled down to reach the "man on the street," partly because the old-fashioned theories are so entrenched and their proponents are so stubborn. The scientists who led the field in the study of intelligence for most of the twentieth century, endlessly arguing the color of the emperor's cloak, had in their ponderous majesty vastly overrated their own intelligence. IQ tests were, and still are, thought of as an accurate barometer of intellectual firepower. This narrow interpretation of intelligence does not even begin to recognize the enormous range of human abilities.

Forward-looking scientists have recognized that there are different kinds of intelligence. Instead of having one big mental computer that can be measured by IQ tests, it turns out that each of us has a unique collection of smaller, highly specialized "brains" that are the reason why you are better than your friend at some things and he or she is better than you at others. Harvard psychologist Howard Gardner has sorted out seven different intelligences that, he says, everyone possesses to a greater or lesser degree. In his excellent book *Frames of Mind*, he argues that each person has a unique cognitive profile that comes from differing strengths in these intelligences. The different intelligences he recognizes include: linguistic, musical, logical-mathematical, spatial, bodily-kinesthetic, interpersonal, and intrapersonal.

Other researchers have come up with their own lists of multiple intelligences. While the lists are different, the central theme of multiple intelligences is the same. While this is all relatively new thinking to the scientific community, it is really just good old basic common sense. While the great old men of psychology were busy having enormous thoughts about minuscule differences between their theories, the average high school kid was tuned into a more accurate viewpoint on human ability. Most kids intuitively realize that their fellow students are naturally good at different things: getting good grades, tinkering with cars, athletics, babeology, organizing people or events, and so forth. No high school kid in his right mind would ever think to put the introverted computer genius in charge of selling ads for the yearbook or ask the wild, frenetic class clown to be the proofreader for the school paper.

When someone really stands out in any particular area, we recognize that they have a "gift." In the last few years, we have begun to understand that all people have their own gifts. We now know that each individual's gift is made up of several innate abilities playing together in harmony like instruments in a band. Now that we have the knowledge and the tools to understand your multiple intelligences, it is possible for you to do a much better job of choosing a career that makes use of these abilities.

Intelligence: A Natural Gift for Doing Anything Well

One of the reasons that many of the scientists never caught up with the average high school student in understanding human ability is that scientists never managed to agree on what the word *intelligence* means in the first place. Right now, they're probably out there somewhere locked in horn-to-horn combat over this weighty issue. You and I have a very practical reason for learning more about innate abilities. Since your goal in reading this book, and mine in writing it, is for you to wind up in a career that you love, let's look at the question of intelligence and ability from a practical and observable viewpoint. First of all, let's use a broader definition of "intelligence." If you consider intelligence to be "an innate capacity for doing something well," it is pretty clear that academic ability is only a small part of the total picture. Some people have a special intelligence of a natural gift for music, athletics, invention, interpersonal relationships, etc. These gifts are just as real and just as important as the combination of abilities that we call "academic ability." Usually, the talents we consider to be gifts are a combination of both the learned and innate. Some may have the innate talent to be a great violinist, but never have the opportunity to learn to play. Or they may be taught in a way that is so contrary to their learning styles that they abandon the instrument before discovering their talent.

Our conventional way of assessing ability is old-fashioned, conservative, constrained. You might find it extremely useful to open up your perspective about what you are naturally good at doing, Anything you have a natural knack for is a talent, an aptitude, a kind of intelligence to be appreciated and considered as a possible piece of the puzzle in designing your career.

What About Learned Skills?

There are two kinds of learned skills, basic and specialized. Basic learned skills consist of all the stuff we have to learn to function successfully as human beings. If we were born with our brains full size and fully developed, women would have to have hips like a rhino. Thankfully, nature thought slimmer hips was a better idea. So we are born with some of our software already installed. Then our brain grows for a few years while our parents and our tribe fill it with what we need to know. For millions of years hominids have taught their children well how to prosper in the environment and the tribe. More than 50 percent of the software we have as adults comes to us this way, through learning basic skills. Almost all humans have the natural talent to learn these basic skills.

Nowadays, we are also trained in highly specialized skills. Most of what you are good at doing is the result of long practice and acquired skill. If you are a "talented" skier, you have spent many years learning to master a technically difficult skill. The technical skills you have acquired are supported by a foundation of innate, inherited ability. Anyone, even a person with only one leg, can learn to become an intermediate skier and have a wonderful, magical time on the slopes. Unless you were raised next door to a ski course and skied constantly, it would be unlikely that you would ever get much beyond the intermediate level unless you had a natural gift for the sport. If you dedicated yourself single-mindedly to becoming an expert, I suppose you could do it. But every time you turned a hard-fought corner in increasing your skills, you would immediately face another difficult challenge. Moving each step up the skill ladder would be very difficult.

In general, people enjoy doing that which they do well. When someone becomes highly skilled at anything they were not forced to learn, it is fairly safe to assume they are expressing a natural gift. It is also safe to assume that if someone regularly spends many hours happily engaged in some hobby activity, they are expressing a natural gift. For someone born with the collection of innate abilities it takes to be a master skier or, for that matter, a master at anything, each progressive skill corner is turned much more easily. The same amount of energy and commitment that would take a less gifted person around one corner would take some-one with a natural gift around ten. So, the way to really get your work life flying is to choose a career for which you have exceptional natural talent and then put in the time and energy to become a real master. Talent and acquired skill are an unbeatable combination.

Are Innate Talents Completely Fixed and Unchangeable?

You can improve on genetically derived abilities by learning to use them fully. You can acquire a body of knowledge, experience, or training that turns ability poten-tial into actuality. You may discover talents you did not know you possessed. But, at this point in time, you cannot create a natural gift in yourself that does not ex-ist now. Innate talent can be improved in very young children. With rigorous, ex-pert training, children can learn at a level so deep that some acquired abilities are indistinguishable from inherited talents. But if you are reading this book, it's too late for you.

There is evidence coming to light that indicates that we may, in the future, dis-cover a way that adults could learn at a level of depth that duplicates innate abil-ity. But we are not there yet, and we won't be anytime soon. The most important year for learning and development is the first year of life, the next most important is the second year, and so on.

The Problem with the Solution

Most creatures are not very adaptable. The birds that live in the woods behind your house would disappear if you were to cut down the trees. If you were to cut down all similar forest environments, the other birds of that species might disap-pear as well. Many creatures inhabit such a narrow ecological niche that a seem-ingly insignificant change in their habitat can doom their species to extinction. Our fellow inhabitants of planet Earth are the ultimate job specialists. Human be-ings, on the other hand, are not only the smartest of creatures but, by far, the most adaptable. We dominate the earth partially because of that amazing adaptability. We seem to be able to make do with whatever Mother Nature throws at us. In the working world, this translates into each of us being able to fill a wide range of jobs. Given sufficient intelligence, the average human can do just about anything with reasonable competence. But there is a big difference between being able to do something and a perfect fit between you and your work. A four-hundred-pound man was once discovered clinging to the top of a tall palm tree in Florida after a

close encounter with an alligator. With typical human adaptability, he had managed to stretch his capabilities way beyond the usual limits.

Our versatility does have its downside, however. Because we are so amazingly adaptable, we've embraced a set of beliefs that causes untold mischief, particularly in our choice of careers. In general, it is believed that if you are intelligent, have the right opportunities, and are interested in the subject matter, you could just as easily be satisfied and successful as a doctor, teacher, computer programmer, or stockbroker. That point of view was perfectly valid in the past, when success was defined as financial security and nothing more. Now that people are waking up to the possibility that work can be deeply fulfilling, challenging, and fun as well as a means to financial security, we need to take a closer look at the assumptions that have guided our career choices.

Throughout history, people have had little opportunity to freely select their careers. They have been constrained by attitudes and circumstantial limitations. To start with, there were a limited number of occupations to choose from. During most of human history, only a small number of occupations was necessary for the smooth functioning of a society. A few thousand years ago, there were approximately five occupations to choose from. Five hundred years ago, the grand total rose to nearly two hundred different occupations. Only recently, and only in the developed world, has the complexity of the social fabric given rise to almost unlimited career possibilities. The U.S. government now identifies more than ten thousand different job titles. In the past people were limited to choices from within the narrow set of options available to members of their caste. In the narrower paradigm of earlier times, most people made career choices based on basic survival. You wanted to be as far away as possible from having the wolf at your door. People often were mostly concerned with picking a career that was secure, made good money, and was looked upon favorably by fellow caste members. Because of human adaptability, they were able to succeed in careers that fulfilled these requirements but had little connection with their individual natural traits. This tendency continues today. Parents whose young lives were affected by hardship and depression still counsel their children that "you're not supposed to like it, just pick something with a secure future."

Consequently, people accept the daily discomfort of a career that does not really fit their talents. They tend to put up with unsuitable, ill-fitting careers because they don't realize that their suffering is unnecessary. I have seen woodpeckers land on a metal flagpole and start tapping away, looking for supper. Each time it took only a few seconds for the bird to realize that it was in the wrong place and fly off. We human beings put up with careers that are, in some ways, as ill-suited as the metal flagpole is for a woodpecker. We can get by. We can survive. But, if you want your life to really soar, you have to find a way to match your natural abilities with your work. Otherwise, you will keep banging away at the metal flagpole, with an empty stomach, wondering why you keep getting migraines.

An Elegant Fit

It is an obvious, empirical truth that when people are doing something they enjoy and do extremely well, they get more done and they do it better. When someone is able to perform at a level of mastery, it is usually a function of making use of acquired skills and experience in conjunction with a strong foundation of natural talent. What is most important is the role of natural talents. People who are both highly successful and continue to love their work, year after year, spend most of their time at work engaged in activities that make use of their strongest abilities. They spend very little time performing functions for which they have no special gift. Their lives are concentrated on doing what they do best. If you think about it, everything on earth, except human beings, does exactly that. What could be more elegant than the fit between duck and pond, tiger and jungle? The people you envy because they are both successful and happy in their work have found their pond, their jungle. Their talents are perfectly matched with what they do.

You are probably not one of those rare people with a big, sensitive career antenna who unerringly makes career decisions early on, or you would not be reading this book. So you are faced with a question: How can you go about doing the best possible job of matching your talents and your work? How can you come closest to duplicating what the people who have succeeded in finding a perfect match for their talents have accomplished?

Self-Assessing Your Natural Talents and Aptitudes

Our culture accidentally provides the tools to learn about some aspects of our individual abilities. For example, after years of gym classes, where you had the opportunity to participate in almost every imaginable kind of athletic activity, you probably know a great deal about your innate athletic talents or the lack thereof. Because you have had such a wide exposure to different athletic activities, you could self-assess fairly accurately. If someone presented you with a survey that asked you to rate yourself in a wide range of different areas of natural athletic ability, you could most likely do a very accurate self-assessment. The same cannot be said for most of the talents and abilities that allow someone to perform brilliantly in some parts of their jobs, only competently in others, and to have a difficult time with other tasks. Although most of us appreciate our unique individuality, few of us have done more than scratch the surface in regard to recognizing and appreciating the unique profile of talents each of us has.

In addition to the problem of not having superaccurate talent-sensing antennae, there are also a couple of other problems. What you know of your talents is based only on what you have done before. If you are in midcareer and plan to choose a new career direction, you probably do not want to limit yourself to choices suggested by what you have learned from your previous experiences. It makes sense to look at a broader and deeper range of possible career options than would be evident by simply reshuffling the deck. If you are a young person making your first career decisions, it is very unlikely that you have the range of experience to even self-assess the basics accurately.

Often, people are most proud of skills they possess that took a great deal of effort to develop. At the same time, they may take for granted the things they are best at doing, because these things come so naturally and easily to them. If you met a fish who could play the piano, it would most likely be extremely proud of its skill, especially since they don't have hands. The fish would probably not be aware that its gift for swimming and breathing underwater was anything special, because these talents come so easily and naturally to it. All of these influences tend to confuse the picture in our self-assessment of our innate abilities.

Constellations of Talents

The other problem with self-assessing is that what we think of as our talents are usually collections of innate abilities working together, rather than the individual talents themselves. People say John Lennon was a genius. They say he had a gift, an extraordinary natural talent. If you think about it, he had many individual talents and personality characteristics that combined, like stars in a constellation, to make up what we think of as his genius. First of all, on the most basic level, he had the underlying musical aptitudes needed by any reasonably competent musician: tonal memory, which is a memory for complex melodies; an accurate sense of pitch; and a great sense of rhythm. These are inherited abilities. If you were born lacking in one of them, forget about making your living as a musician.

Imagine what it would be like if you were trying to make it as a musician, but you couldn't remember the tune or sing on key or had no sense of rhythm. In addition to these basics, John Lennon had many special gifts, just a few of which I will mention. He had the soul of the true revolutionary artist, always true to his vision, never compromising. On the one hand a great sage heart constantly giving everything he had, on the other a streak of rebelliousness and playful cynicism. He had a great gift for language, for subtle wordplay. He had an ability to communicate from the core of the most profound aspects of life, while taking it all lightly. He never lost that sense of wonder, which, when we allow it to dissipate, turns us into perpetual, monolithic adults. He had a lightning fast imagination and wit. He could pierce to the heart of people and issues and situations, see them clearly and from a perspective unlike anyone else's. I could go on, but the point is to idolize you, not John. Just as he had a marvelous collection of individual traits that combined into genius, so do you. One big difference between you and him is that he found a way to have all his abilities play together in perfect harmony, and get paid for it.

When people say they are good at math, or solving problems with people, or writing, they are not describing a single ability, but several working in concert. We see the loaf of bread, not the ingredients. If you think about it, there is not much you can do with a loaf of bread: make sandwiches and French toast, feed the birds. But there are innumerable ways you can combine the basic ingredients: flour, yeast, water, oil, and salt. On the shelves of your supermarket there are hundreds of items that are made from these few ingredients. So the only good way to assess your innate abilities in a way that helps you design a career that will fit you perfectly is to get down to the deepest level, the basic abilities that combine to make up your unique profile of talents. And the one way to do that well is to go through an in-depth career testing program.

Career Testing Programs

I personally think it makes no sense to attempt to make career decisions without being absolutely clear about your talents and aptitudes. You can access all the other pieces of the puzzle through the Inquiries in this book, but to get clarity on this most important area, you need testing. Programs that test innate abilities are very different from the kinds of tests traditionally given by career counselors. Most people who have taken old-fashioned career interest tests say it made no big contribution to their ability to make life/work decisions. Programs that test abilities are entirely different. Since they focus on measuring natural talents, they teach you something really important, something that gives you an edge in making excellent career decisions.

Going through a testing program that measures natural talents and abilities is such a powerfully effective tool that I recommend it to all of my career-decision-making clients. Time after time, clients say they are amazed that they could learn so much about themselves from a series of tests. Midcareer clients quickly realize why they have not achieved the satisfaction or success they wanted. Again and again they say, "I wish I had done this years ago." Younger people, making a first-time choice, say that for the first time they understand which careers would fit them best and why. Clients of all ages learn how to use all their important talents in harmony to create a future that is not a compromise.

If you want to know more about getting your innate abilities tested, contact Rockport Institute. You will find contact information in the back of the book in a section called "Getting in Touch." Rockport offers testing programs worldwide. Many of our affiliates and various other organizations also offer testing programs. If you call, write, or E-mail, we will let you know what is available. The cost of most good testing programs ranges around $500.

The following Inquiry is designed to help you self-assess your innate abilities. You may not have the means or the conviction to go through a testing program, in which case use this Inquiry to learn as much as you can about your abilities. Even if you plan to get tested, you will find it useful. It is, however, no substitute for the real thing. The balance of this chapter introduces you to some of the most important innate talents. You may read these descriptions and know by experience or intuition exactly where you are on each of these scales. It is more likely that you will recognize that you are high or low in a couple or a few of these, but not be sure where you stand in regard to others. Almost certainly, you will not fully understand how your abilities can fit together elegantly in some careers and not so well in others. These descriptions may be sufficient for you to diagnose some of what is missing or ill-fitting about your present work, or serve as the catalyst for insights into what careers would fit you. Still, the best way to really know is to get professionally tested. We did our best to include a complete testing program in *The Pathfinder,* but given the complex nature of the many different tests, it was impossible to do so.

INQUIRY 19

WHAT ARE MY NATURAL TALENTS?

In this Inquiry you will first take a look into what you now perceive as your natural gifts. Then you will read through descriptions of known natural talents to further self-assess your abilities.

1. Make a list of everything that comes naturally to you, for which you seem to have a "knack." Include everything, both work-related and otherwise. Don't include those areas where you think you have developed a skill but have no real natural talent. For example, as a boy I swam competitively on a national level. It would seem, at first glance, that I was a talented swimmer. Actually, I was there because I happened to be on a great team with a great coach and because my dad forced me to go to a very rigorous team practice every morning. Just list those areas in which you feel you are a "natural." What were you known for in school? What do you excel in at work? What do you enjoy most? What work activities do you not consider as work but as fun? What would other people say you were especially good at? Include personality traits as well. They are just as much elements of your "talent profile" as special knacks you may have. You may want to ask people who know you well to contribute to this Inquiry. Ask your spouse, your boss, your parents, and others who may have different points of view from yours.

2. Make another list of everything you are not naturally good at. This is just as important as the former list. A profile of your talents includes both the highs and lows. If you think you are good at almost everything, I can suggest one thing to put on this list: self-assessment.

3. Write out a "talent profile" of yourself. Keep it brief. Here's a sample:
   "I am specially gifted at working with things and objects. I seem to understand them naturally. It does not feel like work to solve problems in designing, building, and repairing objects. For years I did not realize this as a talent because it came to me so easily. I work quickly, seeking the solution to many problems with a sort of accurate intuition. I seem to have

the best solution pop into my head. I am also good at organizing anything. My mind works very rapidly. That is fine for fighting field fires, at which I am excellent and enjoy, but I get bored quickly with anything that becomes repetitive. I also get bored with having the same problems and situation reoccur. I seem to enjoy work only when there is a fast flow of really thorny problems that need a new and creative solution."

4. When you are finished, go on to the descriptions of natural talents that follow. As you read them, keep mentally comparing them with yourself. Is this talent one you are extraordinarily gifted at, above average, average, or not so good at? To get a clear sense of each of these abilities, think of your friends and family. Who is a total klutz in this area? Who is a wizard?

5. When you have read and absorbed these descriptions, go back to your talent profile and rewrite it to include other talents you have now recognized.

6. Which of these talents could play a big part in your career choice?

7. Which are so important that you will include them in your commitment list?

Turn to your Primary Lists (Wants, Commitments and Requirements, and Questions), as well as to your Careers to Consider List. What can you add to those lists now? **What am I sure will definitely be an important component of my future career?** *Remember to go over all the career-choice work you have done so far in your journey through* The Pathfinder.

Descriptions of Natural Talents and Aptitudes

SPATIAL, TANGIBLE, AND NONSPATIAL

Each of us is born with our own natural way of understanding the world around us. The spatial–nonspatial scale provides some important basic information about how you experience and understand your environment, how you perceive the world, and what you understand and work with most naturally and easily. Deciding on a career without being aware of this important distinction has caused untold havoc in the careers of millions of people.

Some people have an inborn talent for understanding and working easily with three-dimensional reality. They are usually happiest in careers where the work is mainly concerned with thinking about or working directly with "things" (objects). Both a biologist and an architect spend most of their time at work thinking about three-dimensional objects even though they may not come in physical contact with the actual objects. Architects without a natural talent for perceiving and working with three-dimensional reality would, in time, almost certainly grow to dislike their careers. Most people with this talent would experience a profound lack of fit with careers that are not spatial. Examples of careers that make use of spatial talent include science, medicine, dentistry, farming, trades such as carpentry and plumbing, mechanics, architecture, interior design, engineering, robotics, inventing, choreography, sculpture, and patent law.

To others, life occurs mainly as concepts that have little to do with three-dimensional reality. This ability is the opposite of spatial talent. Those scoring high on the nonspatial scale are especially gifted in understanding nonphysical, conceptual reality. When spatial people look at a house, they usually concentrate their perceptions on the structural, physical aspects of the house, whereas the nonspatial person may think mainly about the lives of the people who live in the house, its value as an investment, the feeling it projects, or any number of nonphysical perceptions or concepts about the house. Examples of careers that require nonspatial talent are teaching poetry, constitutional law, artificial intelligence, statistics, sociology, linguistics, art criticism, finance, corporate management, sales and marketing, economics.

NON-SPATIAL	TANGIBLES	SPATIAL (3-D)

A third group scores in the middle area, between the spatial and nonspatial people. They fit best in careers that are concerned with tangibles. Many physicians who practice specialties that do not require true three-dimensional ability score in this range. So do many lawyers who practice criminal law, where physical evidence and a chain of tangible events always play important roles. Hands-on, day-to-day management fits this ability, as does career counseling, where clients are coached to make realistic choices about their futures.

ABSTRACT OR CONCRETE?

Some people are naturally result-oriented and driven to seek concrete results. This is obviously an important trait for anyone in a "get the job done" business. Others are perfectly happy to cogitate forever on abstractions. People who score on the abstract end of the scale are usually happiest in work that is theoretical or concept-oriented. Their work does not need to produce tangible results in the world of physical reality. For example, many economists are unperturbed when their predictions about trends turn out to be inaccurate. Their interest is in a reality so abstract that their thinking does not need to refer directly to any practical aspect of reality. When you combine this scale with the spatial–

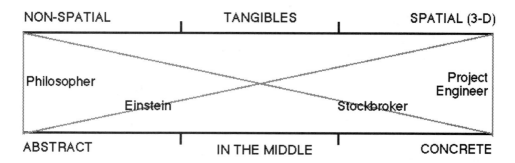

NON-SPATIAL   TANGIBLES   SPATIAL (3-D)

Philosopher

Einstein

Project Engineer

Stockbroker

ABSTRACT   IN THE MIDDLE   CONCRETE

nonspatial scale, you get some excellent clues as to what sorts of careers would fit you best.

Someone with a spatial talent could be concrete, which would be appropriate for an engineer or someone in construction, or they could be abstract, like Albert Einstein. A nonspatial person could be oriented toward producing results, like a stockbroker or corporate manager, or they could be abstract, like a philosopher or Jungian psychologist. Of course, there are many other possible positions on these scales. Career difficulties are almost a certainty if you and your work do not mesh well in these important areas. Doing business with people whose profiles do not mesh with your expectations also causes untold grief. For example, many people who become psychotherapists are nonspatial abstracts. A therapist with this profile might be helpful to someone seeking more understanding or a sounding board. They would not be of much help to someone seeking to produce real concrete changes rapidly.

PROBLEM-SOLVING APTITUDES

When most people consider someone to be a "good problem solver," they are usually unaware that there is more than one kind of problem-solving ability. The most common are diagnostic and analytical reasoning. Each is a very powerful talent for solving certain kinds of problems. People who score high in these aptitudes need to find a daily outlet for them.

DIAGNOSTIC REASONING

Diagnostic reasoning is a gift for quickly seeing a relationship between apparently unrelated facts, for forming an accurate conclusion from a few scattered bits of evidence. It is the ability to leap to accurate conclusions without using a logical, step-by-step approach. It allows a person who possesses it to instantly perceive a link between seemingly unrelated bits of information. It is especially useful in situations where there is no way to logically solve the problem, where an accurate diagnosis must be made without having all of the facts available. Scientists use this ability to create new theories by perceiving relationships and connections between discrete bits of evidence. Newton used diagnostic reasoning when he discovered gravity on that fateful day when the apple fell on his head. If his talent had been in analytical reasoning, his conclusion would more likely have been: You should not sit under apple trees when the apples are ripe and the wind is blowing.

A physician uses this ability to quickly and accurately pinpoint the illness at the root of a group of symptoms. A critic uses it to critique a movie or restaurant, to come to a conclusion that unifies many individual impressions. Diagnostic reasoning is a powerfully active ability that can cause as many problems as it solves. People with this talent need to have a constant flow of new problems. They may have a fascination with learning a new job or skill and then get bored as soon they have it figured out and are not presented with a new problem to sink their teeth into. When high scorers have a career that does not use it regularly, diagnostic reasoning keeps on running and critiques whatever gets in its path: the workplace, the boss, and all too often turns to self-criticism. In many careers, this ability is a liability. For example, in traditional corporate management and other careers that place a premium on maintaining the status quo, the diagnostic problem solver's drive to ferret out unworkability, get to the heart of every problem, and bring these problems, along with suggested solutions, to the attention of senior management, who didn't even recognize there was a problem, is usually considered to be unwanted boat rocking and complaining.

Examples of careers that utilize diagnostic reasoning: emergency room medicine, advertising, comedy, counseling, critical writing, teaching of complex ideas, criticism, repair work where repairing includes diagnosis of problems (such as auto repair), troubleshooting.

ANALYTICAL REASONING

Analytical reasoning is the form of problem solving most trusted in the modern world. People who have this ability solve problems by organizing concepts, information, or things in a logical sequence. People who score high in this ability are happiest in an environment where there is a reccurring need to plan, organize, create order, schedule, or solve logical puzzles. Just as great legs are the key to admission to the Rockettes, analytical reasoning is an absolutely essential aptitude for some careers such as engineering, computers, and editing. Other careers that make use of this ability include data analysis, conference planning, law, business planning, investment analysis, and any profession where significant time is spent organizing resources, schedules, people, or information.

RATE OF IDEA FLOW

Have you noticed that some people never seem to run out of new ideas, plans, or things to say? These individuals would score high on the Rockport Idea Flow Test. A high score in this aptitude indicates a very rapid flow of thoughts and difficulty in concentrating for long periods of time. You can easily recognize this ability in extroverted people because they communicate spontaneously and are able to think quickly on their feet. It is more difficult to pick out this trait in introverted people unless they go through a testing program. A lower score indicates a slower flow of thoughts and a more concentrated, focused approach. In the arts, a modern artist who painted spontaneously and quickly, like Picasso, would be a good example of quick idea flow. At the other, low idea flow end of the spectrum would be an engraver, who would benefit from a mind that naturally and easily focused for long periods of time. In medicine, the emergency room might be a good place for someone with a high flow of ideas, and surgery might be a good speciality for someone with low idea flow. Most people are somewhere between the high and low extremes of the idea flow scale. Each career also has a specific place on the scale. When choosing a career for maximum satisfaction, it is absolutely imperative that your job closely matches your rate of idea flow.

Careers that make use of high idea flow include advertising, sales, classroom teaching, training, lecturing, fiction writing, the improvisational arts, entrepreneurial business, publishing, television, radio, lobbying, reception, and the hospitality industry. A lower score in idea flow suggests a career where an ability to concentrate your attention is an advantage. Persons with lower scores do not have ideas or solutions inferior to those with high scores, they just have fewer of them. This is often an advantage. In business, the high idea flow manager will often keep switching directions in response to his or her wild imagination. A manager with lower idea flow would be more suited to conventional management, where the task is to roll the big snowball up the mountain steadily using standard operating procedures. Would you rather have a surgeon with a wild, tumultuous imagination, or one with an extraordinary ability to concentrate single-mindedly on the tasks at hand? Careers that require a lower score in idea flow include banking, corporate management, research, accounting, engineering, dentistry, and administration.

FORETHOUGHT

This measures your ability to project yourself into the future easily and naturally. A high score suggests a preference for work on projects that continue over a long span of time. In the field of sales, someone with a high score would likely be more satisfied with selling something that took several months of planning and negotiation to complete. Someone with a lower score is usually much happier with tasks that can be completed in a short span of time. The person with a lower score would prefer to see the customer, make the sale, and go on to the next sale.

People with lower scores often have more difficulty in college unless they learn to take this ability into consideration. They have trouble seeing a connection between the paper they are writing now and their future goals. They tend to live in the present and usually have a foggy sense of the distant future. Many of them have no concrete plans that extend into the future. This is not always a disadvantage. People with a lower score have the advantage in work that consists of fulfilling short-term goals rather than extended projects.

VISUAL DEXTERITY

A high score in visual dexterity indicates a gift for working quickly and accurately with the clerical tasks and the pen-and-paper details of the working world. It indicates a special ability to deal with the mounds of paperwork that are a part of professions such as editing, accounting, secretarial work, banking, and law. If you have a high score in this aptitude, you won't necessarily have a passionate love affair with paperwork, but you will be good at getting it done quickly. Those with high scores are terrific proofreaders and extremely detail-oriented. Those with a low score are less gifted in noticing typos and dealing with details. As students, they are often be penalized for their difficulty in crossing every "t" and dotting every "i" correctly. People with a high score often "miss the forest for the trees." They tend to divide life into pieces and parts, thereby missing the "big picture." They think of the forest as made up of a specific, measurable number of trees. Someone with a lower score will usually have a more holistic viewpoint. They will easily grasp the impact of the forest but have less ability to view the forest as individual trees. Most physicians are very high in visual dexterity. They tend to look at ailments of the body as specific symptoms caused by the malfunction of a specific organ. Physicians with an interest in preventative medicine or with a more holistic mind-body interpretation of illness usually score somewhat lower in this measure.

ASSOCIATIVE MEMORY

This test measures an aptitude for learning vocabulary in other languages and memorizing by association. It can be used to learn foreign languages, technical jargon, or computer languages. It is also a useful ability for politicians and others who need to easily remember the names of many people. If you have a low or midrange score in this ability, it does not mean that you cannot learn languages. It will simply take longer for you to memorize vocabulary. A very low score suggests that you should avoid work that involves heavy doses of memorization, such as computer programming.

NUMBER MEMORY

A high score in number memory suggests a gift for remembering numbers and details easily. It is useful in accounting, banking, tax law, and statistics. People with a very high score are usually gifted at remembering a vast range of encyclopedic facts and details. They are often terrific at games like "Trivial Pursuit." This ability is useful to tax lawyers, inventory workers, and all others who need to commit to memory a vast quantity of detailed information.

DESIGN MEMORY

Design memory is an ability that allows the person who possesses it to remember visual images easily. It is useful to architects, who need to remember design details seen previously. It is the secret weapon of those cab drivers who seem to know and remember every inch of a city. After driving to a location once or twice, a person scoring high in this ability will usually be able to give detailed directions from memory.

MANUAL SPEED AND ACCURACY

This is a gift for fast and accurate hand movements. It is a talent obviously necessary for a surgeon or a pianist. If your score is high in this ability, you should, at the very least, have a regular hobby that makes use of this ability, such as wood carving, painting, drawing, cooking, crocheting, theatrical makeup, gardening, calligraphy, darts, instrumental music, etc.

BODY-KINESTHETIC

Body intelligence combines a sensitive perception of the body and the ability to control it with great skill that lets some of us operate with mastery in the physical universe. It is essential for athletes, performers, construction trades workers, farmers, hunters, dancers, soldiers, surgeons, mechanics, dentists, massage therapists, and drummers.

INTUITION

Intuition is knowing or sensing without using rational thought processes or problem-solving abilities. Even though intuition has been the subject of investigation for hundreds of years, we still know nothing about it, how it works, or where it comes from. All we can say for sure is that perceptions, truths, solutions, and new ideas are projected on the screen of our minds from an invisible and unknown source. The only other thing we know about intuition is that it is not an ability that some people have and others don't. When the time comes for a transformation in some aspect of human culture, many people intuit the new paradigm. The one who gets out hammer and nails and actually builds the thing gets the credit, but many others "pick it up" with their intuition antennae. When I was a little boy, I had a flash of insight into the nature of reality that I discovered years later was nearly identical to the unified field theory that Einstein spent most of his adult years trying to prove. "Wow," I thought at the time. Five minutes later, I was back trying unsuccessfully to make an escape-proof pen for box turtles. Probably millions of other people have had the same insight and minutes later returned to their day-to-day turtle pit thoughts. It just goes to show that if you have a great brainstorm, you had better get moving and make something of it. There are millions of other intuition antennae out there twitching in the breeze, just nanoseconds behind you.

CREATIVITY

Everyone has his or her own notion of creativity. Most of my midcareer clients say they want more of it in their work. Sometimes they mean they want more interesting problems to solve. Others want more variety or to use an underutilized set of talents. In the present context, I am speaking of creativity in its purest form: the ability to invent, to create that which did not exist before. Whether it be an artistic work, a scientific breakthrough, or a new way to do business, true creativity is the spark that ignites social evolution. It creates new, previously unimaginable pathways and possibilities. We often mistake self-expression for creativity. Most artists are not really creative, they are self-expressive. True creativity always involves a paradigm change, a transformation and a new way of perceiving or understanding. The ability to invent is the most extraordinary of human aptitudes. It is the one thing that distinguishes us from the other inhabitants of planet Earth. You may not be an Einstein or a Picasso, but you have an untapped reservoir of this most extraordinary ability. You can invent yourself. You can be the author of your life.

ARTISTIC ABILITY

Many people have a special gift for some form of artistic expression. Unfortunately, in the arts there are more talented people than there are jobs. If you have one of the many varieties of artistic ability: writing, music, dance, drawing, sculpting, and so forth, find a way to make one a permanent part of your life, even if you are not gifted enough to make your living with it. If you have really special talent, go for it. Go with it. Let it take over your life. Don't hold back.

INTRAPERSONAL — ACCESS TO YOUR INNER LIFE AND FEELINGS

Some people have almost no access to their inner life. They can distinguish pleasure from pain, but are completely unaware of the constantly changing flow of the tides of their inner life. At the other end of the spectrum are people who are aware of every subtle emotional nuance and who can call upon these distinctions to guide their actions and choices. This keen intrapersonal intelligence is found in the best poets, novelists, actors, painters, therapists, and mentors.

SOCIAL INTELLIGENCE

There are several kinds of social intelligence. You may have a gift for one or more of them. One form is the ability to accurately perceive and understand other's moods, motives, and intentions. Someone with this talent has a kind of interpersonal X-ray vision that enables them to read other people, even if their subjects are attempting to conceal their true thoughts and feelings. Some people have a variety of this ability that works only with individuals, one on one. This is an extremely useful ability for counselors, salespeople, employment interviewers, managers, and police detectives. Others have a gift for understanding and affecting groups. The best politicians, seminar speakers, religious leaders, and teachers possess this "group reading" aptitude. A third form of social intelligence is an ability to get along with others. Some people possess all three varieties of social intelligence. Truly excellent managers have a gift for all three. They can "read people like a book." They pick up subtle signals that allow them to manage individual employees with sensitivity and to understand the ever-changing dynamics of the group they lead. They also get along with people easily and naturally.

Back to Your Lists

Now that you have read about all of these innate abilities, please return to the "What Are My Talents?" Inquiry and rewrite your talent profile to include what you have learned in the last few pages. Do your best to write out a comprehensive statement of what you are naturally gifted at doing. Then, dig into your Primary Lists. What commitments are you ready to make? What questions do you need to answer? What do you want that is not now on your list. Also see if there is anything to enter on your Careers to Consider List. Don't do these Inquiries mechanically. Put your heart and soul into them.

CHAPTER 22
•
MEANING, MISSION, PURPOSE

A vision without a task is but a dream, a task without a vision is drudgery; a vision and a task is the hope of the world.

—FROM AN INSCRIPTION ON AN OLD ENGLISH CHURCH

Why do you get up in the morning and go to work? Do you wake up with the same enthusiasm on workdays as you do on the weekend? Even if your career fits your personality and uses your talents fully, it will not be truly satisfying if you go to work because you have to. Working because you have to pay the bills is just as much a form of bondage as slavery. The chains are subtle, invisible, the enthrallment accepted without much of a struggle. Wage slaves are forced to report to work every weekday morning, against their will, or face the lash of their mortgage company and credit bureau. There are only two practical ways out of this life of servitude. The first is to make so much money that you can buy your freedom. The second is to choose a career you care about. Although you still have to pay your dues and meet your monthly payments, you do not go to work because you must but because you want to.

Ensconced in a new, more meaningful career, you discover that you actually look forward to going to work. Sure, you are still a human being. Little pink wings haven't sprouted from your back. There will be days when you fall out of the wrong side of a bed of nails. Days when wild horses could not drag you out of your funk. But much more often there is a sense of excitement and enthusiasm for the day ahead.

In the next few pages, you will have an opportunity to take a look at what really matters to you, decide how important it is to have your career express this, and to design some important components of your future career. Before we can talk about any of these, we have to lay a little groundwork. What I am going to propose in the next few pages may click as the absolute truth, or it may contradict some of the things you have been taught. Please remember that we're not on a search for universal truth here. We are just working together to get you into a career you will love. There can be many ways of looking at truth, at the meaning of life that seem to conflict with each other. And yet, when we look deeply into our own intuition, these apparently opposite points of view can be equally true.

The real problem is not discovering what is meaningful to you, but finding a way you would be ready, willing, and able to express it in your work. What is difficult is making the transition from understanding to commitment, from realization to action. Although most of us have ready access to what we care about, we often have trouble making the journey from knowing what we care about to actually living our lives as an expression of what matters to us. This next section provides an opportunity to bring the ideal of meaningful work down to earth, where it can grow and flourish.

Meaningful Work

Everyone wants to do work they care about, that they find inherently interesting. Even those rare people who say it doesn't matter would pick doing something they care about before something they didn't. Everyone would rather spring out of bed looking forward to a workday filled with interesting projects than shuffle off to the salt mine. Each of us has our own internal model of what matters, what is interesting and worthwhile. It is highly personal and can be completely different from one person to the next. By "meaningful" you might mean working toward fulfilling your highest ideals, or you might be perfectly satisfied simply doing something you like or feel is especially interesting. Most of us, although we might deny it, believe that what is personally significant to us is what is truly and universally meaningful. We tend to think our own religion, our taste in music, and our understanding of life is just slightly more in touch, and hence more meaningful, than those people who look from a different set of eyes. Bodybuilders cannot understand how ninety-eight-pound weaklings could be perfectly satisfied with their lives. People interested in personal growth often consider folks who do not share their sense of meaning to be less evolved.

Each of us has our own personal perspective on what matters, based on our upbringing, our genetic heritage, the culture we are a part of, and so forth. That which means the most to you may not matter very much to other intelligent, caring people. If each of us has our own idea of what is meaningful, then there are literally billions of somewhat different realities coexisting with each other. If you have any doubt that this is true, see if you can find one single person whose idea of what is meaningful is exactly like yours. Could it be possible that each of these points of view, no matter how radically different from our own, could be just as valid as ours? Could it be that what is meaningful to the family next door is just as intrinsically meaningful as what is important to you and me? How about the guy across the street who is passionate about fishing? What makes saving whales more important than fishing? I suggest that it is one thing and one thing only: Because you say so. What is meaningful to you or me derives every speck of that meaning from our own personal interpretation, not from a committee of angels who voted it onto the list. The enormous variety of different interpretations is what makes us such a rich and varied tribe.

The Game of Life

If each of us has a different viewpoint about of what is meaningful, and other people's points of view are just as real and valid as yours and mine, then all meaning derives from someone's personal interpretation. If you were to travel across the entire universe and explore every corner of it, you might return to tell us that the physicists and mystics got it right; that everything in the universe is exactly as meaningful as everything else. Some stuff is bigger. Other stuff is smaller. Some is closer. Some farther away. There is fast stuff and slow stuff. Some stuff exists. Other stuff doesn't. But nothing means anything by itself. You give it the meaning it has for you. Gandhi or Elvis are not inherently any more meaningful than a lamp. Yes, one or both of them may be more meaningful to you, but not necessarily to your lamp-worshipping next-door neighbors. But, you say, Elvis has done so much more for the world than my lamp. Ah, very true. Good point. But that is more meaningful only to people who believe it is better to do more. The lamp worshipers next door may believe that doing less is better. Let's look at this from a bigger perspective. Imagine the entire universe stretching out forever in all directions with billions of galaxies each containing billions of stars. How meaningful would it be on a cosmic scale if we humans really screwed up completely and turned our beautiful little blue planet into a cinder? Every time we glance up at the stars, we may be looking directly toward millions of planets where the inhabitants used up all their resources and lie mummified on the surface of their former paradise. Tell the truth now, which is more meaningful to you, millions of mummified civilizations or that your credit card is topped out?

If the previous paragraphs ring true to you, then you could invent a new way to look at life as a wondrous game that you are in the midst of playing. What is a game? It is an activity where you take some stuff and, based on a set of rules, give it meaning. You make some things more important than others. In Monopoly, hotels are better than houses. Why? Because the rules say so. If it doesn't matter whether you have more properties or money or hotels, there is no game. The game starts when you decide to play and accept a set of rules. In Monopoly, you agree that it is better to buy Boardwalk than Baltic Avenue. If nothing is more important or meaningful than anything else, there is no game. But, remember, the meaning comes from the rules of the game.

If you know you are playing a game, you can make up new rules or decide to play a new game whenever you want. You are not stuck with the rules that were printed on the box. For example, you could decide that the first person to go broke wins, the most generous player wins, whoever lands on Baltic Avenue wins, or you could just declare everyone a winner. On the other hand, if you think the game you are playing represents the one true reality, you are stuck forever with it. When you are aware that you are in the midst of a game, you can choose to keep playing the same one you have been playing by the same set of rules. You could keep playing the same game and make up new rules (and new meaning.) Or, if you want, you could switch to a completely different game. *It is completely up to you!*

You always have a choice. One would think that everyone living in a culture on the edge of survival, where droughts and famines are a constant threat, would be forced to play only the most ancient games: eat, procreate, seek shelter from the storm, and take care of yourself before all others; but this is not the case. There are people who, at the brink of starvation, are enormously generous, sharing what little they have with others.

One way to make life really exciting is to forget it is a game. It is like going to the movies and seeing a film that is so compelling that you forget you are watching a movie. Your identity as a separate observer disappears. You become so entranced by the action on screen that nothing else exists. You become so completely plugged in to experiencing all the adventures, the joys and tragedies, that you forget that it is a film. In the various life games we play, the same thing happens. We become so entranced with playing the game that we do not notice that it is a game. We forget that whatever we are playing is not the only possible game.

It is both terrifying and enormously liberating to break out of the prison of our beliefs. When you awaken to the possibility and begin to live from the ground of being that everything you have ever believed and that is meaningful to you has no real significance other than what you choose to give to it, the entire universe as you have known it collapses. All that you have ever learned becomes open to question. You find you have no solid ground to stand on. You discover how little of what you think, what you believe, and how you behave you have ever had any choice about. You realize that you have not been the cause of that which happens in your life. You have been the effect of all that you have assumed to be true, real, and meaningful. You realize that your assumption that you have been thinking for yourself all these years has been false; that you have had a free choice about what you think, what you believe, and about the direction of your journey through life just about as much as does a toy electric train on a small, circular track. At the same time, you are for the first time freed from the track you have been running on. (When this happened to Bucky Fuller, he spent the subsequent two years in almost total silence, reconsidering everything he knew, learning to truly think for himself rather than just parrot that which he had heard and read.) Now, you can go where you will; lay your own track in any direction you choose. You can even decide, if you wish, that you will not be a little toy train anymore, even one freed of running on a fixed track. You can reinvent yourself, play new games. You don't have to wait. If you have followed along so far, you can take the next step and take a look at which games you have been playing up until now. When you can stand face to face with the truth, you can begin to invent new games and new rules, or you can wholeheartedly choose to continue playing the ones you are already familiar with.

Here is a list of some of the games we humans play. Every moment of your life is spent playing one or more of them. You may notice that you play most of them at one time or another. Each of us has at least one "master game," a game that has seniority over all others. It is the game you have, probably unknowingly, devoted your life to playing. This game supersedes all the others. It shapes your life, your thinking, your goals and defines what is meaningful to you. As you read through the list, ask yourself, "Which ones do I play? Which ones am I playing now?"

Dark Games

Zombie: Lives a completely mechanical existence, just goes through the motions of living.

Sufferer: Lives in perpetual darkness. Hates the game of life itself, but is in terror of reaching the end.

Criminal: Sees others as a "mark" or as a commodity to manipulate. This includes the professional criminals, many inner-city young people, and many other more socially acceptable criminals. This category includes many supposedly upstanding people who use others for their own ends and hardly notice the suffering they cause. Throughout history there have been plenty of industrial magnates, lawyers, politicians and many others who belong in this category.

The Games People Usually Play

Tribal Primate: Lives exactly the same way people did 100,000 years ago. Gets up in the morning, fulfills a gender role, raises kids, chats with other tribe members, goes to bed. This is the human variation on the basic ancient game of life: eat, procreate, seek shelter from the storm, and survive.

Leaf in the Wind: Goes whichever way life leads, does not make any big decisions. Amazing as it might seem, this game can sometimes lead to high leadership positions.

The Comfort Junkie: Does anything to remain at equilibrium, to avoid pain. This game is often at the core of addictive behaviors, couch potatodom, and risk avoiding. "Always return to equilibrium ASAP" is one the most basic rules of animal physiology and psychology. No wonder it is one of the most favored games of the human race. You play this one often. So does everyone else.

Hog in the Trough: Get more, eat more, have more, buy a bigger one. Wrestle, grunt, and shove to get as much as possible.

Power and Domination: Played on innumerable different fields. Can involve controlling territory, people, or information. A game played by people from many walks of life: from a little child having a tantrum to the macho man, from cops to serial killers, from the high priests of religions to sex sirens.

Security: Being protected from future changes in circumstance is the key. The game is to store lots of nuts against the possibility of famine.

Driven: These people run endlessly around whatever treadmill they are on, never finished, never complete, never at peace.

In Control or Not Out of Control: Controls his or her environment, inside and out. One of the most prevalent games. Played by everyone, nearly always.

The Social Animal: The game is relationships and interplay with other people. The real players of this game have much more of themselves invested in social interaction than most other people do.

Looking Good, or **"I'm cool":** Gets his or her sense of self from peering in the mirror of what they perceive others think of them. "I am what I think I see of me reflected in the eyes of other people."

Rebellion and Compliance: Two sides of the same coin. They do what others want, or exactly the opposite.

I'm the Boss: Runs the show, may be the commander in chief of an empire or just one small goldfish.

The Wise One: Knows all the answers.

Kid at Play: Carpe diem, perennial kid.

The Hedonist: If it feels good, do it. If it doesn't feel good, don't do it.

The Adventurer: Plays daring games, seeks new experiences, unknown territory. This can be played in the external world or within one's own psyche.

The Dreamer: Perfectly happy floating in his or her internal cosmos without needing to bring his or her dreams down to earth.

Dedicated to Truth: The philosopher, seeker of the grail of understanding.

Art and/or Beauty: Devoted to appearance, fashion, design, lovely things, art appreciation.

Problem Solver: Everything is a problem to be solved.

The Performer: Always onstage

The Artist: The self-expressed person who communicates through works of art.

Personal Growth: Attention is turned inward toward self-discovery and improvement. Their psyches and souls are the works of art they are sculpting. May think they should be listed under the following "Games of Contribution" category, but working on one's own self does not necessarily make a contribution to anyone else.

Excellence: The game of producing extraordinary results at whatever you are doing and whoever you are being.

Games of Contribution

Making the World a Better Place: Living from a commitment to contributing to others. Living life to give a gift of well-being to others. (People pushing their religious or political views on others do not belong here. They are playing domination, not contribution.)

Creativity: This game has nothing to do with the field in which it is played. It can just as easily be expressed in sports or business as in the arts. At its essence is visionary magic and the inspired genesis of something new. It involves inventing a new paradigm, bringing a new paradigm to the world, the creation of new possibilities, or new ways of expression. It transforms our world in some way. Pablo Picasso, Thomas Jefferson, the Beatles, and Albert Einstein are all examples of people who played this game. It is not, however, reserved for an elite. You can play anytime. Whenever you open yourself to new possibilities that transform your relationships with yourself, with others, your work, or the world around you, you are playing this game.

Service (agent of the universe): A game that few people are ready to play. The rules of this game ask that you give up your position as the center of the universe in favor of serving. You give up your identity as a psychological being mainly concerned with fulfilling your desires. You give yourself as a gift to the universe to do with you as it will. This is a game you get a chance to play when you are no longer in need of more fulfillment, when you are totally whole and complete. But be careful. Some of the people who say they are playing this game are really up to something else.

INQUIRY 20

WHAT AM I PLAYING FOR?

Most people go through life unaware that they are in the midst of games they play endlessly, for stakes they never consciously chose. Since what is meaningful to you is the direct result of what games you are involved in, please take a few minutes and do an inventory of your game collection.

1. Go through the list of games. Mark all the games you play or have ever played during the course of your life. Don't forget the games you play only occasionally. Even the most awake, aware person may occasionally play a few hands of Zombie. You may find that you play most or all of the games on the list.

2. Go through the list again, putting a different identifying mark next to those games you play often and the ones that are a regular part of your life.

3. Go through the list a third time. This time, you want to get it down to one or two main games. What is that most dominant game, your master game? Which game runs the show? The answer to this question is not hidden somewhere deep within. It should be relatively easy to find because it is the central organizing principle of your life. If more than one game is vying for the championship, you may be able to sort it out by asking yourself, "Which of these do I play all the time, in every situation?" Reveal to yourself which one or ones is/are actually running the show, not which one you would like to play. If you are not excited about the one that you discover has been running the show, you can always make up a new main game. But for the time being, just blow away the fog and do your best to get to the truth.

4. One of the central principles of the concept of "game" is that in a game, the rule book defines one destination as more desirable than the others. Every game has an objective. In Monopoly it is to be the only player who has not gone bankrupt. If there is no destination, there is no game. If, in Monopoly, you just throw the dice when your turn comes and cruise happily around the board without caring if you amass properties, you are not playing Monopoly. Who knows what you are playing? It may be Saint or Lunatic, but it ain't Monopoly. How do you win the games you play? What is the main objective of your biggest and most dominant games? What do you really get from playing that game?

Here is a list of some possible objectives. It is far from complete. Use it to get some hints to help you uncover the objective of your own game. You may notice that these objectives are just more games. Games inside of games inside of games.

- Survive
- Eat, procreate, seek shelter from the storm
- The one who dies with the most toys wins
- Success (whatever that means to you)
- Avoid pain and other unpleasant sensations
- Continue to validate my identity as _____ (good guy, desirable, smart, etc.)
- Be right, avoid being wrong (maybe by making other people wrong)
- Do unto others as you would have them do unto you
- Be taken care of
- Do unto others before they do it to you
- Be entertained. Enjoy. Have fun
- Fit in
- Dominate and avoid domination
- Consistently produce excellent results
- Have people think I am cool
- Make the greatest contribution to humankind that I can

At this very moment you are asking yourself the most powerful question a human being can ask him- or herself: WHAT AM I PLAYING FOR? You are revealing the core of what runs your life. It is not something mysterious. It is so obvious that you may not have noticed it before. It may be the perfect game for you, or it may not be. It may or may not be as noble and idealistic as you would wish. But who said you had to be noble and idealistic, anyway, unless you choose to. You may discover that you want to keep it or change it. Don't worry too much about that right now. Just dig in and figure out what it is. Keep asking WHAT AM I PLAYING FOR? The answer may appear instantly. Or, you may want to spend the next few days inquiring into this. After all, WHAT AM I PLAYING FOR? and WHAT IS THE MEANING OF (MY) LIFE? are the same question. Since philosophers have been working on this one for thousands of years, it wouldn't hurt to spend a couple of days on revealing it to yourself.

5. What are the rules of your most dominant game? At this point you may find it useful to create a section called "My Book of Rules" in your notebook. Only when you are consciously playing your most dominant game and are aware of the rules can you begin to make up new games, new rules, or play the existing game effectively. For example, someone playing the I'm Cool Game might have some rules like, "Whenever I am deciding what to wear, I come to my decision based on what I think the people I will be with will think." Someone playing the I'm the Boss Game might have rules like, "Never get into situations where people who know me as the chief see me as just plain Bob." Someone playing the Creativity Game may have rules like, "There is always a new frontier of unknown possibilities just ahead. My job is to break through and discover them, no matter what the cost to any other part of my life." You will probably find a whole bunch of rules for each game you play. You could spend the next year figuring out all the rules of all the games and writing them down. At the end, you would be completely informed and totally confused. I suggest that you stick to figuring out the rules of your Master Game and perhaps one or two other big ones that affect your life every day.

6. Keep referring back to this Inquiry and the rest of this chapter often. I have been asking myself What am I playing for? several times a day for twenty years. It may be the most powerful question you could ever ask yourself regularly.

Turn to your Primary Lists (Wants, Commitments and Requirements, and Questions), as well as to your Careers to Consider List. What can you add to those lists now? Any new games? Any you have decided to drop into the dustbin?

INQUIRY 21

WHAT GAME WILL I PLAY?

Now you know that you are in the midst of many games. You know what they are and understand the rules. The moment of choice has arrived.

1. Is your dominant game the one you most want to play? If so, congratulations. Your outer life and your inner life are congruent. This most central connection is in tune.

2. If your most dominant game is not the one you want to play most, why not? What is missing?

3. What game would you like to wake up to in the morning and play wholeheartedly, every day, as your most dominant game? This is another question that you may want to spend a day or two working on. In fact, would you like it if I gave you the best homework assignment you ever had? If you accept this assignment, take a one-week vacation sometime very soon. Go someplace serene and beautiful. Relax. Spend the week inquiring into this question and the other ones in this chapter (and having ten times as much fun as you usually do).

4. What careers would best serve to help you to win the senior game you intend to play?

5. What are some of the qualities, functions, activities, and rewards that a job might offer that would help you win the dominant game you intend to play?

6. What are some qualities, functions, activities, rewards that would make it difficult or impossible to win this dominant game?

7. Would you be willing at this time to create any new commitments—to play a new game, to reorder the priorities of the ones you play, to make up some new rules? If so, turn to your Commitments and Requirements List and add them to the list.

8. This is another one of those Inquiries that I recommend you keep working on, at least weekly as you wind your way to your goal. As a kid, you

chose what games to play every day. Now you, and most other people, are stuck playing the same games over and over. What about choosing your games newly, regularly, for the rest of your days? It may not always be practical, but it is certainly a lot of fun.

Choosing Games

When you cease to make a contribution, you begin to die.

— ELEANOR ROOSEVELT

Once you recognize that your life consists of playing a number of games, a powerful transformation can occur. You can literally become someone who did not exist previously. Until now, you have been dangling on strings controlled by the rules of whatever games you were playing. Once you know this, you can choose either to keep playing those games you are already in the middle of, and play them consciously, or to pick some new ones. If you keep the ones you already have, you can then play them 100 percent, without reservation. You can keep the old rules or make up new ones. If you pick new games or new rules, you alter your life forever. It might seem that you would have to spend many years living in a cave, meditating on the meaning of life, to make much progress in transforming what is possible for you and the quality of your life. But you can begin right now. How? Here are three tried-and-true methods to make it much easier to successfully choose new games to play:

1. Completion. The first method is based on the principle that whatever you resist tends to persist. When you can dance the dirty boogie with your life as it really is, unencumbered by resistance and pretense, things tend to change quickly. In this method, you stop trying to change. You embrace your life as it is. You begin by getting very clear what games you are playing now, at this point in your life. Then play the games you are already playing, participating 100 percent. Give them everything you've got, while doing your best to remember that they are games. You will not be able to avoid slipping back into the illusion that there is some cosmic rule about how it is better to own Boardwalk than Baltic Avenue. Once you are usually awake and aware that your games are not the one and only reality, that they are your own creation, then you are no longer a puppet. Once you can choose what you already have, you can make up something new. When you are complete, rather than in a state of unconsciousness or resistance, you can move on, whether that means that you will decide to keep playing the old game or pick a new one.

2. War. Another, much more difficult method is to do battle with your prevalent, unwanted games. If you are involved in a destructive game, this sometimes works. Often though, when you do battle with existing games, the games win and you lose. Usually the preceding and following methods work better unless you are more of a fighter than a lover.

3. Commitment. Make up a new game now and begin to play it 100 percent, from this moment on. Make up some rules and stick to them. Manage the discomfort you feel until your new game settles in. It may take a few months until your new game becomes a habit. Then you will play it automatically, just like the ones you play now.

This book is an expression of methods 1 and 3.

INQUIRY 22

WHAT DOES "DOING MEANINGFUL WORK" MEAN TO YOU?

As we discussed before, doing what is meaningful to you is mainly motivated by self-fulfillment. There may be noble objectives, an ideal fulfilled, evil conquered, and a major contribution to the world made. But the primary motive of doing meaningful work is for you, not for others. The Episcopalian church ladies I know who volunteer their time in a soup kitchen for homeless people are a perfect example. They are lovely, generous women who care deeply about others. In no way do I mean to demean them when I say that they do what they do to fulfill themselves. Yes, they are also motivated by a commitment to making a contribution. But, if serving soup didn't make them feel like the good people they are, they would hang up their ladles and find something else to do.

When you honestly embrace the perfectly normal selfishness that is inherent in doing meaningful work, you can look clearly at what it will take to fulfill you without feeling guilty that you are not living up to some ideal. If you choose to serve your highest ideals, great. If you want to play professional Ping-Pong, affect history by being the prime minister's secret lover, or make world-class cheese steaks, great. If that is what is most meaningful to you, go for it. You do not have to spend the rest of your life feeling guilty because you did not choose to become

Jimmy or Joan of Arc. What is important is to make your own choices as a free agent. What is best for you is what you decide is best for you.

To design a career that is meaningful requires that you be completely honest in appraising your motives. It is not enough to simply look off to the stratospheric heights of your most lofty ideals. You've gotta get down and dirty, be straight with yourself, and design your career so you get what you want as well as make whatever contribution you choose to make. It is better to give and to receive.

There is nothing mysterious about meaning. If you want to know what matters to someone, just ask them. What is meaningful or important to any individual is right there on the surface, not hidden in the murky depths of the unconscious. Let's take a look. Answer as many of these questions as you can. If you have difficulty with one, just push on and come back to it later.

1. What do you mean by "meaningful?" Do you mean that you want to do something you enjoy or work in a field in which you have an interest? Do you mean that you want your work to provide you with certain kinds of rewards or challenges? Do you mean that you want to do work that you believe in, that you think is important or makes some sort of social contribution?

2. List everything that is most meaningful to you. Include things that you might consider doing for a living as well as things you consider to be highly significant, important, or meaningful but unlikely to be the centerpiece of your career. Be specific. "Everything" could include specific fields of endeavor, problems that need to be solved, social ills, things you like to do, places you like to go, activities you are especially passionate about, functions you love to perform, and anything else that falls within the range of what you consider to be meaningful.

3. How important is it for you to do work that is meaningful to you?

4. For some people, it is vitally important that their work be the direct expression of their highest ideals. For other folks, it is not necessary to participate directly in furthering one of those ideals. It is sufficient for them to work in a field that does not have a destructive impact. How important is it that your work be directly or indirectly related to something that is near the top of your "What's Important to Me" list? If so, how directly related?

5. If it is important that you make a direct impact or contribution in an area important to you, what kind of an impact? How much of an impact?

Could you do a job that does not directly make a contribution in an organization that does?

6. What stands in the way of actually doing meaningful work? Write down all important obstacles. For example, here are two common Yeahbuts shared by many people who find that working for socially responsible nonprofit organizations is meaningful: "I will have to work long hours for very little money" and "There are many jobs for people who want to rape, pillage, and loot but few for people who want to do something meaningful." Afterwards, consider each obstacle separately. Brainstorm possible ways of handling the obstacle. Do not listen to your Yeahbuts. Write down everything, even possibilities that seem far-fetched. After you have finished brainstorming, go over all the possible solutions, considering carefully, Would this work? Is it possible? How could I make it happen? Do not act as the agent for your Yeahbuts but rather as an enthusiastic supporter of your ability to handle any challenge, any obstacle.

7. What is sufficiently meaningful that you would actually consider dedicating your work life to it? Once again, remember to access yourself directly instead of looking through the filters of your ideals and standards. Use this section of this Inquiry to sort things out if you are uncertain what would be sufficiently meaningful to satisfy your needs. The following exercise appeared before in the "Temperament, Personality, and Passions" chapter. If you did it then, just review it now. Make a vertical list of everything that you might consider meaningful, prioritized so that the most meaningful things are at the top of the list and things with less significance are at the bottom. You could list different job names, specific fields of endeavor, things you feel would be good to accomplish, or whatever else you think fits into this list. Go through the list again. Reorder it so it is in an absolute hierarchy. In other words, you want each item on the list to be more meaningful than the item directly below it.

8. Now draw a line at the point that separates those things that would be meaningful enough from those that wouldn't. How do you know which is which? You don't. If you did, you wouldn't be doing this exercise. You have to choose on your own. Make the decision yourself. You want to wind up with all the items above the line being things that would be sufficiently meaningful to do as a career, and everything below the line to not fit within that requirement. Remember, in this Inquiry you are looking only at what would be sufficiently meaningful. The careers that wind up at the top of this list do not have to be practical. They do not have to be

something you would want to do. They just have to be sufficiently meaningful. Here's a sample:

population control
educating children in a way that preserves their sense of wonder
educating children to be ready for the challenges of the 21st century
health care for low-income people
publishing good books
<u>creative educational television</u>
ecological balance
create tools for third-world-appropriate technology
helping homeless people
helping families in trouble
marketing ecologically appropriate products
provide opportunities for people to reduce stress in the country

9. Go through this list one more time. See if you can further shorten the list of areas you would consider sufficiently meaningful. Are there any that, although they are meaningful, you know in your heart that you would really never follow through on? Do your best to trim your list down to five or fewer entries. But don't throw away anything that truly belongs on the list.

10. What are the elements that make the ones above the line suitable to you? Is it the subject matter, the furthering of a specific ideal, an elegant fit between aspects of you and the work? Are there other things that might go above the line now that you have looked at why the ones above the line are above the line. If so, write them in. What makes the ones that are not high on your list fail to fully satisfy your requirements.

11. Do you need to produce results in that which is meaningful to you? To what degree do you need to produce results? What sort of results would be meaningful? What degree of results would it take for you to be able to declare yourself successful? Must they be tangible? If so, how tangible?

12. Can you narrow down your selection to one or more top candidates? If so, great. If not, don't worry. You may be perfectly content working in one of several meaningful areas.

13. Do you need to do some research, talk with people, or otherwise find out more about any of your top contenders? If so, what do you need to do? Be specific. What do you need to know to decide or to further narrow down the range of possibilities? What questions do you need to ask and answer? Go do the research and meet me back here when you are complete.

14. Turn to your Commitments List. **What am I sure will definitely be a component of my future career?** If your work must be meaningful, commit to that. If it must be one of the areas above the line, commit to that. Nail down as much as you can. If you can, create a commitment to have your career be about something above the line. If not, what do you have to find out, consider, or decide in order to commit? If you are unable to go all the way to the point of commitment now, go on, do other parts of *The Pathfinder* and come back here later. Keep inquiring into this area. Work to develop more clarity and definition. Making decisions about other pieces of the puzzle may help you narrow it down further. For example, if you decide you are not willing to learn a completely new discipline, that might automatically cross some items off your list.

That's all there is to it. If you have been searching for "meaning," or what is important to you, you just found it. It is not the great mystery it sometimes seems. Some folks spend their lives searching for meaning when it was right there, within reach, all the time. By drawing one simple line, you have taken a stand on doing something meaningful.

On a Mission

When you are on a mission, your energy is directed outward toward producing an outcome. Meaningful work does not necessarily require that you make anything happen. A career with a mission is essentially an action-oriented extension of having a meaningful career. Some of us would be perfectly satisfied to work in a particular field, concentrate on a personal interest, or use certain abilities without the need to produce some result in the world around us. Having a mission could mean converting the cannibals to your religion, saving the whales, working for peace and human rights, becoming a successful editor or family physician, making a couple million bucks, becoming the first female president, or winning an Olympic gold medal. When you are considering what is meaningful to you, it is very useful to get clear whether or not having a sense of mission is important.

INQUIRY 23

A MISSION IN LIFE

1. How important is it that your work involves having a mission, directing your energy toward achieving specific goals? (This is pretty much the same question as number 11 in the last Inquiry. You may want to look back to your answers to that question.)

2. Who are some people you admire who have or had a mission? If they were asked what that mission is or was, what do you think their answer would be?

3. What possible results or outcomes that having a mission could produce might be fulfilling to you? Use this question to brainstorm. Write down whatever surfaces. Don't edit out things that seem beyond your reach or impossible for some reason or another. Some examples: bring back art and music to the classrooms in your area; save two to three million for retirement; have a number-one hit album; bring world population growth down to a sustainable level; keep green areas from becoming parking lots; or edit many wonderful books so they are even better.

4. Go over the previous list and cross out whatever you know you will not actually dedicate yourself to. Be completely honest with yourself. You might cross some out because, as noble or interesting as they seem, they just aren't something you can imagine actually dedicating yourself to. Others may miss the mark for other reasons.

5. Ask yourself why you crossed out the ones you did. What is it about them that took them off the list? This is important information. It may help guide you to focus on which of the ones remaining best fulfill what is important to you.

6. Which of the remaining ones are most fitting, most attractive? Which ones sing your song loud and clear? Mark the ones that rise to the top like cream.

7. What are the elements that make the ones you just marked so attractive to you? Is it the subject matter, the furthering of an ideal, an elegant fit between aspects of you and the work the mission would entail?

8. Can you narrow down your selection to one or more top candidates?

9. Do you need to do some research, talk with people, or otherwise find out more about any of your top contenders? If so, what do you need to do? Be specific. What do you need to know to decide or to further narrow down the range of possibilities? What questions do you need to ask and answer? Go do the research and come back here when you are complete.

Turn to your Primary Lists (Wants, Commitments and Requirements, and Questions), as well as to your Careers to Consider List. What can you add to those lists now? **What am I sure will definitely be an important component of my future career?** *If you know you must have a mission but don't know exactly what it will be, commit to having a mission. If you are sure of some aspects or elements of your mission, write them down.*

If you are unable to go all the way to the point of commitment now, go on, do other parts of *The Pathfinder,* and come back here later. Keep inquiring into this area. Work to develop more clarity and definition.

Purpose

You do not belong to you. You belong to the universe. The significance of you will remain forever obscure to you, but you may assume you are fulfilling your significance if you apply yourself to converting all your experience to highest advantage of others.

— R. BUCKMINSTER FULLER

Several years ago I noticed something unusual about an older man who worked on the garbage truck that serviced my neighborhood. Come rain, shine, or particularly ripe offerings from his clients, he always had boundless enthusiasm and a smile for everyone he met along the way. As time passed, my curiosity soared. Did he love working outdoors? Was he just a naturally cheerful fellow or was he a bit of a lunatic? Finally, I asked. He said that he had worked on a trash truck all of his life. When he was a young man he had always thought that someday he would hang up his trash can and move on to something more in keeping with his dreams. He woke up middle-aged one day and realized that he would spend the rest of his life on the trash truck. He felt that his life didn't amount to anything. After a bout of self-pity, he realized that the reason he felt his life didn't amount to anything had nothing to do with working as a trash man. It was because his life had no purpose. He saw for the first time that he was just a cog in the wheel of fire. Somehow he realized that it was within his power to invent a purpose for his life, to literally create himself as something other than just a trash man. He decided that he would dedicate his life to one thing, "to bring a little ray of sunshine into the lives of everyone I meet."

How can I be useful, of what service can I be? There is something inside me, what can it be?

— VINCENT VAN GOGH

Having meaningful work or work with a mission is essentially a process of satisfying yourself as you are now, finding something you like to do, something that matters to you. Living from a purpose is quite different. It exists in the realm of pure creation and invention. *A purpose is an ongoing commitment to a principle that becomes who you are. It is not a belief or a goal to be achieved, but a place to come from. It is not what you do, but who you are being.* A strange definition, to be sure. Before my trash man created his purpose, he was answering the call of nature and the bill collector, reacting to whatever psychological tapes the gods of chance had decided to play in his brain that morning. When he created his purpose, he literally invented himself as someone new. Now, when he rose in the morning, no matter what mood he awoke to, he found that he could reinvent himself as the guy fulfilling the purpose of bringing a little sunshine into the lives of everyone he met.

I don't know what your destiny will be, but one thing I know: the only ones among you who will be really happy are those who have sought and found how to serve.

— ALBERT SCHWEITZER

Please remember that there is big difference between "meaning" or "mission" and "living from a purpose." The statement you use to describe any of the three could be exactly the same. For example, "to end world hunger" could be a statement of what is meaningful to you, a statement of an objective you are very actively working toward achieving (a mission), or a broad vision that you have literally given you life to and have made more important than getting what you want and being the center of your own personal universe.

What exactly does it mean to live from a purpose? What does it require? *A purpose is an ongoing commitment to a principle that becomes who you are.* The essence of purpose is contribution. You invent a commitment to a principle outside of yourself and larger than yourself. You dedicate yourself to furthering that principle. You literally give yourself to that commitment. It becomes your inner-most self, your reason for being.

It is not a belief or a goal to be achieved, but a place to come from. It is not what you do, but who you are being. A person with the purpose of bringing a lit-tle ray of sunshine into people's lives is never finished. You wouldn't say, "Well, I finally did it. I brought sunshine to five thousand lives. My job is finished. I'm re-tiring from the sunshine business." It is a commitment to a principle and is, there-fore, a place to come from into your life and work. You never arrive. But you are always complete. Purpose becomes the organizing principle of your life or of a part of your life. Instead of checking with your mood or opinions to know what to do, you check in with your purpose. The trash man experienced the same moods that you and I do. But he didn't usually indulge in them. His actions were enlightened by his purpose.

It does not descend on you from high above. You don't find or discover a pur-pose. The only way to have one is to choose one. Were you born with a purpose? Who knows? I have worked with a steady stream of clients who say they want to discover their purpose in life. They say they feel sure that each person is born for some purpose, if only they could discover it. Many of them have been looking for that purpose for a long, long time. I expect that some of them will go to their graves still searching. Then again, I have worked with many people who have cre-ated a purpose for their work.

> ### *Make your work in keeping with your purpose.*
>
> — LEONARDO DA VINCI

When my old mentor Bucky Fuller was a young man, he had a business failure that left him feeling that the best thing he could do for the people he loved was to commit suicide. Just as he was about to end it all, he looked up to the stars and had a revelation. He later said that he realized that he did not own himself, and that he had no right to kill himself. He then dedicated his life to using what he had to offer to make the biggest contribution he could. Then he asked himself what he had to offer. As a result of giving his all, he made so many breakthroughs and dis-coveries that, eventually, his entry in *Who's Who* became the most voluminous of all.

He chose his purpose by looking at what he had to offer. You can wait for the angels to whisper in your ear, or you can have a purposeful life now. If you were born with a purpose, it would seem to me that it would be to use what you have been given to make the fullest contribution you can to your world.

It is not an exalted state. It makes you no better than anyone else. It is, how-ever, a lot more fun than the way most people spend their lives.

You do not have to be a Gandhi, a Mother Teresa or a Martin Luther King Jr.

to create a purpose for your work and live fully from that commitment. If the trash man could do it, so can you. Your purpose could be something lofty: advocating a world view or faith or consciousness that inspires hope in a benevolent cosmos and leads to greater planetary well-being. Or it could be much more down to earth. As a matter of fact, there are probably plenty of people around you who live from purpose. Their purpose may be teach your kids in a way that helps them preserve their sense of wonder, to make the best widgets, or to make your world a better place in some way or another. To have a purpose for your work does not mean dedicating yourself to a narrow range of widely agreed upon ideals. Some of the finest actors and artists, statespeople, and scientists live from a purpose. In fact, many of the people who get to play a big part on the world stage in any area live from a purpose bigger than themselves. Greatness is often born of the passionate dance between a rare talent and a noble purpose. But, the world is filled with many thousands of unknown people who, because they live from a purpose, contribute in their own very special ways to our world. I know a man whose life is completely dedicated to creating the finest steel string guitars that have ever existed. With this purpose he does not get to compromise and cut corners, even when it would save him many hours and no one else would likely ever notice. I know people dedicated to selling with total integrity. With this purpose they have turned the usual manipulative sales relationship with customers into one of contribution. They are also very, very successful because people trust them.

You must be ready, willing, and able to live a life that is not mainly informed by your own needs and desires. As Gandhi said, "Even God cannot talk to a hungry man except in terms of bread." When you live from a created purpose you transform yourself from psychological being to philosophical being. Instead of looking to your personality for your identity and to guide your actions, you look to your commitment to your chosen purpose. Your highest commitment shifts from self-fulfillment to contribution. You begin to invent who you are. When you ask "Who am I?" you are not stuck with your historical identity. The trash man was able to be deeply, profoundly enthusiastic and loving because, rather than succumb to whatever mood blew in with the wind, he was willing to become his own creation every day.

> *When we quit thinking primarily about ourselves and our own self-preservation, we undergo a truly heroic transformation of consciousness.*
>
> — JOSEPH CAMPBELL

It is extraordinary to be able do something you care about, something meaningful. That is enough for most people who seek full self-expression in their work.

Working from purpose is not better, loftier, or more important than anything else. It is simply another game, just like all the other games of life that some people choose to play when they have won whatever games they have been playing in the past. Once people have found themselves, have outgrown the routine of survival-based living, or have become passionately committed to some principle, they sometimes discover that their next step is to learn to invent themselves. If that is what you are seeking, you will know that this section on purpose is for you. If what has been said in the last few paragraphs does not hit you like a ton of bricks, if you do not have a very powerful sense that those words were speaking specifically to you, just go on to the next section.

> *You must be the change you wish to see in the world.*
>
> — MOHANDAS GANDHI

You can create a purpose for any domain of your life. When you dedicate your life to a purpose it transforms who you are in the most fundamental way possible. But you do not have to go all the way over the edge and surrender to the void to have the power of purpose transform various domains of your life. For example, you could have a purpose for your leisure time, your workout, your personal growth, your friendships, your marriage. Since purpose is about contribution, and you are a person, why not create purposes that contribute to you? Here are some examples of purposes from different domains in your life:

College (domain): to grow up into the best me that I can, to have a great time while fully succeeding at what I am doing (purpose).

Playing music: to communicate the entirety of my heart and soul to the audience.

Community service: to assist my community to be more helpful, kinder, and more caring in serving the need of people having serious difficulties; to help homeless people get back on their feet again; to make a difference in other people's lives.

Sex: to give and receive extraordinary, ecstatic erotic pleasure; to communicate fully, creatively, and spiritually with my lover.

Vacation: to experience the heart and soul of other cultures, to play like a child.

Friendship: to be related; to love and support others; to live the Golden Rule with them always.

Couples, groups of people, and organizations can have purposes, too. Just as an individual can invent purposes, so can groups of people. A marriage can be dedicated to a shared ideal, to making some sort of contribution or anything else that extends the intentions of the relationship beyond the usual boundaries. A group of friends can create a purpose so that their interactions are more than just hanging out together. Some examples:

Marriage: to be a model for other people, including our children, of just how great a relationship can be; to contribute to the world around us.

A group of friends: to be family to each other; to support each other to have all of our lives be happy and successful.

The best-run, most successful companies have purposes. They are not just money-making machines. Of course, money is an absolute requirement, but not the one and only reason for the company's existence. As Tom Peters and Robert Waterman wrote in *In Search of Excellence:* "Every excellent company we studied is clear on what it stands for . . ."

A company's purpose might be: to create technological breakthroughs that contribute to humanity; to be the best in our field; to serve the creative spirit of our people so that they can express themselves fully in leading-edge products; superior service.

If you want to see if a company has a purpose other than just to stay in existence, look at its annual report. The report will communicate very clearly what is most important, what is the shared vision of the leadership.

The Benefits of Living from a Purpose

When you are inspired by some great purpose, some extraordinary project, all your thoughts break their bounds: Your mind transcends limitations, your consciousness expands in every direction and you find yourself in a new, great and wonderful world. Dormant forces, faculties and talents become alive, and you discover yourself to be a greater person by far than you ever dreamed yourself to be.

— P A T A N J A L I

Real miracles happen when your work is enlightened by purpose. This very book you are holding in your hands is an example of what can happen when you invent a purpose for your work that is bigger than your personal psychology. Many years ago, I, like the trash man, created a purpose for my life. I promised: "Who I am is a commitment to have people everywhere gain great tools so they can choose work they love, that is creative, and that expresses them fully." At the time I felt I was stepping into something far beyond my ability. I could imagine reading about someone inventing a purposeful life, but I felt out of my depth doing it myself. After all, who was I, a perfectly ordinary self-righteous, tree-hugging, rock and roll refugee from the sixties to take on a completely new context for living and working? Subsequently, I made three promises to one of my mentors, Bucky Fuller, that were expressions of that purpose. I promised that:

1. I will create a body of knowledge that will transform career counseling so that everyone, everywhere can have tools available that allow them to make a career choice that combines all they have to offer into a successful career that is fulfilling, creative, a lot of fun, and maximally useful to humanity.

2. I will train many career counselors, psychologists, and others in this body of knowledge.

3. I will transform the prevalent belief of our culture, so that the culture embraces and puts into practice the concept that people can readily choose a career that fits them perfectly and that they will love.

At the time I made these promises, I did not believe that I could actually make them come true. Nevertheless, I started living from them every day, working to fulfill them in spite of regular attacks of Yeahbuts. In the years before I made these promises, my whims and fancies, my hopes and dreams blew around in circles like leaves in a whirlwind. Once I began to live from a purpose in my work, I noticed that, even though the winds did not stop, there was now a new central core of identity that I had created. Every morning I would wake up like the trash man, to whatever mood and circumstances fate had given me that day. I would reinvent myself as the expression of my purpose rather than just be that old familiar sleepy guy who yearned for nothing more than a cup of coffee. I still do, every day.

What is extraordinary about purpose is that you keep becoming a new person, able to do things you could hardly even imagine previously. That is how this book got written. A couple of years ago, I had never written anything. I couldn't type. I'm left-handed. When I learned to write, teachers still thought that lefties were the spawn of Beelzebub. When they couldn't force us to become God-fearing right handers, they taught us to write with our hands twisted around so that the heel of our hands would drag across the words we had just written. And, of course, they taught us to write with fountain pens so everything would turn into a big illegible smear as your hand dragged across the wet ink. To say the least, the early messages I got about writing were hardly an encouragement. Until recent years, getting me to write a thank-you letter was more difficult than dragging a team of mules into a burning barn.

My third promise to Bucky changed all that. I spent many years working to keep the first two promises. When I got around to the third, I began to wonder how one could go about changing a bad habit of a culture. I had friends who knew some world-class experts in affecting public opinion. All of them were kind enough to offer their sage advice. They all said the same thing: The first thing you have to do is write a book that sells. Nobody will listen to you otherwise. This did not sink in for months. I felt that it was more likely that the moon is made of green cheese than that I could write a book. But every morning I would wake up and remind myself that who I am in my work is the guy fulfilling these three promises, even when I don't feel like it, even when I'd rather go back to bed. Slowly it dawned on me that, in order to keep my third promise, I would actually have to write a book, which also meant that I would have to learn to write. So, because I was totally committed to my purpose, I decided to do it. If I had continued to operate out of doing something meaningful, I would have simply gone on believing that it was impossible for me to write a book. I would have continued to have found ways to express my commitment to other people's career satisfaction that fit snugly and comfortably into a nice warm niche of my identity.

To me, it is a daily miracle that I wrote this book. What is even more amazing is that once I began, all sorts of other miracles started to happen. Within a few months, I had an absolutely wonderful literary agent and had two major publishing companies competing to buy this book. Soon after that, I had found the most extraordinary editor. But the real miracle will be in fulfilling the promise I made.

Singleness of purpose is the most powerful way to move mountains. Normally, folks do that which is within their comfort zone, or at least within the limits of what they think is possible. When your reference point is your purpose rather than your psyche, you seek solutions outside the boundaries you normally live within. You do what works rather than what you feel like. You become almost an unstoppable force of nature. Your effectiveness is not impeded by having to keep your somewhat psycho psyche happy and comfortable.

Things work brilliantly much more of the time. The best, most exciting and most profoundly satisfying marriages I know of are dedicated to a purpose. Why does this contribute to having a marriage work? In most marriages, the quality of the relationship depends mostly on chance. There are precious few commitments that effectively shape the quality of the relationship into something truly extraordinary. It is so easy to let a me-first mentality erode what began as a passionate tango. Little problems tend to pile up in the dark. Uncommunicated things and unresolved transactions form walls that reduce intimacy. When a marriage is dedicated to furthering a purpose, it is necessary to keep it well oiled and working smoothly if the relationship itself is to make a contribution. You discover that if you want the marriage to make a difference, you have to give up playing all these little games that create friction and distance. Instead of hiding problems in the closet, you resolve them, in service of your purpose. A couple who has dedicated their marriage to "being a model for other people, including our children, of just how great a relationship can be" finds it easier to avoid getting stuck in the inevitable problems that arise because they keep referring back to their purpose.

You notice when things are not working much more quickly. You tend to be awake and sensitive to how well you are playing to a degree that is nearly impossible otherwise. If you notice you are heading down a blind alley quickly, you can change course posthaste. The faster you are able to make course corrections in any journey, the better.

Life becomes an exciting adventure. I love those movies where Harrison Ford swings on a vine across the bottomless chasm. It is even more fun to do the swinging yourself. Talk about personal light-speed growth! It is exciting enough to grow and improve gradually, to become slowly, steadily more able to face the slings and arrows of life with flexibility and joy. It is terrific to be able to make goals come true. But, if you want to have excitement, challenge, and deep fulfillment, you've got to jump from the frying pan into the fire. Up the ante from doing something you believe in to giving yourself to a purpose larger than you.

This is the true joy in life, being used for a purpose recognized by yourself as a mighty one: being a force of nature instead of a feverish, selfish little clod of ailments and grievances, complaining that the world will not devote itself to making you happy.
I am of the opinion that my life belongs to the whole community and as long as I live it is my privilege to do for it whatever I can. I want to be thoroughly used up when I die, for the harder I work the more I live. I rejoice in life for its own sake. Life is no "brief candle" to me. It is a sort of splendid torch that I have got hold of for the moment, and I want to make it burn as brightly as possible before handing it on to future generations.

— GEORGE BERNARD SHAW

When life is about caring for the orchard, rather than picking the apples, you get more apples to eat. It is quite paradoxical, but as soon as you give up trying to make yourself happy, you are!

A person starts to live when he can live outside of himself.

— ALBERT EINSTEIN

The Downside

Acting like "a force of nature" is a gigantic pain in the ass. It is much more comfortable to be the innkeeper of your desires rather than the agent of something as demanding and ephemeral as a purpose. This is true for any area of life for which you create a purpose. If your marriage is dedicated to a purpose that demands that the relationship work brilliantly, then you've got be 100 percent accountable for the whole ball of wax. You can't blame it on your partner when things aren't working. You have to do it all yourself. You have to give up hankering for fairness. There is nothing that seems more unjust at times than living from a purpose. Of course, if your partner is doing the same thing and living from purpose, your marriage is likely to be really amazing.

You must reawaken yourself endlessly. Living from purpose does not come easily. It's like driving home late at night and having to shake yourself awake again and again as you catch yourself dozing off. Playing the lead in one's internal soap opera is very compelling. It is familiar, an old game most of us have been playing to perfection for many years. Living from a purpose seems strange at first. You will forget what you are up to thousands of times and have to continually re-create your commitment to your purpose. You quickly discover just how slippery your mind can be at returning to the same old used to be.

You give over control of your life to your purpose and allow it to dominate you. You do what your purpose calls for instead of what you feel like doing.

It is often uncomfortable. Because you do what needs to be done instead of what you feel like doing, you often wind up in situations where what you need to do seems impossible.

INQUIRY 24

CHOOSE A PURPOSE, THEN GO LIVE IT

1. **First of all, decide if you are ready to live from a purpose.** This is a way of life much like mountain climbing: It is very exciting, you often tingle from head to toe with the sheer joy of life, you get to see the world and yourself from a place you could not otherwise reach. It is, however, much more demanding than the way you are used to living. You find that you are often hanging from a cliff with an endless drop below. Before you take this on, make sure you are not fooling yourself. If you want to live from a purpose mainly to get some benefit or reward for yourself, you are looking for meaningful work, not purposeful work. You do not, however, have to be selfless or humble to live from a purpose. Throughout history, most of the people who demonstrate the best examples of purposeful living have had big, healthy egos. As long as the purpose is bigger than the ego, fine.

2. **Find a principle you would be willing to dedicate yourself to.** Pick something where the ongoing fulfillment of the purpose uses you fully and naturally. Your talents and personality together form a tool that has the best chance of moving mountains. It also helps if you have a very strong natural passion for making a contribution in this area. Choose the area you care about most, or use some other selection criteria of your own. If you find that selecting a principle to dedicate yourself is extremely difficult, you are probably not quite ready to live from a purpose.

3. **Use the power of language to craft your purpose precisely.** Get it as sharp and clear as a laser beam. Keep working on it until, when you say it, it can almost burn a hole through the wall with its clarity and power. Remember, a purpose is not a goal. It is the expression of a principle. Craft the words so that they remind you that your purpose is a place to come from, not someplace to get to. "To make a million a year" is a mission, a goal, not a purpose. "To be a great example to my children" can be a purpose. If you can invent it now, live it now, and from it can issue an endless stream of appropriate actions, then it could be a purpose.

4. **Declare it as your purpose.** Make a definite commitment to become your purpose. For example, "I am a commitment to bringing together East and

West through communication and media." "I am a commitment to people having careers that fit them perfectly so their lives will be creative, purposeful, and fun." "I am a commitment to using ethical salesmanship to get products to people that make a real difference in their lives." Perhaps you could even have a little ceremony to induct yourself into your purpose.

5. **Work out the best possible ways to express your purpose.** Then get to work. From a clear purpose comes potent actions. Sit down, figure out what would move things most powerfully in the direction of your purpose. Then get to work and do whatever it takes.

6. **Manage your life day by day and moment to moment so that you are "on purpose" as much as possible.** Find ways to remind yourself of your purpose. You will constantly forget you are living from a purpose and get lost in the day-to-day routine. Purpose has to be continually renewed.

·

CHAPTER 23

VALUES AND REWARDS

You get much more than a paycheck from your work. If most of your important values are rewarded, you are well on the way to a very satisfying life.

INQUIRY 25

VALUES

---

1. Please take a few minutes to go through the following values checklist. Put a mark in the circle in front of all the values that are personally important to you. Don't worry about the boxes and columns that appear after a particular value. We'll get to those later. Mark all of your values, not just ones that are related to work. This list is just a starting point. Your most important values may not be on this list. Write in other important values that are not listed. Please do this now. **Please do not read further until you have completed this step.**

Values Chart

VALUE	Ideal	Standard	Want	True Value	Life Value	Work Value	Priority
○ ACHIEVEMENT OR ACCOMPLISHMENT							
○ ACKNOWLEDGEMENT							
○ ADVANCEMENT							
○ ADVENTURE							
○ AFFECTION							
○ ALIVENESS / VITALITY							
○ ART OR THE ARTS							
○ AUTONOMY							
○ AVOID BEING DOMINATED							
○ AVOID PAIN							
○ BE A GOOD MEMBER OF MY RELIGION							
○ BE A GOOD PARENT OR CHILD							
○ BE A VALUED MEMBER OF THE TEAM							
○ BE ENGAGED FULLY WITH LIFE							
○ BE IN CONTROL							
○ BE RIGHT							
○ BE THE BEST							
○ BE TRUSTED							
○ BEAUTY							
○ BELONG TO THE GROUP							
○ BUILD A BUSINESS							
○ CARING							
○ CHALLENGE							
○ CHALLENGE STATUS QUO							
○ CHILDREN							
○ COMPETING							
○ CONNECTION							
○ CONTRIBUTE TO OTHERS							
○ CONTROL MY ENVIRONMENT							
○ COOPERATION							
○ COURAGE							
○ CREATIVITY							
○ CULTURE							
○ DARING							
○ DIGNITY							
○ DO GOOD							

Values Chart

VALUE	Ideal	Standard	Want	True Value	Life Value	Work Value	Priority
◯ DO THE RIGHT THING							
◯ DO THINGS MY WAY							
◯ DIE WITH THE MOST TOYS							
◯ ELEGANCE							
◯ EMPOWERMENT							
◯ ENLIGHTENMENT							
◯ ENTREPRENEURSHIP							
◯ EQUALITY							
◯ EQUITY							
◯ ESTEEM (OF OTHERS)							
◯ EXCELLENCE							
◯ EXCITEMENT							
◯ EXPRESS MY SEXUALITY FULLY							
◯ FAME							
◯ FAMILY HAPPINESS							
◯ FEEL GOOD							
◯ FINANCIAL SECURITY							
◯ FIX BROKEN THINGS OR SYSTEMS							
◯ FRANKNESS/CANDOR							
◯ FREEDOM							
◯ FRIENDSHIP							
◯ FUN AND LAUGHTER							
◯ FULFILLMENT							
◯ GETTING AHEAD							
◯ GIVE OF MYSELF							
◯ GOODNESS (OR BADNESS)							
◯ HAPPINESS							
◯ HARD WORK							
◯ HARMONY OF RHETORIC AND ACTION							
◯ HEALTH							
◯ HELPING							
◯ HELPING THE LESS FORTUNATE							
◯ HONESTY							
◯ HUMOR							
◯ ICONOCLASM							
◯ I'LL SHOW THEM							

Values Chart

VALUE	Ideal	Standard	Want	True Value	Life Value	Work Value	Priority
○ INCLUSIVITY							
○ INDEPENDENCE							
○ INNER HARMONY							
○ INNOVATION							
○ INTEGRITY							
○ INTERESTING EXPERIENCES							
○ INTIMACY							
○ INVENTING							
○ JOY							
○ JUSTICE							
○ KEEP THINGS THE SAME							
○ LEADERSHIP							
○ LEARNING							
○ LEISURE TIME							
○ LOOK GOOD							
○ LOVE							
○ LOYALTY							
○ MAKE MONEY							
○ MARRIAGE							
○ MASTERY							
○ OPPORTUNITY							
○ ORDER							
○ PEACE							
○ PERSEVERANCE							
○ PERSONAL APPEARANCE							
○ PERSONAL DEVELOPMENT							
○ PLAY							
○ PLAYFULNESS							
○ PLEASURE/SENSUAL GRATIFICATION							
○ PREPARE FOR RETIREMENT							
○ PRIVACY							
○ QUALITY							
○ REACH FOR THE STARS							
○ RECOGNITION							
○ RE-CREATE THE CAREER OF A PARENT							
○ RELIABILITY							

Values Chart

VALUE	Ideal	Standard	Want	True Value	Life Value	Work Value	Priority
○ RESPECT							
○ REVOLUTION							
○ SAFETY							
○ SAVING/INVESTING							
○ SECURITY							
○ SEEK TRUTH							
○ SELF-CONTROL							
○ SELF-ESTEEM							
○ SELF-EXPRESSION							
○ SELF-RELIANCE							
○ SELF-RESPECT							
○ SERVICE							
○ SET AN EXAMPLE FOR OTHERS							
○ SEX							
○ SIMPLICITY							
○ SOCIALIZING							
○ SOCIAL ADVANCEMENT							
○ SOLVING PROBLEMS							
○ SPIRITUAL DEVELOPMENT							
○ SPIRITUAL VALUES							
○ SPONTANEITY/IMPROVISATION							
○ STRENGTH							
○ SYNERGY							
○ TEAM SPIRIT							
○ TRUTH							
○ UNIQUENESS							
○ USING MY TALENTS							
○ WEALTH							
○ WINNING							
○ WISDOM							
○ WORLD HOPPING							
○ YOUTH							
○ OTHER							
○ OTHER							
○ OTHER							
○ OTHER							

What Are Values?

Many career-counseling programs are based on "human values." You are asked to consider what values are important to you and then to design a career based on them. But what exactly is a value? According to the dictionary, a value is a *principle, standard or quality held by an individual, group, or society.* Notice that the definition does not make any mention of the individual, group, or society actually living by their values. American society holds certain traditional values including equal rights for each individual, freedom of speech, truth, justice, fair play, etc. The heroes in comics live by these values. How about the rest of us? Our foreign policy record suggests that we sometimes live by an entirely different set of values. When individuals are polled about their values, their answers rarely reflect the ones they actually live by. What's going on here? Are these people consciously lying? I don't think so. The problem is that the very concept of values is fuzzy. Let's see if we can sort this out in a way that gets our hands on the steering wheel.

The point of this present discussion is to encourage you to become aware of, separate, and distinguish the several very different elements that we lump together and call "values." Attempting to become clear about your values and then making career decisions appropriate to them is extremely difficult so long as what you call your values are an undifferentiated mass. If you can separate them into clearer categories, you'll better know the front end of the bull from the back. You will be able to choose which values will enhance your life and provide a sense of direction. Then you will be the source of, the creator of the values you live by.

Values, Dissected and Classified

Ideals An ideal is *a conception or model of something perfect that exists only in concept, not in reality.* It is the ultimate aim, not how we actually live. The ideal person always strives toward his or her ideals. Extraordinary people often do. Many of us do little more than complain about how other people don't live up to the ideals that we don't live up to either.

Having ideals gives us a vision of a perfect life to strive for. If you use your ideals as a reference point to pull you up toward an ideal life, so much the better. One of the most powerful commitments you could ever make would be to dedicate yourself to constantly improve in the direction of the lofty heights of your ideals. It would transform your life again and again and again.

On the other hand, expecting that you are supposed to always live up to your ideals is a recipe for disaster. You will never live up to your ideals. You're not supposed to. That's why they are called ideals. If you indulge in demeaning your present reality by comparing it with your ideals, you nullify the opportunity that having ideals offers. If you are a musician, what is the point of selling yourself short by comparing yourself with Mozart or Dylan?

Standards A standard is *a level of performance or attainment used as a measure of adequacy.* It is a judgment or conclusion that something should be other than the way it actually is. For example, many people subscribe to a standard that "life should be fair." Whenever life isn't fair, they get upset, disturbed. They feel that something is wrong. But, in fact, life is usually, randomly unfair. It always has been that way. The good guys don't necessarily finish first, except in the movies. Bad people do not usually get their comeuppance. Expecting that our standards should be met, by ourselves and others, is a form of self-righteousness of which we are all guilty. We have standards about almost everything—standards about how people should look, dress and behave, how the government should work, how people should raise their children. We have standards about haircuts and bread, music, and manners. We have standards about ourselves, our work, our relationships. The only things we don't have standards about are the things we haven't thought about yet.

How do you recognize a standard? Simple, it always contains a "should." If you "should" be taller, better looking, farther along in life, better educated, younger, older, more successful, richer, more caring, have more or better friends, or have a better sex life, you are face to face with a standard. If you think the world "should" be more peaceful, more just, or less polluted, there's a standard lurking about. The problem is that nothing is ever the way it should be. It's always the way it is. "Should" only exists when something doesn't come up to your measure of adequacy.

Wants and Preferences Some values may simply be wants and preferences. For example, you may have marked adventure as one of your values in the previous exercise. This may not be an important ideal or a "should." It may simply be something that you want or prefer to have as a part of your career, if possible. What's the difference between a want and a preference? A want has more of a charge behind it, more need, more urgency, more attachment than a preference does.

True Values Your true values are those that you live by or are willing to commit to live by. Right now, most of them are probably just another form of preexisting commitments. They may be virtuous or noble, but many of them were dropped on you by your family and culture. The real opportunity is to be able to choose your own set of true values.

Some of your true values apply universally to all aspects of your life. You may, for example, hold honesty and integrity as important values that are just as important at work as they are in the rest of your life. Some other life values may be very important to you but need not necessarily be fulfilled or expressed at work. For example, you may get enough adventure in your leisure-time activities, such as skydiving.

To help you gain a clearer perspective as you go through this Inquiry, let's also divide values into work-related values and ones that are not work-related:

Work Values These are the values that are intimately connected with your work. Some of them may be universal life values and others may apply only to work. Sometimes your work values may be completely different than those in the rest of your life. For example, you may be highly competitive at work, always going for victory and staying ahead of the pack, while at home you are docile and totally noncompetitive.

Non-work Values These are values that you do not need to fulfill or express at work.

2. Go through the previous values checklist. Of the ones you marked as values important to you, consider which of your values are actually ideals, standards, wants or preferences, the first three boxes. Mark the appropriate box with a check. **Please do not read further until you have completed this step.**

   Now that you have separated and categorized the very different concepts we lump together as values, you can more easily choose which values to keep and which to discard. You do not have to live up to an ideal or standard just because it is on your list. Your past does not need to command your future. The time has come to do some deep spring cleaning. Dump the stuff you don't really want.

3. Go through the values checklist again. Cross off the ones you are willing to throw out. Choose freely which values to keep and which to dump. Just because your papa held keeping up with Mr. Jones as a standard doesn't mean that you have to renew your subscription.

4. Go through your tattered list of values again. Check the "True Value" box after each of the values that you are willing to live by. If one of your most important values is not on the list, write it in. Don't mark the ones you think you should have, the best or most noble ones. Mark only the ones that actually, truly guide your life.

   Here's how you can tell. If saving for a rainy day is one of your top values, you will be actively engaged in saving, or you will be consistently striving to change your circumstances to make saving possible. If you are in great pain about not saving and you're not fully engaged in resourceful, creative action to remedy the situation, then saving is only a standard or an ideal.

This is not the time to attempt to "look good" to yourself by marking idealistic values that drive your life less than other less noble values may. For example, according to advertising psychologists there are five reasons that people are motivated to buy what they buy and do what they do. These are powerful background motivators that people forget when they make up values lists. We tend to forget about them because we don't "feel good" admitting we are motivated by these things. These powerful motivators are: looking good, feeling good, being right, feeling safe, avoiding pain. If you do not have at least some of these in your true values list, I think that you may be fooling yourself.

5. Go through the values that you have marked as true values. Separate them into work values and nonwork values. Mark the appropriate column. Many of your values may fit into both work and nonwork categories.

6. Now that you have sorted out the true values you actually live by and from, you may wish to create some new ones. Look to see if you would be willing to add any new values to your list. Please, no New Year's resolutions! Add only those values that you have not been living from that you are now willing to adopt fully and completely as your own. For example, you may have recognized that "saving for a rainy day" has actually been a standard, not a true value. You can forge it into a true value by choosing it and then living from it from this moment hence. There may also be values that you have lived by in the rest of your life, but not at work, that you are now willing to forge into work values as well.

7. Prioritize your true values that are also work values. Here's how to do it. Values are hierarchical. People will always sacrifice a lower, but still very important value to protect or uphold a higher value. Some basically honest senior government officials have in the past resorted to lying when faced with a choice between loyalty to their administration and honesty. That's because loyalty, keeping their jobs, or some other value were higher on their scales than honesty.

Go over the work values you have marked. Which is your number one, most important true work value? Which value would you never sacrifice under any circumstances? Mark it #1 in the "Priority" column of your values checklist. Which is next most important? Which is third, and so forth? Write down the appropriate number in the "Priority" column. Use a pencil because you may need to make changes as you prioritize your values. Continue to prioritize your top work values. Don't worry if you can't absolutely prioritize them. Just do the best you can.

If your top values are all noble and high-minded, you may be fooling yourself. Could you be counted on to be completely honest even if you would be terminally embarrassed if you told the truth? What if you would lose your job if you told the truth? What if you would lose your life? For many people, avoiding losing their jobs is a higher value than honesty. That does not mean they are devoid of integrity. They may always be honest except when confronted with the possible loss of their jobs. Dig in and get face to face with your top work values now. You may want to take a few days to work on this exercise.

8. Open your notebook and create a new section entitled "True Work Values." Write your prioritized important true values into this section. You will be writing about each of these, so leave plenty of room. Three or four entries per page should be just about right.

9. Then dig in to each of them and get clear about what you really mean. For example, if one of your values is security, what exactly does security mean to you? Do you mean a million in the bank, a job that's impossible to be fired from, headhunters constantly knocking at your door, or working in a safe neighborhood?

10. Turn to your Commitments and Requirements List. Are you ready to commit to having all or some of your true work values fulfilled in your new career?

INQUIRY 26

REWARDS

One of the rewards you get from your work is a paycheck. If the only work-related value that mattered to you was money, you could simply pick the career that provided you with the biggest bucks. But for work to be fulfilling, it must contribute much more than money. It must reward or express your most important work values. The rewards that mean the most are those that are the direct fulfillment of your important workplace values. If, for example, "acknowledgment" is an important workplace value, you will not perform at your best or experience an ongoing sense of satisfaction in a job where the management style is to correct mistakes rather than recognize accomplishment.

1. Go back through your "True Work Values" section. Ask this question about each one. "What specifically do you mean?" For example, if one of your values was "a fat paycheck," what exactly do you mean by that? Be very specific. This is a very useful question, since a leading causes of job dissatisfaction is a mismatch between the rewards the job offers and personal values.

2. Turn to your Commitments and Requirements List. Are you ready to make any promises to yourself related to values and rewards?

CHAPTER 24

•

EIGHT GREAT CAREERS

By now, your Commitments and Requirements List probably has enough specificity to make this Inquiry extremely helpful in identifying some other pieces of the puzzle, and perhaps further narrowing the field of careers worthy of your consideration. Even if your Commitments and Requirements List contains only entries that are of personal importance to you, but do not help to define your future career (like "have a window that opens in my office"), this Inquiry may be useful in creating some more specific commitments. In this Inquiry, you will be comparing and contrasting several careers that you find both attractive and possible to get further clarity about what is most important to you. It may be that none of these eight careers turns out to be your final choice. In this Inquiry, you are exploring you, not making a decision about what to do with your life.

INQUIRY 27

EIGHT GREAT CAREERS

---

1. Start a new section in your notebook for this Inquiry. Two pages per career should be sufficient, so make sure you have sixteen or more pages available in this section.

2. Think of eight careers that are as close as possible to being a perfect fit with everything important to you—your talents, personality, dreams, plans, goals. Most of these careers should be a practical possibility as well. Don't use careers that are an impossible dream you are sure you are unwilling to stretch to attain. *Take the time and effort to come up with a great list.* Start with careers on your Careers to Consider List. Make sure they meet the criteria of being close to a perfect fit. You can also simply make these up, select them from a list you have of careers that fit a particular ability or characteristic you possess, ask friends, or otherwise create them. You may have to spend a day or more in the career section of your library to come up with eight really good ones. If you can't come up with all eight after a couple of full days of research, include some that are

a less than perfect fit. Why so many? You are going to compare and contrast each with the others. The more you have, the better able you will be to do that well. Make sure none of them involve making compromises you are unwilling to make. See that each is a rich, multilayered tapestry woven from everything you know to be an important part of your future career. Make them as varied as possible. Be sure to include any possible careers you are now seriously considering. Write the name of each of these careers at the top of a page in your notebook. Each career will need two pages. Work on this Inquiry one career at a time. Explore the various steps of this Inquiry for one of the eight careers. Then come back and work on another. Repeat until you have done all eight *completely*.

3. Write a description of the first career on your list. Describe it in a way that brings it to life for you. Write this description to breathe life into this career. You want your description to be rich and multisensory so that you are actually able to see yourself, in your mind's eye, in the midst of this career. You want to be able to see, feel, hear, and touch it. Write down the day-to-day activities, the nature and purpose of the work, functions performed, the physical location, the abilities and traits you would make use of. The more multisensory you make your description, the more real it will be for you. It is not necessary to know the real nature of the careers you are describing. This exercise is about your perceptions and what is important to you. Just do your best in describing what you think the work would be like.

4. Draw a vertical line down the middle of the second page for each of the eight careers. Above the left column, write "HOT." Write "NOT HOT" above the right-hand column. Then begin to look critically at all aspects of the career. First, answer the question: What's hot? Write down everything positive about the career, what is attractive to you, what fits, what feels good, what fulfills your goals, etc. Dig deep. Don't just take the obvious, easy answers. Consider everything about this potential career and how it might contribute to you, and you to it. The point of this is to mine all the gold from every possible vein. If one of your "hots" involves working with people, ask yourself other questions concerning people. How many people? How often? What sort of people? Why be with them? What's the result of our interactions? Next, do the same thing with everything that is "not hot" about the potential career. Spend enough time to explore fully. You may want to use the long list of questions at the back of the "Questions" chapter to help you work on this Inquiry. *The exercise should take several hours to complete.*

5. Collect all the important "hots" from all the individual pages on one master "hots" page. Do the same with "nots." Then prioritize the ten most important entries in each master list.

6. Go back over the eight careers. Compare and contrast each with the others. How are they different? What "hots" and "nots" run through several of them as themes? How important are these themes to you? What careers have risen to the top? Which have sunk to the bottom? Why? Ask yourself, "What further questions does this Inquiry bring to light?

7. Ask yourself, "Would I be willing to generate any new commitments based on doing this Inquiry? What elements of these careers, what entries on the lists am I willing to commit to now? *Turn to your Primary Lists (Wants, Commitments and Requirements, and Questions), as well as to your Careers to Consider List. What can you add to those lists now?* **What am I sure will definitely be an important component of my future career?**

8. I sometimes use this Inquiry twice with a client: once when everything is still foggy, and again a little later on when the career has taken more shape. You might want to do the same thing.

•

CHAPTER 25

50,000-MILE CHECKUP

50,000-MILE CHECKUP

You are now well along the way through the career-choice process. Let's take a few minutes to check on how you are progressing. So far, you have used many Inquiries, all of which are supposed to help you look into the many areas that play a part in having a career that is deeply satisfying. To gauge how you are progressing, take a look through your Commitments and Requirements List. See if the commitments you have written down so far are beginning to shape what you will do with your life. That will help you tell how far down the trail you have traveled.

Write out the commitments you have so far as a statement that describes your future career as well as you can. Make sure you include commitments you haven't yet written down as well as ones from as many areas of inquiry as possible: personality traits, innate talents, etc. Here is an example:

> I will have a career that is true to my ENFP nature and my maestro personality, working directly with people or organizations that are essentially healthy, but want to improve their performance. It will be in a consulting, coaching, teaching capacity that makes constant use of my high diagnostic reasoning, and fast-moving imagination. My husband and I will definitely move to the bay area within the next year. When we arrive, I will enroll in a master's program, if it proves necessary, to learn the discipline I choose. In the next few weeks I will do whatever research it takes to narrow my choice further, first of all to investigate disciplines that work with individuals and ones where I would be consulting with organizations.

If you have this much specificity, you are well on your way to making your choice. On the other hand, your Commitments List might sound more like this:

> I will work with friendly, positive people in a position that allows for growth and rewards me for my skill and productivity, rather than on my political

skill. I will have a window that opens and have plenty of spare time for other aspects of my life.

If yours is more like the second list, it may be useful to notice that when you read this description, you really don't get any clue about what that person will be doing. All of their commitments are obviously valid and very important to them. Nevertheless, the statement is not going to be very helpful to them in pinning down their future career. What's more, it also sounds like they may be reacting to unpleasant elements of their present job or past ones, rather than carving out new territory and designing their future.

If your list basically sounds like the first list, you are in good shape. Go on to the next chapter. If your list reminds you more of the second list, it is time to declare a breakdown, and figure out how to generate more directive commitments.

Your difficulty may stem from a focus on hunting for preexisting requirements rather than creating new commitments and making bold decisions, lack of practice in taking a stand and making it happen, and attacks of Yeahbuts. It could be that you have not been participating 100 percent in this process. It could be that you didn't understand until right now how important it is to focus on commitments that actually shape your future. Or it might be that you care more about elements that, although important to you, do not carry you in giant steps down the trail to a final decision. Whatever the cause, you need to realize that the way things are going now, you are unlikely to get to your goal. You have to find a way to do that which you have been unable to do so far. Here are possible solutions:

1. Figure out the source of your difficulty. What is going on? Just ask yourself. You probably know where you fell short. If that doesn't help, reread the "If You Get Stuck" chapter and see if it helps diagnose what has happened.

2. If you figure out the source of your difficulty, go back to the chapters that are appropriate to help you through.

3. If you are not sure, you may want to re-up your commitment to getting to your goal and start the whole process all over again, from the beginning.

4. You could hire an expert career coach to guide you through the rapids to your goal.

CHAPTER 26

•

THEY PAY YOU TO
PERFORM SPECIFIC FUNCTIONS

The whole point of working is to perform a function, produce a specific result, or fill a particular role. It is bewildering to consider the myriad possibilities available in the more than 10,000 different job titles that have been identified by the federal government. The point of this chapter is to help you define which functions you will perform and what parts you will play in the theater of the material world.

If you were to lay down in the grass with a magnifying glass and study a nest of ants, you would quickly notice that their society is divided into easy to recognize functional roles. Some ants guard the door, others gather food, or serve the queen. It seems more complicated for us. But if you could step back and observe human career functions with a telescope from the moon, the enormous variety of things we do in our work would become almost as easy to categorize as the jobs in an ant nest.

Most careers are concentrated on performing between one and three specialized functions most of the time. Some of these functions are *directly people-oriented*. Other people are the central focus of the work. The customer-service representative, the supervisor, the therapist, and the teacher all perform functions whose purpose is directly and centrally focused on people. Some functions are centered around *data, information, and ideas*. An artist, a computer programmer, and a secretary all perform functions that mainly involve data/information/ideas. In the final category, work centers on *things/objects and the physical world*. Stevedores, brain surgeons, carpenters, and architects all fit in this category.

Of course, many careers involve more than one function. Most of the time, the important functions in a particular career cluster in one of these three categories. Usually, each career has an obvious senior function. Other, more junior functions may support the senior function. For example, a journalist's senior function is writing news stories, a "data/information" function. Even though journalists may spend a large portion of their day interviewing people, the final product and central focus of the job is data/information—the story. Take a few minutes to consider the careers of people you know and work you have done. Look for the central functions. What is the main point, the main product? What are the supporting functions?

Sometimes, the main functional category a job fits into is open to interpretation. Some careers include multiple functions. A professor of engineering engages in all the functional categories. He or she teaches groups of students, advises and supports individual students. Research, writing, and scoring exams is a data function. In a highly spatial, three-dimensional field like engineering, "things" are never very far away. Even though all the functional categories are a part of this career, for most professors of engineering, one function is most important. A professor could particularly love working with the students directly, or a passion for close contact with the world of things might be foremost.

In the past, many physicians considered themselves to be healers, a people function, first and foremost. Nowadays, the practice of medicine is primarily a things function. The modern physician is a mechanic, a technical expert in the diagnosis and treatment of disease, the repair and replacement of body parts. Even though the thrust of medical education is to produce highly trained mechanics, an individual can always choose to be a healer first, a people function. However, if you are considering a career in medicine and are mainly interested in being a healer of people, you might find yourself in an alien environment in a modern hospital or medical practice. Even though the senior function of a particular career is open to your own interpretation, remember to be realistic when you design the functions of your future career. If you are not deeply interested in the highly technical diagnosis and repair of body parts, don't become a physician. If you don't love selling, don't become a salesperson. It is not enough to love the product or interacting with other people. Since you will be selling the product all day, every day, the senior function of all sales jobs is selling, not advising, consulting, or knowing a great deal about some service or product.

People often make the mistake of choosing a career with subject matter they love, but performing functions that are not the most natural for them. Just because you love carpets woven by nomads in the Persian deserts doesn't necessarily mean you will love selling them, or studying them, or weaving them. The trick is to find a way to have it all: to perform a set of functions you really enjoy, combined with subject matter that you are passionate about. Do everything you can to find a way to do both. Don't assume that you will have to make a compromise until you have searched to the ends of the earth to find a way to have both function and subject matter fit you well. If you have to emphasize one over the other, putting more emphasis on functions is usually the way to go. Interests are highly changeable and suggestible. On the other hand, the natural gifts you have for performing various functions are hardwired. The point of this chapter is not to discover what functions you use so that you can reproduce them in your new career. It is to discover what constellation of functions are best for you, and, hopefully, to commit to having work where you get to perform them, all of the time.

In the following Inquiry, you are going to have a chance to decide what functions you will perform in your future career. Give everything you have to this

Inquiry. It is an especially important one because if you can pin down the functions you will perform, you will have solved a few large pieces of the puzzle.

For everything else living on the earth, genetics inflexibly dictates their function. Only we humans can make up our own minds. Nevertheless, most people naturally perform a narrow range of functions that link them to specific careers, without being aware they are doing so. Some of us are natural promoters, organizers, inventors, entrepreneurs, improvisational speakers, tool users, builders, dancers, and so forth. The goal in the following Inquiry is to narrow down the function or functions you will perform in your future career to the point where you can say: "I am a _____." The idea is to become clearer about what functions are your best and most natural forms of self-expression. If you had a huge key on your back, like a wind-up toy, and they wound you up each morning and turned you loose, what would you do? What do you do naturally, without being asked? What are the functions you just can't help doing when an opportunity is presented? If you aren't sure, just do the best you can. It's fine to mark something you think you would excel in but aren't sure.

Have you ever known of an animal that was the slightest bit unclear about its natural functions? Probably not. On the other hand, we humans spend so much time thinking and so little time observing directly that it is little wonder we often suffer from a lack of insight about what functions express us best. In this exercise, do your best to notice and report which functions express you best. Even if you are stuck in a career that doesn't really fit, you probably have found a way to do that which comes naturally, either at work or after work. Someone whose natural functions lean toward educating people, but who is stuck in a secretarial job, may become the person in the office who gravitates to training new secretaries. Another secretary who is a natural counselor/therapist may be the person everyone trusts to listen to their problems and advise them. Your activities and interests outside of work also provide clues about what functions express you most naturally.

Some folks hate to box themselves into just one function or two or three. They say they want to perform a wide range of functions in their work. The point of this Inquiry is not to cut you off from doing many activities at work, but to decide where most of your time and energy will be concentrated. Almost everyone, no matter how creative, brilliant, or successful, has work that concentrates on a very small number of functions, usually no more than three. Even Leonardo daVinci concentrated his energy on a few functions: drawing, designing, and investigating the physical world. Yes, he did many, many things. But most of them expressed these few functions or played a lesser role in his extraordinary career. This doesn't mean you will not get to do many other things as significant parts of your work or your life outside of work. In fact, there is no reason why you cannot do everything on the following functions list, if you so desire.

PRIMARY JOB FUNCTIONS

1. Go through the list of functional groupings that follow. Put a mark on the line in front of the subcategories that express or describe you best. Ideally, this is more a matter of noticing, observing, and witnessing what you do well naturally and enjoy doing than it is a matter of checking off preferences. Remember, you are doing your best to reveal which functions express you naturally. These are not necessarily functions in which you have experience or training. You will most likely have found a way to perform them regularly in some area of your life. Do not mark more than a *grand total* of ten to fifteen subcategories. This means a total of ten to fifteen in the entire Inquiry, not ten to fifteen in each section. Sometimes several similar functions are listed on one line. If some words describe the function you are focusing on better than others, circle the words that communicate best. Even though you may be good at, or make use of many functions, just mark the most important ones. Check only the ones that really stand out. You might want to have a talk with your friends and family. Show them this these pages. They may have noticed some things about you that you so take for granted they are completely invisible to you.

   If you are a young person with little experience, you may have difficulty honing your functions to a sharp point. If so, just do the best you can. Mark down functions you are attracted to or think you may have a knack for.

   If you are older and have spent a large chunk of your working life performing a group of functions that do not fit or express you well, this exercise may take more thought. You may want to run this Inquiry past some other people who know you well, including people who are intimately familiar with you at the workplace. Take this exercise as far as you can. Get as much definition as possible.

2. Once you are finished, go through the list and rate your talent or ability in each of the subcategories you marked. Mark the number in front of the subcategory. Five is the highest rating, 1 the lowest. After that, go on to the instructions that follow this list.

PEOPLE-ORIENTED FUNCTIONS
USED PRIMARILY WITH INDIVIDUALS

—①②③④⑤ Mentoring, one-on-one teaching, instructing, training, tutoring
—①②③④⑤ Counseling, coaching, empowering
—①②③④⑤ Healing, treating the diseases or problems of, rehabilitating
—①②③④⑤ Encouraging, supporting
—①②③④⑤ Providing emotional support
—①②③④⑤ Advising, consulting
—①②③④⑤ Assessing, evaluating
—①②③④⑤ Diagnosing, analyzing, or understanding an individual's needs, mood, motives, responses, behavior, etc.
—①②③④⑤ Using intuition or nonverbal clues to understand individuals
—①②③④⑤ Observing, studying the behaviors of
—①②③④⑤ Persuading, selling, motivating, influencing, enrolling, recruiting
—①②③④⑤ Using your personal charisma
—①②③④⑤ Giving pleasure to
—①②③④⑤ Cultivating and maintaining relationships
—①②③④⑤ Selecting, screening, hiring
—①②③④⑤ Managing, supervising
—①②③④⑤ Giving instructions, providing information
—①②③④⑤ Listening
—①②③④⑤ Interviewing
—①②③④⑤ Communicating verbally
—①②③④⑤ Bringing together, introducing
—①②③④⑤ Negotiating between individuals, arbitrating
—①②③④⑤ Enabling, assisting other people to locate information
—①②③④⑤ Helping, serving, providing for needs of individuals
—①②③④⑤ Entertaining, amusing, giving pleasure to, conversing with, hosting
—①②③④⑤ Assisting
—①②③④⑤ Other _____
—①②③④⑤ Other _____

USED PRIMARILY WITH GROUPS, ORGANIZATIONS, THE PUBLIC OR HUMANITY

—①②③④⑤ Empowering, enabling a group
—①②③④⑤ Inspiring a group
—①②③④⑤ Instructing, teaching, training a group
—①②③④⑤ Healing
—①②③④⑤ Managing, leading a group, organization, company
—①②③④⑤ Initiating, creating, founding a group of people, company, etc.

___①②③④⑤ Supervising, captaining a group or team
___①②③④⑤ Team member such as a member of a work group, athlete, orchestra member
___①②③④⑤ Leading group in recreation, games, exercise, travel, rehabilitation
___①②③④⑤ Negotiating between groups, resolving conflicts or disputes, bringing conflicting groups together
___①②③④⑤ Facilitating, guiding a group
___①②③④⑤ Persuading, motivating, convincing, or selling to a group
___①②③④⑤ Using your personal charisma
___①②③④⑤ Networking
___①②③④⑤ Communicating verbally with groups, public speaking or communicating verbally through the media
___①②③④⑤ Communicating with people via art, music, writing, or other art forms
___①②③④⑤ Diagnosing, analyzing, or understanding a group's existing or potential needs, mood, motives, responses, behavior, etc.
___①②③④⑤ Using intuition or nonverbal clues to understand a group or individuals in a group setting
___①②③④⑤ Consulting to affect a group or organization's productivity, behavior, etc.
___①②③④⑤ Advising a group, providing expertise
___①②③④⑤ Designing events or educational experiences
___①②③④⑤ Creating activities, games
___①②③④⑤ Hosting, entertaining socially
___①②③④⑤ Amusing, providing entertainment or pleasure to
___①②③④⑤ Performing, acting
___①②③④⑤ Presenting to people via TV, films, seminars, speeches
___①②③④⑤ Selecting, screening prospective members or employees
___①②③④⑤ Assisting, serving, helping
___①②③④⑤ Other_____
___①②③④⑤ Other_____

INFORMATION, DATA, MEDIA, KNOWLEDGE, WISDOM, ART, OR IDEA FUNCTIONS

___①②③④⑤ Idea-generating, creating , inventing, imagining
___①②③④⑤ Drawing, painting, filming, photographing
___①②③④⑤ Creating software or similar works
___①②③④⑤ Creating original works of art

___①②③④⑤ Performing, acting

___①②③④⑤ Presenting to people via TV, films, seminars, speeches

___①②③④⑤ Creating visual or written presentations or presentations using other media

___①②③④⑤ Writing fiction

___①②③④⑤ Writing nonfiction, critical writing

___①②③④⑤ Technical writing

___①②③④⑤ Creating marketing materials, advertisements, etc.

___①②③④⑤ Designing events or educational experiences

___①②③④⑤ Creating activities, games

___①②③④⑤ Research to develop new ideas, theories, etc.

___①②③④⑤ Mastery of a specialized body of knowledge, expertise, wisdom, lore

___①②③④⑤ Brainstorming

___①②③④⑤ Diagnosing by seeing the relationship between clues

___①②③④⑤ Perceiving patterns in data, events, or processes or accurately evaluating information

___①②③④⑤ Seeing through masses of information to the central principles or most important facts

___①②③④⑤ Breaking masses of data down into component parts

___①②③④⑤ Synthesizing: combining parts to form a whole

___①②③④⑤ Systematizing, prioritizing, or organizing information

___①②③④⑤ Information engineering, computer programming

___①②③④⑤ Judging, evaluating, or appraising information

___①②③④⑤ Making recommendations

___①②③④⑤ Organizing information, projects, or events

___①②③④⑤ Planning, strategizing

___①②③④⑤ Researching by gathering or compiling information

___①②③④⑤ Researching via observing behavior or phenomena

___①②③④⑤ Using physical senses to evaluate information

___①②③④⑤ Translating, interpreting to other language, media, or style

___①②③④⑤ Interpreting other people's concepts, ideas

___①②③④⑤ Making decisions about data

___①②③④⑤ Adapting information to suit another purpose

___①②③④⑤ Combining existing ideas or concepts into new ones

___①②③④⑤ Editing, improving

___①②③④⑤ Retrieving information, researching, compiling information

___①②③④⑤ Copying, entering in computer

___①②③④⑤ Comparing, proofing

___①②③④⑤ Mathematics, working with numbers, statistics, formulae

___①②③④⑤ Accounting

___①②③④⑤ Record keeping, storing, filing

___①②③④⑤ Other_____

___①②③④⑤ Other_____

FUNCTIONS RELATED TO THINGS,

OBJECTS, THE PHYSICAL WORLD

___①②③④⑤ Understanding complex physical systems, the sciences, technology

___①②③④⑤ Creating new theories, understanding or interpreting of physical systems

___①②③④⑤ Inventing, creating, designing original devices or objects

___①②③④⑤ Creating works of art

___①②③④⑤ Diagnosing and repairing mechanical systems (such as a mechanic or physician)

___①②③④⑤ Repairing or restoring things, maintaining

___①②③④⑤ Assembling

___①②③④⑤ Choosing, arranging objects artistically

___①②③④⑤ Eye for design, color, texture, or proportion

___①②③④⑤ Sensual acuity of sight, sound, smell, taste, or feel

___①②③④⑤ Evaluating, appraising

___①②③④⑤ Sculpting, shaping, tooling

___①②③④⑤ Crafting (combining artistic and motor skills to fashion things)

___①②③④⑤ Fine hand dexterity (as used by surgeon, tailor, artist, etc.)

___①②③④⑤ Massaging, touching, hands-on healing

___①②③④⑤ Dancing

___①②③④⑤ Directing films or plays, choreographing, storyboarding

___①②③④⑤ Skilled, precision use of tools

___①②③④⑤ Manufacturing, mass-producing

___①②③④⑤ Cooking

___①②③④⑤ Using physical skill and dexterity in athletics, etc.

___①②③④⑤ Operating an airplane, ship, boat, truck, or car

___①②③④⑤ Navigating, orienteering, pathfinding

___①②③④⑤ Using large tools such as bulldozers and other construction machinery, tanks

___①②③④⑤ Constructing buildings or other large objects

___①②③④⑤ Farming, gardening, raising or tending plants or animals

___①②③④⑤ Operating, controlling, or guiding machines

___①②③④⑤ Tending machines

___①②③④⑤ Acute awareness of surroundings, physical environment,

___①②③④⑤ Street wisdom, acute alertness to threats to survival

___①②③④⑤ Hunting, trapping, fishing
___①②③④⑤ Fighting
___①②③④⑤ Installing
___①②③④⑤ Cleaning, preparing, washing, dusting
___①②③④⑤ Moving, storing, warehousing, carrying, lifting, handling
___①②③④⑤ Other_____
___①②③④⑤ Other_____

3. When you have finished following the previous instructions, review the categories you marked. Select the most important functions and underline or highlight them. Do not mark more than a grand total of ten from the entire list of functions. Then narrow from ten to somewhere around five final, most important, most fitting functions. Narrow down your selections as much as possible. Get to the real essentials

4. Look through the work you have done so far in this exercise. Can you pick out any themes? Do most of the entries concentrate in one of the major categories? For example, you may discover that your entries are concentrated on working with groups of people. Delve deep to see what else you can discover. Do you have a preference for a certain size group? Do you want to work with them face to face or in a more abstract way?

5. By now, you may be able to designate one or more functions as you own perfect "senior" function. Or you may just be able to pin it down to the point of picking which major category you will concentrate on: people, information, or things. You may be able to decide that your senior, most important category is "speaking in front of groups of people" or " planning events." You may have discovered that there is more than one important function at the top of your list. Or, there may be various possible combinations of functions. Sometimes, these may fit together easily and obviously. Sometimes not. If not, go on to step 6 of this Inquiry, in which you experiment with various combinations to clarify further. In this step, you use a method that is very similar to the way you would go about rearranging the furniture in your living room. Most people find it is impossible to visualize how furniture would look without actually moving it around and trying various combinations. You will do the same thing with various combinations of functions. If you are fairly clear about which functions are most important and how they fit together with one another, skip step 6.

6. Make a couple of pages of your notebook into a form like the one on the next page, with a senior function column on the left, a secondary func-

tions column on the right. Pick a likely candidate for your first senior job function. Write the main category it falls into on the first line on the left-hand column. Then write in the function on the line below, as shown at number 1 in the illustration. Then do the same thing for possible supporting functions, as shown at number 2 in the illustration. Continue to experiment. Write down as many possible combinations as you can think of, starting at number 3 in the illustration and continuing down the page until you have exhausted all reasonable possibilities. Experiment, play, consider possibilities, enjoy. Keep playing with various combinations until you have a sense of what combination or combinations suit you best. As you try out various possibilities, consider how the functions fit together. Even though most careers have one senior function, you might want to experiment with combinations where there is more than one senior function. Perhaps you will find that some seemingly unlikely combination clicks.

7. What careers are suggested by the combinations of functions you like best? Brainstorm! Make up as many careers as you can that might express your best combination of functions. At this point, you may need to do some research. You may not know what careers use the combinations you like best. The ideal way to get ideas is to ask as many people as you can. Your friends may have some good ideas. People who work directly in fields that use a similar combination may be a useful source of information.

Senior Function	Secondary or Supporting Functions
People (individuals)	Things, objects
Managing, supervising	Manufacturing, designing
Things, objects	Things, objects
Manufacturing	Inventing, designing

8. Make one or more pie charts that illustrate what functions you would like to use in your future career. Do not restrict your slices to the major, primary, and secondary functions. Add in smaller slices for whatever other functions you want to include. And, don't forget about lunch, kibitzing,

etc. At this point, you may be quite clear about what functions you want to perform. If not, use pie charts as a way of exploring further. Try out various combinations.

9. Turn to your Commitments and Requirements List and your Questions List. Bring them up to date with what you have decided, discovered, or revealed from this Inquiry.

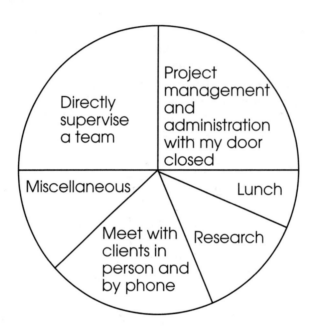

CHAPTER 27

•

HUMAN ECOLOGY—WORKPLACE ENVIRONMENTS

When the subject of ecology comes up, it is usually in reference to environmental deterioration or how we are destroying an ecological niche by altering its delicate balance. In the suburban jungle, to archetypal white-collar Bob, it all seems a little abstract, like bad news from far away. He turns off the TV, vaguely distressed by the news feature about syringes floating up on the shore again. He goes to bed and dreams of beaches. In the morning he is off on his one hour bumper-to-bumper commute in a sea of fellow drivers. Many of them, like Bob, are feeling both competitive and benumbed. All the way to work he worries that he may fall victim to the "downsizing" that has reduced his department by 50 percent. His stomach churns. Because the workload hasn't diminished, he has been ordered to shoulder twice the responsibility. He is still tired and stressed out from the pressure and isn't thinking clearly. Every day it gets a little more difficult. It seems like the workday never ends. Plus, no matter how much he does, he never gets any praise. His boss seems to have learned his supervisory skills at the Cotton Fields School of Management, where you sit on a big white horse and point out all the mistakes your employees make while instilling as much fear and uncertainty as possible.

In the midst of all this turmoil, Bob has not noticed that he is part of an ecosystem. He is an organism in the midst of various environments that alter the course and quality of his every moment. He attributes his exhaustion and grumpiness to some of the parts of his environment: the boss, the long hours. He never recognizes that it is not quite as simple as that. It's not just one thing or another. It is the impact his entire ecosystem has on him. The stressors he notices and complains about are just the tip of the iceberg. Beneath the surface there are other, more subtle, environmental factors that affect his peace of mind, clarity of thought, creativity, and physical health. How does he deal with it? He simply accepts his fate with a shrug and pays the price that his personal ecological disaster zone extracts, and so, to some degree, do most of the rest of us. Once again, our adaptability and resilience are our downfall. If, in order to be reasonably productive, we humans needed an environment nearly perfectly designed for us, there would be more human ecologists working in big business than accountants. But, we continue to prove somewhere in our world every day that we can survive nearly anything except total starvation.

We put up with destructive environments because we think we must. In career planning, the quality of the workplace environment is often the first thing to be sacrificed for the sake of other goals. "I'll put up with any degree of discomfort to reach my goal" is considered an admirable philosophy. Sometimes the traditional climb up the career ladder requires you to temporarily pay heavy dues. "Temporarily" is the key word. For every person who temporarily puts up with an ill-suited environment as part of a clearly focused plan, there are ten who wind up permanently stuck, glued by stasis like flies on flypaper. People end up in these ecological cesspools permanently because they were not sufficiently committed to working in a supportive environment, or because they did not understand the impact an adverse work environment would have on the overall quality of their lives.

Sometimes it's just good old crazy thinking that gets people into a mess. I know a man who wakes up at 4:30 A.M., does the chores on his ten-acre country place, drives a two-hour commute into the city every morning, works a ten-hour day at a job he doesn't like, arrives back home at 8 P.M., enjoys living in the country for two hours before he falls asleep. Nearly every weekend he brings a big pile of work home. Is it worth it? Speaking from the shade of his furrowed brow, he says it is. I can't help thinking that he pays a hefty price for his few hours of pleasure. Instead of designing a career from the ground up that included living in the country and the time to enjoy it, he just added the farm on top of an already stressful career, thinking it would be the cure. The real subject of this chapter is stress. The point of considering your workplace environment is more than just hanging around in a place you like. It is to design a personal ecosystem that manages stress well.

Low-Stress Living

Nobody ever has anything good to say about stress. It is right up there with mosquitoes on the list of the major nuisances Mother Nature made. Nevertheless, it is virtually impossible to have a life that is stress free. Life becomes stress free the moment you die. When we sit in a sylvan glade and absorb the peace of the deep forest, we do not realize that all balanced ecosystems have numerous stressors. One component of a balanced system is its ability to process stress successfully. As your own personal career ecologist, you want to design a career ecosystem that melts, dissolves, and dissipates stress, so that it doesn't build up inside of you.

Stress is not a complicated subject. Picture yourself as a talking tube with a hole in each end, like this:

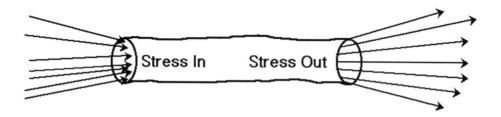

The stress goes in one end and, hopefully, out the other. So long as the exit hole is as big as the entrance hole, everything is fine. The stress that enters gets back out again. When the amount of stress coming into is more than the system can handle, it builds up and is stored in the body, like this:

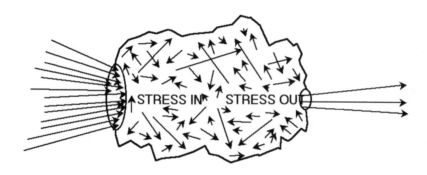

If you choose a career that is fairly low stress, you will not have to master processing stress through your system. If you pick work that involves a lot of challenge, it will, most likely, generate more stress. If this is the case, or, if getting to your goal involves spending a few years in a stressful environment, you will have to design into your career plan a way to deal with it. There are just three ways to deal with stress:

Minimize the stressors in your environment. The very best is to choose a career that fits you perfectly in as many areas as possible: talents, personality, and so forth. Or, you could just pick a career that is naturally low in stress.

Keep the stresses in the environment from getting to you. Close your office door, wear earplugs and dark sunglasses, or develop some compassion for your boss.

Learn ways to let out the stress that gets in. There are many ways to dissipate career-related stress, to actually dissolve it by opening up the exit sphincter so the stress flows out of your system: have nurturing relationships, a sense of humor, an environment at home that melts stress. Do a lot of aerobic exercise and use stress-relieving practices such as meditation and hatha yoga.

If you just can remember that you are a tube with a hole on each end, it should be relatively easy to figure out how to design your career so that stress will not be a big problem.

Designing Your Workplace Ecosystem

Are you ready to become your own personal ecologist? Human ecology is the science concerned with understanding the relationships between humans and their physical and social environments. To design a career that fits, you need to consider both the physical and social environments of your work life. The physical environment ranges from the big geographical picture, where you live, to the micro, the noise level and the color of the paint in your office. The social environment includes everything from the socioeconomics of where you live to the customary mood of the people who you work with (including you). To be your own human ecologist takes more observation than study. Your heart knows what fits and what doesn't. You could easily sit down right now and invent a workplace environment that would be perfect for you. On the other hand, most folks are willing to settle for unnecessary compromises because it seems too difficult and challenging to have it all fit together perfectly. As usual, it is a question of commitment. If it is really important that you love your work, you will definitely need to make the environment just as important as all the other vital pieces of the puzzle.

These days, you not only have to think about designing a career by considering the present workplace environments, but also about what will likely take place in the future. Years ago, while trapped in a small tent by a howling blizzard, my friend Andy read a story to me where people living in an icy wilderness had to spend all of their lives searching for enough firewood to barely heat their huts. It was an ultimate horror story that is now beginning to come more true every day as world population soars and resources become ever more precious. It now takes a working couple to have the same lifestyle my parents enjoyed, with only dad bringing home a paycheck. So think about the future and design it into your plan.

It is one thing to pay heavy dues now for a wonderful future that you have carefully planned. It is yet another to fool yourself that you are paying temporary dues when, in reality, you are just in a bad place. When I founded Rockport Institute many years ago, I put every penny into research. That meant living at the office for a while. The office was in downtown Washington, D.C., just up Pennsylvania Avenue from the White House. Whenever the president needed a pack of gum in the middle of the night, a whole fleet of vehicles would go screaming by just a few feet away with the sirens going full tilt. There was a big noisy student bar close by, and the young dudes used our corner for all-night games of chest thumping, hurling, and yelling. I used earphones, shades, exercise, and meditation to deal with that incredibly stress-provoking corner. All the while, I knew it was temporary. Now, many years later, I'm sitting in my office overlooking a lake and flower gardens and listening to mockingbirds and wood thrushes sing. Was it worth it to put up with that terrible downtown environment in the beginning? Oh yes! Would I have gone berserk if I had not had a clear vision of where I was going? Oh yes!

INQUIRY 30

DESIGNING YOUR

WORKPLACE ECOSYSTEM

The list of questions in the "Questions" chapter contains many that are environment-related. Go back through them. What environmental elements are most important to you? What affects you negatively? What would be the ideal environment? What stressors would you be willing to deal with in your work environment? How much? How often? Remember that it is impossible to have a stress-free environment. Your job is to design your environment so that it fits in with what you can and are willing to handle. For example, to you, it might be ideal to work at home and never have to deal with rush-hour traffic. Are you willing to commit to this perfect situation, or will you make some sort of compromise? If so, how far will you drive? Make sure you assess carefully. What shape are you in after a commute of fifteen minutes? A half hour? An hour? Please look at all the other environment-related question in this same way.

When you are finished, turn to your Primary Lists (Wants, Commitments and Requirements, and Questions), as well as to your Careers to Consider List. What can you add to those lists? **What am I sure will definitely be an important component of my future career?**

CHAPTER 28

•

MAKING THE FINAL CHOICE

Many years ago, I used to help a dairy farmer with his midsummer haying. It was a long, hot, sweaty, prickly process of throwing heavy bales high onto a farm wagon and then unloading them into the barn. At the end of the day, we would all gather around, totally exhausted, and heave the last wagonload of bales high into the dusty hayloft. As we got down to the very last bale of the day, someone would inevitably invoke the ancient hay maker's joke and exclaim: "Here it is! I found it! Here's that bale we were looking for!"

You have now reached the end of your long and prickly journey through the career-choice process. The is the place you hoped to arrive at from the very beginning. If you have built a sufficiently strong group of commitments and requirements, have answered all your important questions, and have continued to refine your Careers to Consider List, you should now be ready to make the final choice. If you are not sure you are ready, go back through your Primary Lists and see if you have forgotten anything important.

For some of you, the final decision will not be too challenging. The choice may be fairly obvious. Or, you may now have to choose between more than one career that fits all of your specifications. If that is the case and you have reached the moment of choice, you may want to reread the "Making Decisions, A Short Course" chapter to help you get off the horns of your dilemma. This is your life, and your choice to make. There is no right answer or perfect career.

I suggest that, after all the work you have done, you are the one person in the universe who is capable and prepared to make this choice. All you have to do is do it. It is your final created commitment. "I will be a . . ."

The Yeahbuts may be telling you to leave your options open. If you do, you will still be in the midst of uncertainty. There are only a few special situations when it may be appropriate to have your final choice include more than one specific career:

- More than one very similar jobs would be equally appealing, and you are willing to split your job hunt between them.
- You live in or plan to move to a geographical area where choices and jobs are very limited. In this case, you may need to keep your focus a little wider than one single career option.

- You are a college student and feel that you have narrowed your choice sufficiently for the present, and want to get some more experience or maturity under your belt before you make the final decision.

Unless your situation is similar to one of these scenarios, reluctance to make one final choice is probably just an attack of Yeahbuts. You can't make your dreams into your life until you decide. So, take a deep breath and go for it!

When the choice is made, you may not feel excited or relieved. If your choice extends you out into new territory, you may feel apprehensive or suffer an even more massive attack of yeahbuts than usual. There is a phenomenon all salespeople know about that they call "buyers remorse." This is a special form of Yeahbut that attacks once a decision has been made. If this happens, don't let it sway your resolve. In fact, you may have doubts surface regularly. This is perfectly normal. If you read the biographies of people who have accomplished extraordinary feats, you will realize that doubts are almost inevitable. Once I asked my explorer friend John Goddard if he had suffered from attacks of doubts in the midst of expeditions into new territory. He said that at times the doubts were constant, especially at times of great difficulty and duress. I suggest that you treat them like mosquitoes. Know that you will have to put up with them, that they will draw some blood. But do not let them keep you from your destination.

Once the choice has been made, remember that there is one more step in the career-choice process. Go out and celebrate! Nobody deserves it more than you.

Turn to your Primary Lists (Wants, Commitments and Requirements, and Questions), as well as to your Careers to Consider List. What can you add to those lists now? What will my future career be? If you have made a final choice, don't forget to add a celebration to your Commitments List.

•

CHAPTER 29

MASTERING PERSONAL MARKETING

Now that you have decided what you are going to do, it's time to get out there and make it happen. This chapter is about personal marketing. If you understand the basic principles of marketing yourself, you will be much more effective, whether you are job hunting or trying to gain admittance into the perfect graduate school program. I will discuss personal marketing in the context of a job hunt. The principles are equally useful no matter what you use them for.

To Master Personal Marketing

Forget about the traditional approaches to job hunting. They are woefully ineffective. Don't waste your time combing the literature for tips that will make your search fast and painless. They won't. The ideal situation in any job hunt is to have several potential employers lined up at your door, competing to have you accept their high-quality job offers. Does this seem unrealistic? If it does, you have already shot yourself in the foot. You have crippled your efforts before you are even out of the gate. In this chapter, you will learn the most essential principles of personal marketing. By focusing on principles instead of tips, you get to the heart of the matter.

Masters in any area of endeavor do not need to worry much about technique. They don't have to concern themselves with remembering a long list of rules and tips. They come from the deepest principles of their art or craft. When essential principles are your ground of being, you do the right thing naturally. Find an example in your own life that proves that what I am saying is true. It doesn't need to be something extraordinary. It could be something as common as riding bikes when you were a kid. You do not have to be an exceptional bicyclist to come from a ground of being of mastery. Nearly all kids who grow up with bikes are masters. They come from the essential principles. They do not have to think about what to do next. They do the right thing naturally, even in situations that are new and dangerous.

In many areas of endeavor, such as bikes and violins, it takes practice to develop mastery. The principles can only be absorbed through practice. Fortunately, this is not true of personal marketing. You can absorb the principles quickly, directly, and use them immediately to improve your job hunt. This chapter could be expanded into a book of several hundred pages. You won't find answers to all of your specific job-hunting questions here. But if you let the material in this chapter really sink in, you will be able to answer many of your questions without outside help. As you read through this chapter, what it says will most likely "click." You will recognize this stuff as true. Then all you have to do is overcome the tug of equilibrium and inertia in order to wage a very powerful, effective job-hunt campaign.

Abundance

Scarcity and abundance are opposing states of mind. I used to visit all the old folks in a nursing home in Camden, Maine, on Christmas day. Each of these folks had an identical room, with identical furniture and an identical view. I would walk into one room and be subjected to a torrent of complaints: the room was too small, the view inadequate, etc. In the next room I would find a cheerful person enjoying the abundance of his nice room and terrific view. When you are forced to live within fixed circumstances, a state of mind of abundance produces a completely different day-to-day life than does a point of view of scarcity. It allows you to generate circumstances that otherwise could never occur. If you look at job hunting from scarcity, you will probably conduct a campaign trying to come up with one decent job offer. Why not set your goal much higher at the very beginning? Why not something like, "Have several excellent job offers to choose from within the next three months." If you are fully committed to multiple offers, you will get out there and kick up a bigger storm of creativity and action than you would if you were looking for one.

Job-Hunt Effectiveness

The one most basic principle of job hunting is that every step in the process is a form of personal marketing. The person who gets the job is often the one who does the best job of marketing him- or herself, rather than the person most qualified. To compete successfully, you have to understand why one person gets selected over another and design your campaign so that you will be that person. Each phase of the job hunt provides an opportunity for you to come up with a creative strategy to boost the effectiveness of your campaign.

Presenting yourself in the best possible light takes a good suit, a great résumé, and an understanding of how to increase your odds of being the person selected.

In the next chapter, we will take care of the résumé. Right now, let's get you high up on the mountain of candidates.

Your success in the job hunt is dependent on the two axes of the chart below. The horizontal axis is the "Number of Transactions." If you apply for 200 jobs, you will have ten times the chance of landing one than if you apply for twenty jobs. If you spend twenty hours per week actively building a network, you will have ten times the chance of landing a job than if you network two hours per week. Double the transactions; double your chances. What could be more simple?

I'm a great believer in luck, and I find that the harder I work, the more of it I have.

— THOMAS JEFFERSON

The other axis is the "Quality of Transactions." "Hot," high-quality transactions all depend on having relationships with people who will help you or on being

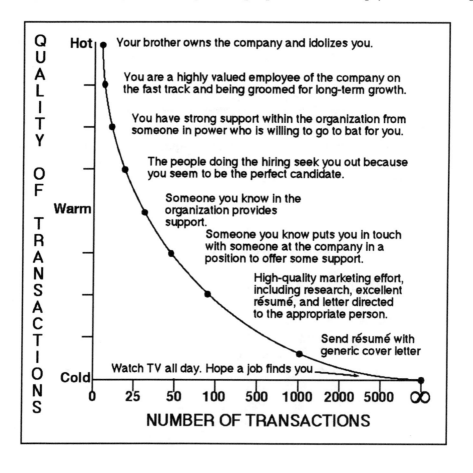

perceived as an exceptional candidate. At the top of the chart, you have a relative who owns the company and idolizes you. In this case you have everything going for you: There is a strong sense of relatedness and the perception that you are the best candidate. We will discuss both of these subjects a little later. If you are operating in this "blazing hot" zone, you probably will get a job offer with only one transaction. The higher you operate on the quality scale, the fewer transactions it will take per job offer. Conversely, as you descend down the quality scale, the number of transactions necessary to land a job multiplies at an enormous rate. Once you have descended into the pits of job hunting, where you mass mail résumés with generic cover letters, you are now up to an average of at least 1,000 transactions per offer, maybe more. Notice that increasing the quality of your marketing effort has an enormous effect on the number of transactions necessary. One step up the quality ladder brings the number of transactions down to around 100. When someone says that they do not have time to put out a full-blast marketing effort, they must not know the paradox of job hunting: The more time and energy you give to job hunting, the less time and energy it takes to land the job. Not only will you have a job sooner, but it will also take less total time and effort. So, if you don't have time to job hunt, give it all the time you have.

If possible, make finding your new job a full-time job. If you are working, you are going to have to arrange to work fewer hours or days, take a lot of sick days, or spend your time at your present job hunting for a new one on the phone. Unless you are very financially secure, quitting your job to have the time to job hunt may be counterproductive, because people tend to get a little desperate when they are unemployed and are more likely to pick the wrong job. After giving so much thought to designing your future career, you do not want to con yourself into accepting the wrong job because you feel vulnerable.

Rejection

Most of us job hunt from a point of view that saps our effectiveness from the very beginning. Take a few moments and imagine what it would be like if you were offered every job you applied for. Then the hunt would just be a matter of doing some research to see where you might like to work, meeting with potential employers to clarify whether or not there would be a perfect fit between you and the job, negotiating benefits, and accepting the one you wanted. Most people would have a great time "shopping" for the perfect job. It would be like shopping for anything else you were excited about. Take a minute and notice how you feel when you are shopping for something that really turns you on: a special gift, a book, clothes, a car, a guitar, or whatever. Feel that feeling. On the other hand, job hunting probably feels more like being blindfolded and tied to a post in front of a firing squad.

What makes job hunting feel like the firing squad is that we have dumped it into a mental pigeonhole along with other unwanted, unpleasant experiences. Job hunters become like characters in *The Wizard of Oz,* cowed and diminished by beliefs: "If I only had a heart." "If I only had a brain." "If I only had the right stuff to compete, the right degree, ten more years of experience, and a better network." The fly in the ointment is rejection. It is unlikely that you will be offered every job. You may be rejected again and again before you find the job you want. It happens to everyone. Even Madonna gets turned down. No one likes to be rejected. Years ago, a woman I was dating broke up with me just as I was going to break up with her. I felt betrayed and rejected even though I got exactly what I wanted. My feelings made no sense, but that didn't reduce their impact one bit. Because feelings arise automatically, it is unlikely you will learn to call up some inner force that will make them go away. If you job hunt, you will be rejected and feel rejected. The key is to transform the hunt by approaching it from a new point of view, where rejection has much less impact, where you are the cause, rather than the effect of the stream of events. Instead of being a leaf in the wind, hoping to run across a job that wants you, become an active force of your intentions and seek to create multiple excellent job offers to choose from.

If you design and plan your job hunt carefully, taking into consideration all the realities, the twists and turns of circumstance and fate, you will be able to concentrate on effective action rather than reacting to discomfort and potential rejection. Remember that some of the most powerful criteria driving human behavior are: feeling safe, being right, feeling good, looking good, and avoiding pain. In a traditional job hunt, all of these criteria take a beating. You don't feel safe because you are exposing yourself to rejection. You don't experience being right when you are invalidated by not being chosen. You don't feel good about all the uncertainty inherent in the hunt. You don't look good if they don't want you. Most people unconsciously conduct their job hunt based on these criteria rather than what works. A stiff and uncomfortable dance with rejection ensues, with the job hunter concentrating on avoiding having their toes stepped on rather than really swinging out. They say something like, "I'm not comfortable calling people I don't know." That is a perfectly valid statement, but when it affects their actions, they lose. When the commitment is to feeling safe, the previous statement gets translated to, "I won't call people I don't know." When the commitment is to results, you may voice the same complaint, but it will be while you are dialing the phone.

It's all a matter of perspective. If you were shopping for a special article of clothing, you might try on many candidates before you picked the final one. Are you rejecting the clothes that don't fit or look right, or are they rejecting you? Most job hunters feel more like clothes on the rack than someone shopping for the perfect fit. By turning your job hunt into an intentional project, a game of your own design, potential employers become the candidates, instead of you. They become part of your movie, rather than you a bit player in theirs.

Turn Your Job Hunt into a Project

When you design your hunt as a project, and make a commitment to achieving exceptional results, you will almost certainly find that you have to do some things that don't come easily. Within the context of a project, your actions are driven by your commitment to results rather than by your feelings. Once you have made a definite commitment to a specific result, planned how to get there, listed all the steps in order, all you have to do is wake up each morning and do what your list tells you to do. It is a matter of implementing a creative action plan that gets you most effectively to your goal instead of doing that which is within your everyday bag of tricks. Job hunting is one of those areas of life where the ends definitely do justify the means.

What you want to do is to get your effectiveness up as high as possible, reduce the mistakes, get you in the best position to succeed as soon as possible, with the minimum of difficulty and distress. To do that means learning a lot about the art of designing and implementing projects. I suggest that you reread the "Goals and Projects" chapter and use it as a guide to designing your job hunt.

Creating Agreement

Career changers ask, "Why would an employer hire me when I have no experience in the field I want to go into? Even if they did, wouldn't I have to go all the way back to square one, compete with younger people for a low-level job, and take a big pay cut? How can I deal with this problem successfully?"

First-time career choosers ask, "How can increase my chances of being the person who gets the job. How can I stand out from the crowd as an exceptional candidate?"

What makes a movie star a star? How did a madman like Hitler take over the minds of an entire nation? Why is a diamond worth more than a grain of sand? Why is a swan more beautiful than a chicken? All of these questions are answerable when you understand the principle of "agreement." A diamond is worth more than a grain of sand for only one reason: People agree that it is. Most cultures agree that uncommon objects are more valuable than plentiful things. There are also agreements about what is beautiful and what isn't. What makes a dandelion a weed is that people agree that it is. It is actually more sensible to imagine a culture where homeowners spent their weekends trying to reach landscaping perfection by achieving a lawn speckled with thousands of beautiful yellow dandelions than it is to imagine our own where endless hours are devoted to wiping out every last one.

No matter how deeply and passionately a president of the United States may want to chart a course that makes significant changes and improve the lives of the citizenry, the reality is that he or she has to make decisions that generate agreement. This person, who has more power than anyone else in the country, has to be more circumspect in what he says than anyone else, because he cannot risk saying things that drain his hard-won reservoir of agreement.

Agreement is one the most powerful forces in the world, not only in shaping our culture, but also in defining who we are, what we believe, and how we behave. I was told about an experiment where people were brought, one at a time, into a specially constructed, completely dark room, where the floor, walls, and ceiling had been painted flat black. A person was guided to the one chair in the room, asked to sit down, and look toward the far wall. On this wall two dots of laser light were then projected. Because the air had been filtered so there was no dust in the air, all the participant could see was the two distant points of light. The participant was asked to estimate how far apart the two dots were. Some of them guessed the lights were two feet apart, others guessed twenty feet apart. Since they had no clues to help them estimate how far away the wall was, their answers were enormously varied. Later on, the same experiment was repeated, this time with small groups of people. Several people were asked to sit in the room at the same time. They were asked to give their answers out loud, so that the other participants could hear them. What happened then gives us a very strong clue into the incredible power of agreement in our lives. The answers the groups gave were constrained to a much narrower range. The first person would guess that the points of light were four feet apart, the next person might say five feet apart, and the following person three feet apart. Gone was the wide-ranging diversity of opinion. The participants were unknowingly influenced by the incredible power of agreement into believing in opinions that came from something other than their own, individual thinking. In this case, it would be fair to say that reality equals agreement. In addition to revealing much about how our opinions are formed, this experiment provides a clue about how you can make a change into a new field or be seen in the best light in your job hunt.

You gain admittance into any group, social or professional, by creating agreement. Some fields, such as medicine or law require a piece of paper, a license to practice, that automatically generates agreement that you are an insider in that field. Without the paper, you are excluded.

Fortunately for you, most careers do not have such specific entry requirements. Whether you are seen as an insider or an outsider in that field is a matter of perception. Here's how it works. Let's say your hobby is exploring coastal waters in

a kayak. One day, you find yourself on a plane sitting next to someone who is also an inveterate sea kayaker. Soon you would be deep into a conversation that would be difficult for an outsider to understand. You would both agree that the other was an "insider," make certain assumptions about them, and use language in a special insider's code. Both of you would have, without thinking about it, included the other inside of a "sphere of agreement." Every field of endeavor has around it a similar sphere of agreement. When two chefs, two cops, or two film directors meet, they do exactly the same thing as the sea kayakers: make some assumptions and automatically include the other as an insider.

Let's say that you started to date a kayaker and felt left out of the conversation whenever another kayaker was around. You might resolve the problem by "creating agreement." You might go kayaking a few times with your friend, read some books, start to act like a kayaker, look like one, think like one, talk like one, and move like one. Then you would be included within the sea kayakers' "sphere of agreement," because you had actually become a kayaker. They would think of you as an insider, an accepted member of the group. Now let's say there was a spy who wanted to get close to the sea kayaker's lover for some nefarious purpose. They wouldn't waste time taking kayak voyages. They would just read the right books and magazines, and talk with other sea kayakers to get a feel for the sport and its jargon. Then they could speak the language well enough to pass themselves off as a kayaker, and so be perceived as an insider by the kayakers, and gain their trust. They would gain admission into the sphere of agreement. What is useful to take from these examples is that you are considered an "insider" or a "member" based on agreement, not necessarily on some measurement of your long years of experience.

Now that you know that the way into a new career area is to create agreement, let's talk about how to go about doing it. Take a look at the illustration. The domelike structure represents a "sphere of agreement." Notice that it has many layers, like an onion. The outermost layer is the beginners' circle. It is where new graduates or tyros begin the journey toward the innermost layer, "the inner circle." Within the inner circle are the people who have generated the most agreement. They are the leaders or masters of this particular field. Remember, they are not necessarily the most experienced, the wisest, or most capable. Many people who permanently inhabit the middle layers of the sphere of agreement in any field of endeavor may be just as wise and just as experienced as those who reach the inner circle. Members of the inner circle are there because of one thing and one thing only: Other people in the field agree that they should be there. What these people are good at is creating agreement.

Most of us seek to enter a new field in the least effective way possible. It goes something like this. You, shown bowing to the guardian of the gate, (the personnel department), with résumé in hand, present yourself to the dragon, who guards the door into the new field. The door leads to the outermost beginners' circle. We learn this method when, as newly minted college graduates, we prostrate ourselves, with degree and résumé in hand before various job interviewers, asking them to please, please let us in. Our résumés and degrees communicate loud and clear the only agreement we have collected so far consists of the college courses we took.

Recent graduates have one thing going in their favor. Organizations expect to populate the beginners' circle with them, so the traditional path through the guardian's door works for the ones with the best degrees, résumés, and interviewing skills. Midcareer changers have a more difficult problem. Since they do not have any direct work experience in the field they wish to enter, they do not fit within the standard guidelines.

The guardian of the gate selects potential candidates mechanically, by comparing résumé data. They are sieving a vast pool of minnows, looking for the biggest and best ones. They want minnows that fit the specs perfectly. If you don't, you will get dumped back in the pool, even if you would be perfect for the job, because they don't want to take a chance on anything unusual. Remember, the personnel department is part of the administrative function, usually one of the most risk-averse part of any organization. They want to make sure that their butts are covered. If you come to work one day with an Uzi and blow away everyone on the fourth floor, they want to be able to explain that it was not their fault. You did, after all, have the best résumé.

So, if the pathway through the front door into the beginners' circle is not the best way in, what is? I once had a fifteen-year-old high school student come to me as a client. He was mathematically gifted, and had decided to become a math professor. He told me that only one-third of the people who earn a Ph.D. in math actually find jobs that make use of their hard-earned doctorates. He wanted to get a head start and make sure he was one of the people who find a job. Together, we came up with a plan. He did a little research and identified the three best-known mathematicians in the area, the ones in the middle of the inner circle. Then he called each of them and asked if he could meet with them for a few minutes to make a proposal. At the first meeting, with the mathematician he most respected, he offered to work for him for two hours every Saturday. He said all he wanted in exchange was to have a half hour each week to ask questions about math. This was an offer that was impossible to refuse. Even the most exalted mathematicians have the same grungy messes in their garages and basements that we average mortals do, plus he would get to help this gifted and innovative kid in the field they both loved. Soon, my client had a mentor and supporter. Eventually, through his mentor, he met some of the other leading mathematicians, who were reminded of themselves at an earlier age, and they, too, became his boosters, and stuck with him through his college career. During his undergraduate years, he looked from the point of view that he already was a mathematician, rather than a lowly math student, and took on creative projects, where the other students just did what they were told. The rest, as they say, is history. He combined the following methods to increase his chances of being selected. These apply equally to career changers and first-time job hunters.

Some Practical Tips for Getting in the Sphere

Here are a few suggestions to help you create agreement that you are already in the sphere:

- **Be what you want to do.** Most people who make a career change and then seek a job in the new field, walk into interviews with the point of view that "I am not a (*fill in job title here*). But maybe they will hire me so I can learn to become one." If that is where you are coming from, they will hear your message loud and clear. But there is another possibility. It is to so thoroughly absorb everything about your intended career that you know it like a pro. If you know it as well as a pro, then declare yourself as a pro. You simply say, "I am a corporate trainer," and mean it. This is not a matter of making up some words. You have to fill yourself completely with the new career. You have to live it and breathe it and do everything you need to do in order to know it well, as a brand-new insider. Once you declare yourself to be a corporate trainer, begin do the things that trainers do. If you act like a trainer, walk like a trainer, talk like a trainer, read what they read, hang out where they do, have friends who are trainers, join trade associations, attend conventions and seminars, get a friend who owns a company to let you train their people, then all that's left to do is to get a job as a trainer. Your motive is not to fool anyone, but to simply do what works and go with the flow of the universe.

  When my young mathematician friend got to college, he immediately did what is natural for someone "being" a mathematician. He made friends with the math professors and became a part of their circle. He was soon engaged in creative, independent, advanced studies. When he finished his undergraduate years, he had no trouble gaining admission to the best Ph.D. program because he was already deep within the sphere of agreement, had demonstrated real mastery, and had built a powerful network of supporters that began when he was in high school. The best way to get in is to be in.

  "Being" what you want to do is one big secret to gaining entry into any sphere of agreement. Instead of going in the front door, you beam yourself up into the middle of it. This works just as well in other areas of your life. If you come from a ground of being of abundance, what you do and what you have issues forth from abundance. If you come from scarcity, scarcity is what you shall have.

- **Read extensively about your new field.** Learn it thoroughly by reading all pertinent books including academic texts, how-to books, trade journals, and books by leaders in the field.

- **Attend conventions and seminars.** They are the perfect opportunity to meet people. Everyone you meet will automatically confer insider status on you. You will be surrounded by all the key players. All of them are just a handshake away from becoming a member of your network of support. In addition, the miniseminars, panel discussions, and access to vendors will provide an extraordinary educational experience.

- **Create a network of supporters in the field.** This is so important that it deserves an in-depth discussion, which you will run into later in this chapter.
- **Do projects that place you inside the sphere.** Your résumé should show you to be an insider, if possible. A creative résumé can focus attention on your strengths in a way that beams you aboard, but it always helps to have actual experience in the field you wish to enter. There is no better way to demonstrate being inside than having actual work experience. Perhaps you could volunteer or convince a friend who owns a business to let you do whatever you want to do for the company or you could provide consulting for them. Or you could start your own tiny company. Even if you have very few patients at Bob's Drive-in Discount Brain Surgery Clinic, you can put it in your résumé that you worked as a surgeon there. You do not necessarily have to reveal that you started the company or that your only patient was the neighbor's cat.
- **Create cooperative, nonadversarial relationships and transactions.** A job interview is almost always an adversarial situation. You are trying to sell something to them. They are trying to sell something to you. You and the interviewer are psychologically on opposite sides of the table. Learn to create relationships that do not have an adversarial component. Notice how different it feels when you look at the left side of the illustration below than it does when you look at the right side. When you must enter an adversarial transaction, learn to turn it to a cooperative one.

  There are many ways you could create relationships that are nonadversarial and, at the same time, automatically beam you aboard. For example, you could write an article for a trade magazine or newsletter, most of which are always hungrily searching for good articles. Pick an interesting, slightly controversial topical subject. Interview several people in the middle of the inner circle, placed just slightly below God, and preferably in a position to hire you. Quote them extensively in your article.

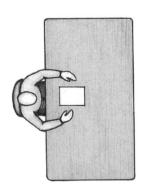

These relationships start off on a completely different footing than if you were asking them for a job. You are on the same side of the psychological desk, asking them questions that show just how far inside the sphere you are. In this relationship you are perceived as an insider who will further cement their position in the middle of the inner circle by lionizing them in print. At some later date you can get back in touch with them and ask them to support you, or at the very least ask them for names of people you might get in touch with.

Then, when you call the people they suggested, you can say, Mr. X (just slightly below God) suggested that I call you. If you interview several people, you are likely to have good chemistry with at least one of them. They may be willing to do more and really go to bat for you. This and other similar methods don't work nearly as well if you cheat. You really do have to be prepared thoroughly. You have to "be" inside the sphere. You have to do so much reading and research that you know both the theoretical and practical aspects the field thoroughly. You should have a couple of projects you have done in the field as a volunteer on your résumé, if possible.

When you must participate in an adversarial transaction, such as a job interview, you can turn it around by being nonadversarial. Your best chance for achieving this is to create a personal relationship with the interviewer by sharing yourself, by being honest and forthright. They are used to interviewing people who are on the defensive, smile frozen on face, trying their best to answer every question perfectly while revealing as little as possible. Revealing yourself does not mean airing your dirty laundry. You do not have to tell them about your foibles or about the two years you spent wandering in the Himalayas if you don't want to do so. To reveal yourself means being who you are rather than some persona you manufactured to look good in the interviewers' eyes. If you treat them like someone you just met who is a close friend of your best friend, that should break the adversarial ice.

- **Use creative approaches.** These few tips only scratch the surface of what is possible. Don't rely on these tips for your answers. You need to develop your own creative solutions that perfectly fit your situation. Don't be afraid to be outrageous. Once there was a man who had trouble getting by the secretaries of the high-powered people he wanted to reach. He wanted to speak with them to offer something that he thought would be a unique opportunity for them to take advantage of. Secretary troubles didn't stop him, however. A few days later, each of the high-powered folks received a box delivered by courier. On it was a note that said: "I have been trying to get through to you to tell you about_____, which I think you will be very interested in hearing about. In the attached box is a trained homing pigeon. If you want to hear more about our offer, just take the box to your window and release the pigeon. It will bring a message to me that I should contact you right away. If you aren't interested, please accept the pigeon as my gift to you." He had a 100-percent response rate. Every single one of his potential customers released the pigeon. Most were amused and quite willing to speak with him.

INQUIRY 31
THE NETWORKING GAME

The purpose of the Networking Game is to create a powerfully effective network for you that leads to multiple high-quality job offers. Remember that the two axes on the Job Hunting Effectiveness graph earlier in this chapter are Number of Transactions and Quality of Transactions. This game is concerned with creating some sizzling heat in the quality of your transactions. It transforms networking from something difficult and confusing into a game that many people find they enjoy. Even those who don't like playing the game will discover that that can generate results at networking where previously they wouldn't tread.

If you are a job hunter, the usual personal marketing methods you use fall somewhere on the "Quality of Transactions" axis. Notice that your job-hunting effectiveness depends directly on the warmth and strength of your relationships with people who can help you and on their degree of commitment to your cause. That automatically enrolls you in the Networking Game, whether you wish to play or not. Your style of play may be to say " I pass" every time your turn rolls around, but you are in the game nevertheless, like it or not. If you are willing to send out résumés only to job listings you found somewhere, or to use other cold approaches near the bottom of the effectiveness scale, your turn may come around more than a thousand times before you win the game. Or, what is more likely, is that you will get desperate and accept a job that you don't really want.

No matter how reluctant you are to assertively market yourself by putting forth an effective networking campaign, you've just got to do it if you are committed to landing a really excellent job. Since you are already in the game, you might as well play it consciously and play it to win. Ask anyone you know who is a master of networking. They will tell you that they do exactly the same things this game asks of you, with only minor stylistic differences. Although there are folks who are natural-born schmoozers with networking flowing in their veins, you can learn to play extremely well, as long as you don't let yourself get trampled by Yeahbuts and fearful feelings. It comes down to the same old question: Which is more important, being safe and comfortable, or getting results?

Finding Players for Your Networking Game

1. **Make a list of people you know who could possibly help you.** Write down absolutely everyone who might be able to help you directly or refer or recommend you to someone who could. No editing. Let's say, for example, you want into break into documentary films. You should write down everyone you know except those who you are absolutely sure do not know any one in documentary films. In other words, if someone has told me specifically, "I do not know anyone in documentary films, and I don't know anyone who knows anyone in documentary films. Plus, I wouldn't help you if you were the last person left on earth, " I might not put this person on my list. Otherwise, include almost everyone. In building a network it is better to be active, intentional, and inclusive than smart. When you get too smart, you do not think to include the guy who works in your next-door neighbor's garden, who also works for an award-winning independent film producer-director. Include college and high school classmates, your family, friends of your family, your friends, your friend's friends, former professors, former employers, sports partners, neighbors, the parents of the kids on your kid's team. When you are finished, you have created a network. You may think it doesn't look like much, but it is better than no network or a tiny one made up of your three best friends. After all, you've got to start somewhere.

2. **Keep adding people to your network.** Increase the quality of people participating in your network while at the same time keeping the numbers up. What you want is both quality and quantity. To make sure your network does not shrink to nothing, you have to have a certain critical mass of participants. If you have only ten people to tap, your network is always face to face with extinction. It is the same with endangered species. If there are only a few individuals left of a particular animal, the first job is to initiate a breeding program to get the numbers up.

How many people did you write down as possible players? If you came up with more than, say, fifty people, you have a small but manageable network. If you came up with 100 or more, you are in good shape. If you have fewer than 100, you need to get to work building numbers right away. Decide on a specific minimum number of participants. One hundred would be a good number for most people. Later on, as you play the networking game, if your numbers fall below 100, you know your team is headed for extinction. The point here is not to be fussy or overly anal, but to make sure the boat is not sinking. If you can do this without counting and keeping track, fine.

3. **Create a "super list" of stars in this field.** The point of this list is to remind you to be unreasonable. One of the most effective networking methods is to increase the quality of participants as you build numbers. Seek out people who can help you in some substantial way. Even though your original network may have the neighbor's gardener as a possible supporter, the chances are pretty small that the gardener will be of much help. The people who could be most helpful are the most central luminaries in the field you seek to enter. They are the people in the middle of the "sphere of agreement" we discussed in the "Creating Agreement" section of this chapter. These anointed ones could, with one phone call, possibly get you the job you want.

Take a few minutes to create a list entitled, "Powerful People." Include people who are leaders in the field you want to enter, people who would be most able to help you, irrespective of other factors. If you wanted to break into films, you might put Steven Spielberg and a few other major players at the top. Also include people you know or might have a connection with, who may not be at the very top of the field but are somehow in a position to help you considerably. The people who inhabit the inner circles of the sphere of agreement will be the same people whose support would rate most highly on the Job-Hunt Effectiveness Chart. Why not spend your time going after their support? Next, get the support of some of these major players. (Before you do that, make sure that what you have to offer is worthy of their attention.)

Does this sound completely out of the question? Imagine for a minute that the person you most love has been kidnapped by the forces of evil. You find a note that says, "You have one month to get a great job in your new field, or else your loved one will be fed to the crocodiles." Wouldn't your reservations about contacting the most potentially helpful people disappear instantly? Wouldn't you do whatever it would take to save them? Well, this is exactly the situation you are in right now, except it is your life that is at stake!

Even if what I have just said seems completely outrageous, the point is still valid. Put your networking energy into finding, contacting, getting to know, and generating agreement about how terrific you are with people as close to the "inner circles" as you possibly can. Please don't feel you are less than sufficient if making friends with the gods of your chosen field seems out of the question. I'm really communicating principles, not tips.

Getting the underlying principle is what is most useful. If playing at a certain level of "inner circle" seems impossibly huge, work at a level that is as far into the sphere of agreement as you can muster the courage to handle. Put your energy into getting to know the head of the department you want to work in, not the file clerk; the project director, not the most junior engineer. In making your participant list, you may discover that you don't know who could be most helpful. In which case, it is time for some research.

People building a network often lament that they are not as fortunate as those folks who have a good "old boy" or "old girl" network. These networks are mostly fantasy. A network is a network is a network. Your job is to create a hot network of support. Old school chums are just one kind of support you could call on. These old friends may be hot contacts. But there are many other ways to generate warmth. Someone you could meet tomorrow may become completely enrolled in your cause and do far more to help you than any old school friend. It is all a matter of enrollment.

The more creative you are, the better it will work out. Shake out the stiffness. Loosen up. Think of some really outrageous ways to build your network. For example, if you still like the idea of an old boy or old girl network, get creative about it. Don't just rely on the people you knew at school. Everyone who went to your college, whose heart is still beating, is a potential source of support. Many of them will be willing to help when they find out that you both went to the same school. Call the alumni office. Find out who works in the field you are entering. If they won't tell you, do further research. Get a complete list of alumni. Find out who is the chair of the reunion committee for each class. Call each of them. They will know who is doing what or who would know the answers to your inquiries. Let your fingers do the walking, not your brain. You are definitely not going to feel like calling 100 fellow alums you have never spoken to before. But, as they say, feel the fear and do it anyway.

4. **Rate your team of supporters.** Let's take a look at the quality of your network. Go through your list and rate each person. Some people will get one star, two stars, or three stars. Some will get nothing. If some of the terms used seem to come from a low-grade horror movie, remember, this is a game. The idea is to lighten up and enjoy networking.

A *Three Star* supporter is someone who is extremely dedicated, self-actualized, and useful in helping/supporting you, or is someone who has extraordinary resources that will be willingly put in your service. These are people who will champion your cause to the point of really going out of their way for you They remain conscious of their commitment to your cause without management. They are your most solid supporters. Three-Stars are created, not born. Your father, mother, husband or wife, or best friend might already be three-star supporters, but maybe not. These most valuable people do not necessarily have to have contacts or other special access. Some three-star participants may just be people who love you to death and will stand with you, support you to be your best, be a sounding board or a shoulder to cry on.

A *two-star* supporter is someone who is dedicated and useful to your success in finding the job you want, is willing to stretch out and go to bat for you but needs active management to remain a useful resource. Two-stars need phone calls to keep them interested and committed. They will forget about you quickly if you are not actively managing them.

A *one-star* is someone who is, for one reason or another, a possibly useful member of your network but is not participating in a powerful way. Most people have a network of support that consists almost entirely of one-star contacts. Old college buddies who might answer some questions about their organizations, give you some names of useful people to contact, or go to bat for you in a limited way, such as to recommend you to their company, would get one star. The difference between a one-star and a two-star is that the two-star will go farther out of their way, put more energy and commitment into helping you, or be in a position where their help can provide extraordinary benefits to get you to your goal.

It may be that many people on your list get no stars. They are the *unborn,* people who are not, as yet, playing. Each represents a spark of possibility not yet tapped. They are people you haven't contacted yet and do not know if they will support you.

The final category is the *dead.* These are the people you would absolutely not contact. You are sure they wouldn't help you. Some of them may be people you have killed off as potential supporters for one reason or another. Perhaps they have written you off completely for some other reason. You have managed to kill off any possibility that they may help you in some way. These are truly dead, beyond resurrection. Most of the people you consider to be dead are only dead in your imagination. To be included in this category, a person must simply be someone you would not contact. Most of the people you would not contact are not folks you have killed off but people you are too shy to call on. They are actually members of the ranks of the unborn. People tend to bury many of their potential supporters in unmarked graves along with the actual dead because they so fear rejection. There is no reason why you can't ask people you used to date or work with for some support. There is no reason why you should not call the film producer whose car you totaled or the former supervisor you never got along with. There is no reason why you cannot find a way to contact and get support from the most powerful people in the field you want to get into. Except for fear of rejection. The worst they can do is say no. But when you, through mismanagement, kill off a supporter, erase them from your list. Then learn from the situation; how can you avoid this happening again in the future?

5. **Play the game by making requests.** You win the Networking Game by making requests of the people in your network and eliciting promises from them that wind up with you having several excellent job offers to choose from. Most people network in a very timid way. When they have a contact in a powerful position in the organization they wish to work for, they waste this influential contact by asking them for information. You don't want information. You want a job! Requests are one of the most powerful tools you have to move your life forward. "Will you marry me?" your applications to colleges, and cover letters sent along with your résumé are all requests. Designing requests is a learned skill. Most people do not realize the power of designing and communicating potent requests. Each of us has a built-in, internal, automatic request designer. Unfortunately, it is programmed to come up with safe, comfortable, pathetically reasonable requests. Either you design your requests proactively or it will do it for you. When you design a request, ask yourself, "What do I really want? If I had no qualms at all, what would I ask this person for?" Once again, the only reason people avoid making more outrageous requests is that they fear they will be rejected. They avoid making strong requests by thinking, "I don't want to impose on people." "It's too pushy." "I'm not that kind of person." "I don't know anyone." "I would feel uncomfortable." All of these thoughts are all nothing but Yeahbuts provided to you by your friendly internal survival system, to avoid the near-death experience of rejection. We tend to take "no" personally. If you make a big request of someone and they say no, it doesn't mean you are unworthy. It just means, "No, I do not agree to honor your request." A good networker will then make another, smaller request. If you remove all the significance from the process of making requests, here's what happens:

You make a request. They do one of three things. They agree to fulfill your request, they say no, or they make a counteroffer. Most people fold their cards if they get a no answer. Don't do it. Make a smaller request instead.

Request—"Will you be my love slave forever?"
Reply—"Not a chance."
Request—"How about just for tonight?"

Reply—"Nope."
Request—"Want to go have a cup of coffee together?"
Reply—"OK, let's do it!"

The secret of getting favorable responses to your requests is the ability to create a state of relatedness. The more related you and the other person are, the more likely they are to be willing to fulfill your request. If you ask random people on the street to give you a hundred dollars, you will have few takers. If you ask your best friend, he or she would not refuse. Relatedness is not a function of time previously spent together. You and your boss may have cohabited in the same office for the last ten years and have no real relatedness. On the other hand, some people are capable of creating relatedness almost instantly. Even though many of the people who do this naturally are expressing an innate talent, you can learn to do it, too. The best way to create relatedness is to come from relatedness instead of trying to make it happen. In other words, start communicating with the other person, assuming relatedness. Share yourself with them. Let them find out who you are. Lighten up. Be friendly, personal. Be more interested than interesting. You don't need to impress them. Instead, let them get to know you. Even though they may expect a certain business-like formality, break through it as soon as you can.

When you communicate with people you do not know, or know well, your real objective is to create a relationship, a friendship, a mutual concern. Only within a state of relatedness will people be willing to go out of their way for you. There is no way you can fake it. You need to start looking at relatedness in a new way, as a state that can be created rather than something that just grows by itself over time. Since the bases for relatedness are intimacy and generosity, they are what you have to offer the other person. Both intimacy and generosity are places to come from, not to get to. Don't be a taker. The way to be a great networker is to be a willing and generous participant in other people's networks. Share yourself with them. If you are always willing to give more than you take and don't give in to your Yeahbuts, you could turn yourself into a really spectacular networker. As a networker, you are in the relationship business. These people do not need you, and they will help you only to the extent that they experience being related with you. If this "creating relatedness" is all a new concept to you, go out and practice creating relationships with everyone you meet for the next week. When you buy a pack of gum, create a state of relatedness with the clerk. Find common ground with them. Acknowledge them. Assume the best. Call them by name. Communicate with enthusiasm. When the cop stops you for speeding, create a friendship instead of arguing.

Before you begin to actively play the networking game, get clear exactly what you want the people in your network to do for you. Sit down and brainstorm a list of ideas for possible outcomes. At one end of the spectrum, you could ask them to become your champion and strongly advocate your candidacy to the CEO. At the other end, you could ask them for a little information on what they do in their job. There are many things you could request of them in between these two polar ends of the spectrum of possible requests. Before you pick up the phone or meet with someone, have a definite intended result for the call in mind. Make each conversation a powerful expression of playing the networking game. Make sure you know what you want. Make sure you ask for what you want. One request to make of every single person you contact is, "Who do you know that might . . . ?" Always work on building your network. After each transaction, rate the conversation. What worked? What didn't work? How can you improve next time?

Chess players guard their most powerful pieces carefully. If they have to put a piece in danger, they sacrifice a pawn. You want to do the same thing. Marshall your forces skillfully. Make use of the people in your network appropriately. Reserve the most powerfully useful participants until it is time to use them to maximum benefit. Otherwise you will waste them on trivia. If your best friend's dad is the director of an organization in the field you want to get into, do not call him while you are doing basic information gathering. Don't let him see you as a know-nothing outsider. Wait until you have thoroughly mastered everything you need to handle to enter your new field. Wait until you are extremely knowledgeable and sure of yourself. Then make a big request. Ask him to champion your cause, to really go to bat for you.

6. **Manage your network.** You manage your network by creating more one-star participants in your game from the endless sea of the unborn. At the same time, you work on transforming one-star participants into two-star and three-star players. It's a little like increasing your number of houses in Monopoly, heading toward having hotels. You raise the number of stars of a participant in your network by generating their commitment to your success in finding a great job. Commitment isn't lip service. It is dedication and action. As you know, the way to get them on your team is to build authentic relationships.

When you begin the game, your network may not be very strong. Still, I suggest that you play the game as if you were in the Olympics. If the neighbor's gardener is not likely to be able to help you, why even ask him? Because he might help. You've got to work with the resources you have available. Second, and most important, you are learning to play a game where you must do what is needed, not what you feel like doing. You want to get to the point where you do what is next on your list whole-heartedly, rather than listen to the endless chorus of internal Yeahbuts that judge and evaluate your every move and seek to have you do only what is comfortable and nonconfronting.

Not Ready to Job Hunt Yet?

If you are not ready to go job hunting now, I assume you feel you need to do something to prepare for your chosen career. Unless you are planning for a career in a highly technical area, you may not need to go back to school to learn how to do the job in the area you have selected. A few well-chosen books will teach you more practical how-to information in most fields than you will get in ten years of graduate school. If you think you will learn to be an excellent therapist in a master's program in counseling or learn to be a journalist in journalism school, I suggest that you ask professionals in the field you are thinking of entering just how much of the subject matter covered in advanced-degree programs is useful in the real world. You will hear a chorus of "not much, not much."

The most compelling reason to get an advanced degree for most career changers is to generate agreement. An appropriate master's degree is a very useful chunk of agreement that can help vault you into your new career. But before you decide to go back to school, make sure you are going for the right reasons. Oftentimes, you can create agreement in other, more efficient ways. For example, if you want to get into the field of public relations and publicity, having natural talent and a personality that suits the job, doing a few volunteer projects for friends' businesses, creating a network of support, and effective personal marketing may be all you need to gain entry.

When you are planning how to get from here to there, find out what you need to know to be effective in the new field. Do whatever you have to do to learn the job. Be skeptical of people who tell you will learn how to do it in school. Remember that you will learn 90 percent of what you need to know on the job, in all fields, even in brain surgery. Obviously, there are many fields, like brain surgery, where you absolutely must go back to school to learn the craft. But make sure you are going back to school for the right reasons. And, if you do decide to go, don't walk in as a beginner. Like my young mathematician friend, *be* a professional in your new field on your first day in school. Don't expect that a graduate program will teach you what you need to know. You will have to take charge, design your own education, and convince your professors to let you do creative projects that will allow you to master as much of your new field as possible.

If you are not ready to job hunt now, and are not planning to go back to school, I assume that you need to spend some time learning the new field on your own and creating a network and agreement. I suggest that you plan out a strategy now, with specific steps and completion dates, to keep you on track and to make sure you do not lose sight of your goal.

CHAPTER 30

•

HOW TO WRITE AN EXCEPTIONAL RÉSUMÉ

This chapter presents the basic principles of writing powerful and effective résumés. It will not answer all your questions or guide you completely through this complex subject. It would take a full-length book to get across everything important. A great résumé does not necessarily follow the rules that you hear through the grapevine. It does not have to be one page or follow some special format. Every résumé is a one-of-a-kind communication. It should be appropriate to your situation and do exactly what you want it to do. Let's cut to the chase in this brief guide and focus on the most basic principles of writing a highly effective résumé.

This résumé guide is most appropriate for people looking for a job in the United States. In the U.S. the rules of job hunting are much more relaxed than they are in most of Europe and Asia. You can do a lot more active personal marketing here. In Europe and Asia and for those in the U.S. seeking jobs in some professions such as law, academia, and highly technical engineering and computer fields, you will have to tone down my advice a few notches and follow the traditional, conservative format accepted in your field. But even when your presentation must fit a narrow set of rules, you can still use the principles in this chapter to make your presentation more effective than your competition's.

Writing a great résumé involves facing up to some good news and some bad news. The good news is that, with a little extra effort, you can create a résumé that makes you really stand out as a superior candidate for a job you are seeking. Not one résumé in a hundred follows the principles that stir the interest of prospective employers. So, even if you face fierce competition, with a well-written résumé you should be invited to interview more often than many people more qualified than you.

The bad news is that your present résumé is probably much more inadequate than you now realize. You will have to learn how to think and write in a style that will be completely new to you. To understand what I mean, let's take a look at the purpose of your résumé. Why do you have one in the first place? What is it supposed to do for you? Here's an imaginary scenario. You apply for a job that seems absolutely perfect for you. You send your résumé with a cover letter to the prospective employer. Plenty of other people think the job sounds great, too, and apply for it. A few days later, the employer is staring at a pile of several hundred résumés. Several hundred? you ask. Isn't that an inflated number? Not really. A job offer often attracts between 100 and 1,000 résumés these days. So you are facing a great deal of competition. OK, back to the fantasy and the prospective employer staring at the huge stack of résumés. These people aren't any more excited about going through this pile of dry, boring documents than you would be. But, they have to do it, so they dig in. After a few minutes, they are getting sleepy. They are not really focusing any longer. Then, they run across your résumé. As soon as they start reading it, they perk up. The more they read, the more interested, awake, and turned on they become. Most résumés in the pile have gotten only a quick glance. But yours gets read, from beginning to end. Then, it gets put on top of the tiny pile of résumés that made the first cut. These are the people who will be asked in to interview. In this mini résumé-writing guide, what I hope to do is to give you the basic tools to take this out of the realm of fantasy and into your everyday life.

The Number-One Purpose of a Résumé

The résumé is a tool with one specific purpose: to get you an interview. If it doesn't, it isn't an effective résumé. A résumé is an advertisement, nothing more or less. A great résumé doesn't just tell prospective employers what you have done, it makes the same assertion that all good ads do: *If you buy this product, you will get these specific, direct benefits.* It presents you in the best light. It convinces the employer that you have what it takes to be successful in this new position or career. It is so pleasing to the eye that the reader is enticed to pick up and read it. It whets the appetite, stimulates interest in meeting you and learning more about you. It inspires the prospective employer to pick up the phone and ask you to come in for an interview.

Other Possible Reasons to Have a Résumé

- To pass the employer's screening process (requisite educational level, number of years of experience, etc.); to give basic facts that might favorably influence the employer (companies worked for, personal interests, etc.).
- To establish you as a professional person with high standards and excellent writing skills, based on the fact that the résumé is so well done.
- To help in other phases of the job-hunting process: to give to friends and contacts who may in turn pass them on to potential employers; to give to your job-hunting contacts and professional references, to provide background information.

What It Isn't

It is a mistake to think of your résumé as a history of your past, as a personal statement, or as a means of self-expression. Sure, most of the content of any résumé is focused on your job history. But write from the intention to create interest, to persuade the employer to call you. If you write with that goal, your final product will be very different than if you write to inform or catalog your job history.

Most people write a résumé because everyone knows that you have to have one to get a job. They write their résumé grudgingly, to fulfill this obligation. Writing the résumé is only slightly below filling out income tax forms in the hierarchy of worldly delights. If you realize that a great résumé can be your ticket to getting exactly the job you want, you may be able to muster some genuine enthusiasm for creating a real masterpiece, rather than the feeble products most people turn out.

What if I'm Not Sure of My Job Target?

If you are hunting for a job but are not sure you are on a career path that is perfect for you, you are making a big and unnecessary compromise. You are probably going to wind up in something that doesn't fit you very well, that you are not really going to enjoy, and that you will most likely leave within three years. Doesn't sound like much of a life to me? How about you? Are you willing to keep putting up with pinning your fate on the random turnings of the wheel? You need to start over at the beginning of *The Pathfinder* and swing out a little more in choosing the path of your future lifework.

How to Knock the Socks off the Prospective Employer

Research has shown that only one interview is granted for every fifty to 100 résumés received by the average employer. Research also tells us that your résumé will be quickly scanned, rather than read. Ten to twenty seconds is all the time you have to persuade a prospective employer to read further. What this means is that the decision to interview a candidate is usually based on an overall first impression of the résumé, a quick screening that so impresses the reader and so convinces him or her of the candidate's qualifications that an interview ensues. As a result, the top half of the first page of your résumé will either make you or break you. By the time they have read the first few lines, you have either caught their interest, or your résumé has failed. That is why I say that your résumé is an ad. You hope it will have the same result as a well-written ad: to get the reader to respond.

To write an effective résumé, you have to learn how to write powerful, but subtle advertising copy. Not only that, but you must sell a product in which you have large personal investment: you. What's worse, given the fact that most of us do not think in a marketing-oriented way naturally, you are probably not looking forward to selling anything, let alone yourself. But if you want to increase your job-hunting effectiveness as much as possible, you would be wise to learn to write a spectacular résumé. You do not need to hard sell or make any claims that are not absolutely true. You do need to get over your modesty and unwillingness to toot your own horn. People more often buy the best-advertised product than the best product. That is good news if you are willing to learn to create an excellent résumé. With a little extra effort, you will find that you will usually get a better response from prospective employers than people with better credentials.

Focus on the Employer's Needs, Not Yours

Imagine that you are the person who will be doing the hiring. This person is not some anonymous paper pusher deep in the bowels of the personnel department. Usually the person who makes the hiring decision is also the person who is responsible for the bottom-line productivity of the project or group you hope to be a part of. This is a person who cares deeply how well the job will be done. You need to write your résumé to appeal directly to them. Ask yourself: *What would make someone the perfect candidate? What special abilities would this person have? What would set a truly exceptional candidate apart from a merely good one? What does the employer really want?* If you are seeking a job in a field you know well, you probably already know what would make someone a superior candidate. If you are not sure, you can gather hints from the help-wanted ad you are answering, from asking other people who work in the same company or the same field. You could even call the prospective employer and ask what they want. Don't make wild guesses unless you have to. It is very important to do this step well. If you are not addressing their real needs, they will not respond to your résumé. Putting yourself in the moccasins of the person doing the hiring is the first and most important step in writing a résumé that markets you rather than describes your history. Every succeeding step in producing a finished document should be part of your overall intention to convey to the prospective employer that you are a truly exceptional candidate.

Plan First

Focus your writing efforts. Get clear what the employer is looking for and what you have to offer before you begin your résumé. Write your answers to the above-mentioned question, *What would make someone the perfect candidate?* on notebook paper, one answer per page. Prioritize the sheets of paper, based on which qualities or abilities you think would be most important to the person doing the hiring. Then, starting with the top-priority page, fill the rest of that page, or as much of it as you can, with brainstorming about why you are the person who best fulfills the employer's needs. Write down everything you have ever done that demonstrates that you fit perfectly with what is wanted and needed by the prospective employer. The whole idea is to loosen up your thinking enough so that you will be able to see some new connections between what you have done and what the employer is looking for. You need not confine yourself to work-related accomplishments. Use your entire life as the palette to paint with. If Sunday school or your former gang are the only places you have had a chance to demonstrate your special gift for teaching and leadership, fine. The point is to cover all possible ways of thinking about and communicating what you do well. What are the talents you bring to the marketplace? What do you have to offer the prospective employer? If you are making a career change or are a young person and new to the job market, you are going to have to be especially creative in getting across what makes you stand out. These brainstorming pages will be the raw material from which you craft your résumé. One important part of the planning process is to decide which résumé format fits your needs best. Don't automatically assume that a traditional format will work best for you. More about that later.

A Great Résumé Has Two Sections

In the first, you make *assertions* about your abilities, your qualities, and your achievements. You write powerful, but honest advertising copy that makes the reader immediately perk up and realize that you are someone special. The second section, *the evidence section,* is where you back up your assertions with evidence that you actually did what you said you did. This is where you list and describe the jobs you have held, your education, etc. This is all the stuff you are obliged to include. Most résumés are just the evidence section, with no assertions. If you have trouble getting to sleep, just read a few résumés each night just before going to bed. Your troubles will disappear! Nothing puts people to sleep better than the average résumé. The juice is in the assertions section. When a prospective employer finishes reading your résumé, you want them to immediately reach for the phone to invite you in to interview. The résumés you have written in the past have probably been a gallant effort to inform the reader. You don't want them informed. You want them interested and excited. In fact, it is best to only hint at some things. Leave the reader wanting more. Leave them with a hint of mystery. That way, they have even more reason to reach for the phone. The assertions section usually has two or three subsections. In all of them, your job is to communicate, assert, and declare that you are the best possible candidate for the job and that you are hotter than a picnic on Mercury.

You start by naming your intended job. This may be in a separate *objective section,* or may be folded into the second section, the *summary.* If you are making a change to a new field or are a young person not fully established in a career, start with a separate objective section.

The Objective

Ideally, your résumé should be pointed toward conveying why you are the perfect candidate for one specific job or job title. Good advertising is directed toward a very specific target audience. When a car company is trying to sell their inexpensive compact to an older audience, they show grandpa and grandma stuffing the car with happy, shiny grandchildren, and talk about how safe and economical the car is. When they advertise the exact same car to the youth market, they show it going around corners on two wheels, with plenty of drums and power chords thundering in the background. You want to focus your résumé just as specifically.

Targeting your résumé requires that you be absolutely clear about your career direction, or, at least, that you appear to be clear. The way to demonstrate your clarity of direction or apparent clarity is to have the first major topic of your résumé be your OBJECTIVE. Let's look at a real-world example. Suppose the owner of a small software company puts an ad in the paper seeking an experienced software salesperson. A week later they have received 500 résumés. The applicants have a bewildering variety of backgrounds. The employer has no way of knowing whether any of them is really interested in selling software. They remember all the jobs they applied for that they didn't really want. They know that many of the résumés they received are from people who are just using a shotgun approach, casting their seeds to the winds. Then they come across a résumé in the pile that starts with the following:

OBJECTIVE : a software sales position in an organization where an extraordinary record of generating new accounts, exceeding sales targets, and enthusiastic customer relations would be needed.

This wakes them up. They are immediately interested. This first sentence conveys some very important and powerful messages: "I want exactly the job you are offering. I am a superior candidate because I have the qualities that are most important to you. I want to make a contribution to your company." This works well because the employer is smart enough to know that someone who wants to do exactly what you are offering will be much more likely to succeed than someone who doesn't. And will probably be a lot more pleasant to work with as well. Secondly, this candidate has done a good job of establishing why he or she is the perfect candidate in their first sentence. They have thought about what qualities would make a candidate stand out. They have started communicating that they are that person immediately. What's more, they are communicating from the point of view of making a contribution to the employer. They are not writing from a self-centered point of view. Even when people are savvy enough to have an objective, they often make the mistake of saying something like, "a position where I can hone my skill as a scissors sharpener," or something similar. The employer is interested in hiring you for what you can do for them, not for fulfilling your private goals and agenda.

Here's how to write your objective. First of all, decide on a specific job title toward which to direct your objective. Go back to your list of answers to the question "How can I demonstrate that I am the perfect candidate?" What are the two or three qualities, abilities, or achievements that would make a candidate stand out as truly exceptional for that specific job? The person in the above example recognized that the prospective employer, being a small, growing software company, would be very interested in candidates with an ability to generate new accounts. So, they made that the very first point they got across in their résumé. Be sure the objective is to the point. Do not use fluffy phrases that are obvious or do not mean anything, such as: "allowing the ability to enhance potential and utilize experience in new challenges." An objective may be broad and still somewhat undefined in some cases, such as: "a midlevel management position in the hospitality or entertainment industry." Remember, your résumé will get only a few seconds attention, at best! You have to generate interest right away, in the first sentence they lay their eyes on. Having an objective statement that really sizzles, is highly effective. And it's simple to do. One format is:

OBJECTIVE: An X position in an organization where Y and Z would be needed.

X is the name of the position you seek. Y and Z are the most compelling qualities, abilities, or achievements that will really make you stand out above the crowd of applicants. The research you have previously done to find out what is most important to the employer will provide the information to fill in Y and Z.

If you are not really sure what job you are after, you should adapt your résumé to each type of job you apply for. There is nothing wrong with having several different résumés, each with a different objective, each specifically crafted for a different type of position. You may even want to change some parts of your résumé for each job you apply for. Have an objective that is perfectly matched with the job you are applying for. Remember, you are writing advertising copy, not your life story.

You do not need to use a separate objective section if you are looking for a job in your present field. You will include your objective in your summary section. The point of using an objective is to create a specific psychological response in the mind of the reader. If you are making a career change or are a young person, you want the employer to immediately focus on where you are going, rather than where you have been. If you are looking for another job in your present field, it is more important to stress your qualities, achievements, and abilities first.

A Few Examples of Separate Objective Sections

- Senior staff position with a bank that offers the opportunity to utilize my expertise in commercial real estate lending and strategic management.
- An entry-level position in the hospitality industry where a background in advertising and public relations would be needed.
- A position teaching English as a second language where a special ability to motivate and communicate effectively with students would be needed.

The Summary

The summary or summary of qualifications consists of several concise statements that focus the reader's attention on the most important qualities, achievements, and abilities you have to offer, those qualities that are the most compelling demonstrations of why they should hire you instead of the other candidates. It gives you a brief opportunity to telegraph a few of your most sterling qualities. It is your one and only chance to attract and hold their attention, to get across what is most important, and to entice the employer to keep reading. This is the spiciest part of the résumé. This may be the only section fully read by the employer, so it should be very strong and convincing. The summary is the one place to include professional characteristics (extremely energetic, a gift for solving complex problems in a fast-paced environment, a natural salesman, exceptional interpersonal skills, committed to excellence, etc.) that may be helpful in winning the interview. Gear every word in the summary to your targeted goal.

How to write a summary? Go back to your lists that answer the question What would make someone the ideal candidate? Look for the qualities the employer will care about most. Then look at what you wrote about why you are the perfect person to fill their need. Pick the stuff that best demonstrates why they should hire you. Assemble it into your summary section. The most common ingredients of a well-written summary are as follows. Of course, you would not use all these ingredients in one summary. Use the ones that highlight you best.

A short phrase describing your profession

Followed by a statement of broad or specialized expertise

Followed by two or three additional statements related to any of the following:

breadth or depth of skills
unique mix of skills
range of environments in which you have experience
a special or well-documented accomplishment
a history of awards, promotions, or superior-performance commendations
one or more professional or appropriate personal characteristics
a sentence describing professional objective or interest.

Notice that the following examples show how to incorporate your objective in the summary section. If you are making a career change, your summary section should show how what you have done in the past prepares you to do what you seek to do in the future. If you are a young person new to the job market, your summary will be based more on ability than experience.

A Few Examples of Summary Sections

"Highly motivated, creative, and versatile real estate executive with seven years of experience in property acquisition, development, and construction, as well as the management of large apartment complexes. Especially skilled at building effective, productive working relationships with clients and staff. Excellent management, negotiation, and public relations skills. Seeking a challenging management position in the real estate field that offers extensive contact with the public."

"Over ten years as an organizational catalyst/training design consultant with a track record of producing extraordinary results for more than twenty national and community-based organizations. A commitment to human development and community service."

"Energetic self-starter with excellent analytical, organizational, and creative skills."

"Financial management executive with nearly ten years of experience in banking and international trade, finance, investments, and economic policy. Innovative in structuring credit enhancement for corporate and municipal financing. Skilled negotiator with strong management, sales, and marketing background. Areas of expertise include . . ." (a bulleted list would follow this paragraph.)

"Health-care professional experienced in management, program development, and policy making in the United States as well as in several developing countries. Expertise in emergency medical services. A talent for analyzing problems, developing and simplifying procedures, and finding innovative solutions. Proven ability to motivate and work effectively with persons from other cultures and all walks of life. Skilled in working within a foreign environment with limited resources."

"Commander-Chief Executive Officer of the U.S. Navy, Atlantic Fleet. Expertise in all areas of management, with a proven record of unprecedented accomplishment. History of the highest naval awards and rapid promotion. Proven senior-level experience in executive decision making, policy direction, strategic business planning, Congressional relations, financial and personnel management, research and development, and aerospace engineering. Extensive knowledge of government military requirements in systems and equipment. Committed to the highest levels of professional and personal excellence."

"Performing artist with a rich baritone voice and unusual range, specializing in classical, spiritual, and gospel music. Featured soloist for two nationally televised events. Accomplished pianist. Extensive performance experience includes television, concert tours, and club acts. Available for commercial recording and live performances."

Skills and Accomplishments

In this final part of the assertions section of your résumé, you go into more detail. You are still writing to enroll readers, not to inform them. Basically, you do exactly what you did in the previous section, except that you go into more detail. In the summary, you focused on your most special highlights. Now you tell the rest of the best of your story. Let them know what results you produced, what happened as a result of your efforts, what you are especially gifted or experienced at doing. Flesh out the most important highlights in your summary.

You are still writing to do what every good advertisement does, communicating the following: If you buy this product, you will get these direct benefits. If it doesn't contribute to furthering this communication, don't bother to say it. Remember, not too much detail. Preserve a bit of mystery. Don't tell them everything.

Sometimes the skills and accomplishments section is a separate section. In a chronological résumé, it becomes the first few phrases of the descriptions of the various jobs you have held. We will cover that when we discuss the different types of résumés. When it is a separate section, it can have several possible titles, depending on your situation:

SKILLS and ACCOMPLISHMENTS
ACCOMPLISHMENTS
SUMMARY of ACCOMPLISHMENTS
SELECTED ACCOMPLISHMENTS
RECENT ACCOMPLISHMENTS
AREAS of ACCOMPLISHMENT and EXPERIENCE
AREAS of EXPERTISE
CAREER HIGHLIGHTS
PROFESSIONAL HIGHLIGHTS
ADDITIONAL SKILLS and ACCOMPLISHMENTS

There are a number of different ways to structure skills and accomplishments sections. In all of these styles, put your skills and accomplishments in order of importance for the desired career goal. If you have many skills, the last skill paragraph might be called "Additional Skills."

Here are a few ways you could structure your skills and accomplishments section:

1. A listing of skills or accomplishments or a combination of both, with bullets.

Example:

Selected Skills and Accomplishments

- Raised $1,900 in 21 days in canvassing and advocacy on environmental, health, and consumer issues.
- Conducted legal research for four Assistant U.S. Attorneys, for the U.S. Attorney's office
- Coordinated Board of Directors and Community Advisory Board of community mental health center. Later commended as "the best thing that ever happened to that job."

2. A listing of major skill headings with accomplishments under each. The accomplishments can be a bulleted list or in paragraph form. The material under the headings should include mention of accomplishments that prove each skill.

Example:

Selected Accomplishments

National Training Project / Conference Management

Director of "Outreach on Housing," a national public education/training project funded by USAID, foundations, and all the major church denominations. Designed, managed, and promoted 3-day training conferences in cities throughout the U.S. Planned and managed 32 nationwide training seminars and a 5-day annual conference for university vice-presidents and business executives.

Program Design: Universities

Invited by Miscatonic University President H.P. Lovecraft to develop new directions and programs for the University's Office of Summer Educational Programs, first Director of Miscatonic's "Pre-college Program," first editor of "Midnight at Miscatonic."

3. A list of bulleted accomplishments or skill paragraphs under each job (in a chronological résumé).

Example:

Director of Sales and Marketing   **1986–1994**
DELAWARE TRADE INTERNATIONAL, INC.   Wilmington, DE
Promoted from Sales Representative within one year of joining company to Director of Sales and Marketing. Responsible for international sales of raw materials, as well as printing and graphic arts equipment. Oversaw five sales managers. Was in charge of direct sales and marketing in seventeen countries throughout Europe and the Middle East.

- Recruited, trained, and managed sales staff. Developed marketing strategy, prepared sales projections, and established quotas. Selected and contracted with overseas subagents to achieve international market penetration.
- Negotiated and finalized long-term contractual agreements with suppliers on behalf of clients. Oversaw all aspects of transactions, including letters of credit, international financing, preparation of import/export documentation, and shipping/freight forwarding.
- Planned and administered sales and marketing budget, and maintained sole profit/loss responsibility. Within first year, doubled company's revenues and produced $7–$9 million in annual sales during the next eight years.

Evidence

There isn't really a section on a résumé called "evidence." By evidence, we mean all the mandatory information you must include on your résumé: chronological work history with dates, education, affiliations, list of software mastered, etc. All this is best placed in the second half of the résumé. Put the hot stuff at the beginning and all this less exciting information afterward. It gives the employer the details about where you worked, how long, your education, etc. This is the standard stuff that any résumé book can help you with, so we will not cover it here in detail. We divided the résumé into a "hot" assertions section and a more staid "evidence" section for the sake of communicating that a great résumé is not information but advertising. A great résumé has no evidence section. It is all one big assertions section. In other words, every single word is crafted to have the desired effect, to get them to pick up the phone and call you. It is all one big ad disguised as a history of your working life. The decisions you make on what information to emphasize and what to deemphasize should be based on considering every word of your résumé to be an important part of the assertions section. The evidence includes some or all of the following sections:

Experience

List jobs in reverse chronological order. Don't go into detail on the jobs early in your career; focus on the most recent and/or relevant jobs. (Summarize a number of the earliest jobs in one line or very short paragraph, or list only the bare facts with no position description.) Decide which is, overall, more impressive: your job titles or the names of the firms you worked for; then consistently begin with the more impressive of the two, perhaps using boldface type.

You may want to describe the firm in a phrase in parentheses if this will impress the reader. Put dates in italics at the end of the job, to deemphasize them; don't include months, unless the job was held less than a year. Include military service, internships, and major volunteer roles, if desired, because the section is labeled "Experience. " It does not mean that you were paid.

Other headings: "Professional History" or "Professional Experience," not "Employment History" or "Work History," both of which sound more lower level.

Education

List education in reverse chronological order, degrees or licenses first, followed by certificates and advanced training. Set degrees apart so they are easily seen. Put in boldface whatever will be most impressive. Don't include any details about college except major and awards, unless you are in still in college or just recently graduated. Include grade point average only if over 3.4. List selected course work if this will help convince the reader of your qualifications for the targeted job.

Do include advanced training, but be selective with the information, summarizing the information and including only what will be impressive for the reader. No degree received yet? If you are working on a degree, include the degree and the expected date of completion in parentheses.

If you didn't finish college, start with a phrase describing the field studied, then the school, then the dates. (The fact that there was no degree may be missed.)

Other headings might include "Education and Training," "Education and Licenses," "Legal Education / Undergraduate Education" (for attorneys).

Awards

If the only awards received were in school, put these under the education section. Mention what the award was for if you can (or just "for outstanding accomplishment" or "outstanding performance"). This section is almost a must if you have received awards. If you have received commendations or praise from some very senior source, you could call this section "Awards and Commendations." In that case, go ahead and quote the source.

Professional Affiliations

Include only those that are current and will be relevant and impressive. Include leadership roles, if appropriate. (This is where you could convey your status as a member of a minority targeted for special consideration by employers, if there is a professional association to show it.) This section can be combined with "Community Leadership" as "Professional and Community Memberships."

Community Leadership

This is good to include if the leadership roles or accomplishments are related to the job target and can show skills acquired, for example a loan officer hoping to become a financial investment counselor who was the financial manager charged with investing the funds of a community organization. Any Board of Directors membership or chairmanship would be good to include. Be careful with political affiliations, as they could be a plus or minus with an employer or company.

Publications

Include only if published. Summarize if there are many.

Comments from Supervisors

Include only if very exceptional. Heavily edit for key phrases.

Personal Interests

Advantages: Can indicate a skill or area or knowledge that is related to the goal, such as photography for someone in public relations; carpentry and woodworking for someone in construction management. Can show well-roundedness, good physical health, or knowledge of a subject related to the goal. Can create common ground or spark conversation in an interview.

Disadvantages: Are usually irrelevant to the job goal and résumé purpose, and may be meaningless or an interview turnoff ("TV and Reading," "Fundraising for the Hell's Angels").

You probably should not include a personal-interests section. Your reason for including it is most likely that you want to tell them about you. But, as you know, this is an ad. If this section would powerfully move the employer to understand why you would be the best candidate, include it, otherwise, forget about it.

May also be called "Interests and Hobbies," or just "Interests."

References

You may put "References available upon request" at the end of your résumé, if you wish. This is a standard close (centered at bottom in italics), but is not necessary—it is usually assumed. Do not include actual names of references. A references list can be done as a separate sheet and brought to the interview to be given to the employer, if requested.

A Few Guidelines for a Better Presentation

Visually enticing—a work of art. Simple, clean structure. Very easy to read. Symmetrical. Balanced. Uncrowded. As much white space between sections of writing as possible; sections of writing that are no longer than six lines, and shorter, if possible. Maximum use of italics, capital letters, bullets, boldface, and underlining, with uniformity and consistency. Absolute parallelism in design decisions: If a period is at the end of one job's dates, a period should be at the end of all jobs' dates; if a degree is in boldface, all degrees should be in boldface.

As mentioned above, the résumé's first impression is most important. It should be exceptionally visually appealing to be inviting to the reader. Remember to think of the résumé as an advertisement.

Absolutely no errors. No typographical errors. No spelling errors. No grammar, syntax, or punctuation errors. No errors of fact.

All the basic, expected information is included. A résumé must have the following key information: your name, address, and phone number (immediately identifiable and at the top of the first page); a listing of all jobs held since beginning your career, in reverse chronological order; educational degrees, including the highest degree received, in reverse chronological order. Additional, targeted information will, of course, accompany this. Much of the information people commonly put on a résumé can be omitted, but these basics are mandatory.

Jobs listed should include a title, the name of the firm, the city and state where the firm is located, and the years you held this job. Jobs earlier in a career can be summarized or omitted if prior to the highest degree, and extra part-time jobs can be omitted. If no educational degrees have been completed, you are still expected to include some mention of education (professional study or training, partial study toward a degree, etc.) acquired after high school.

It is targeted. A résumé should be targeted to your goal—to the ideal next step in your career. First you should get clear what your job goal is, what the ideal position or positions would be. Then you should figure out what key skills, areas of expertise, knowledge, or body of experience the employer will be looking for in the candidate. Then gear the résumé structure and inclusions around this target, proving these key qualifications. If you have no clear goal, take the skills (or knowledge) you most enjoy or would like to use or develop in your next career step and build the résumé around these.

Strengths are highlighted, weaknesses deemphasized. Focus on whatever is strongest and most impressive in order to tell the prospective employer exactly why they should choose you. Make careful and strategic choices as to how to organize, order, and convey your skills and background. Consider whether to include the information at all, its placement in the overall structure of the résumé, location on the page itself or within a section, ordering of information, more impressive ways of phrasing the information, use of design elements (such as boldface to highlight, italics to minimize, ample surrounding space to draw the eye to certain things).

An initial focus. A résumé needs an initial focus created to help the reader. The reader will not want to read through every word in order to figure out what your profession is and what you can do. Think of the résumé as an essay with a title and a summative opening sentence.

An initial focus may be as simple as the name of your profession ("Commercial Real Estate Agent," "Résumé Writer") centered under your name and address; it may be in the form of an objective; it may be in the form of a summary statement; or, better, a summary statement beginning with a phrase identifying your profession.

Use of power words. For every skill, accomplishment, or job described, use the most active impressive verb (which is also accurate) you can think of. Begin the sentence with this verb, except when you must vary the sentence structure to avoid repetitious writing.

A List of Power Verbs

accelerated
accomplished
achieved
acquired
added
addressed
administered
advised
allocated
analyzed
answered
appeared
applied
appointed
appraised
approved
arranged
assessed
assigned
assisted
assumed
assured
audited
awarded
bought
briefed
broadened
brought
budgeted
built
cataloged
caused
changed
chaired
clarified
classified
closed

collected
combined
commented
communicated
compared
compiled
completed
computed
conceived
concluded
conducted
conceptualized
considered
consolidated
constructed
consulted
continued
contracted
controlled
converted
coordinated
corrected
counseled
counted
created
critiqued
cut
dealt
decided
defined
delegated
delivered
demonstrated
described
designed
determined
developed

devised
diagnosed
directed
discussed
distributed
documented
doubled
drafted
earned
edited
effected
eliminated
endorsed
enlarged
enlisted
ensured
entered
established
estimated
evaluated
examined
executed
expanded
expedited
experienced
experimented
explained
explored
expressed
extended
filed
filled
financed
focused
forecast
formulated
found

founded
gathered
generated
graded
granted
guided
halved
handled
helped
identified
implemented
improved
incorporated
increased
indexed
initiated
influenced
innovated
inspected
installed
instituted
instructed
insured
interpreted
interviewed
introduced
invented
invested
investigated
involved
issued
joined
kept
launched
learned
leased
lectured
led
licensed

listed
logged
made
maintained
managed
matched
measured
mediated
met
modified
monitored
motivated
moved
named
negotiated
observed
opened
operated
ordered
organized
oversaw
participated
perceived
performed
persuaded
planned
prepared
presented
processed
procured
programmed
prohibited
projected
promoted
proposed
provided
published
purchased
pursued

qualified
ranked
rated
received
recommended
reconciled
recruited
redesigned
reduced
regulated
related
reorganized
replaced
replied
reported
represented
researched
resolved
responded
revamped
reviewed
revised
saved
scheduled
selected
served
serviced
set
set up
simplified
sold
solved
sorted
sought
sparked
specified
spoke
staffed
started

streamlined
strengthened
stressed
stretched
structured
studied
submitted
substituted
succeeded
suggested
summarized
superseded
supervised
surveyed
systematized
tackled

targeted
taught
terminated
tested
toured
traced
tracked
traded
trained
transferred
transformed
translated
transported
traveled
treated
trimmed

tripled
turned
uncovered
unified
unraveled
updated
used
utilized
verified
visited
waged
widened
won
worked
wrote

Some Other Power Words

ability
capable
capability
capacity
competence
competent
complete
completely
consistent
contributions
developing
educated
efficient
effective
effectiveness
enlarging
equipped
excellent
exceptional

expanding
experienced
global
increasing
knowledgeable
major
mature
maturity
nationwide
outstanding
performance
positive
potential
productive
proficient
profitable
proven
qualified
record

repeatedly
resourceful
responsible
results
significant
significantly
sound
specialist
stable
substantial
substantially
successful
thorough
thoroughly
versatile
vigorous
well educated
well rounded
worldwide

Results-oriented. Wherever possible, prove that you have the desired qualifications through a clear, strong statement of accomplishments, rather than a statement of potentials, talents, or responsibilities. Indicate results of work done, and quantify these accomplishments whenever appropriate. For example: "Initiated and directed complete automation of the Personnel Department, resulting in time-cost savings of over 25 percent." Additionally, preface skill-and-experience statements with the adjectives "proven" and "demonstrated" to create this results orientation.

Concise, to the point. Keep sentences as short and direct as possible. Eliminate any extraneous information and any repetitions. Don't use three examples when one will suffice. Say what you want to say in the most direct words possible, rather than trying to impress with bigger words or more complex sentences. For example: "coordinated eight citywide fundraising events, raising 250 percent more than expected goal," rather than "was involved in the coordination of six fundraising dinners and two fundraising walkathons, which attracted participants throughout St. Louis and were so extremely successful that they raised $5,000 (well beyond the $2,000 goal)."

Vary longer sentences (if these are necessary) with short, punchy sentences. Use phrases rather than full sentences when phrases are possible, and start sentences with verbs, eliminating pronouns (I, he, or she). Vary words—don't repeat a verb or adjective twice in the same writing block or paragraph. Use commas liberally to clarify meaning and make reading easier. Remain consistent in writing decisions, for example, use of abbreviations and capitalizations.

Length. Everyone freely gives advice on résumé length. Most of these self-declared experts say a résumé should always be one page. That makes no more sense than it does to say an ad or a poem should automatically be one page. Your résumé can be 500 pages long if you can keep the reader's undivided attention and interest that long, and at the same time create a psychological excitement that leads prospective employers to pick up the phone and call you when they finish your weighty tome. Don't blindly follow rules! Do what works. Sometimes it is appropriate to have a three-pager. But unless your life has been filled with a wide assortment of extraordinary achievements, make it shorter. One page is best, if you can cram it all into one page. Most *Fortune* 500 CEOs have a one- or two-page résumé. It could be said that the larger your accomplishments, the easier to communicate them in few words. Look to others in your profession to see if there is an established agreement about résumé length in your field. The only useful rule is to not write one more word than you need to get them to pick up the phone and call you. Don't bore them with the details. Leave them wanting more.

Length of consulting résumés. In a consulting résumé, you are expected to shovel it as deep as you possibly can. If you are selling your own consulting services, make it sizzle, just like any other résumé, but include a little more detail, such as a list of well-known clients, powerful quotes from former clients about how fantastic you are, etc. If you are seeking a job with a consulting firm that will package you along with others as part of a proposal, get out your biggest shovel and go to town. Include everything except the name of your goldfish. A full list of publications, skills, assignments, other experience, and every bit of educational crapola that you can manage to tie into your work. The philosophy here is more is better.

Voice and verb tense. Résumés can be written using either the first- or the third-person voice. Whichever you choose, use it consistently. Verb tenses are varied and based on accurate reporting. If the accomplishment has been completed, it should be past tense. If the task is still underway, it should be present tense. If the skill is something that has been used and will continue to be used, use present tense ("conduct presentations on member recruitment to professional and trade associations"). A way of smoothing out transitions is to use the past continuous ("have conducted over 20 presentations . . .").

No lengthy blocks of writing. A good rule is to have no more than six lines of writing in any one writing block or paragraph (summary, skill section, accomplishment statement, job description, etc.). If any more than this is necessary, start a new section or a new paragraph.

Ordering of experience and education sections. Experience sections should come before education, in almost every case. This is because you have more qualifications developed from your experience than from your education. The exceptions would be (1.) if you have just received or are completing a degree in a new professional field, if this new degree study proves stronger qualifications than does your work experience; (2.) lawyers, who have the peculiar professional tradition of listing their law degrees first; (3.) an undergraduate student; or (4.) someone who has just completed a particularly impressive degree from a particularly impressive school, even if they are staying in the same field, for example, a MBA from Harvard.

Telephone numbers. Be sure the telephone number on the résumé will, without exception, be answered by a person or an answering machine, Monday through Friday, 8 A.M. to 6 P.M. You do not want to lose the prize interview merely because there was no answer to your phone, and the caller gave up. Include the area code of the telephone number. If you don't have an answering machine, get one. Include E-mail and fax numbers, if you have them.

Production. Use a laser printer or other printer that produces high-quality results. The résumé should look typeset. Do not compromise. Your résumé will look pathetic next to ones that have a typeset appearance. Use a standard conservative typeface (font) in 10 or 11 point. Produced to the sharpest printing quality—no faded or broken letters; Off-white / cream or bright white 8½ x 11 inch paper, in the highest quality affordable. If you are applying for a senior-level position, use Crane's paper. An absolutely clean paper—no smudges. No staples. Generous border. Don't have your résumé look like you squeezed too much on the page.

A Few More Tips

- Try not to include anything on the résumé that could turn the employer off, anything that is controversial (political, etc.) or could be taken in a negative light.
- Put the most important information in the first line of a writing block or paragraph—the first line is read most.
- Use bold caps for your name on page one. Put your name at the top of page two, on a two-page résumé. Put section headings, skill headings, titles, or companies (if impressive), degrees, and school names (if impressive) in boldface.
- Spell out numbers under and including 10; use numerical form for numbers over and including 11 (as a general rule). Spell out abbreviations unless they are unquestioningly obvious.

What Not to Put on a Résumé

The word "Résumé" at the top of the résumé
Fluffy, rambling "objective" statements
Salary information
Full addresses and zip codes of former employers
Reasons for leaving jobs
A "personal" section, or personal statistics
Names of supervisors
References

Accuracy, Honesty, Stretching the Truth

Make sure that you can back up what you say. Keep the claims you make within the range of your own integrity. There is nothing wrong with pumping things up in your résumé so you communicate who you are and what you can do at your very best. In fact, you are being foolish if you seek to convey a careful, balanced portrayal of yourself. You want to knock their socks off!

Questions a Great Professional Résumé Writer Would Ask You

What key qualifications will the employer be looking for?
What qualifications will be most important to them that you possess?
Which of these are your greatest strengths?
What are the highlights of your career to date that should be emphasized?
What should be deemphasized?
What things about you and your background make you stand out?
What are your strongest areas of skill and expertise? Knowledge? Experience?
What are some other skills you possess—perhaps more auxiliary skills?
What are characteristics you possess that make you a strong candidate—
   things like innovative, hard-working, strong interpersonal skills, ability to
   handle multiple projects simultaneously under tight deadlines?
What are the three or four things you feel have been your greatest accomplishments? What was produced as a result of your greatest accomplishments?
Can you quantify the results you produced in numerical or other specific terms?
What were the two or three accomplishments of that particular job?
What were the key skills you used in that job—what did you do in each of those skill areas?
What sort of results are particularly impressive to people in your field?
What results have you produced in these areas?
What are the buzz words that people in your field expect you to use that should be included in your résumé?

Basic Résumé Formats

There are three basic types of résumés: Chronological, Functional, and Combined Chronological-Functional. To see what these styles look like, get a résumé book. They are usually terrible guides for how to write an excellent résumé, but they are good for seeing different formats.

CHRONOLOGICAL

The chronological résumé is the more traditional structure for a résumé. The experience section is the focus of the résumé, with each job (or the last several jobs) described in some detail. There is no major section of skills or accomplishments at the beginning of the résumé. This structure is primarily used when you are staying in the same profession, in the same type of work, particularly in very conservative fields. It is also used in certain fields such as law and academia. It is recommended that the chronological résumé always have an objective or summary, to focus the reader.

The order of information usually is: objective first, then a summary section, followed by a detailed work history in reverse chronological order, then education and other supplementary information. (See books that specialize in, and have many examples of, résumés, to get a better sense of how information fits into specific formats.)

The advantages: May appeal to older, more traditional readers, and work best in very conservative fields. Makes it easier to understand what you did in what job. May help the name of the employer stand out more, if this is impressive.

FUNCTIONAL

The functional résumé highlights major skills and accomplishments. Readers see clearly what you can do for them, without their having to read through the job descriptions to find out. It helps target the résumé into a new direction or field. By combining the most salable and appropriate key skills and qualifications from your entire work history, it helps to prove you will be successful in this new direction or field. Actual company names and positions are in a subordinate position, with no description under each.

There are many different types of formats for functional résumés. The functional résumé is a must for career changers, but is very appropriate for generalists, for those with spotty or divergent careers, for those with a wide range of skills in their given profession, for students, for military officers, for returning homemakers, and for those who want to make slight shifts in their career direction.

A functional résumé starts with an objective, then a summary section, followed by a longer section that communicates why you are the most perfect candidate available. This could be called "skills and accomplishments," "selected accomplishments," or "career highlights." This is followed by a listing of your work history, without detailed explanations of each job, in reverse chronological order. In a functional résumé, you tell your tale up front and then include education and other supplementary information at the end.

Advantages: It will help you most in reaching for a new goal or direction. It is a very effective type of résumé, and is highly recommended. The disadvantages are that it is hard to know what the applicant did in which job, which may be a negative to some conservative interviewers.

COMBINED

A combined résumé includes elements of both the chronological and functional formats. It may be a shorter chronology of job descriptions preceded by a skills and accomplishments section (or with a longer summary including a skills list or a list of qualifications). Or it may be a standard functional résumé with emphasis on the skills and accomplishments section and a detailed job description under each different job held.

There are obvious advantages to this combined approach. It maximizes the advantages of both kinds of résumés, avoiding the potential turn off of either type. One disadvantage is that they tend to be longer résumés. Another is that they may be repetitious—accomplishments and skills may have to be repeated in both the functional section and the chronological job descriptions.

GETTING IN TOUCH

As you know, I strongly recommend that you go through a testing program that measures your most important natural talents and innate abilities. Without a crystal-clear understanding of these natural gifts, your chances of making a truly excellent career choice are greatly reduced. We provide this kind of testing worldwide, as do other organizations. Please write or call to learn more. Most testing organizations charge somewhere around $500. (These programs are completely different from the old-fashioned testing offered by your local career counselor.)

If you find that you need more assistance than *The Pathfinder* can offer, and want personal one-on-one coaching, please get in touch with us at Rockport Institute. Rockport offers the Career Choice Program, which can take you all the way to making your final career decisions. Our network of independent affiliated career coaches, trained in Rockport's leading-edge methodologies, may make it possible for you to work in person with someone in your local area.

We also provide the following services:

- Advanced training in career coaching to career counselors, psychologists, human resources professionals, clergy, high schools, colleges, and others with a commitment to excellence in career guidance.
- Personal consulting for CEOs and other senior professionals on both corporate and personal issues. Personal and professional coaching for artists, musicians, dancers, and other creative professionals.

You can reach us at:

ROCKPORT INSTITUTE, LTD.
10124 Lakewood Drive
Rockville, MD 20850, USA

301-340-6600

Find us on the Internet by searching for Rockport Institute using your favorite search engine.

John Goddard, my favorite goal setter, explorer, and lecturer, gives presentations to groups, from professional groups to school assemblies. He also leads adventures into the wilds. You can reach him at:

4224 Beulah Drive
La Canada, CA 91011

Captain Neal Parker, my favorite crusty sea captain, takes passengers on overnight cruises aboard his beautiful schooner yacht *Wendameen.*

P.O. Box 252
Rockland, ME 04841
207-594-1751

Mac Lore, the illustrator, can be contacted by writing to the author.

For information on the Myers-Briggs Type Indicator, call: Consulting Psychologists Press 800-624-1765. Ask for customer service.

AN INVITATION

The best software in your computer is probably not version 1.0. Most likely, your software has gone through several versions, each one improved by suggestions from users. It has become customary for users to let the software developer know of ways their product could be improved. This custom has not crossed over to the world of book publishing, yet. Let's get it started now! Think of this book as software for the mind. My commitment is to have *The Pathfinder* continually improve. To do this, I need your help. Please accept my invitation to participate in making this the best guide to choosing a career on the planet. All suggestions, ideas, critiques are more than welcome.

ACKNOWLEDGMENTS

MY MENTORS

My mom and dad—for love and genes.

John Sebastian—itinerant jug-band musician, high school roommate, first soul brother who opened the doors to the magic world beyond Wallingford.

Sam Lightnin' Hopkins—great friend, long gone, still missed. Po' me.

Werner and Randy MacNamara—Thank you, thank you, for everything and nothing.

Bucky Fuller—who got me into all of this.

I. J. Grandes del Mazo—Foxy Peruvian Yoda. Thank you, Toto.

My miraculous wife, Mitra, favorite (and sexiest) mentor of all.

MY INSPIRATIONS

Erin, Newsha, and Neema; Jeff and Mac; Aunt Carol and Uncle Jim; Yoghoub and Azar; Roya, Sam Boogandoo, Crip, Muggleduffy, Curly, and all the crew in pet heaven. The Beatles, who showed me how mastery, magic, joy, commitment, and irreverence can play together in perfect harmony. Dylan, Robert Johnson, Rembrandt, Vermeer, Mark Knopfler, Ravi Shankar, Steven Spielberg, John Grinder, Richard Goldberg, W. Edwards Deming, Johnson O'Connor, e.e. cummings, Rumi, Sid Gautama, and Yeshua the carpenter (two career changers).

THIS BOOK IS IN YOUR HANDS BECAUSE OF THESE GREAT PEOPLE. THANK YOU SO MUCH!

Two phenomenal supporters: my amazing agent Stephanie Tade and Becky Cabaza, my truly exceptional editor. You are both hot, hot, hot!

My wonderful clients, who taught me everything in this book.

The volunteer editors who generously contributed their wisdom: Sheryl Peltin Etelson, Sheila Cahill, Robyn King, Mitra Mortazavi Lore, Paula Rubin, Anthony Spadafore, and Stephanie Tade. Also, thanks to Nancy Fish, Sirah Vettese, Sandy Shotwell, Dan Pence, Claire Spector, Patti Skinner, Barry Saiff, Jeff Lore, and Bill Clinton. A portion of the first draft of the résumés chapter (structural options and guidelines) was written by Alden Lancaster many years ago as an internal Rockport Institute document.

Thank you, Matt Groening! Thank you, Anne Murray (widow of the great mountaineer and author of one of the best quotes of all time, W. H. [Bill] Murray)

The concepts shown in the "The Machinery of Human Behavior" illustration and the idea for that illustration are from the work of I. J. Grandes del Mazo.

I have done my best to find the copyright holders of the quotations in this book. If something has not been attributed or is quoted incorrectly, please let me know.

Rockport Institute, the Rockport Institute logo, the Career Choice Program, Career Choice, the Networking Game, the Career Testing Program, Pathfinder, Career Pathfinder, the Pathfinder Program, the terms "tribal" and "maestro" and the titles of all the Inquiries in this book are service marks and trademarks of Rockport Institute, Ltd. and Nicholas Ayars Lore.

ABOUT THE AUTHOR

As the director of Rockport Institute, NICHOLAS LORE is a mentor to many of the most gifted career, personal, and business coaches and counselors around the world. He coaches individuals of all ages choosing a new career direction, and serves as a personal consultant to CEOs who want their organizations filled with happy, committed, productive people. He has been a corporate CEO, manufacturing plant manager, entrepreneur, researcher in the field of psychology, market gardener, blues singer and guitar player, well driller, and newspaper boy.

INDEX

abilities, *see* talents, natural
abstraction, 252–53
abundance mentality, 325, 334
academic ability, 242
accomplishment cycles, 181–89
accountability, 101
adaptability, 244–46, 317
addictions, 130–31, 132, 135
Adventurer Game, 266
after-work activities, 233–34
agreement, sphere of, 239–37,
    339–40, 345
Alcoholics Anonymous (AA), 132
altruism, 91
ambition, 129–30
analysis, 141, 145, 147, 151
analytical reasoning, 254
answers:
    inside source for, 77, 78–79, 81, 100
    made-up, 77–78, 79, 81
    outside source for, 77, 79, 81
    uncertainty and, 191–92
apprehension, 54, 61, 66–67
Aristotle, 17
Art and/or Beauty Game, 266
Artist Game, 266
artistic ability, 258
associations, trade, 96
associative memory, 256
assumptions, 191
attention span, 239
awards, 360

Barron-Tieger, Barbara, 212
behavior, 157–62

commitment and, 162
cycle of, 160, 161
machinery of, 157–62
negative, 135, 161
pattern of, 106
reinforcement of, 160, 161–62
Being There, 97
Berra, Yogi, 38
body-kinesthetic, 257
book learning, 94, 147
boundaries, 24, 28–29, 37
brain:
    human, 77, 122–25
    left vs. right, 77
    mammal, 120, 123
    reptile, 118–19, 120, 123
brainstorming, 76, 78, 103, 111,
    152, 174, 274, 315, 344
breakthroughs, 99–100
Brown, Eva May, 103
Buddhism, 192
Bushido code, 123–24

Campbell, Joseph, 19, 281
"career hell," 11, 13
careers:
    access to, 89
    childhood expectations of, 7–9
    contribution of, 12, 13, 19, 28,
        91, 161–62, 266–67, 272,
        273–74, 280–81, 282, 285–86
    description of, 304–5
    design of, 31–32, 40, 51–53, 57,
        113–14, 154–55, 161, 163, 198,
        201–372